Learning the Language
of Global Citizenship

Learning the Language of Global Citizenship

Service-Learning in Applied Linguistics

Edited by

Adrian J. Wurr
University of North Carolina–Greensboro

Josef Hellebrandt
Santa Clara University

ANKER PUBLISHING COMPANY, INC.
Bolton, Massachusetts

Learning the Language of Global Citizenship
Service-Learning in Applied Linguistics

ISBN 978-1-933371-06-1

Composition by Julie Phinney
Cover design by Thomjon Borges

Anker Publishing Company, Inc.
563 Main Street
P.O. Box 249
Bolton, MA 01740-0249 USA

www.ankerpub.com

Library of Congress Cataloging-in-Publication Data
Learning the language of global citizenship : service-learning in applied linguistics /
    edited by Adrian J. Wurr, Josef Hellebrandt.
        p. cm.
  Includes bibliographical references and index.
        ISBN-13: 978-1-933371-06-1
    1. Language and languages—Study and teaching.   2. Student service.   3. Inter-
    cultural communication.   I. Wurr, Adrian J.   II. Hellebrandt, Josef.

P53.L4315 2006
418.0071—dc22   2006034250

Adrian dedicates this work to his parents, who as immigrants
inspired in their children a greater interest
and understanding
of the world.

Josef is grateful to his wife and mother
for their insights to tolerate others.

Table of Contents

About the Authors

■ The Editors

Adrian Wurr is assistant professor of English and service-learning faculty fellow emeritus at the University of North Carolina–Greensboro, where he teaches courses in applied linguistics, composition, and English education. His research interests include Teaching English to Speakers of Other Languages (TESOL), service-learning, literacy studies, and program administration. He has published numerous scholarly articles in the U.S. and abroad, including forthcoming works in *TESOL Quarterly* and *Reflections*, the premiere national, peer-reviewed journal devoted to the study of community-based writing. He serves as the associate editor for the online journal, *The Reading Matrix,* and as a consultant on the Campus Compact Research and Scholarship Initiative in North Carolina. In spring 2007, Dr. Wurr will begin a five-month Fulbright TESOL Lecturing position in Vietnam.

Josef Hellebrandt (Ph.D., Purdue University) is associate professor of Spanish and chair of the Department of Modern Languages and Literatures at Santa Clara University. His research focuses on service-learning in Spanish and civic engagement. Drawing on his collaborations with service-learning researchers and practitioners throughout the United States, he published *Construyendo Puentes (Building Bridges): Concepts and Models for Service-Learning in Spanish* (coeditor: Lucía Varona, 1999) within the American Association for Higher Education's series on service-learning in the disciplines and *Juntos: Community Partnerships in Spanish and Portuguese* (coeditors: Jonathan Arries and Lucía Varona, 2004). In addition to his professional work, he serves on the board of a nonprofit Saturday morning school for German in San Jose, California.

■ The Contributors

José G. Centeno, is an assistant professor in the speech-language pathology and audiology program at St. John's University, New York. He has extensively worked as a speech-language pathologist in New York City and published on bilingualism issues of Spanish-English bilinguals in the U.S. and on stroke-related language impairments in monolingual Spanish speakers. He has also been a frequent presenter at national and international conferences and participated in state, national, and international professional committees on bilingual/multicultural populations. His current research and professional interests focus on stroke-related impairments and aspects of service delivery in monolingual Spanish/bilingual Spanish-English adults.

Rosario Díaz-Greenberg is associate professor of multicultural education at California State University–San Marcos. She is the author of *The Emergence of Voice in Latino High School Students* (Peter Lang, 1995), as well as numerous articles on service-learning, education, and social justice.

Howard Grabois is currently assistant professor at Purdue University. He had always been a terrible language learner until he did an extensive bicycle tour in France at the age of 24. Once he discovered the joys of language learning, he spent the better part of a decade living in Spain and other Mediterranean countries, where he worked as an ESL teacher. He earned his Ph.D from Cornell University and is currently involved in the design and coordination of language programs.

Aileen Hale is assistant professor of bilingual education at Boise State University. She has extensive experience teaching and researching ESL and service-learning theory and pedagogy. She has received several grants for the integration of service-learning in higher education and K–12 schools. Her most notable publication is "Service-Learning and Spanish: A Missing Link" in *Construyendo Puentes (Building Bridges): Concepts and Models for Service-Learning in*

Spanish, published in 1999 as part of the American Association for Higher Education's series on service-learning in the disciplines.

Mary Hutchinson is a senior lecturer in English at the Penn State University Lehigh Valley Campus and has taught an assortment of courses over the years, including developmental writing, rhetoric and composition, business writing and advanced business writing, editorial processes, applied linguistics, and communication and information technology. She currently serves as the first-year seminar coordinator and is the former director of the Lehigh Valley Writing Project, a federally funded national writing program, which provides professional development opportunities for K–college teachers with the goal of increasing the reading, writing, and critical thinking skills of students.

Jessie Moore Kapper is assistant professor of English at Elon University in North Carolina, where she teaches TESOL and professional writing and rhetoric courses. Laura Clapp, Cindy Lefferts, Melissa Taylor, and Nikki Wasikowski are students at Elon University. Missy Schwandt is an alumna of the school.

Fu-An Lin is currently a doctoral candidate in foreign language education at the University of Texas–Austin. She has taught at English programs in Taiwan and in the state of Texas. Her research interests are teacher knowledge, TESOL teacher education, adult student achievement, and English grammar instruction.

Denise Overfield (Ph.D., Hispanic applied linguistics and methodology, University of Pittsburgh) is associate professor of Spanish and chair of the Department of Foreign Languages and Literatures at the University of West Georgia. She teaches courses in teacher education and Spanish and has written and lectured on service-learning in foreign language learning. Her interest in service learning stems from her experiences as a Peace Corps volunteer.

Chin-Sook Pak (Ph.D., romance linguistics, University of Michigan) is associate professor of Spanish at Ball State University in Muncie, Indiana. Her research interests are in cross-cultural discourse analysis of newspaper genres and community-based learning. Most of the Spanish language and linguistics classes that she teaches incorporate a community-based learning component. She also regularly teaches an interdisciplinary service-learning honors colloquium. She is the recipient of the Outstanding Teaching Award (Ball State University) and the Brian Douglas Hiltunen Faculty Award for Outstanding Contribution to the Scholarship of Engagement (Indiana Campus Compact).

James M. Perren attended university in Spain, Japan, California, and Pennsylvania. He has taught courses in English as a second language, public speaking, service-learning, technology for educators, intercultural communication, and teacher training. He has published a book chapter on a new model for intercultural teacher training as well as several other minor publications. James has given academic presentations in Brazil, Canada, Hong Kong, Japan, the U.S., and Vietnam. James is currently completing his doctorate in Education/TESOL at Temple University in Philadelphia, Pennsylvania.

Ruth Spack is professor of English and ESOL director at Bentley College. She has published numerous articles and books, including *Guidelines* (2nd ed., Cambridge University Press, 1999), *The International Story* (Cambridge University Press, 1994), *Negotiating Academic Literacies* (Lawrence Erlbaum Associates, 1998), and *Crossing the Curriculum* (Lawrence Erlbaum Associates, 2004). Her scholarly monograph, *America's Second Tongue: American Indian Education and the Ownership of English, 1860–1900* (University of Nebraska Press, 2002) was awarded the Modern Language Association's Mina P. Shaughnessy Prize for Outstanding Research Publication in the Field of Teaching English Language and Literature and was named a CHOICE Outstanding Academic Title by the Association of Academic Colleges and Universities.

Darci L. Strother is professor of Spanish at California State University–San Marcos. She has been involved in service-learning since 1995. She is the author of *Family Matters—A Study of On-and Off-Stage Marriage and Family Relations in Seventeenth-Century Spain* (Iberica, 1999), and has published numerous articles in the fields of Golden Age Spanish Literature, as well as world language pedagogy and professional development.

Stuart Stewart (M.A. Spanish, Texas A & M University; Ph.D. linguistics, Louisiana State University) is assistant professor of Spanish and linguistics at Southeastern Louisiana University where she teaches courses in language, linguistics, and language teaching methodology. She serves as coordinator of field experiences for foreign language education majors and has served as director of the foreign language resource center and the department's summer study abroad program in Costa Rica. Her research interests include critical pedagogy, discourse analysis, foreign language teaching, migrant health, and service-learning.

Amy Szarkowski teaches at Miyazaki International College in Miyazaki, Japan. She received her Ph.D. in clinical psychology from Gallaudet University, the only liberal arts college in the world dedicated to the education of Deaf students. A hearing person herself, she immersed herself in Deaf Culture and since that time has had the opportunity to travel to many parts of the world, continuing her investigation of Deaf Cultures. She was granted a Fulbright award to study in Rome, Italy, at the Italian National Research Center, and is currently living in Japan and studying Japanese Sign Language. A strong advocate of service-learning, Dr. Szarkowski works to incorporate it into many of her classes.

Joby Blaine Taylor directs the Shriver Peaceworker Program, a graduate service-learning program for returned Peace Corps volunteers based at the Shriver Center in Baltimore, Maryland. He received his Ph.D. from the interdisciplinary language, literacy, and culture program at the University of Maryland–Baltimore County, and he has previously published on the language of service in the *Michigan Journal of Community Service Learning*. He lives in Baltimore City.

Gresilda A. Tilley-Lubbs, (Ph.D., second language education) is assistant professor of second language education/ESL at Virginia Polytechnic Institute and State University.

Robin Glenn Walker is currently an instructor of English at Fayetteville Technical Community College. She attended graduate school at the University of North Carolina–Greensboro during the writing of the initial drafts of this article. Her interests are learning communities, service-learning, community-based literacy programs, and TESOL. She has taught TESOL to various individuals in immigrant communities, a workplace development course on English grammar for business communication, cognitively challenged adults, and various levels of college English. She is creating a learning communities class involving developmental English and first-year college study skills for Fayetteville Technical Community College. For further information about this article, the author can be reached at walkerr@faytechcc.edu

Erin Whittig is an adjunct professor of English at Boise State University (BSU). She was the primary researcher as the instructor for ESL-101. In addition to ESL-101 and mainstream 101 courses, Erin employs service-learning in the second-semester composition course at BSU, which introduces students to community-based research.

Preface

The origin of this volume lies in a project that began almost a decade ago. That project was the American Association for Higher Education's (AAHE) series on service-learning in the academic disciplines. Early in 1995, a new faculty-based organization under the aegis of Campus Compact, the nation's only higher education association devoted primarily to civic engagement, called for the development of a series of volumes on service-learning in individual academic areas. Responsibility for funding and organizing the series quickly passed to AAHE, and by 2000 the undertaking had reached completion—the largest publication project in the association's history.

A key contributor to the AAHE series was one of the coeditors of the present volume, Josef Hellebrandt. Although it seems hard to believe, only a decade has passed since one had to make a case for the relevance of service-learning to courses in Spanish. One can only assume faculty had become so accustomed to seeing the campus as the locale for academic work that even the proximity of a Spanish-speaking community seemed irrelevant to student learning!

The work done by Hellebrandt and his colleagues to link the study of Spanish and Hispanic cultures to the priorities and needs of real Hispanic communities was ground breaking. The following volume, edited by Adrian Wurr and Josef Hellebrandt, is also ground breaking, but in a different way, since it reflects a new set of circumstances both inside and beyond the academy. While one of the primary goals of the AAHE series was to demonstrate service-learning's academic legitimacy within individual disciplinary areas, the present volume has been able to take advantage of a far more receptive intellectual climate to reach out to a truly global scholarly community. In the chapters that follow, one finds programs, courses, and issues related to language acquisition in a wide variety of forums, domestic and international. Questions related to the tension between primary and secondary language use and acquisition find illustration not only in the case of Spanish speakers in the United States, but also in situations outside the English-speaking world.

But scope of interest is not the only important difference. Because our understanding and acceptance of the potential benefits of community-based work has grown so much during the past decade, the present volume is able to address, in addition to program and course models, a broad range of theoretical issues. Indeed, its attention to research goes far beyond anything that can be found in most of its discipline-related predecessors. This is not surprising. Even a cursory glance at the list of dissertation abstracts published by the National Service-Learning Clearing House (http://servicelearning.org/resources/online_documents/research/) makes it clear that service-learning as practice has opened up important new areas of research. Indeed, one major initiative launched since the publication of the AAHE series is an annual International Service-Learning Research conference.

Ironically, this growth in service-learning's intellectual and academic ambitions has coincided with a very different kind of growth outside the academy: a growth in the numbers of peoples crossing international borders. As Castles and Miller's comprehensive study *The Age of Migration: International Population Movements in the Modern World* (3rd ed., Guilford Press, 2003) demonstrates, the movement of peoples—legally and illegally—is now so ubiquitous it is in many ways redefining the modern world. This phenomenon has not only continued unabated over the period of service-learning's growth, but has taken on a new urgency in the United States thanks to the debate about illegal immigration and questions of national and international security. A similar sense of urgency can be found in other countries as well.

Thus, this book could not appear at a more opportune time. Even as the service-learning movement becomes more international, the need for new ways of thinking about and dealing with international phenomena becomes clear. As scholars and educators who believe community and civic engagement is one of the most important academic developments of our time, I welcome this volume—both for what it is and for the trends it may facilitate.

Edward Zlotkowski
Former AAHE Series Editor
Professor of English, Bentley College
June 2006

Introduction and Overview: Language for Community Engagement at Home and Abroad

Adrian J. Wurr, Josef Hellebrandt

Language is one of the most basic and essential characteristics of human beings. Indeed, the ability to use language effectively as a means of communication in society is thought to be the significant difference between humans and other animals. "Language is one of the strongest markers of group identity, and linguistic conflict one of the bitterest sources of discord," notes language educator Lynne Díaz-Rico (2004). "This makes the role of speech communities—and those who manage, instruct, and transform them—into some of the world's strongest potential forces for cohesion and division" (p. 376). It therefore seems appropriate that a volume focusing on service-learning in applied linguistics begins by looking at language in society and the role language educators worldwide play in shaping that world into a peaceful and just one for all.

Language is often at the heart of many social issues and current events that capture headlines worldwide. Language use and education are often in the news in the United States. The Linguistics Society of America's (n.d.) web site lists an average of 48 major media stories concerning language over the last three years. Similarly, Robin Lakoff's book, *The Language Wars* (2000), analyzes some of the more significant and persistent issues of the last decade involving language. She describes and analyses the ways in which language plays a crucial role in events such as the rise of political correctness in American higher education (e.g., free speech and tenure decisions), conflicting definitions and views of sexual harassment (e.g., the Clarence Thomas and Anita Hill controversy), and the use of Ebonics or other minority languages in classrooms and educational materials (e.g., the Oakland, California, school board decision to require the use of Ebonics in its public schools as well as English-only amendments in California and Arizona). Lakoff also notes the ways in which O. J. Simpson and Hillary Rodham Clinton both successfully reclaimed their public identities for sociopolitical purposes by narrating significant events in their life in ways that captured the public imagination. More recently, we have seen the self-declared "Education President" George W. Bush shift his attention from what *Newsweek* referred to as "The Reading Wars" (Kantrowitz & Hammill, 1990) to a long-term war on terrorism, in which the lack of expertise in critical foreign languages such as Arabic, Vietnamese, and Thai is considered by the U.S. Senate to be a matter of national security since this lack hampers information gathering and analysis (S. Res. 28, 2005).

Elsewhere in the world, language issues are no less prominent in the media. Bernard Spolsky (2006) recalls several incidents of national significance occurring within a month of each other in different parts of the world:

> In October 2004, a commission chaired by Claude Thélot that had been charged with organizing a national debate on the future of French schooling recommended that English no longer be treated as just one of a number of foreign languages taught in the system; rather, in recognition of its role as the international language of communication, it should be considered together with French and mathematics as the core curriculum. A month later, the Russian Constitutional Court ruled that Tartarstan cannot switch the Tartar's language's alphabet from Cyrillic to Latin, saying that regional authorities have no jurisdiction over the alphabets of ethnic groups and peoples. In Canada, some 40 years after the Official Languages Act, fewer than 10 percent of non-francophones claim to be bilingual, and

the newspapers are starting to ask why the federal government is spending so much money on attempts to change the situation. At the same time, in Boston, a health clinic gave in to pressure from the U.S. Equal Opportunity Commission and the National Labor Relations Board and cancelled a policy that forbade its employees speaking Spanish with each other. (p. 15)

While these issues may come to the average person's mind most immediately with regard to language and education, two parallel issues of long-standing interest to language educators and service-learning scholars bear further discussion: the achievement gap and civic participation. While at first glance these two issues may appear different, we would like to argue that they are in fact very similar, and in ways that language and service-learning scholars are perhaps best positioned to understand and address.

■ The Achievement Gap

The achievement gap between different ethnic student populations has been implicated in varying levels of participation, retention, and success among these groups in public schools (Neal, 2005; Jencks & Phillips, 1998; Singham, 2005; Vernez, Krop, & Rydell, 1999), while declining civic participation rates as measured by such indicators as voter turnout, charitable giving, and volunteerism have been a topic of concern for service-learning scholars for some time (Astin, Sax, & Avalos, 1999; Hahn, 1999). What connects these two issues are the discourse skills necessary to participate fully and succeed in each setting. To understand this connection more completely requires some discussion of the discourse skills required in each setting. Focusing first on school settings, we discuss the language skills necessary for academic success, such as the ability to argue, analyze, and compare and contrast, which Jim Cummins (1981b) of the Ontario Institute for Studies in Education refers to as Cognitive Academic Language Proficiency (CALP). We then turn to the public sector and consider the role civic literacy plays in civic engagement, and the discourse skills utilized in both.

CALP refers to the general academic language proficiency that can be gained in one's first, second, or additional language. Though the concept is most often applied to second language learning and instruction, CALP is equally important to academic success for all children whose home language or dialect differs from the language of instruction, as work by Mina Shaughnessy (1977) and Mike Rose (1990) with basic writers, and Shirley Brice Heath's (1983) research on home, school, and community discourse patterns in a working-class mill town illustrates. Essentially, CALP involves "the ability to communicate messages that are precise and explicit in tasks that are context-reduced and cognitively demanding" (Ellis, 1994, p. 696). Beyond vocabulary and sentence-level grammar, CALP involves higher-order thinking and discourse skills related to communication, conceptualization, critical thinking, context, and culture (Díaz-Rico & Weed, 2002).

Second language acquisition research has shown that even under ideal situations, it takes six or more years for the academic language proficiencies (CALP) of a child learning English as a second language to match those of his or her same-age peers (Collier, 1987; Cummins, 1981a; Hakuta, Butler, & Witt, 2000). Teachers of English to Speakers of Other Languages, Inc. (TESOL, Inc.), the largest professional organization for English language educators, summarized this research in its 1999 position statement on the acquisition of academic proficiency in English:

> In the past decade, research has shown that content-based instruction that focuses on the development of academic language proficiency is critical for success in school. LEP [Limited English Proficient] students are expected to learn academic content in English in order to compete academically with their native-English-speaking peers.

For most LEP students, 2 years is the general time-frame for acquiring social language skills in English. The acquisition of academic language proficiency, on the other hand, is more demanding and takes LEP students from 6 to 9 years to achieve parity with their native English language peers. (p. 2)

While the 14th Amendment to the U.S. Constitution guarantees all children equal access to public education, and the Bilingual Education Acts of 1968 through 1994 reaffirm that these rights apply specifically to language minority students (Leibowitz, 1982; Weise & García, 1998),[1] state and local school districts are generally allowed to decide how to implement the mandates of the law, particularly with regard to the goals for language instruction, whether that be to develop proficiencies in the first and second language in additive bilingual education programs, or to transition students from their first language to English as a second language in a set amount of time (i.e., "structured immersion" or "transitional bilingual education"); the goal of these latter programs is monolingualism and hence they are considered "subtractive bilingual education" models. California's Proposition 227, passed in 1998, differs from federal laws governing the rights of language minority students to equal educational opportunities in its attempt to legislate specific instructional models. Proposition 227 explicitly prohibits schools from providing bilingual education unless parents specifically request it and restricts such instruction to structured immersion lasting no more than one school year (Adamson, 2005, p. 216). Given what is known about the length of time required to acquire CALP in a second language, such legislation makes it difficult for language minority students to compete on equal footing with their native-English-speaking peers.

Historically, during times of peak immigration there is a decline in the acceptance of bilingualism. Increased

immigration tends to create a feeling of instability, perhaps due to the unsettling aura of change, apparent job
competition, or fear of an inability to communicate with
immigrants. This feeling of instability often leads to fear
of the unknown and an insistence on using the status quo
language, English. (Fitzgerald, 1993; Portes & Rumbaut,
1996; as cited in Weise & García, 1998, p. 6)

Current immigration figures from the national census in
2000 strongly suggest the United States as a whole, and the Midwest and South in particular, is well poised for such a backlash
against linguistic diversity at the moment. Census 2000 found
an unprecedented 18% of the American population now live
in households where English is not the primary language (Shin
& Bruno, 2003). States vary in this percentage, with California
leading at 40%, followed by New Mexico at 36%, and Texas at
32%. However, English language learners and their families are
increasingly living in places like the Midwest and the South that
are less experienced than border states in accommodating diverse
populations. Of the ten states that saw the largest increase in
their Hispanic population in the 2000 census, nine are in the
Midwest or South. North Carolina led the nation with a 394%
increase in the Latino population between 1990 and 2000, with
93 of its 100 counties reporting increases greater than 100%,
and many in the Piedmont area where Adrian Wurr lives have
witnessed increases of more than 500% (Bender, 2004). Such
dramatic demographic changes have caught many schools and
public institutions by surprise, and the response is often too little
too late to meet demands.

With inadequate resources and a shortage of qualified language educators an endemic problem in American schools, large
numbers of linguistically and culturally diverse students inevitably
sink rather than swim in public schools. In Michelle Fine's (1991)
important book, *Framing Dropouts,* she discusses the unrealized

intentions of the Bilingual Education Acts and notes the findings of the Educational Priorities Panel of 1985: "There were enough licensed New York City high school teachers to serve fewer than 25 percent of LEP-identified students in science, 18 percent in math, and 46 percent in social studies" (p. 256). More recently, Díaz-Rico (2004) has noted, "There are many English learners among the 50 percent yearly dropout population of the Boston public school system, or the 70 percent dropout population in the New York public schools" (p. 11). Indeed, many educators now use the term *pushed-out* rather than dropout to refer to students who are victimized by not-so-benign educational policies that limit the chances of educational success for minority language and culture students (Derwing, DeCorby, Ichikawa, & Jamieson, 1999; Lee & Burkam, 2003).

In sum, second language acquisition research has shown that even under ideal situations it takes at least six years for the academic language proficiencies of a child learning English as a second language to match those of his or her same-age peers. Lack of the necessary language and discourse skills inhibits equal access to and participation in public education for language minority students. Ultimately, this leads to withdrawal from schooling and contributes to the achievement gap in school retention and success between mainstream and minority students.

■ Multilingualism as Resource

Yet with great challenges also come great opportunities. While some have responded to changes in the cultural landscape of America with renewed calls for assimilation and national unity under a single language, the shock of 9/11 and increased competition in the global marketplace have caused others to question the wisdom of American monolingualism (Edwards, 2001; Pratt, 2003; Stanton, 2005; Tonkin, 2001).

The importance of knowing multiple languages, and of knowing the world better through language, has become increasingly clear to many political and educational leaders in America. In the name of national security, Congress declared 2005 the "Year of Foreign Language Study" (S. Res. 28, 2005). The U.S. Department of Defense (2005), in collaboration with industry, academic, and professional language association representatives, issued a white paper on the need for the study of languages in the national interest. Two professional language organizations—the Joint National Committee for Languages (JNCL) and the National Council for Languages and International Studies (NCLIS), with more than a quarter million members in the government, academic, and private sectors—produced position statements that reaffirmed their belief that

> Language and international education are clearly in the public and national interest. . . . Only with language competence can Americans hope to conduct effective trade policy, expand international trade, ensure the integrity of national defense, enhance international communication, and develop a truly broad-based education for all citizens. (JNCL & NCLIS, 2005)

But Mary Louise Pratt's (2003) article, "Building a New Public Idea About Language," speaks more directly to the concerns of language and service-learning scholars. Pratt argues that multilingualism should be seen as a form of civic literacy in the global community and a necessary skill for global citizenship. Describing monolingualism as a handicap, she asserts that "If scholars and teachers of languages are to seize upon the opening [created by national security concerns], they will make themselves heard as advocates not for particular languages but for the importance of knowing the world through languages" (p. 6). Arguing that language professionals are ideally suited to advocate such views given their personal and professional experience, Pratt concludes that we

> need to make the case for language learning as an aspect of educated citizenship. I believe we need to make that case in as many ways as possible, right now. Language education is far too big an issue to be contained by national security concerns alone. If a new public idea is vigorously asserted, it can help generate resources that will help make its promise a reality. (p. 6)

Pratt effectively makes the case for language education in general and multilingualism in particular as the most effective way to better meet the needs of the global community, and does so in terms that service-learning scholars can easily understand and appreciate. We wish to heed and extend Pratt's call by linking her argument more explicitly to parallel concerns of service-learning scholars with regard to enhancing democratic values and civic engagement through civic education and service-learning.

▪ Civic Literacy

Civic education, broadly defined, refers to developing students' competence and motivation to engage actively in public problem solving in their communities as well as in the larger world. While there are different ways of measuring civic engagement, voter turnout and rates of volunteerism are commonly used. Polls and other public research conducted over the last few decades have consistently shown that the majority of eligible voters in America do not vote and even fewer volunteer in their communities. The groups of most importance to educators are school-age children, particularly since experiences in adolescence have a formative influence on identity development and actions later in life (Erikson, 1968).

Declining rates of civic engagement are not unique to the United States, either. Over the last few decades, citizens of many Western democracies have become increasingly cynical about political leaders and their trust in government is at historic lows. For example, Hahn's (1999) comparative study of civic education in six countries found that in response to the statement, "most people in government are honest," "only 15% of the Danish students and 12% of the Dutch students agreed; in the other four countries fewer than 10% of students agreed" (p. 246). Similarly, the Center for Information and Research on Civic Learning and Engagement (CIRCLE) reports youth voter turnout rates have declined by every measure over the last 30 years (Levine & Lopez, 2002). At the same time, however, rates of volunteerism among youth are up: Close to 60% of the 18–24 year olds surveyed in a 1994 National Association of Secretaries of State study said they volunteer on a regular basis. Volunteer work was typically reported as a one-on-one activity at a soup kitchen, hospital, or school (National Association of Secretaries of State, 2004). While political contexts vary from setting to setting, and from country to country, we need to consider better ways to help students overcome the service-politics split at home and abroad.

Rutgers University professor Tobi Walker (2003) believes part of the reason for the service-politics split is a failure to transfer skills learned in local service projects to activism on the national and international level. Based upon informal research she has conducted over the years, people of all ages and walks of life value community service but are turned off by politics. Students in her classes "wanted to 'make a difference' and they believed the best way to do that was helping another person one-on-one. Working on policy, challenging decision-making structures, or engaging mainstream institutions rarely entered their thinking" (Walker, p. 171). Such observations reinforce the need for carefully designed service-learning experiences that not only reflect upon the macro-level societal issues that shape their local service experiences, but also help students act upon these insights in concrete and tangible ways.

Educators and political leaders have noted for some time the need for schools to provide carefully designed service-learning opportunities to enhance civic engagement. Research over the years clearly shows service-learning not only enhances academic learning but also increases civic participation (Eyler, Giles, Stenson, & Gray, 2001). Developing students' civic identity, as well as their civic discourse and participation skills, is central to effective civic education (Boggs, 1992; Kirlin, 2003; Mattson, Frantzich, Ball, Battistoni, & Hackett, 2000).

Civic identity consists of one's social relationships and actions as well as a sense of personal efficacy, and a belief in advancing the public good. Yates and Youniss (1998) draw upon Erikson's (1968) work in social psychology to argue that "civic experiences in youth can become reference points that aid in the formation of political understandings and engagement" (p. 495). Kirlin's (2003) review of the research concurs on the critical role participation in clubs and service organizations plays in fostering lifelong civic engagement, but points out that a key element in civic experiences, whether participating in a chess club or serving in a soup kitchen, is autonomy in deciding the nature and scope of one's personal involvement. This helps explain why previous studies (Verba, Schlozman, & Brady, 1995; Conway & Damico, 2001) have found participation in school sports to be negatively correlated to civic engagement during adulthood, according to Kirlin:

> Organized sports provide little opportunity for civic skill development: the goal (winning) is predetermined, and adults undertake the planning for the season, organize the matches, and do most of the coaching. Opportunities for students to organize themselves, decide on objectives, and collectively make decisions are limited. (p. 166)

If personal agency and autonomy in determining the nature and scope of engagement are critical factors in shaping formative experiences in civic identity, then possessing the communication and participation skills necessary to successfully negotiate community ventures becomes even more important. Kirlin (2003) offers an initial breakdown of some underlying background knowledge and cognitive skills necessary to effective participation in civic discourse. The civic discourse skills and their underlying cognitive skills or schema include: 1) monitoring public events and issues (e.g., understand distinctions between three sectors of society—public, nonprofit, and private; understand context for events and issues—what happened and why; capacity to acquire and thoughtfully review news—read the local newspaper); 2) deliberating about public policy issues (e.g., think critically about issues; understand multiple perspectives on issues); and 3) interacting with other citizens to promote personal and common interests (e.g., understand democratic society—collective decision making as norm; capacity to articulate individual perspective and interests) (Kirlin, 2003, p. 167). Kirlin's taxonomy of civic discourse skills provides a good initial sketch of an area in need of more research, and one about which the contributors in this anthology have much to say by illustrating how such civic discourse skills can and should be applied in the global arena.[2]

Additionally, Wurr (in press) found that linguistically and culturally diverse learners in particular needed additional instruction and support in developing the civic discourse skills necessary to complete service-learning projects successfully. In two separate studies, a pilot and main study involving native (NS) and non-native (NNS) English-speaking college students, he explored how students from diverse sociolinguistic backgrounds responded to and gained from service-learning. The results were mixed, with the initial study indicating NNS students often experience more difficulty finding and successfully completing work in the community while the main study found a similar group of NNS students to expect and gain more from service-learning activities than a comparative group of NS students. Intervention techniques were seen as instrumental in helping NNS students overcome sociolinguistic barriers to civic participation. Background knowledge on service organizations in America, interactional patterns and performance routines are likely to occur at a service site (e.g., interviewing, conducting surveys, and taking field notes), and an understanding of the historical and cultural values and traditions associated with volunteering in America helped prepare all students—especially NNS students with relatively little prior service-learning experience. Students more familiar with volunteerism and the service industry in American society can more readily draw upon this knowledge to help them complete the task at hand.

Just as the lack of the necessary language and discourse skills leads minority students to drop out of school in greater numbers than others, so too does it prevent them from effectively participating in American society, according to CIRCLE research released in 2002. Though the 2005 presidential elections marked a sharp increase in youth voter turnout rates for all ethnic groups, and for African Americans in particular, minority youth are still less likely than their same-age white peers to vote, to register to vote, to volunteer, or to feel they can make a difference in solving the problems of their community (Lopez, Kirby, & Sagoff, 2005). Voter turnout figures from CIRCLE's "The Youth Vote 2004" fact sheet are shown in Figure A.

Language minority students are not the only ones silenced in American schools and society. All students lacking the necessary civic literacy skills are at risk of being pushed out of participating in American democracy, and all Americans are at risk of being pushed out of the global marketplace due to a lack of expertise in universal civic literacy skills. Indeed, the overwhelming consensus among political, educational, and corporate leaders is that in order to maintain its role as a world leader, America must do a better

Figure A. Voter Turnout Figures

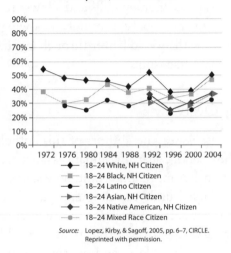

Graph 7: 18–24 Year Old Citizen Voter Turnout by Race, Presidential Years

Source: Lopez, Kirby, & Sagoff, 2005, pp. 6–7, CIRCLE. Reprinted with permission.

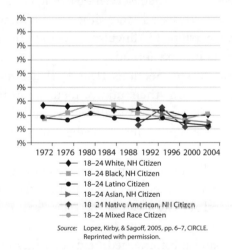

Graph 7: 18–24 Year Old Citizen Voter Turnout by Race, Midterm Years

Source: Lopez, Kirby, & Sagoff, 2005, pp. 6–7, CIRCLE. Reprinted with permission.

Source: Lopez, Kirby, & Sagoff, 2005, pp. 6–7, CIRCLE. Reprinted with permission.

job preparing multilingual professional and political leaders comfortable operating in multicultural environments. Multilingualism enhances universal civic literacy skills and allows greater access to, and participation in, the global community. Knowing multiple languages and knowing the world better through language are essential skills for global citizenship.

■ Anthology Overview

In taking up these issues, the authors of this anthology not only demonstrate how service-learning enhances language learning and civic participation, but more important, how service-learning can enhance international understanding and global civic participation skills. The first section provides the theoretical framework for developing service-learning projects in applied linguistics. In order for linguists to be able to address some of the educational and social problems related to the demographic and enrollment trends described above, their service-learning efforts need to be well defined, research based, and aimed at building sustainable community partnerships for linguistically and culturally diverse communities at home and abroad.

The contributors in Sections II and III use many of these same theories to inform their praxis, focusing in particular on service-learning with culturally and linguistically diverse populations. The courses and programs described highlight the saliency of using service-learning to enhance students' awareness and understanding of linguistic diversity and to apply this knowledge in meaningful ways to their personal and professional development at home and abroad.

The research reports in the final section of the book represent the largest and most engaged fields of study in applied linguistics—Spanish, TESOL teacher education, and composition studies. Together with the other empirically based research studies included in this anthology, they help document some of the research findings from the field. Given the challenges inherent in service-learning research, these studies are noteworthy for their efforts to document the impact of service-learning on students, faculty, and community partners in carefully designed studies that move beyond anecdote and teacher testimony to qualified claims supported by empirical data.

◼ Endnotes

1) The major legislative thrust of the Bilingual Education Act, that language minority children have a right to free public education, was folded in the No Child Left Behind Act in 2001. The No Child Left Behind Act attempts to ensure that the instruction language minority students receive is comprehensible through assessment of their learning outcomes compared to other student populations.

2) There may be some precedent for the concept of universal civic discourse skills, that is, skills that can be transferred from one community setting to another since some reading skills are believed to be universal. See Wurr (2002) for a discussion of case studies that highlight some of these in second language readers.

◼ References

Adamson, H. D. (2005). *Language minority students in American schools: An education in English*. Mahwah, NJ: Lawrence Erlbaum Associates.

Astin, A. W., Sax, L. J., & Avalos, J. (1999). Long term effects of volunteerism during the undergraduate years. *The Review of Higher Education, 22*(2), 187–202.

Bender, D. E. (2004, October). *Documenting migration transitions: Redesigning curriculum to include service learning and communicative Spanish*. Paper presented at College of William and Mary Sharpe Colloquium on service-learning with immigrant and minority language communities, Washington, DC.

Boggs, D. L. (1992). *Adult civic education* (Rep. EDO-CE-92-129). Columbus, OH: Clearinghouse on Adult, Career, and Vocational Education. (ERIC Document Reproduction Service No. ED 350 489)

Collier, V. (1987). Age and rate of acquisition of second language for academic purposes. *TESOL Quarterly, 21*(4), 617–641.

Conway, M., & Damico, A. J. (2001, September). *Building blocks: The relationship between high school and adult association life.* Paper presented at the annual meeting of the American Political Science Association, San Francisco, CA.

Cummins, J. (1981a). Age on arrival and immigrant second language learning in Canada: A reassessment. *Applied Linguistics, 2*(2), 132–149.

Cummins, J. (1981b). *Bilingualism and minority children.* Ontario, Canada: Ontario Institute for Studies in Education.

Derwing, T. M., DeCorby, E., Ichikawa, J., & Jamieson, K. (1999). Some factors that affect the success of ESL high school students. *Canadian Modern Language Review/La Revue canadienne des langues vivantes, 55*(4), 532–547.

Díaz-Rico, L. T (2004). *Teaching English language learners: Strategies and methods.* Boston, MA: Allyn & Bacon.

Díaz-Rico, L. T., & Weed, K. Z. (2002). *The crosscultural, language, and academic development handbook* (2nd ed.). Boston, MA: Allyn & Bacon.

Edwards, J. (2001). Languages and language learning in the face of World English. *ADFL, 32*(2), 10–15.

Ellis, R. (1994). *The study of second language acquisition.* Oxford, U.K.: Oxford University Press.

Erikson, E. H. (1968). *Identity: Youth and crisis.* New York, NY: Norton.

Eyler, J. S., Giles, D. E., Stenson, C. M., & Gray, C. J. (2001). *At a glance: What we know about the effects of service-learning on college students, faculty, institutions and communities, 1993–2000* (3rd ed.). Scotts Valley, CA: Learn and Serve National Service-Learning Clearinghouse.

Fine, M. (1991). *Framing dropouts: Notes on the politics of an urban public high school.* New York, NY: SUNY Press.

Hahn, C. L. (1999). Citizenship education: An empirical study of policy, practices, and outcomes. *Oxford Review of Education, 25*(1/2), 231–250.

Hakuta, K., Butler, Y. G., & Witt, D. (2000). *How long does it take English learners to attain proficiency?* (Policy Report 2000–1). Santa Barbara, CA: University of California Linguistic Minority Research Institute.

Heath, S. B. (1983). *Ways with words: Language, life, and work in communities and classrooms.* Cambridge, U.K: Cambridge University Press.

Jencks, C., & Phillips, M. (1998). The black-white test score gap: An introduction. In C. Jencks & M. Phillips (Eds.), *The black-white test score gap* (pp. 1–51). Washington, DC: Brookings Institution.

Joint National Committee for Languages, & National Council for Languages and International Studies. (2005). *Mission statement.* Retrieved October 3, 2006, from: www.languagepolicy.org

Kantrowitz, B., & Hammill, R. (1990). The reading wars. *Newsweek, 116*(10), 8–12.

Kirlin, M. (2003). Civic skill building: The missing component in service programs? In Campus Compact, *Introduction to service-learning toolkit: Readings and resources for faculty* (2nd ed., pp. 163–169). Providence, RI: Author. (Reprinted from *PS: Political Science and Politics, 35*(3), 571–575)

Lakoff, R. T. (2000). *The language wars.* Berkeley, CA: University of California Press.

Lee, V. E., & Burkam, D. T. (2003). Dropping out of high school: The role of school organization and structure. *American Educational Research Journal, 40,* 353–393.

Leibowitz, A. H. (1982). *Federal recognition of the rights of minority language groups.* Rosslyn, VA: National Clearinghouse for Bilingual Education.

Levine, P., & Lopez, M. H. (2002). *Youth voter turnout has declined, by any measure.* College Park, MD: Center for Information & Research on Civic Learning & Engagement.

Linguistics Society of America. (n.d.) *Linguistics in the news.* Retrieved October 3, 2006, from: www.lsadc.org/info/ling-news.cfm

Lopez, M. H., Kirby, E., & Sagoff, J. (2005). *The youth vote 2004.* College Park, MD: Center for Information & Research on Civic Learning & Engagement.

Mattson, K., Frantzich, S., Ball, W. J., Battistoni, R. M., & Hackett, R. (2000, November). *Education for civic leadership.* Retrieved October 3, 2006, from: http://publicleaders.tcnj.edu/roundtable_11_30_00.htm

National Association of Secretaries of State. (2004). *Fact sheet: Voter participation among youth and minorities.* Retrieved October 3, 2006, from: www.nass.org/Young%20Voter%20Fact%20Sheet.pdf

Neal, D. (2005). *Why has black-white skill convergence stopped?* (Working Paper No. 11090) Cambridge, MA: National Bureau of Economic Research.

Pratt, M. L. (2003). Building a new public idea about language. *ADFL, 34*(3), 5–9.

Rose, M. (1990). *Lives on the boundary.* New York, NY: Penguin.

S. Res. 28, 109th Cong. (2005). (enacted).

Shaughnessy, M. (1977). *Errors and expectations: A guide for the teachers of basic writing.* New York, NY: Oxford University Press.

Shin, H. B., & Bruno, R. (2003). *Language use and English-speaking ability: 2000. Census 2000 brief.* Retrieved October 3, 2006, from: www .census.gov/prod/2003pubs/c2kbr-29.pdf

Singham, M. (2005). *The achievement gap in U.S. education: Canaries in the mine.* Lanham, MD: Rowman & Littlefield Education.

Spolsky, B. (2006). Does the US need a language policy, or is English enough? Language policies in the US and abroad. In A. L. Heining-Boynton (Ed.), *2005–2015: Realizing our vision of languages for all* (pp. 15–38). Upper Saddle River, NJ: Prentice Hall.

Stanton, D. C. (2005). On linguistic human rights and the United States "foreign" language crisis. *ADFL, 36*(2), 5–13.

Teachers of English to Speakers of Other Languages. (1999). *Position statement on the acquisition of academic proficiency in English.* Retrieved October 3, 2006, from: www.tesol.org/s_tesol/bin.asp?CID=32&DID=378&DOC=FILE.PDF

Tonkin, H. (2001). Language learning, globalism, and the role of English. *ADFL, 32*(2), 5–9.

U. S. Department of Defense. (2005). *A call to action for foreign language capabilities*. Washington, DC: Defense Pentagon.

Verba, S., Schlozman, K. L., & Brady, H. E. (1995). *Voice and equality: Voluntarism in American politics*. Cambridge, MA: Harvard University Press.

Vernez, G., Krop, R. A., & Rydell, C. P. (1999). *Closing the education gap: Benefits and costs*. Santa Monica, CA: RAND.

Walker, T. (2003). The service/politics split: Rethinking service to teach political engagement. In Campus Compact, *Introduction to service-learning toolkit: Readings and resources for faculty* (2nd ed., pp. 171–174). Providence, RI: Author. (Reprinted from *PS: Political Science and Politics, 33*(3), 646–649)

Weise, A., & García, E. E. (1998). The Bilingual Education Act: Language minority students and equal educational opportunity. *Bilingual Research Journal, 22*(1), 1–18.

Wurr, A. J. (2002). Reading in a second language: A reading problem or a language problem? *Journal of College Reading and Learning, 33*(2), 157–169.

Wurr, A. J. (in press). Composing cultural diversity and civic literacy: English language learners as service providers. *Reflections: A Journal on Writing, Service-Learning, and Community Literacy, 5*(3).

Yates, M., & Youniss, J. (1998). Community service and political identity development in adolescents. *Journal of Social Issues, 54,* 495–512.

Section I

Conceptual Essays

As service-learning courses have become a mainstay at many college and university campuses, it has also become necessary to keep its practitioners—students, faculty, and community participants—current on how the field of applied linguistics defines, justifies, and envisions its expanding use of service-learning. Professionals in the field regularly refer to two landmark publications, which have helped them advance service-learning: *Principles of Good Practice in Combining Service and Learning* (National Service-Learning Clearinghouse, 1996), resulting from the 1989 Wingspread Conference, and *Standards for Foreign Language Learning in the 21st Century*, published in 1996 by the American Council on the Teaching of Foreign Languages. Nevertheless, in order for applied linguists to be able to address some of the educational and social problems related to the demographic and enrollment trends described in the introductory chapter, their service-learning efforts need to be well defined, research based, and aimed at building sustainable community partnerships for linguistically and culturally diverse communities at home and abroad.

In Chapter 1 Joby Blaine Taylor offers a much-needed etymological overview of the term *service*. Directing our attention to the 56 different usages of the verb *serve* and 38 of the noun *service* as

1

documented in the 1989 *Oxford English Dictionary*, Taylor makes a convincing case for carefully examining the word's particular meanings and variation over time. In instances where faculty and service-learning directors may be asked to calculate a federal grant's "return on the nation's investment," Taylor argues, they need to be familiar with the term's multiple semantic meanings, such as "service as charity," "service as public service," "service to country," and also "service as economics." Only then, he maintains, will service-learning practitioners become knowledgeable and informed participants in the debates surrounding the term *service* in national service and service-learning.

In Chapter 2 Chin-Sook Pak reports on promising findings in motivation research. Drawing on the results from two interdisciplinary service-learning seminars at Ball State University, the author analyzed student reflection activities and papers and determined that service-learning classrooms feature many of the motivational strategies that have been found beneficial for motivating second language learners. This includes, for example, promoting group cohesiveness and cooperation, and presenting learners with meaningful tasks and learning materials. The author's conclusion that "service-learning pedagogy can naturally incorporate a greater number of motivational strategies for learning Spanish than traditional classes" provides further support for Spanish faculty seeking to adopt service-learning in their classes.

In Chapter 3 Denise Overfield argues that properly structured service-learning experiences can create a space for acquiring a second language in the classroom and in the community. She illustrates how nursing students taking an introductory Spanish for health care workers class can improve their health care knowledge through a carefully designed service-learning experience at a county health department while at the same time advancing their Spanish proficiency. Overfield shows how closely sociocultural theory connects with service-learning pedagogy, which helps the reader understand how native and nonnative speakers interact with each other, negotiate meaning, and assist the learner's language acquisition in a unique cultural and social setting.

In the last chapter of this section, Stuart Stewart describes several service-learning projects she and her students undertake as they co-construct new knowledge about the history and current conditions of Hispanics living in the United States and new identities as advocates for change. Using a critical pedagogy framework in connection with National Standards for Foreign Language Learning, her work illustrates well the concept of empowerment on many levels, and helps show how a single person, course, or program can serve as a catalyst for others in the community to come together to solve common concerns.

1

What's the Service in Service-Learning? Historicizing as a Means of Understanding

Joby Blaine Taylor

> *A main source of our failure to understand is that we do not command a clear view of the use of our words.*
>
> —Ludwig Wittgenstein,
> *Philosophical Investigations* (1953, p. 49)

■ Keyword Investigation: Definition as Origin or History

> *It is common practice to speak of the "proper" or "strict" meaning of a word by reference to its origins. . . . The original meanings of words are always interesting. But what is often most interesting is the subsequent variation.*
>
> —Raymond Williams, *Keywords* (1985, p. 21)

One way to think about a word is as a nugget of truth that describes some piece of the world. Under this model, a word's meaning is its essence; it just needs uncovering. Definitions are durable and context free. The metaphor for this approach to semantics (i.e., the search for word meaning) is that of a gold mine. This metaphor operates within the larger conceptual frame that Michael Reddy (1993) critiqued as the "language as a conduit" metaphor. If words are gold nuggets—or any form of hard currency—then language is a system of value and exchange. The research path that proceeds from the mining metaphor in semantics highlights etymology as a kind of etiology, a quest for the word's original and truest meaning. In the etymon lies the gold. Definition, it follows, is properly about origin.

Another way to think about a word is as a window or lens for viewing a particular social context. Definitions reveal word meaning as used in particular times and places. However, this gazing metaphor should not hide the interactive character of language. Language, like all cultural systems, not only describes a world that we look out on, but also interprets and shapes that world. A window frames a view and a lens focuses an image. They are interpretive tools, tools for sense-making and social formation. Under these metaphors a word's meaning and value are naturally expected to vary greatly over the course of a language's history as well as across situations.[1] Words are cultural symbols with more or less currency depending on the resonance of their conceptual metaphors with the historical and social context of their usage. A word's earliest meaning is one example in what is typically a long and complex semantic history. Etymology is not the pick-and-shovel work of a miner digging for gold nuggets (i.e., true etymons) and discarding the tailings (i.e., variant meanings) along the way. A more instructive metaphor for etymology is an archaeology dig, sifting down through the historical strata with attention to the various layers and with the point of reconstructing a semantic narrative. An etymon, as the "deepest" recoverable layer in a word's story, is an important component of historical linguistic study, but it does not contain a word's essence. Most often etymology reveals the limits of our historical record and stops short of a verifiable "origin."

The word *service*, which will be the topic of the following pages, comes into English usage from French and brings an even earlier story of usage from Latin. Before these Romantic precedents, the term's history fades back into "Indo-European," an unrecorded proto-language reconstructed through acts of scholarly imagination. One etymological speculation is that *serve*, like *slave* (i.e., derived from Slavs), may have its roots in the name of a specific enslaved group, perhaps an Italian or Etruscan tribe conquered by the early Romans. These proper names for groups of people would have subsequently been generalized into a reference to a broader servant or slave class. The story of human language is deeper than human records, and our reconstructions of the past have interpretive and instrumental aspects. Etymology is less about corrective semantics—getting back to the truest sense of a word from a history of semantic devolution—and more about pragmatic semantics: building more sophisticated descriptions and interpretations that serve as tools for understanding and doing things in the present. The elusive etymon is one meaning among many meanings, a window into historical and social context. Definition is historicization.

Service and Serving: Roots and Variation

From the highest subject to the lowest, no man chuses to serve for nothing.

—BURN *Poor Laws*
(1764, in *Oxford English Dictionary*, 2006 [*OED*])

The noun *service* and the verb *to serve* encompass a broad semantic range. My objective is to investigate several of the terms' core meanings that have influenced the conceptualization of service-learning and national service. Much of the confusion and conflict over the questions "What is national service?" and "What is service-learning?" are rooted in semantic variations already existing in the term *service* when it was adopted for these modern compounds. Problems result when one or more of these semantic traditions of *service* are drawn upon with essentialist confidence without recognizing that *service* has a complex history. Subtle nuances of meaning in a term such as *service* can have significant practical consequences, especially when the term becomes the backbone of national and academic discourses. The result, in the phrase that inspired Raymond Williams's (1985) classic reference work *Keywords*, is that many of the definers in these discourses are "not speaking the same language" (p. 11).

Service, according to the *OED* (2006), "has supplied the place of a noun of action to its cognate verb *serve*."[2] The word enters English at the turn of the 12th century through the Old French term *service*, which, in turn, came from the Latin *servitium*. A great many English terms share this etymological history. Old French, a Latinate language with Germanic influences, came into contact with English after the Norman conquest of England in 1066, becoming a powerful influence on the development of Middle English (ME) language. English absorbed some 10,000 French words between the 11th and 16th centuries (Claiborne, 1990, p. 22).

The Latin cognate for the noun *servitium* is the verb *servire*, which became the Old French *servir* and through this entered English as *serve* (or its ME variants *serrfenn* or *serven*) documented by 1175. Etymologically, both the noun and verb in English ultimately derive from the Latin word *servus* meaning "slave." The word *serf*, still in use today, carries this original reference to a member of the slave class, as does, to a lesser degree, the common word *servant*. The root definitions of *serve* and *service* refer to a specific type of class-based activity. *Service*, in this earliest traceable meaning, is what the underclass does to aid the upper class. That the *service* in *service-learning* commonly refers to activities of an inverted charity-based nature, in which the privileged upper class provides aid to a needy underclass, is an example of the utter semantic plasticity of language. *Service* implies a social hierarchy, but, ironically, the direction of the aid aspect of *service* can run either up or down the rungs of this class ladder depending on the context of use. *Service* contains its own antonym. The movement from bottom-up to top-down helping is only part of the complex story of *service* that underpins the confusion and debates in national service and service-learning.

The *OED* (2006) documents 56 different usages of the verb *serve* and 38 of the noun *service*. Given the fact that their earliest documented English uses refer to specialized religious meanings, the terms appear to have entered English with multiple meanings already up and running. The *OED* distinguishes and documents five basic groups of usages of the verb *serve*. First, *to serve* continues the early etymological sense of its Old French and Latin precedents, meaning "to be a servant, to render service." Interestingly, the earliest documented uses of this sense in English are religious references to serving God dated to ca. 1175. Second, *to serve* can mean "to be subordinate, serviceable, or useful; to answer a purpose." This use is documented in English by 1225, which places it roughly in the same period of ME usage, and is a figurative application of the former class-based sense of service to other things, as in, "my work served its purpose." Third, *serve* is often used to mean "to minister to a person at table; hence, to supply, furnish, present with a commodity." Documented by 1250, this sense is a semantic specialization of the broader class-based activity of serving to refer specifically to waiting on those at a meal. These specializations are a natural result of the proximity and high visibility of the labor of house servants (i.e., as distinct from field servants). This specialized category of *service* enters another round of semantic generalization in which the term is extended to refer to any act of providing a commodity; ultimately, the term *service* becomes the source for concepts and terms like *customer service*, *service industry*, and *food services*. Fourth, *to serve* can mean "to dish up food; to deal out, present." This sense of the word *to serve*, which was documented around 1400, is closely related to the previous *domestic service* usage; except, in this case, it is the commodity itself which is said *to be served* (i.e., served up) rather than the person. Here the semantic shift is from active to passive voice. While this accommodates the reality of serving food to a table of people, it is also an interesting example of utilizing grammar to avoid the direct acknowledgment of the subordinate role of serving another person. Fifth, *to serve* is used to mean "to treat in a specified manner." This sense is documented as early as 1275 as a development of the qualitative notion that one could be well or ill served. It is a semantic generalization of the etymological sense, softening, if not eliminating, any reference to social class. In today's English, it is largely colloquial, as in the phrase, "it *serves* me right."

Similarly, the *OED* distinguishes and documents five basic meanings for the noun *service*. First, directly connected to the Old French and Latin precedent meaning "the condition of being a servant; the fact of serving a master" (e.g., "I was put into his service"). Again, interestingly, the earliest English use carries the specialized religious sense documented from 1230. The second meaning of *service* involves a subtle but important variation on this original sense, moving the meaning from a condition of servitude (i.e., a kind of ontological category) to a type of activity (i.e., a performative category). Here *service* refers to "the work or duty of a servant; the action of serving a master" (e.g., "I did him service as his aide"). It is documented early, first appearing about 1200. This distinction between a social status and a type of social action opens the term, through semantic specialization, to a number of non-class-based activities such as *national service, military service,* and also *public service*. Third, *service* has a number of specialized religious uses, as in "the service of God," "a religious service," or a "service book." A reference to a religious service ca. 1100 remains the earliest documented use of either of the terms *service* or *serve*, appearing within a generation of the Norman arrival. Fourth, *service* can mean "help, benefit, advantage, use." This meaning involves a semantic generalization of the specialized help provided by servants to refer to any kind of help or benefit provided by any class of person. This is the semantic stream, documented from the 14th century, from which *service as charity* and the *service* of *community service* have their primary source. It is the class-neutral bridge that allows for the reversal of the hierarchy of *service*. The notion of *service as charity* involves an additional round of semantic specialization by which *service* comes to mean "help provided to those most in need." Fifth, and finally, *service* can mean "waiting at table, a supply of food; hence, a supply of commodities, etc." Documented from 1300, this parallels the third sense of the verb *to serve* and is the precedent for current *service industry* usage.

Across these ten interrelated semantic streams of the verb and noun, the earliest documented English use is of *service* (i.e., "serfise") ca. 1100 as a technical reference to a specific Christian ritual, a *religious service*. Both the noun and verb have multiple documented uses of this sense in the later 12th century. Although a number of different semantic uses of the terms date to roughly the first century of Norman rule, it is interesting to note that a *marriage service* or *baptismal service* or *serving God* are among the first wave of inherited meanings. For service to have arrived in English with this already highly specialized meaning, it first had to undergo a number of shifts from the root meaning "service to a master" (i.e., the condition of servanthood). Many of these diverse meanings of *service* appear to have been concurrent already in 12th- and, certainly, 13th-century English. This means that some of the historical shifts of meaning were likely inherited in English as part of the deeper linguistic story of French and Latin.

Metaphor is the chief agent in this semantic change process. To arrive at *service* meaning "a religious ritual," for example, requires an initial semantic change from "service to a master" to "service to God." The conceptual metaphor supporting this transition is *God as Master*, which, through divine omnipotence, then places all human beings in service, not just those on the lowest socioeconomic rung. God makes a servant of everyone. A second semantic change through metaphor extends *service* from referring only to a general condition relating humans to God to include references to specific ritual activities archetypical of this human condition, namely religious services. In order for this kind of specialized metaphor to work as an agent of semantic change, a term must have a high degree of cultural currency. That is, the associations highlighted and focused by the metaphor depend upon popular assumptions about the term's meaning. For *service* to have the highly specialized meaning of "Catholic Mass" found in this earliest documented English usage means that it arrived with a richly layered semantic history. *Service* was already emblematic of a range of activities performed in service to God, activities that paralleled a host of exercises performed for earthly masters. That *service* entered English as a specialized term is not surprising because the movement of language borrowing from that time period involved common English folk interacting with a ruling French class. In Robert Claiborne's (1990) summary:

> The earliest French infusions into English were mostly the kinds of words that common folk naturally pick up from their rulers: terms of government, the law, warfare, and the church, all of which were dominated by the new Norman elite. (p. 21)

By the 13th century semantic streams of English use are documented in which *service* and *serve* developed or, more likely, recovered, a great semantic flexibility. Its uses included a variety of religious meanings, diverse diplomatic and political meanings, references to the ontological and performative versions of the servanthood meaning, specializations of this early meaning referring specifically to *domestic service* and, more specifically again, *table service*. *Service*, meaning "to help or benefit someone," appears in print by the 16th century, providing precedent for the semantic class reversal of *service* from *slavery* to *charity*. While the earliest documentations of this general "help" meaning do not openly carry the sense of class inversion, neither do they do exclude it. Berner, writing in 1533, says: "the grete seruyce that he hathe done to me shall be euen ryght well rewarded" (*OED*). In 1603, William Shakespeare (1991) writes in *Measure for Measure* (I.ii.181) "I pre'thee (Lucio) doe me this kinde seruice." Along this same timeline the term *charity* had come to predominantly mean "helping the needy" by the 16th century and by the 17th century the abstracted notion of a *charity institution* had come into use (Williams, 1985, p. 54). This convergence of *service* and *charity* reflects the sociocultural shifts and arising needs resulting from the transition from feudalism to capitalism; that is, from an agrarian social order to multiple specialized orders in densely organized cities.

■ Service: Modern Compounds

No one can give the date for the birth of any language. Each looms up imperceptibly out of a horizonless past. Languages thus appear rooted beyond almost anything else in contemporary societies. At the same time, nothing connects us affectively to the dead more than language.

—Benedict Anderson, *Imagined Communities*
(1983, pp. 144–145)

Several hundred years of mixed usage in English support today's compound concepts of *public service, national service, military service, customer service, divine service, community service,* and *charitable service.* In contemporary American life the word *service* is used both popularly and professionally with general and technical meanings and purposes. In government and media we speak of *public service.* The emphasis provided by the specifying term *public* accents the distinction between *public* and *private.* Public services are supported by tax revenues—which, in principle, are at least drawn from across the citizenry—and not by private enterprise. *Public servants* are those persons at local, state, or federal levels who are supported by public funds to operate public interest programs. They may be elected, appointed, or hired; or, they may be volunteers, but their service is to the state and its general citizenry. This meaning stands in the long-developed lineage of *service to country or a sovereign*. It is implied that public services are provided for the general public good, not for the private interests of a subgroup. *Webster's Dictionary* (1985) dates its definitions of *public service* to ca. 1570 and of a *public servant* to ca. 1676.

In economic language, modern English refers to the *service sector, service industries, customer service,* and *service economy.* This lineage is also the source of compounds like *service charge,* which is for services in addition to the basic fee; *service station,* which is where one stops for car repairs; and, *service road,* a road that parallels an expressway and permits special access to the adjacent community. Generally, this semantic stream distinguishes between various economic systems. An agricultural economy, in which value resides in the existence or production of hard goods, is distinguished from an industrial economy, in which value is added to raw materials by manufacturing and processing new products from them, which is further distinguished from a service economy, in which value is created through aspects of presentation and delivery. *Service* coupled with *economy* highlights the importance of packaging, delivery, and customer interface. This meaning derives from and further develops the etymological semantic sense of *service as servanthood* that specialized to mean "waiting tables" and then generalized again to mean the "providing of commodities."

In state matters we speak of *national service* and *military service.* By 1700, one could simply refer to *the Service* and *military* was understood. Like *service* and *religion, service* and *military* developed such strong associations that the second term could be dropped. *The Service* is a shorthand borne of widespread use, giving the terms *serviceman* and *servicewoman* to refer to members of the military, and *service medals* as shorthand for awards for exemplary military action.

The justice system prescribes *community service* hours in an interesting compound that intends both punishment and reparation for misdemeanor offenses. *Service,* in this case, refers to forced labor or the punishment aspect, but also implies that *service* repairs the social and material damage caused by the offense, and can reform the offender as well. *Community service* combines the original sense of *service as servitude* with the tradition of *public service* in which one works for the state to improve it. Beyond its justice usage, the compound *community service* has another semantic tradition that aligns it with a range of volunteer activities performed as charity to individuals or society. It is this lineage preserved in official designations like the *Corporation for National and Community Service* and the *Michigan Journal of Community Service Learning* that has been and remains a deep source for and influence on *national service* and *service-learning*, to which I will return.

Religious meanings of *service* also continue to have currency. In contemporary English usage one can still attend *church services*; and, in the same Roman Catholic tradition that informed the earliest uses of *service* in English, one can still *serve Mass*.

In summary, there are five primary semantic strands for *service* in current English usage, all of which relate to centuries of precedent and development. *Service to country and community* includes semantic traditions of military, diplomatic, public, and community service. *Service to God* includes the general and specialized religious references of *service*. *Service to superiors* includes the condition and activities of providing aid from a lower to upper class. *Charitable service* includes those helping activities moving in the inverse direction from upper to lower class. The inequality implied here can be based in distinctions other than socioeconomic class, for example, serving those with disease or disabilities. Finally, *service industry* includes those activities that add or create economic value through service.

This backdrop of etymological and contemporary domains of *service* meanings sets the stage for the discussions of the meanings of *national service* and *service-learning*. Contemporary confusions and conflicts result, in part, because the conceptualization of *national service* and *service-learning* draws from across these streams, compounding and mixing conceptual metaphors in the process.

■ Service-Learning: The Making of a Neologism

> *We are far from fully comprehending, much less agreeing on, exactly what service-learning ought to be or what it ought to do.*

> —Goodwin Liu (1999, p. xiii)

The compound term *service-learning* was coined by Bill Ramsay and Robert Sigmon in the mid 1960s in reference to internship programs in social and economic development sponsored by the Oak Ridge Associated Universities in Tennessee (Pollack, 1997). An early definition, "the accomplishment of tasks that meet genuine human needs in combination with conscious educational growth" (Stanton, Giles, & Cruz, 1999, p. 2) was composed in 1969, and can be found in publications of the Southern Regional Education Board. However, as is often the case with new terms, *service-learning* has numerous and contested uses and meanings. Stanton et al. (1999), early and important voices in the field, state:

> The definition of service-learning is problematic because it must express the joining of two different, complex processes: service and learning. It is complicated further because those who use the term and practice the pedagogy often have different and conflicting goals. (p. 207)

Service-learning variously refers to a *philosophy*, namely, a pragmatic alternative to the foundational epistemology of traditional Western philosophy; a *pedagogy*, one espousing socially situated experiential learning over didactic classroom instruction; and a *program*, various grassroots social problem-solving activities bringing together students and community members.[3] In 1990, Jane Kendall noted that in her literature review for the path-breaking three-volume *Combining Service and Learning,* she encountered 147 different terms for the activities falling under her purview. These ranged from *action research* to *collaborative learning* to *public service* to *servant leadership.* She says, "Even in a debate that lasts for decades, one has to choose some words in order to communicate. I have chosen 'service-learning' as the primary term that most closely expresses what this work is about" (pp. 19–20).

The early pioneers of service-learning drew from various philosophical, pedagogical, and programmatic traditions that when joined under the designation *service-learning* represented more than one of *service's* semantic streams. One of the emerging leaders in the field, Goodwin Liu (1999), warns against treating the neologism *service-learning* as if its meaning sprung from thin air:

> To characterize service-learning as a new development in education is inaccurate at best and presumptuous at worst. The concept (if not the label) has an impressive pedigree that includes the university-based extension programs of the 1860s land grant movement, John Dewey's philosophical pragmatism during the early decades of this century, and the campus and community-based organizing initiatives in the 1960s civil rights movement. (p. xiii)

As he mentions, one key source informing the development of *service-learning* was John Dewey's Pragmatism. Dewey's philosophy argued that epistemology is a tool for living and is worked out through interaction with the world. From this perspective, *service-learning as a philosophy* embodies the notion that knowledge is worked out in social contexts toward the end of solving problems. Service poses complex and real problems for experiential learning.

Dewey's theory of progressive democracy was related to this problem-based epistemology and distributed the responsibility of social problem solving to all citizens. From this perspective, *service-*

learning as a program is a model for citizenship education through civic engagement. Civics, like any area of learning, is experientially set and problem based. This idea has begun to take institutional root in American higher education. In the mid 1980s, Campus Compact, a coalition of higher education presidents commit- ted to linking citizenship education with community service in their institutional mission, began with three members. By 2005 it counted nearly 1,000 members.

Finally, Dewey's pedagogical position, which followed from his theories of knowledge and society, was that teachers should guide students as they construct meaning through engaging in real prob- lem solving in social experiential settings. In contrast to traditional didactic approaches, this model is student centered; the Deweyan teacher is a facilitator, not an authority, and the classroom is an experience, typically just an impoverished one. In 1983, David Kolb adapted Dewey's understanding of human inquiry to develop an influential four-stage model of experiential learning, which par- tially informed what today has become the National Society for Experiential Education.[4] In this respect, *service-learning as a peda- gogy* is a subset of the experiential learning model, one that adopts service as its specific experiential learning context.

Another source of influence on *service-learning* as it developed in higher education came from earlier models of applied scholar- ship such as the land-grant colleges of the middle 19th century, in which the mission of the institution was to engage the resources of higher education toward identifying and solving social problems. This tradition has been revived recently through Ernest Boyer's (1994) call for a "New American College" in which he envisioned the transformation of institutions of higher education into inter- disciplinary institutes conjoining theory and practice in their com- mon effort to resolve pressing social issues.

With source influences as broad as these, one naturally expects debates over terminology and semantics. While numerous seman- tic issues remain, the debates over the name for this developing philosophy, pedagogy, and program have been largely resolved. While the field's leading journal, *The Michigan Journal of Community Service Learning* (formed in 1993), still retains a variant (i.e., *service learning* prefaced with *community* and without a connecting hyphen), the term *service-learning* has been institutionalized. *Service-learning* was the term codified in the National and Community Service Act of 1990. The National and Community Service Trust Act of 1993 further created the Corporation for National Service (CNS), a U.S. department on par politically, and in collaborative relationship with, the Department of Education. Heads of the two departments recently drafted a joint "Declaration of Principles" that states, "We believe it is important to emphasize the common enterprise of school improvement and the national service movement. *Service-learning* is the bridge" (italics added, Riley & Wofford, 2000, p. 670). Learn and Serve America (LSA), a branch of CNS, is now entering its second decade of providing grants, technical assistance, and training for service-learning programs at all levels of schooling across the country.

Service-learning appears now as the keyword in book titles in the field—for instance, *Service-Learning: The Essence of the Pedagogy* (Billig & Furco, 2002), *Service-Learning: A Movement's Pioneers Reflect on its Origins, Practice, and Future* (Stanton et al., 1999), and *Where's the Learning in Service-Learning?* (Eyler & Giles, 1999). It is also becoming increasingly distinguished in higher education through changing staff titles. Where previously community service and volunteerism were branches of student affairs, titles like "Director of Service-Learning" and "Chair of Service-Learning" are becoming increasingly common. There has also been an increase in academic conferences dedicated to the field under the title *service-learning*, notably in 2001, the First Annual International Service-Learning Research Conference, hosted by UC Berkeley. Writing in 1999, Stanton, Giles, and Cruz state, "The past decade has been breathtaking for service-learning. . . . Service-learning pedagogy is now advocated by students, faculty, presidents of colleges and universities, and even by Congress and the president of the United States" (p. xv). In short, the term, though not yet included in general dictionaries, has been adopted at all political and educational levels in the U.S. Service-learning exists in somewhat of a liminal state, established as an accepted neologism, but with many and contested semantic interpretations.

■ Service-Learning Semantics: Confusion and Conflicts

> *What is really happening through these critical encounters . . . is a process quite central in the development of a language when, in certain words, tones and rhythms, meanings are offered, felt for, tested, confirmed, asserted, qualified, [and] changed.*

> —Raymond Williams, *Keywords* (1985, pp. 11–12)

Having traced the etymological origins and various semantic trajectories of *service* and also having reviewed the sources and history of the newly instituted term *service-learning*, I would now like to explore some of the issues and debates in the emerging field of service-learning by relating them to the differing semantic strands of *service* itself. The Latin root of *service* defined the activities of servants toward masters. The inversion of meaning that later identified *service* as *charity* proceeds by a metaphoric analogy: As I am served by those beneath me, so I too serve a power greater than myself, a God or a Sovereign, or a Country/Nation. Hence *service* is applied beyond the servant class to include even the king who engages in service to the divine. Furthermore, this ultimate authority requires, whether by faith, mandate, or contract, that I act to help those around me who are in need. This opens a semantic window for the reversal of *service* hierarchy, *service* to those of a lower socioeconomic class than oneself. It depends on one's estimation of *charity* whether this development is a positive one or not, but, normative judgments aside, charity is typically a conservative concept. Charity preserves socioeconomic class distinctions even as it argues for a kinder, gentler upper class.

Many of the founders of what came to be termed *service-learning* programs were grounded not in a *service* tradition but rather in John Dewey's tradition of progressive democracy whose citizenship model held as its goal the elimination of such class distinctions. In a series of interviews with early practitioners, Stanton, Giles, and Cruz (1999) found that a number "expressed serious reservations about the term *service-learning* itself, and the implications of noblesse oblige, and power and control, that it contains" (p. 207). The premier—perhaps endemic now that it is institutionalized—semantic problem with *service-learning* is that the *service* it adopted was widely associated with the *service as charity* tradition, while in contrast, the field's seminal sources and pioneers were solidly against such programs of charity. The first term identifying the field carries both a reference to social inequality and a deep tension about what programmatically to do about it. Dewey himself argued against the dangers of paternalistic charity and these later advocates of Deweyan progressivism feared guilt by association with the socially conservative understandings of *service*.[5] Service-learning that is framed by *service as charity* implies support for the hierarchy that ranks persons and communities. Dewey thought that *service* ought to be about leveling asymmetrical social relations, not acting charitably within them.

Nadine Cruz (1990), an early service-learning leader, has argued that, especially in the context of international programs, the *service as charity* meaning reinforces unequal relationships rather than equalizing them. Cruz states, "I think it is possible to empower learners (through service learning) and not promote the common good (by reinforcing a sense of inferiority among those 'served' or a false sense of power among those who 'serve')" (p. 323). These attempts to effect a shift in the meaning of *service* in *service-learning* are part of an ongoing debate in which the concept of *service* has been understood as existing along a value continuum. For Dewey and those in his tradition of progressive democracy, *service as charity* represents one end, that of naïve, socially conservative, or even destructive instances of social activity. At the other end, *service as progressive social change* represents mature, socially reformative *service*. According to Stanton, Cruz, and Giles (1999), this means that true service implies a two-way street of giving and receiving; service seeks mutuality. They attempt to differentiate this in the linguistic move from *service* to *service-learning*: "Service-learning advocates differentiate their practice from volunteer service by evoking the concept of reciprocity between server and served as well" (p. 3).

Dewey's influence on service-learning also leads many of its advocates to oppose the implication that *service as charity* consists only of privatized individual acts. If the above debate was against *service's* class conservatism and toward radical pedagogy for social change, then this second debate argues against private acts of service and toward *service as a citizenship duty*. In this case, however, unlike the first, there are precedent semantic meanings of *service* that could be aptly applied. This Deweyan tradition could arguably extend the meaning of *public service* beyond just traditional paid public servants to include all students and interns who participate in service-learning programs. In the case of service-learning programs with a national scope, there is also the deeply historical semantic tradition of *service to country and community* upon which to draw for these public interpretations of service. Service-learning, then, has historical precedent from which to develop itself into programs of citizenship learning through civic engagement. While the semantic tradition of *service as charity* focuses on the individual act, the semantic tradition of *service to country and community* has always included a broad public service mission.

Yet another of the *service as charity* implications is the conclusion that the service in service-learning must be voluntary and unpaid. This leads to the perception of conflict in cases where students are recompensed for their activity; their altruistic intentions seem compromised. This fuels debates about what dollar amount would constitute an internship as opposed to volunteer service-learning and whether it is possible to reimburse students for mileage as they drive to city schools to volunteer tutor. More important, such a semantic reduction ensures that *service-learning* cannot be applied to vocational fields; that is, *service* cannot be one's life work, only a spare time activity. This reduction of *service* to *volunteerism* reinforces an association of *service-learning* with a privileged classism, restricting participation to those who can afford to be volunteers. Mike Goldstein, another early founder of service-learning whose critical voice was captured by Stanton, Giles, and Cruz (1999), states:

> What troubles me in the semantic war is the issue of compensation—that giving of service is the reward. . . . That's a wonderful idea. . . . But most students today can't afford to do that. . . . At Urban Corps it was an absolute article of faith that students were going to be compensated, because otherwise it was going to look like all the other volunteer programs: a lily-white, middle-class, nice thing to do. This notion that if you get paid, you're less worthy than a volunteer is nonsense. It's overtly discriminatory. (p. 210)

This is another conflict in which the historical precedent of *service as public service* and its broader tradition of *service to country and community* can be recovered and applied beyond political officeholders. There is little debate about whether public servants should be paid (although there is debate when they vote themselves a raise!) and for decades, national service programs like the Peace Corps, and more recently AmeriCorps, have provided modest living stipends to support service participation.

Another interesting conflict arising from this volunteer connotation results when service is instituted as a required activity. For example, in 1993 the Maryland State Department of Education instituted a high school graduation requirement of 75 hours of service-learning, the first state to adopt such a mandate. My experience with my own students arriving from Maryland high schools is that they identify the *service* in *service-learning* predominantly with the semantic tradition of *charity* resulting in their critical view that the state has adopted the oxymoron *service as forced volunteerism*. In an almost unanimous chorus these students state that service-learning is a good experience but should not be "required" because those who do not want to participate voluntarily will miss the point anyway and could easily end up doing others a *disservice* in the process.

The emergence of service-learning, rooted in Deweyan concepts, at faith-based institutions of higher education, has also produced debates about the meaning of such service activities. Many of these institutions draw their missions from the deep tradition of *service as divine service*. For example, in the Christian tradition, *service* carries a "preference for the poor" and is linked closely to the semantic tradition of *service as charity*. However, proponents argue that the tradition of religious charity, from which "shallower" secular charity meanings derived, is more closely tied to the "deeper" meaning preserved in the Latin *caritas*. Charity is not just superficial class-based do-gooding, but is a legitimate and needed tradition of caring for those most in need (Foos, 1998; Morton, 1995). Still there remains the question about normative intent in faith-based service-learning initiatives. Critics of Christian service argue that it carries an evangelical intent. Nadine Cruz (as cited in Stanton et al., 1999) asks, "What does it mean to do service out of a missionary narcissism?" (p. 208). How secular must a "social gospel" become before its object is social change and not proselytism? These are questions that service-learning advocates at faith-based institutions must answer if they seek inclusion in the broader field of service-learning.

A final area of semantic confusion and conflict involves the interface of national service and service-learning. One reason for the quick and dramatic expansion and institutionalization of service-learning in higher education has been the distribution of many millions of federal grant dollars through the Corporation for National and Community Service's Learn and Serve America initiatives. The national service selection and sponsorship of service-learning gives it a great deal of weight in the semantics of framing and evaluating these programs. However, *national service* draws from semantic streams of *service* that service-learning advocates do not typically acknowledge. For example, *service to country* has for many centuries been closely tied to *military service.* The U.S. has a century-long tradition of *national service* dating from William James's 1906 (1983) address "The Moral Equivalent of War," and referring to citizen activities informed by the discipline of *military service,* but directed toward the general improvement of society. This tradition runs through the Civilian Conservation Corps of the 1930s, the Peace Corps from the 1960s, AmeriCorps beginning in the 1990s, and the Citizen Corps created after September 11, 2001. All of these programs, in James's rhetorical lineage, have been framed as metaphoric wars enlisting citizens in the fight against social problems (Taylor, 2002). *Service as war* has been a predominant framing metaphor for *national service.*

In the 1990s business language began underpinning the description and evaluation of national service. This drew legitimacy from two early meanings of service: *service as public service* and *service as economics.* The first supported that tax dollars were hard at work supporting public services and the second that those tax dollars, like our aspirations for private investments, were efficiently adding value and increasing profit through service programs.

These frames have practical purposes. The discourse framing *national service as war* creates a sense of civic urgency and the need for national solidarity. The discourse framing *national service as business* aims to cultivate trust in national leaders and government structures and create a citizen "company man" identification as stakeholders and stockholders. Citizen volunteers add value and create a return on investment. The discourse framing *national service as citizenship* uses service participation as a tool for engaging and framing membership identity and loyalty. Service is the dues paid for membership, and manufacturing new citizens through service becomes an extended citizen duty. Good politicians (or their rhetoricians) know that they can access these various semantic traditions, creatively borrowing here and implying there, to support strategic national ends.

The critical question in the semantic interplay between *national service* and *service learning* is: What is the role of the nation? If a nation's primary raison d'être is "protection" then these several metaphors of national service are simply function. A nation fights its enemies; hence, national service is war, both metaphoric and real. A nation guards its assets and creates wealth; hence, national service is business. A nation preserves its membership and identity; hence, national service is citizenship. It is only to be expected that when coupled with these "national" purposes *service* will be appropriated under these metaphors. Being cognizant of this allows service-learning advocates to question or limit their framing potency in contexts where these metaphors are inappropriate. Service-learning advocates would intuitively recognize the limitations of framing *service as war*: that it reduces and oversimplifies complex social issues, that it focuses on attacking problems over collaborative and sustainable work, et cetera, but they have yet to recognize this implication of closely associating with this tradition of *national service*. Similarly, service-learning program coordinators become frustrated and cynical with evaluation forms for federal grants whose focus is calculating a "return on the nation's investment." They realize that student experience and program effectiveness cannot be reduced to a bottom dollar, yet these concerns have not yet been articulated to government funding agencies. These upcoming debates can be given clarity through the recognition that the involved parties are drawing from different semantic traditions of the same word, *service*.

■ Definition? Implications and Conclusions

*We get somewhere in history by weaving metaphor upon meta-
phor and then riding upon our carpet. . . . Perhaps time is simply the accretion of metaphor upon metaphor.*

—Edward Berggren (1994, p. 30)

There is no denotation that flows naturally from the term *service*. Rather, there are meanings for the term that entered English
nearly a millennium ago already importing a complex semantic
history and which were subsequently developed and semantically
nuanced even further. The debates about the meaning of *service*
in *service-learning* are not then about semantic essence but about
the struggle for normative and political currency. Definers of service-learning, in articulating what they mean, are more precisely
expressing what they want. There is a political economy to the
determination of meaning. *Service* as it refers to a host of "helping"
activities is sufficiently abstract so that its meaning in actual usage
is subject to great influence by its association with other concepts.
Pairing *service* with concepts such as Master, God, Nation, Poor,
might yield the cognitive metaphors *service is slavery, service is evan-
gelism, service is soldiering,* or *service is charity* respectively, each with
dramatic semantic differences.

Keith Morton (1995) has argued that service-learning need
not choose *social change* models over *charity* models, but rather
could conceive deep instances of each. Rather than getting mired
in a quest for the "correct" definition, he suggests that context be
the guide to choosing the appropriate paradigm. If a service activity involves political advocacy around a key issue or empowering
a specific community, then articulating *service* as "social change" is
the appropriate and best choice for developing a program that does
what it intends. If student service involves one-on-one mentoring, then articulating *service* as "charitable helping of others" may
be appropriate. Service-learning will better move from theory to

practice if its advocates articulate purposeful, contextually appropriate definitions, that is, self-conscious metaphors for service. A natural starting point is to recover and redescribe the various semantic traditions of *service* itself. Because *service* has many meanings, *service-learning* is even more layered given the complexities of the compound joining *service* to *learning*. Connecting the meanings of *service-learning* with precedent meanings of *service* is a helpful means of understanding confusions and conflicts in the field. If the history of the word's range of meanings is forgotten then the debaters really are, as Williams (1985) put it, "speaking different languages."

Given the institutionalization of the term *service-learning*, debaters of this neologism's meaning have the full semantic fields of both terms available as the starting point for forming purposeful metaphors for their activities. Considering the breadth of the service-learning concept, these may be philosophically purposeful, focusing on the way in which knowledge is constructed through service; they may be pedagogically purposeful, focusing on the way in which learning and teaching occur in service contexts; or, programmatically purposeful, framing and reflecting the context of service. Semantic debates ought to remain central to this process, not as an attempt to prescribe an essentialist definition, but rather as the critical expression of a call that definitions be historically informed, self-consciously developed, and well chosen to fit their context.

■ Endnotes

1) Diachronic variations, or differences over time, are the subject matter of historical linguistics. Synchronic variations, or differences across cultures and situations, are the subject matter of sociolinguistics.

2) *OED* references are to the online edition, a database without pagination. Specific examples of historical usage for all of the

meanings of *service* I describe may be found in the noun and verb entries in the *OED*.

3) The question of pedagogy highlights the term *learning* in service-learning. While it is beyond this project to explore its subtleties it deserves an etymological note. Learning is from the Old English *leornian* "to study," whose original meaning, given Indo-European cognates, seems to have been "to follow a track." The Latin *lira* keeps this sense, and interestingly the Latin verb *delirare* (i.e., to lose the track) means madness (English *delirium*). That is, to stop learning would interestingly mean to go insane.

4) Hesser (1996) notes that the National Center for Public Service Internship Programs and the Society for Field Experience Education were formed in 1971 and 1972 respectively, then merged in 1979 to form the National Society for Internships and Experiential Education (NSIEE), which is now known simply as the NSEE. That is, internships and public service, as well as experiential education, informed the historical development of NSEE. I would like to thank the editors of this volume for this historical note.

5) See John Saltmarsh (1996) on Dewey's critique of charity.

■ References

Anderson, B. (1983). *Imagined communities: Reflections on the origin and spread of nationalism*. London, U.K.: Verso.

Berggren, E. (1994). Deconstruction and nothingness: Some cross-cultural lessons on teaching comparative world civilization. In R. Martusewicz & W. Reynolds (Eds.), *Inside out: Contemporary critical perspectives in education* (pp. 210–236). New York, NY: St. Martin's Press.

Billig, S., & Furco, A. (Eds.). (2002). *Service-learning: The essence of the pedagogy*. Greenwich, RI: Information Age Publishing.

Boyer, E. (1994, March 9). Creating the New American College. *The Chronicle of Higher Education*, p. A48.

Claiborne, T. (1990). *Roots of English: A reader's handbook of word origins*. New York, NY: Anchor Books.

Cruz, N. (1990). A challenge to the notion of service. In J. Kendall, et al. (Eds.), *Combining service and learning: A resource book for community and public service* (pp. 321–323). Raleigh, NC: National Society for Internships and Experiential Education.

Eyler, J., & Giles, D. E. Jr. (1999). *Where's the learning in service-learning?* San Francisco, CA: Jossey-Bass.

Foos, C. (1998). The "different voice" of service. *Michigan Journal of Community Service Learning, 5,* 14–21.

Hesser, G. (1996). A brief national history of service-learning. In V. M. Littlefield (Ed.), *Community service-learning at Augsburg College: A handbook for instructors, version 2.0* (p. 1–7). Minneapolis, MN: Augsburg College Center for Faculty Development.

James, W. (1983). The moral equivalent of war. In F. Burkhardt & F. Bowers (Eds.), *The works of William James: Essays in religion and morality* (pp. 162–173). Cambridge, MA: Harvard University Press. (Original work published 1906)

Kendall, J. (Ed.). (1990). *Combining service and learning: Vol. 1. A resource book for community and public service*. Raleigh, NC: National Society for Internships and Experiential Education.

Kolb, D. (1983). *Experiential learning: Experience as the source of learning and development*. New York, NY: Prentice Hall.

Liu, G. (1999). Foreword. In T. Stanton, D. Giles, Jr., & N. Cruz (Eds.), *Service-learning: A movement's pioneers reflect on its origins, practice, and future* (pp. xi–xiv). San Francisco, CA: Jossey-Bass.

Morton, K. (1995). The irony of service: Charity, project, and social change in service-learning. *Michigan Journal of Community Service Learning, 2,* 19–32.

National and Community Service Act of 1990, S. 1430, 103d Cong. (1990).

National and Community Service Trust Act of 1993, HR. 2010, 103d Cong. (1993).

Oxford English Dictionary Online. (2006). Retrieved October 3, 2006, from: http://dictionary.oed.com

Pollack, S. (1997). *Three decades of service-learning in higher education (1966–1996): The contested emergence of an organizational field.* Unpublished doctoral dissertation, Stanford University.

Reddy, M. (1993). The conduit metaphor: A case of frame conflict in our language about language. In A. Ortony (Ed.), *Metaphor and thought* (2nd ed., pp. 164–201). New York, NY: Cambridge University Press.

Riley, R., & Wofford, H. (2000). The reaffirmation of The Declaration of Principles. *Phi Delta Kappan, 81*(9), 670–673.

Saltmarsh, J. (1996). Education for critical citizenship: John Dewey's contribution to the pedagogy of community service learning. *Michigan Journal of Community Service Learning, 3,* 13–21.

Shakespeare, W. (1991). *Measure for measure* (B. Gibbons, Ed.). New York, NY: Cambridge University Press.

Stanton, T. K., Giles, D. E., Jr., & Cruz, N. I. (1999). *Service-learning: A movement's pioneers reflect on its origins, practice, and future.* San Francisco, CA: Jossey-Bass.

Taylor, J. (2002). Metaphors we serve by: Investigating the conceptual metaphors framing national and community service and service-learning. *Michigan Journal of Community Service Learning, 9*(1), 45–57.

Webster's Ninth New Collegiate Dictionary. (1985). Springfield, MA: Merriam-Webster.

Williams, R. (1985.) *Keywords: A vocabulary of culture and society.* New York, NY: Oxford University Press.

Wittgenstein, L. (1953). *Philosophical investigations.* (G. Anscombe, Trans.) New York, NY: Macmillan.

2

The Service-Learning Classroom and Motivational Strategies for Learning Spanish: Discoveries From Two Interdisciplinary Community-Centered Seminars

Chin-Sook Pak

The past several decades of motivation research in the second/ foreign language (L2) field have provided language teachers with various frameworks for understanding the complexity of factors that can affect students' motivation for learning an L2 (Clément, Dörnyei, & Noels, 1994; Crookes & Schmidt, 1991; Dörnyei, 1994, 2001b; Gardner, 1979, 1985; Gardner & Lambert, 1972; Williams & Burden, 1997). From social factors such as students' perception of the target language, culture, and community to educational factors such as course, teacher, and learner-related variables within a classroom setting, motivation serves as a driving force not only to initiate but also to sustain L2 learning processes. As a result, strategies to develop motivation-sensitive teaching practices have received considerable attention (e.g., Chambers, 1999; Dörnyei, 2001a; Dörnyei & Csizér, 1998; Oxford & Shearin, 1994).

The aim of this chapter is to examine motivational strategies for learning Spanish in the context of service-learning classrooms. The "counter-normative" nature of service-learning pedagogy (Clayton & Ash, 2004; Howard, 1998) is known to create some discomfort for both the faculty and students as they learn to move away from individualism, instructor control, and predictability of traditional classrooms to self-critical analysis, shared responsibility, civic engagement, and active learning of "messy" service-learning classrooms involving community partners. However, such shifts in the perspective of the classroom can positively affect motivation for L2 learning. Based on data from student reflection papers gathered from two interdisciplinary service-learning seminars conducted in Spanish at Ball State University, this chapter investigates specific motivational strategies that are natural outcomes of the service-learning classroom. Although motivational strategies for language learning were not purposefully included in the design and delivery of both seminars, a large number of them were found to be inherent in these service-learning seminars.

▪ Motivational Studies and Second/Foreign Language Learning

Motivation in the context of second language acquisition can be understood as "the combination of effort plus desire to achieve the goal of learning plus favorable attitudes towards learning the language" (Gardner, 1985, p. 10). In this definition, the successful language learner will need not only desire but also effort and satisfaction with the learning tasks. The framework for understanding motivation in language learning has its roots in various fields in psychology. The most influential earlier studies in motivation were conducted by a group of social psychologists who examined the relationship between attitudes and motivations and achievement of language learners in bilingual settings of Canada and offered the well-known "integrative vs. instrumental" conceptualization of motivation in L2 learning (Gardner & Lambert, 1972; Gardner, 1979). An integrative orientation (i.e., reasons for studying) is associated with the learner who wishes to identify himself/herself with the culture(s) that speak that language. An instrumental orientation is related to pragmatic interests such as better employment opportunities, passing an exam, or gaining promotion. The social psychological perspectives on motivation have highlighted the superiority of the integrative aspect, asserting that the attitudes and orientations of the learner toward the community of speakers of the target language are the most important factors influencing his/her learning of that language. In his influential Socio-Educational Model of language learning, Gardner (1985) thus examines "the integrative motive" that is affected by two principal sets of variables thought to influence motivation: "integrativeness" (e.g., attitudes toward the target language group, interest in foreign languages, and integrative orientations) and attitudes toward the learning situation (e.g., attitudes toward the language course and language teacher).

Research since the 1990s has broadened theoretical perspectives to incorporate other psychological approaches to understanding the complexity of L2 learning motivation. Representative works by such scholars as Crookes and Schmidt (1991), Dörnyei (1994, 2001b), Oxford and Shearin (1994), Tremblay and Gardner (1995), and Williams and Burden (1997), while not ignoring the importance of the social dimension, have investigated the connection between L2 language learning and theories of motivation in cognitive/educational psychology. A few examples of these theories include expectancy-value, self-efficacy, self-determination, and goal-setting theories. Expectancy-value theories suggest that learners will be motivated if they expect success and value the outcomes (Wigfield & Eccles, 2000). Self-efficacy theory implies that learners' judgment of how well they can perform (i.e., confidence) will determine their choice of activities and the effort and persistence placed on them (Bandura, 1997). Self-determination theory distinguishes intrinsic motivation (e.g., personal pleasure/satisfaction) from extrinsic motivation (e.g., good grades or avoiding punishment) and insinuates that learners' motivation will be greater if their activities are more self-determined rather than dictated (Deci & Ryan, 1985). Finally, goal-setting theory suggests that learners' performance is greater if goals are specific, challenging, and meaningful to them (Locke & Latham, 1990). Thus, the incorporation of a wide array of motivation theories from general psychology has led to the conceptualization of broader frameworks for understanding L2 motivation, which in turn has produced a number of works aimed at facilitating motivation-sensitive teaching practices.

Zoltán Dörnyei's (2001a) *Motivational Strategies in the Language Classroom* will serve as the primary text of reference in this discussion of specific motivation strategies for learning Spanish in service-learning courses. Dörnyei provides the most comprehensive list of practical classroom strategies to date. He defines motivational strategies as "techniques that promote the individual's goal-oriented behavior ... those motivational influences that are consciously exerted to achieve some systematic and enduring positive effect" (p. 28). Dörnyei offers 35 possible strategies based on four key components of his process-oriented framework of motivational teaching practice in the L2 classroom: creating the basic motivational condition (e.g., appropriate teacher behaviors, classroom environment, group dynamics); generating initial motivation (e.g., enhancing learners' language-related values and attitudes, their expectancy of success and goal-orientedness, relevant teaching materials); maintaining and protecting motivation (e.g., stimulating and enjoyable tasks, specific goals, self-esteem, positive social image, learner autonomy); and encouraging retrospective self-evaluation (e.g., motivational attribution and feedback, learner satisfaction, and rewards). These motivational strategies will be examined in detail in the context of the service-learning classroom.

■ Service-Learning and Student Learning Outcomes

With a greater number of campuses committing to civic purposes of higher education, there has been a surge of interest in service-learning pedagogy across disciplines. Service-learning is a form of experiential education whose pedagogy involves engagement, reflection, and reciprocity. The service tasks meet specific community needs and students are presented with a mechanism for reflection that connects their community service experience to course content and citizenship. Bringle and Hatcher (1995) note that this is "in contrast to co-curricular and extracurricular service, from which learning may occur, but for which there is no formal evaluation and documentation of academic learning" (p. 112). The underlying concept of reciprocity in service-learning highlights its democratic and communal process where every party involved is both teacher/learner and server/served. Thus, successful service-learning programs must meet three criteria: 1) enhanced academic learning; 2) relevant and meaningful service with the community; and 3) purposeful civic learning (Howard, 2001).

Implementation of service-learning courses, however, creates challenges for both teacher and students. Howard (1998) refers to it as counternormative pedagogy that "qualitatively changes the norms and relationships of the teaching-learning process" (p. 22). Discomfort and dissonance surface as both the instructor and students must cope with "'real world' messiness and unpredictability, complexities of the social change process, personal and intellectual risks inherent in reflection, and shared control and responsibility implicit in partnerships" (Clayton & Ash, 2004, p. 59). Indeed, service-learning pushes students from individualistic self-orientation to commitment to the broader good in the community and from being passive recipients of information in a classroom tightly controlled by the instructor to becoming active coinvestigators engaged in critical analysis of their social reality in the context of unpredictable real-life situations. These shifts in the perspective of the classroom, if embraced by the instructor and students, can positively affect the quality of the student learning experience.

Benefits of service-learning endeavors on student learning outcomes are well documented. Research findings suggest that there are significant personal, social, and cognitive learning outcomes (Eyler & Giles, 1999). In their examination of studies, programs, and reports on the effects of service-learning on higher education and communities from 1993–2000, Eyler, Giles, Stenson, and Gray (2001) summarize that service-learning has a positive effect on students' sense of personal efficacy, personal identity, spiritual growth, moral development, interpersonal development, ability to work well with others, leadership and communication skills, reduction of stereotypes, facilitation of cultural and racial understanding, sense of social responsibility and citizenship skills, ability to apply what they have learned in the "real world," demonstration of complexity of understanding, problem analysis, critical thinking, cognitive development, and so forth.

Benefits of service-learning pedagogy in the context of those who teach and study Spanish as an L2 have also been demonstrated by a growing number of practitioners and by research presented in the United States. For example, along with numerous articles steadily published in such journals as *Foreign Language Annals* and *Hispania,* the American Association of Higher Education (AAHE) has a monograph on service-learning and Spanish, *Construyendo Puentes (Building Bridges)* (Hellebrandt & Varona, 1999) and the American Association of Teachers of Spanish and Portuguese has dedicated one of its volumes in the annual professional development series to service-learning, *Juntos: Community Partnerships in Spanish and Portuguese* (Hellebrandt, Arries, & Varona, 2004). Such explosion of interest in service-learning by those who teach Spanish can be attributed to the significant Hispanic presence in the country and consequently, growing opportunities to work with native speakers of Spanish in local communities. In particular, service-learning tasks have been considered an effective pedagogical tool for meeting the "Fives Cs" of *Standards of Foreign Language Learning in the 21st Century* as stipulated by the American Council on Teaching of Foreign Languages (ACTFL). These goals are *communicate* in languages other than English; gain knowledge and understanding of other *cultures; connect* with other disciplines and acquire information; develop insights into the nature of language and culture (i.e., *comparisons*); and participate in multilingual *communities* at home and around the world. As Hale (1999) suggests, service-learning can serve as a "missing link" between meeting these goals and the traditional classroom where students have limited opportunities to engage in real communication or to acquire culture competence. A Spanish course with a well-designed service-learning component can provide students with opportunities that allow them to "learn *with* speakers of the language rather than *about* them" (Plann, 2002, p. 332).

Research on the effects of service-learning on students who study Spanish suggests significant positive learning outcomes. A successful service-learning experience depends on factors such as duration, intensity, and placement of the service; quality and quantity of reflective activities that facilitate the application of service to academic content and vice versa; and quality feedback from professors and community partners on students' self-reported learning, use of skills taught in courses, and commitment to service. Practitioners of service-learning have noted numerous positive student learning outcomes: increase in communicative competence (e.g., intensity and diversity of students' exposure to cultural and linguistic materials); increase in self-confidence (e.g., sense of fulfillment, enjoyment, and pride through contact with native speakers); further interest in the language and culture (e.g., strengthening students' desire to minor/major in Spanish); increase in cultural awareness and reduction of stereotypes (e.g., exposure to diversity; more reflective critical analysis of students' social reality, and positive attitudes toward Spanish speakers and their cultures); sense of solidarity, friendships, and closeness with classmates, instructor, and the community; connection with other disciplines; development of active learning skills; and meeting the goals of the national standards for foreign language learning (Beebe & De Costa, 1993; Hale, 1999; Jorge, 2004; Long, 2003; Mullaney, 1999; Olazagasti-Segovia, 2004; Overfield, 1997; Plann, 2002; Polansky, 2004; Tilley-Lubbs, 2004; Varona, 1999; Varona & Bauluz, 2004).

Morris (2001), in his evaluation of a service-learning program at the University of Minnesota, has conducted interviews and surveys with the participating students to study its impact on learner motivation and attitudes toward Spanish, Spanish speakers, and their cultures. His study shows significant positive changes in students' response between pre- and post-service-learning surveys. For example, students rated higher in all the categories on desire to interact with Spanish speakers, to continue studying Spanish beyond the requirements, to improve their understanding of the cultures that use Spanish, and even to support a foreign language requirement, etc. Thus, Morris concludes that "face to face contact with local native Spanish speakers had a positive effect on the participant's motivation and attitudes towards learning Spanish and towards Spanish speakers and their culture" (p. 252).

■ The Service-Learning Seminars at Ball State University

I have had the privilege of teaching two interdisciplinary service-learning seminars at Ball State University. These two seminars, conducted in Spanish, varied in the intensity of the service-learning experience: "Servir y aprender" was a 15-credit, project-driven seminar offered during the fall semester of 2003, and "¿Hablas español? Connecting with our Hispanic Community" was a three-credit honors colloquium taught during the spring semester of 2005. The goals of both seminars were to become better informed about a number of historical, social, legal, economic, and cross-cultural issues as they relate to the growing Hispanic presence in the U.S. (and particularly in Indiana); to develop meaningful relationships via services to community organizations or Hispanic community members; and to provide meaningful and authentic contexts for language acquisition. As is characteristic of service-learning courses, the seminars also aimed at meeting other academic and civic learning goals such as developing critical-thinking, problem-solving and organization skills, interpersonal learning, diversity, social responsibility, citizenship, and leadership skills.

The 15-credit immersion service-learning seminar was taught through the Virginia B. Ball Center for Creative Inquiry at the university. The center supports four faculty members each year to teach interdisciplinary seminars, each with 15 students. Each seminar must explore the connections among the arts, humanities, science, and technology; create a product to illustrate their collaborative research and interdisciplinary study; and present their product to the community in a public forum. Working together with community sponsors, each group of faculty and students creates a product (e.g., an exhibit, performance, or publication) to engage the community in public dialogue. The students enrolled in the seminars come from various disciplines and backgrounds and carry their full load of "courses" for the semester at the Center.

In "Servir y aprender," 15 Ball State students and I conducted community action research that took us into businesses, churches, schools, police stations, courtrooms, jails, and victim support and advocacy agencies around Hamilton County, in central Indiana. Students provided a number of interested agencies and organizations with weekly services. The community partnership work included interpreting and translating written documents; teaching survival English to jail inmates and conveying their concerns to the authorities; listening to and surveying concerns by interviewing numerous local Hispanic community members at churches, homes, and schools; and working alongside Spanish-speaking employees at a factory and serving as liaisons to non-Spanish-speaking managers. As an outcome of their community service and research, the students identified common issues where recently arrived, working-class Hispanic immigrants can unintentionally stumble into conflict. The culminating seminar product was the creation of *Sobrevivir*, a series of four educational soap operas or telenovelas (see www.bsu.edu/vbc/sem_20032004_fall_pak.htm). These videos (in Spanish with English subtitles, 40 minutes) are being used to inform the mainstream and new immigrant communities about some of the common issues related to driving without a license, public intoxication, seeking medical care, and domestic violence.

In the three-credit honors colloquium, "¿Hablas español? Connecting with our Hispanic community," 12 students worked with three local working-class Hispanic immigrant families by assisting them with a number of everyday needs for both the children and adults. These service tasks included helping to access the public transportation system, developing literacy and basic computer skills, mentoring the children, exploring educational resources for all age groups, tutoring survival English language skills for the adults, interpreting and explaining written documents, and forming meaningful friendships. By intimately working with each member in the family, the class examined not only a number of economic, political, and social issues related to the growing Hispanic population in the region but also a wide spectrum of challenges an immigrant family faces as it struggles to integrate itself into American society. At the end of the semester, half the class shared their learning experience at a service-learning conference organized by Indiana Campus Compact, and the other half worked together to write a press release on the outcomes of their community partnership experience for local papers. Finally, the class chose to draft and send a letter to urge the government to support DREAM ACT, which calls for assisting undocumented minors who have grown up in this country, graduated from high school, and have no criminal record, to attend college and legalize their immigration status. The class met three hours per week, and students completed 20–30 service hours during the semester.

Students in both seminars had majors from a variety of disciplines such as history, English literature, criminal justice and criminology, education, telecommunications, theatre, political science, environmental sciences, and Spanish. Students' Spanish language background also varied from those who had completed only two years of college-level Spanish to those who had experienced a semester or year of study abroad in a Spanish-speaking country. A small percentage of the students constituted heritage speakers (first-to third-generation Hispanic immigrants) with varying degrees of Spanish language proficiency. Although the class was conducted in Spanish, English was permitted to facilitate class discussions involving guest speakers with limited Spanish language proficiency.

Language support (e.g., explicit instruction of grammar/discourse strategies) was provided depending on the need. For example, at various intervals during the semester, the class reviewed detailed usages of the preterit/imperfect, the future, and the subjunctive to facilitate class discussions and weekly journal writing, in which students described their weekly service activities, interpreted and reacted to them, and shared their plans for future encounters with the community partners. Although many reading materials were in English (e.g., government reports, research articles), students also regularly read a substantial number of articles in Spanish, especially from dailies published in such cities as Los Angeles, Chicago, and New York, as well as in other local newspapers and magazines.

An important component in both seminars was ongoing reflection activities that included class discussions, weekly journals, pre- and post-seminar personal essays, and a final reflection paper. Class discussions contributed to identifying patterns of discoveries as well as seeking solutions to potential challenges. Weekly journals described and evaluated the details of students' weekly seminar experience. The reflective activities were facilitated by ongoing documentation of their learning via developing a service-learning portfolio that organized the reading list, notes, lesson plans for services, and weekly journals. All reflective activities were done in Spanish with the exception of the final reflection paper in which students could choose the language and were asked to evaluate their overall service-learning experience by examining their service-learning portfolio.

Given their community immersion experience, students in both seminars reported an increase in their motivation to use and improve their Spanish language skills. The next section will closely examine motivational strategies for Spanish language learning as documented in students' written reflection work. According to Long (2003), "diary studies have gained considerable acceptance in the field of second language acquisition because they are useful for identifying attitudes, motivation, and other variables relevant to the learning/teaching process" (p. 225).

■ Service-Learning and Motivational Strategies for Learning Spanish

In one of the principal works that offers practical pedagogical strategies to positively influence learners' attitudes and motivation, Dörnyei (2001a) provides an extensive inventory of motivational strategies useful for the language classroom. Although he warns that the effectiveness of these strategies depends on the learning conditions determined by such factors as cultural background, age, proficiency, and relationship to the target language, Dörnyei offers 35 strategies aimed at creating the basic motivational conditions, generating initial motivation, maintaining and protecting motivation, and encouraging retrospective self-evaluation.

The first group of motivational strategies is intended to create the basic motivational conditions that are conducive to developing appropriate teacher behaviors and a good relationship with the students, a pleasant and supportive classroom atmosphere, and a cohesive learner group with appropriate group norms. Highlighting the teacher's own behavior as the most important motivational tool, Dörnyei suggests ways in which teachers can positively influence and relate to students. These strategies include demonstrating enthusiasm and sharing the value of and satisfaction attained from L2 learning, showing high expectation of what students can achieve, developing a personal relationship with the students, creating a supportive atmosphere in the classroom by encouraging risk-taking and tolerance, developing group cohesiveness by promoting group activities both inside and outside the classroom, formulating group norms and having them discussed and accepted by the learners, and having the group norms consistently observed.

The service-learning classroom as exemplified by the two seminars embraced all of these strategies, although they had not been purposefully integrated into the design of both seminars. Because the seminars involved concrete, hands-on service tasks in the community, from the very beginning of the semester, the students understood the importance of using and improving Spanish in order to provide meaningful services. The expectations for quality work were made clear. The direct contact with native speakers in the community also increased their enthusiasm and willingness to work more rigorously to improve their language skills than they would have in the traditional language classrooms. The students also worked together both in and outside of the classroom in groups, taking risks in unfamiliar territories and understanding that their success depended on the group. As a consequence, they were willing to tolerate differences and support each other. Furthermore, the students became coinvestigators, creating a shared sense of ownership of the class. Due to this codependency, I was able to develop a much closer personal relationship with the students. Below are some examples of students' reflection collected from their papers:

> Another meaningful relationship I formed was with my professor and the rest of my classmates. Since this was a new type of class for everyone, it was very important to work together to get ideas from one another as well as to support each other in all our endeavors.

> We gave each other advice, shared resources, and listened to each other. I get a sense of family from this class.

We soon learned everyone's personalities, tendencies, strengths and weaknesses as well as how to pull together as a class even when some of us were not getting along.

I believe that camaraderie formed among us because we all shared that same drive to do something about issues we had been studying. Since the topics discussed were often grave and overwhelming, having a group of fellow class-mates was comforting.

This was the first class I have experienced through three years of college in which there was an overriding sense of concern and compassion for everyone else in the room. The distinction, I would propose, is due to the nature of the project upon which we had embarked to complete. Rather than competing for grades in a more traditional classroom setting, we were focused on accomplishing a greater humanitarian goal.

Dörnyei's second group of motivational strategies is aimed at generating initial motivation. These include suggestions to enhance the learners' language-related values and attitudes, to increase the learners' expectancy of success, to increase the learners' goal orientedness, to make the teaching materials relevant to the learners, and to create realistic learner beliefs. Examples of specific strategies include presenting peer role models, raising the learners' intrinsic interest in the L2 learning process, promoting "integrative" values with the L2 and its speakers, increasing the awareness of the instrumental values (e.g., career enhancement), increasing the students' expectancy of success, and formulating explicit class goals.

In both of my seminars, the interdisciplinary nature of learn-ing/serving required us to seek guest speakers with different sets of expertise who provided the class with new perspectives and skills.

The speakers were community professionals, volunteers, agency representatives, faculty, and students with previous service-learning experience with Spanish-speaking communities in the area. The direct contact with native speakers in the community was conducive to increasing the "integrative" values of students' learning.

As students learned first hand about the impact of the growing Hispanic presence in the United States and the desperate need for bilingual professionals in so many sectors of governmental, business, religious, health, and social service organizations, they became further aware of the instrumental values associated with knowing Spanish. Students negotiated and adjusted goals for their service tasks and discussed what would constitute a meaningful learning experience. The teaching materials were designed to meet students' service and learning needs. Students also contributed by selecting their own reading materials and sharing them with the class. Finally, students formed and evaluated realistic expectations of their Spanish learning.

> In this class, not only is there motivation to learn the language, but there is also a sense of, "Why wouldn't I want to know how to speak Spanish?" The fact that we were able to put our skills to use in real-world settings and communicate with people outside of our classroom is a great way to acquire a second language.

> In the past my motivation to learn Spanish was selfish. I knew that it would make me much more marketable in the business world and probably allow me to command a higher salary. Now, however, while I still do want to learn Spanish for the business aspect, there is also a much more important reason . . . I simply want to be able to communicate with millions of other people . . . I want to be able to communicate with them to help them, to learn from them, and to just be a friendly person towards them.

The difference between learning in a traditional classroom and [this seminar] is that we had the real world in our assignments. What we were doing mattered and we had to uphold and raise our standards.

We immersed [ourselves] in their [Hispanic] world and thus in their language. We spoke Spanish in their contexts and not in the contexts of a Spanish classroom with a book full of verb conjugations. The relationships were authentic as was the communication we maintained.

The third group of motivational strategies is directed at maintaining and protecting motivation. These strategies encourage teachers to make learning stimulating and enjoyable, to present tasks in a motivating way, to set specific learner goals, to protect the learner's self-esteem, to increase their self-confidence, to allow learners to maintain a positive social image, to promote cooperation among the learners, to create learner autonomy, and to promote self-motivation learner strategies. In order to make learning more stimulating and enjoyable, Dörnyei suggests that teachers break the monotony of classroom events and enlist students as active task participants. In the service-learning classroom, the partnership work with the community constantly influences the direction of students' activities; there is no room for monotony given the fact the students must cope with changing needs of the community. In both seminars, students had to address unexpected events and issues:

Throughout the course of the semester, we were faced with countless problems that needed our attention. However, these were not your everyday problems that had a simple step-by-step solution. Therefore, we were forced to use our problem-solving skills to come up with inventive ways of dealing with the issues.

The service-learning process was useful in promoting and stimulating different manners of thought and perception. Beliefs that were previously held . . . were able to be approached from multiple viewpoints and to be criticized normatively.

The interdisciplinary nature of this seminar was one of the most valuable tools of our class. Because of this aspect of the class I was learning and doing things I never thought I would.

All learning materials and activities were aimed at helping the students to better connect with the community while using and improving their Spanish language skills. For example, in order to better express their emotions and describe their reaction to their service experiences, students were more willing to learn the subjunctive. In order to better assess the relevant issues related to serving our Hispanic community members, students regularly read and shared articles from such newspapers as *La Opinión* (from Los Angeles) and *El Diario/La Prensa* (from New York City). Students also made constant adjustments to their plans—what they could realistically achieve during the limited amount of time given during the semester:

I also discovered that this is a gargantuan task and one can quickly and easily become overwhelmed simply thinking about it. This is why I am going to try to focus on simple, achievable goals that I have control over.

Dörnyei also suggests providing learners with multiple opportunities to experience success and build confidence by helping students reduce language anxiety. The unpredictable and interdisciplinary nature of service-learning projects can create much anxiety initially. At the beginning of the seminars, many of my students worried whether their Spanish skills were good enough to work with their community partners. Many of them also never had any meaningful direct contact with Spanish-speaking community members. Furthermore, some students felt frustrated in dealing with the uncertainties and unpredictability of the outcomes. However, the direct contact with native speakers wanting to work with students, the relationship-building opportunities, and supportive environment resulting from group dependency strengthened their determination to persevere, to overcome the anxiety, and to build their confidence:

> Through speaking with María [not real name] and the class, I have been able to construct statements with greater ease and accuracy and to speak with greater confidence. In fact, I remember correctly using the preterit for, perhaps, the first time in class. I was so proud . . . Because of the one incident, I trusted myself with the tense more and attempted to use it more often, even though I did not always use it correctly.

> This class has provided the single most beneficial opportunity I have ever experienced . . . I discovered throughout this semester that one's ability to speak well in another language is based heavily upon his confidence and assertion in that speech.

> While I wouldn't say that I can communicate with ease, I think I can safely say that I am able to communicate without anxiety. This is a direct result of the experience I have had with native Spanish speakers and how appreciative and warm they are because of the fact that I am attempting to speak their language.

This class greatly improved my motivation to use Spanish. . . . In the past, any time the teacher was not near me, I spoke English . . . I now catch myself trying to use my Spanish wherever possible, such as at work. When I have just finished speaking Spanish, I have trouble switching back into English. I even sometimes think in Spanish, which is something I had never done before. Probably the most dramatic evidence of my improved Spanish is the decrease I have experienced in anxiety level.

The service-learning tasks, furthermore, provided students with the opportunities to maintain a positive social image as students developed meaningful relationships with their community partners, class peers, and instructor. Most important, service-learning pedagogy promotes learner autonomy. The instructor is no longer the information provider but a coinvestigator who works alongside the students.

Kate and I formed a very special bond because we were involved in the same experience. For instance, we both were apprehensive to speak and listen to Spanish on a weekly basis, but we worked together and encouraged each other which immediately alleviated all worries because we knew we were in it together.

Before I began working with her and her family, I did not know that I would leave having a new friend. At the beginning, we did not trust each other nor did we know anything about one other, but as the semester continued, we grew close together.

We decided what we were going to teach our community partners and how we were going to go about doing so. We had to find the necessary resources on our own . . . we pooled our resources with the rest of the class so that they could then use them.

What I really like about this seminar is that it truly was a learning process every step of the way for us students and our professor. There was always a new problem to overcome and another conflict to work out.

One of the unique features of the semester was the individual autonomy given to each student. For the first time, the instructor seemed on a more level playing field with the students and provided guidance more than instruction.

The final group of motivational strategies is intended to encourage students to positively self-evaluate their learning experience. These strategies include promoting motivational attributions, providing motivational feedback, increasing learner satisfaction, and offering rewards and grades in a motivating manner. In the service-learning seminars, the students were engaged in ongoing reflection activities throughout the semester. At the end of the service activity, the students were asked to reread their weekly journals and evaluate their learning experience. They attributed their success to their effort, cooperation, and risk-taking. They received supportive feedback from their peers, community partners, and the instructor. They experienced satisfaction with development of more confidence and involvement in hands-on tasks affecting real-life situations. And finally they received meaningful rewards:

If I were to choose the single most meaningful aspect of the experiences created through this class, it would be that students were pushed perpetually to think and engage others in ways that were previously unknown, unorthodox, and uncomfortable.

I noticed that my writing proficiency increased as well. At the beginning of the class, it took me somewhere between two and three hours to write a single [journal entry], but by the end of the semester, it only took me a little over an hour.

Beyond this once in a lifetime learning experience, I have found that I have made special friends that I will remember for a lifetime. I've been able to learn the life of students with diverse backgrounds and other disciplines. Our hard work and weeks of stress proved a testing ground for our dedication to the project and the strength of our friendship.

The fact is, helping María with important problems and also learning from her unique experiences will be something that I will remember forever, not the grade I received on a test.

I am now much more aware of the communities in which I live . . . I see the multitudes of different ethnicities and cultures and I want to learn about them. Essentially, I now want to be a *part* of my community, rather than simply be *in* my community.

It has given me insight on real life situations and has given me an outlook on life which I was blinded from before. This seminar has changed my career decision and goals for higher education.

In summary, the majority of motivational strategies provided by Dörnyei were inherent in my two interdisciplinary service-learning seminars. By working as coinvestigators in the community within real-life contexts, striving to provide relevant and meaningful services, developing meaningful relationships with their peers, instructor, guest speakers, and community partners, and taking an active part in their learning process, the students reported higher drive, effort, and satisfaction in learning Spanish.

■ Conclusions

After elaborating and offering numerous motivational strategies that language teachers can use with foreign- or second-language learners, Dörnyei (2001a) states that it is not possible for a teacher to incorporate all of them. Instead, the author asserts that even he has "consistently applied only a fraction of the long list of strategies discussed earlier," and encourages teachers to focus on quality with "a few well-chosen strategies that suit both you and your learners" to become "good enough motivators" (p. 136). What is surprising about the service-learning classroom is that its pedagogical goals can naturally incorporate, not just a few, but many if not the majority of the strategies mentioned. By bringing together faculty, students, and community partners, concentrating on the greater good beyond the boundaries of one discipline, creating connections between service and learning, and documenting the learning process through rigorous reflection activities, service-learning pedagogy can create optimal conditions for learning Spanish as an L2. The service-learning classroom can promote stronger faculty-student relationships, develop group cohesiveness and cooperation, strengthen students' integrative and instrumental orientations, present meaningful tasks and learning materials, make learning more stimulating and enjoyable, promote learner autonomy, and finally, increase learner satisfaction.

The service-learning classroom, however, must address several challenges. Its success depends on understanding and embracing the shift of perspectives on teaching and learning processes. Effective implementation of service-learning tasks and satisfactory learning outcomes also depends on factors such as service quality and intensity, quality and frequency of student reflection activities and feedback from the teacher and the community partners, proper application of the skills taught in courses, and commitment to service by all parties involved. Coordinating activities with community partners and adjusting class activities to cope with changing needs may make the service-learning classroom more labor-intensive and time-consuming than the traditional classroom. Nevertheless, when the goals and tasks are meaningful and there is a clear sense of shared ownership, students may demonstrate an unexpected capacity to learn and to serve, and they can be the ones who raise the standards.

The present study has examined motivation strategies for language learning in the context of two unique interdisciplinary seminars conducted in Spanish. In order to validate the claims made in this paper regarding the numerous motivational strategies that are inherent in the service-learning classroom, future research will need to investigate how L2 motivation is affected by service-learning pedagogy within already established language courses in the curriculum.

■ References

Bandura, A. (1997). *Self-efficacy: The exercise of control.* New York, NY: Freeman.

Beebe, R. M., & De Costa, E. M. (1993). The Santa Clara University Eastside Project: Community service and the Spanish classroom. *Hispania, 76,* 884–891.

Bringle, R., & Hatcher, J. (1995). A service learning curriculum for faculty. *Michigan Journal of Community Service Learning, 2,* 112–122.

Chambers, G. N. (1999). *Motivating language learners.* Clevedon, U.K.: Multilingual Matters.

Clayton, P. H., & Ash, S. L. (2004). Shifts in perspective: Capitalizing on the counter-normative nature of service-learning. *Michigan Journal of Community Service-Learning, 11*(1), 59–70.

Clément, R. Z., Dörnyei, Z., & Noels, K. A. (1994). Motivation, self-confidence, and group cohesion in the foreign language classroom. *Language Learning, 44,* 417–448.

Crookes, G., & Schmidt, R. W. (1991). Motivating: Reopening the research agenda. *Language Learning, 41,* 469–512.

Deci, E., & Ryan, R. (1985). *Intrinsic motivation and self-determination in human behavior.* New York, NY: Plenum.

Dörnyei, Z. (1994). Motivation and motivating in the foreign language classroom. *Modern Language Journal, 78,* 273–284.

Dörnyei, Z. (2001a). *Motivational strategies in the language classroom.* Cambridge, U.K.: Cambridge University Press.

Dörnyei, Z. (2001b). *Teaching and researching motivation.* Harlow, U.K.: Longman.

Dörnyei, Z., & Csizér, K. (1998). Ten commandments for motivating language learners: Results of an empirical study. *Language Teaching Research, 2*(3), 203–229.

Eyler, J., & Giles, D. E., Jr. (1999). *Where's the learning in service-learning?* San Francisco, CA: Jossey-Bass.

Eyler, J. S., Giles, D. E., Stenson, C. M., & Gray, C. J. (2001). *At a glance: What we know about the effects of service-learning on college students, faculty, institutions and communities, 1993–2000* (3rd ed.). Scotts Valley, CA: Learn and Serve National Service-Learning Clearinghouse.

Gardner, R. C. (1979). Social psychological aspects of second language acquisition. In H. Giles & R. St. Clair (Eds.), *Language and Social Psychology* (pp. 193–220). Oxford, U.K.: Blackwell.

Gardner, R. C. (1985). *Social psychology and second language learning: The role of attitudes and motivation.* London, U.K.: Edward Arnold.

Gardner, R. C. & Lambert, W. E. (1972). *Attitudes and motivation in second language learning.* Rowley, MA: Newbury House.

Hale, A. (1999). Service-learning and Spanish: A missing link. In J. Hellebrandt, & L. T. Varona (Eds.), *Construyendo puentes (building bridges):*

Concepts and models for service-learning in Spanish (pp. 9–32). Washington, DC: American Association for Higher Education.

Hellebrandt, J., & Varona, L. T. (Eds.). (1999). *Construyendo puentes (building bridges): Concepts and models for service-learning in Spanish.* Washington, DC: American Association for Higher Education.

Hellebrandt, J., Arries, J., & Varona, L. (Eds.). (2004). *Juntos: Community partnerships in Spanish and Portuguese.* Boston, MA: Heinle.

Howard, J. (1998). Academic service learning: A counternormative pedagogy. In R. Rhoads & J. Howard (Eds.), *Academic service-learning: A pedagogy of action and reflection* (pp. 21–30). San Francisco, CA: Jossey-Bass.

Howard, J. (2001). *Service-learning course design workbook. A companion volume to Michigan Journal of Community Service Learning.* Ann Arbor, MI: University of Michigan, Office of Community Service Learning.

Jorge, E. (2004). Dialogue and power: Collaborative language curriculum development. In J. Hellebrandt, J. Arries, & L. T. Varona (Eds.), *Juntos: Community partnerships in Spanish and Portuguese* (pp. 17–28). Boston, MA: Heinle.

Locke, E. A., & Latham, G. P. (1990). *A theory of goal setting and task performance.* Englewood Cliffs, NJ: Prentice Hall.

Long, D. R. (2003). Spanish in the community: Students reflect on Hispanic cultures in the United States. *Foreign Language Annals, 36*(2), 223–232.

Morris, F. A. (2001). Serving the community and learning a foreign language: Evaluating a service-learning programme. *Language, Culture, and Curriculum, 14*(3), 24–255.

Mullaney, J. (1999). Service-learning and language-acquisition theory and practice. In J. Hellebrandt & L. T. Varona (Eds.), *Construyendo puentes (building bridges): Concepts and models for service-learning in Spanish* (pp. 49–60). Washington, DC: American Association for Higher Education.

Olazagasti-Segovia, E. (2004). Second language acquisition, academic service-learning, and learners' transformation. In J. Hellebrandt, J.

Arries, & L. T. Varona (Eds.), *Juntos: Community partnerships in Spanish and Portuguese* (pp. 5–16). Boston, MA: Heinle.

Overfield, D. M. (1997). From the margins to the mainstream: Foreign language education and community-based learning. *Foreign Language Annals, 30,* 485–491.

Oxford, R. L., & Shearin, J. (1994). Language learning motivation: Expanding the theoretical framework. *Modern Language Journal, 78,* 12–28.

Plann, S. J. (2002). Latinos and literacy: An upper-division Spanish course with service learning. *Hispania, 85,* 330–338.

Polansky, S. G. (2004). Tutoring for community outreach: A course model for language learning and bridge building between universities and public schools. *Foreign Language Annals, 37,* 367–373.

Tilley-Lubbs, G. A. (2004). Cross the border through service-learning: The power of cross-cultural relationships. In J. Hellebrandt, J. Arries, & L. T. Varona (Eds.), *Juntos: Community partnerships in Spanish and Portuguese* (pp. 36–56). Boston, MA: Heinle.

Tremblay, P. E., & Gardner, R. C. (1995). Expanding the motivation construct in language learning. *Modern Language Journal, 79,* 505–520.

Varona, L. T. (1999). La comunidad en el aula y el aula en la comunidad: un modelo. *Hispania, 82,* 806–815.

Varona, L. T., & Bauluz, M. V. (2004). When everyday life becomes the focus of attention in intermediate Spanish courses. In J. Hellebrandt, J. Arries, & L. T. Varona (Eds.), *Juntos: Community partnerships in Spanish and Portuguese* (pp. 69–82). Boston, MA: Heinle.

Wigfield, A., & Eccles, J. (2000). Expectancy-value theory of achievement motivation. *Contemporary Educational Psychology, 25,* 68–81.

Williams, M., & Burden, R. (1997). *Psychology for language teachers: A social constructivist approach.* Cambridge, U.K.: Cambridge University Press.

3

Conceptualizing Service-Learning as a Second Language Acquisition Space: Directions for Research

Denise M. Overfield

The development of service-learning pedagogy for foreign language learners is a relatively recent phenomenon that coincides with a shift over the past 20 years in second language acquisition research. The latter has moved from an approach that focuses on the learner as an individual who is deficient in his/her knowledge of the target language to one that emphasizes the learner as a participant in a social setting (for example, the foreign language classroom) and examines how that setting shapes and is shaped by linguistic, educational, and social practices (see Frawley & Lantolf, 1985; Hall & Davis, 1995; Lantolf & Appel, 1994; Ohta, 2000; Platt & Brooks, 2002). In this body of work, classroom discourse analysis provides much revealing information regarding second language acquisition specifically and cognitive development in general.

Historically, many learning theories have stemmed primarily from the belief that the learner is a vessel who must be filled with knowledge (Kozulin, Gindis, Ageyev, & Miller, 2003; Sfard, 1998). Much recent educational research, however, has used sociocultural theory as a starting point for examining the role that learners play in the educational process. This theory, which stems from Vygotsky's (1978) work, moves educational processes from an individual standpoint to a perspective that emphasizes the ways in which culture, social roles, and language (among other things) affect the development of learners. According to sociocultural theory, all human cognition and learning are social and cultural rather than individual phenomena (Kozulin et al., 2003). This perspective emphasizes that the learner is inextricably linked to the cultural and historical conditions in which he or she learns and maintains that the learner is the single most powerful influence on her or his own learning. No amount of experimental or instructional manipulation, such as structured input or information tasks, can override the learner's agency (Donato, 2000). Learners assume control of their own participatory activities with the support of both other learners and the teacher (van Lier, 2000).

This perspective, though, conflicts with traditional notions of classroom power. Pica (1987) states that interactive practices in the classroom reflect unequal power structures as determined by the knowledge base of the expert, or teacher, who, because he or she "knows" more, wields more control in the classroom. However, Hall, Hendricks, and Orr (2004) point out that this statement assumes that the expert's primary responsibility in an interaction is to provide linguistic support "via clarification requests and comprehension checks to their non-native speaking counterparts" (p. 64), and the task of novice speakers is to react to the linguistic aid provided by the expert. Pica's statement also assumes that linguistic knowledge alone determines how and what type of learning occurs. However, when given expanded opportunities, novice speakers do not simply react to information and cues given to them. For instance, Donato (2000) points out that "classroom group work is best conceived as internal goal-direction actions of the students rather than passive adherence to external task demands" (p. 41). Donato goes on to say that the utterances of the teacher and other learners are not input but rather "social practices of assistance" (p. 46) that create and influence the learning space. Group dynamics, for example, determine how members of a group operationalize an activity. As they work to express meaning within a given context, whether it is in the classroom while speaking to a teacher or as interns in a health department giving eye exams, learners work to establish their role, understand that of other participants in the interaction, and attempt to define the direction of the interaction with their collaborators. Sociocultural theory (SCT) perspectives assume that language development is a nonlinear process, with "breaks, innovation, and unpredictability as the norm" (Lantolf, 2005, p. 337) and acknowledge the importance of individual, social, and cultural contexts in the learning process.

Related to this general framework are activity theory and emergent grammar. The former posits that advanced forms of human activity are the direct result of the goals and motives of the activity participants (Lantolf, 2005). The ways that learners participate in activities cannot be predicted; therefore, the very nature of specific activities will vary depending on who the participants are and when they participate. Emergent grammar stems from the perspective that human beings are not born with an innate ability to "acquire" grammar; rather, one's ability to use grammatical structures in different ways in different contexts is directly related to the sociocultural contexts in which the communicative acts take place. Hopper (1998) says that the concept of emergent grammar suggests that

> structure, or regularity, comes out of discourse and is shaped by discourse in an ongoing process. Grammar is, in this view, simply a name for certain categories of observed repetitions in discourse. It is . . . not to be understood as a prerequisite for discourse . . . [but emerges] out of face-to-face interaction in ways that reflect the individual speakers' past experience of these forms, and their assessment of the present context. (p. 156)

Lantolf (2005) says that within this perspective, second language learning is a way of utilizing and enhancing communication tools we already possess, thus enabling participation in many more communicative activities. Given this, there is no "end point" at which a speaker may be perceived as having attained a final goal in acquisition. Instead, the learner constantly uses and eventually transforms communicative tools as he uses them in different contexts with different people in different ways.

To fully appreciate the social context of language, Gee (1996) says we must focus on the idea of a discourse. A discourse is a way of "behaving, interacting, valuing, thinking, believing, [and] speaking" (p. viii) that is accepted as the realization of a particular role by specific groups of people. For instance, a stockbroker dresses in a particular way and uses particular ways of speaking when at work in a financial institution, but when she is relaxing on the weekend with her friends, she dresses in another way and uses other words, gestures, and intonation when speaking to them. To engage in her professional discourse while socializing with friends would result in a dissonance that creates discomfort for all parties.

This recognition of the connection of how context, communicative purpose, and interactive practices influence and determine each other is manifested in the National Standards for Foreign Language Education Project (1999). The shift in SLA research frameworks, as well as increased political pressure on professional organizations as a result of the 1989 Education Summit (Díaz-Rico, 2004), resulted in the adoption of the Standards as a basic framework for language education. The framework of communicative modes that is included in the Standards document emphasizes that an understanding of cultural perspectives, products, and practices, in addition to knowledge of the linguistic system, is crucial to the ability to interact with individuals (National Standards for Foreign Language Education Project). Included in the Standards is the Communities Standard, which states that learners use the language both within and beyond their communities and for personal, lifelong enjoyment. Motivated in part by this conceptualization of language that goes beyond the linguistic system and also emphasizes the local and international contexts of a target language, many foreign language (FL) educators now seek to incorporate basic principles of service-learning pedagogy as a way to create a wider variety of cultural and linguistic opportunities for learners.

The combination of this research, which will be discussed later in this paper, with the development of the Standards has stimulated educators to explore a variety of language teaching techniques that acknowledge both the learner's agency and the social and historical factors that influence his linguistic and cognitive development. Service-learning, which links theory to actual community contexts in order to enhance learner understanding of the theory, is one of these techniques.

Service-learning in the language classroom is still a relatively new concept, but it offers rich opportunities for researchers who study second language acquisition. Service-learning pedagogy starts with the belief that learning only occurs through a cycle of action and reflection, that a true learning experience links emotions and intellect, and that personal and interpersonal development are linked to academic and cognitive development (Cone & Harris, 1996; Eyler & Giles, 1999). Language, both inside the classroom and outside of it, forms the basis of the learning experience because it is the tool that creates these links. For this reason, this chapter proposes that the unique cultural, social, and individual components of service-learning pedagogy provide a learning space that highlights the linguistic, cultural, and social aspects of a language-based event, and it situates second language learners in the center of that. A framework that conceptualizes service-learning as second language acquisition and utilizes a sociocultural point of view may provide rich data regarding the learning and linguistic processes that learners use and create as part of their development.

■ Defining the Learning Space

Marton, Runesson, and Tsui (2004) describe the object of learning in a classroom as what a learner tries to learn and the space of learning as "a specific characterization of the interaction in the classroom" (p. 22). This space is an experiential one that widens as the teacher provides the learners with multiple opportunities to explore the object of learning. The opportunities that a learner has, of course, directly influence the learner's social, cognitive, and emotional development and thus the extent to which they master the object of learning. However, teachers and learners create the learning space together; neither the teacher alone nor the learners alone can create possibilities for learning, and this joint responsibility for the creation of the learning space is predicated on a joint collaboration of meaning (Tsui, 2004).

For example, a classroom is one manifestation of the learner's environment, and pair or group work in a classroom is an example of how learners work with each other and collaborate to create meaning while engaged in organized activities. A classmate in the group might know more about the topic or task at hand and thus be considered a type of expert, while another learner in the group is, in comparison, a novice. The expert, with the aid of an organized task that another expert (the teacher) designs, can help lead the novice to higher levels of understanding through the use of explanations, examples, paraphrasing, and questions. Other interactive processes in which learners and teachers may engage include the development and testing of theories, retelling stories, and giving instructions. It is only through the collaboration of all involved that opportunities to participate in these processes exist.

These processes, or instructional conversations, are language-based episodes that reconstruct informal conversations in a formal educational setting (Donato, 2000). These conversations exist on two levels: They may draw attention to coherence, turn-taking, and spontaneity, yet they also may focus on curricular information, activate previous knowledge in the learner, provide direct instruction, or use questions to help students modify, elaborate, or restate their own thoughts. These conversations not only socialize learners into the target language in rich ways and provide models for non-classroom-based target language use, but they also provide a framework for the analysis of classroom discourse that captures a broader array of information regarding linguistic and cognitive development (Donato, 2000).

In fact, Hall (1997) suggests that one of the primary aims of sociocultural second language acquisition research is to construct a theory of second or foreign language (L2) classroom practice in order to provide insight into the types of conditions that affect the L2 learner's social and psychological identities both as a learner of "and communicator in the target language" (p. 304). In order to achieve this understanding, we must identify and characterize the types of communicative practices, or the characteristics of learning spaces, in L2 classrooms. This involves a study of both the content and discursive characteristics of instructional conversations. Understanding the different types of interactive practices in which learners and teachers engage, as well as identifying the consequences of those different practices, will help us develop more effective pedagogical theories and activities to create better L2 classrooms.

For instance, Hall (1995), in her examination of the target language discourse in one high school Spanish class, points out that the communicative practices that teachers and other expert language speakers use in a classroom environment can hinder or facilitate the learner's L2 interactional development. Both what and how the teacher says what she says define the space of learning and thus may hinder or enhance the learner's understanding of the object of learning (the target language). Classroom talk that relies on prompts to elicit a mechanical response in a passive learner, or language that consists primarily of repetitive speech, or metalinguistic topics or creates socially jarring instances (such as a lack of topic transition or rejoinders) creates limited opportunities for learners to participate in topic development and management. The learner's role is severely limited in such an environment.

This idea that learners need cues and must respond to them appropriately in order to develop their linguistic skills does not consider the role of mediation in the learner's development. Mediation, or the ways in which individuals engage in processes to assist their cognitive development and understanding of concepts, is a critical part in the formation of any learning space, and the availability and use of mediational tools in the learner's environment significantly affect the ways in which participants interact. These tools include textbooks, visuals, interaction with others, and opportunities to engage in organized learning activities, and they serve to assist and support the learner as he attempts to make sense of the world around him (Shrum & Glisan, 2004).

Clearly, language is a critical mediational tool for learners. Engagement in a task not only provides opportunities for the learner to learn language, but it also provides the opportunity to learn through language (Wells, 1999). As participants negotiate, define, describe, classify, or test information, they do it with words, and those words are used in specific contexts. As noted earlier, these contexts, in addition to individual factors such as motivation, will determine what words the learners choose to employ and how. Language, therefore, does not just represent experience, it also creates experience, and understanding how it does so is critical to understanding how the object of learning is realized in a classroom—or in any learning space (Marton, Runesson, & Tsui, 2004).

Mediation depends on the active role of the learner, and it helps the learner avoid developing incomplete or inaccurate concepts that might occur through solely independent exploration. Service-learning pedagogy relies on the use of language to mediate and create. While language mediation exists in all learning environments, service-learning pedagogy creates opportunities for learners to participate in a variety of markedly different cultural contexts, and it recognizes and brings to the fore the transformation of the learner as she participates in these contexts.

◼ Service-Learning Pedagogy in a Language Learning Context

Underwood, Welsh, Gauvain, and Duffy (2000) describe service-learning as a type of learning through apprenticeship. Starting with the assumption that cognition is a collaborative process "embedded in sociocultural activity" (p. 9), they describe service-learning as a

> dynamic social relationship in which novices engage with more expert participants in productive activity that serves multiple goals and needs, including those of the more skilled participants. In short, the novice learns through active assistance with the intent of meaningful and useful productions . . . the novices gain experience and knowledge that enable them to participate more competently with skilled partners. (pp. 9–10)

Lantolf (2000) states that in cases where experts come together with novices, the novices do not merely copy the capabilities that they see in the expert. Instead, they start by imitating these capabilities and then, through collaboration with other novices and experts, transform this knowledge as it becomes their own. The novice is not expected to reproduce what he or she learns from the expert; rather, the treatment of the novice as a communicative being, instead of as a passive one, results in the creation of new ways of understanding.

The critical components in this transformation are concrete experience, reflective observation, abstract conceptualization, and active experimentation (Kolb, 1984). Participants engage in this cycle by negotiating their roles in the community and classroom, defining and describing their experiences, and testing theories. The student and teacher thus use concrete experiences in the community as a basis for reflection, and they use these reflections to create and integrate concepts. They then take these concepts and use them to solve problems. At all stages of the cycle, the students negotiate their roles with the community, define and describe issues that arise, and test theories. These attempted solutions, or concrete experiences, form the basis for the next cycle (Morris, 2001; Kolb, 1984).

For instance, if a community and a service-learning classroom work to develop a newsletter for the community in order to help the community organize itself, the next step might be an examination of the effectiveness of the newsletter and the development of ways to improve it and create additional means for communication within the community. While a variety of mediational tools are important in this experience, all phases of the cycle include tasks that center on the use of language as a means of shaping the learning space. Effective service-learning is never an add-on—the same is true for any effective pedagogical approach. Service-learning programs must be designed, and classroom experiences must prepare for, support, and build on the community activities of the learners (Cone & Harris, 1996).

Service-learning differs from other types of experiential learning in its emphasis on service and the central role that such service plays in transforming the learner's understanding of concepts. While the learner in a service-learning classroom begins with an idea of what he wishes to accomplish, that goal changes as he comes into contact with individuals in the community and reflects on those experiences. Rockquemore and Shaffer (2000) have found that learners who engage in service-learning experiences move through three stages. The first of these, shock, results from cognitive dissonance from interacting with individuals in a context with which they are not familiar. Another way of describing this is with Gee's (1996) definition of discourse. As he says, language makes no sense when isolated from an overall discourse. Service-learning experiences are meant to introduce learners to another discourse, and a learner who does not know the practices, values, and language of a discourse will understandably experience discomfort as she acquires that discourse. The second stage is normalization, and this occurs as the learner develops relationships with members of the community and starts to connect community experiences with classroom content. Rockquemore and Shaffer describe this as a shift from a "descriptive to an integrative format" (p. 21). The final stage is engagement, at which learners question and analyze their own assumptions, "reframe their perspectives and beliefs, and determine if their behavior in the future should be modified, based upon what they have learned" (p. 21). It is in this stage that one sees behaviors that are the result of shifts in the way that the learner understands the world around him. These behaviors may manifest themselves as advocacy for social change, or they manifest themselves in the words, gestures, and activities that the learner utilizes as he engages with members of the community.

The classroom teacher who utilizes service-learning pedagogy designs activities and sequences them so that community members and classroom learners work together to define needs and fulfill them. However, she accepts at all times the fact that her activities are a plan that could easily change based on personalities, time of day, or a change in the community's or learner's priorities. Certainly these changes occur in any classroom. Service-learning pedagogy, however, accepts this fluidity and accepts that what may have been the intended outcome may never occur. Even if that happens, however, there are learning outcomes, and the learner must find that outcome with the aid of the teacher.

Simply observing community manifestations of social issues or language use does not in itself constitute service-learning. For example, undergraduate nursing majors who are enrolled in a community nursing course may participate in a service-learning component in a local health department where they apply what they have learned in the classroom by administering basic exams to low-income residents of a community. They glean knowledge from that experience and reflect on it in a variety of ways in the classroom, which may lead to more effective action during their next community experience. This action may consist of the ways in which diagnoses and/or treatments are made, or the ways in which the health care worker learns to communicate more effectively with the client. The learner, who is a novice in the sense that he has only recently been introduced to the issues that he will confront in the community, is also an expert in the sense that he has knowledge or skills that the community needs. Instructional conversations in this context activate and build on the prior knowledge of learners, model problems and encourage learners to propose solutions, and centralize the learner through the use of questioning and reflection. The community, meanwhile, comprises experts who are familiar with the real-world manifestations of issues and problems that teachers and students address in the classroom

In fact, one of the most important characteristics of effective service-learning programs is the power of the community's voice. Learners must address needs that the community defines and address them in socially and culturally appropriate ways even as they struggle to understand them. This interaction between experts and novices is a significant source of learning. As Wells (1999) says:

> knowledge construction and theory development most frequently occur in the context of a problem of some significance and take the form of a dialogue in which solutions are proposed and responded to with additions and extensions or objections and counterproposals from others. (p. 51)

Language is clearly an intrinsic part of this negotiation, and all parties use it in different ways to define the area of engagement.

Until fairly recently, the object of learning in a learning space that utilized service-learning was often a social issue such as the lack of educational support for at-risk students in an urban school and ways to address that issue (Calderon & Farrell, 1996; Eyler & Giles, 1999; Maybach, 1996; Root, 1994). Students who address such issues do so with the aid of their native language and interact with individuals (classmates, teachers, and community members) who likely share a common native language. However, the increasing use of a sociocultural approach to language acquisition research, the creation of the national standards, and the rise in service-learning programs in general have converged to create conditions in which more language educators utilize service-learning in a foreign language learning context. What is unique about layering service-learning with foreign language learning is that the object of learning (the target language) is also the space of learning. The learner thus uses both the native and target languages to mediate and create experience. While this is certainly true of second language classrooms in general, in a traditional classroom the centrality of the learner as a cultural being and manager of her own learning is not always assumed.

For instance, if we take the earlier example of nursing students engaged in service-learning at a county health department, and we also add that the nursing students are beginning Spanish students enrolled in a course designed for health care workers, we create a language learning space in which the nursing students learn a new discourse as they develop and communicate their health care knowledge. The native speakers who are the nursing students' clients must work to understand what the students say as well as establish their own meaning. As the groups involved in the service-learning experience negotiate to establish the roles that each will play in the experience, the classroom teacher provides ways of supporting the novice speakers as they do so. The teacher must provide ways of preparing the novice for the task, support the learner during the community experience, then lead the learner through a reflective process that will in turn lead to a more sophisticated understanding of the components of interaction so that the learner moves to increasingly sophisticated levels of interaction. Journals, classroom role-playing, discussion, and community visitors to the classroom are all ways of supporting and leading the learner through the process. The service-learning component in a foreign language course thus provides a space in which a group of experts and novices (and those labels shift as the topic and language do in the interactions) interact at a variety of levels in various contexts.

■ Directions for Research

Thus far, most of the literature that links service-learning pedagogy and foreign language learning has focused on program design and learner motivation and attitudes (Kaplan & Pérez-Gamboa, 2003; Long, 2003; Overfield, 1997; Polansky, 2004). In the latter area, results have been uniformly positive. Mullaney (1999) provides examples of student comments in which the students describe how their Spanish improved or how they had developed a better understanding of linguistic issues as a result of their participation in a project that linked Hispanic ESL students with native English speakers who were learning Spanish. Hale (1999) also quotes students who say that hands-on experiences are far superior to the activities in which they engage in the classroom. In her study, she describes how several students who had participated in service-learning experiences enrolled in additional Spanish classes but dropped out due to "boring book work, labs, and repetitive out-of-context drills" (p. 22). The students said that if these additional classes had incorporated a service-learning approach, they would have continued, but the traditional format discouraged them.

It is revealing that the learners characterize their classrooms in this way. Research over the past two decades in second language acquisition (SLA) has led to the development of classroom techniques that include problem-solving activities, discussions, and the frequent use of pair and group work to simulate the "real world" (Pica, 1987). Yet there is a sense on the part of many students that classroom language and interaction is inauthentic or insufficient (Barnes-Karol, 1995; Morris, 2001). While it is unlikely that a learner would express it in this way, it appears that what is missing is a learning space in which experts and novices have opportunities to create mutually agreed-upon interactive practices that can be expanded or revised as needs arise. It is this kind of space that learners who participate in nontraditional settings find both challenging and motivational. Students express dissatisfaction with the use of reproductive tasks in a classroom versus creative tasks in which they define how to approach and resolve them.

This conceptualization of the classroom as one in which creative tasks are central creates a space for learning in which the language system, or object of learning, is not simply a series of prompts to which the learner must respond as instructed. As Lantolf (2000) points out, what ultimately matters is how individual learners decide to engage with a task. We have already seen that this motivation affects how learners decide to engage in tasks that they consider "traditional," but we have not seen extended, discourse-based research that examines their engagement with service-learning based activities.

One possible direction for research in this field is whether and how the increased motivation that researchers have already documented with foreign language learners and service-learning experiences reveals changes in the types of activities that learners create and experience. For instance, it may be that increased motivation and a sense of agency in the learning process may result in learners demonstrating the tendency to initiate spontaneous questions or volunteer information in order to establish relationships with community members. At this point, these are only speculative points, but it is entirely possible that the development of such a willingness to adopt and perhaps transform language to suit a particular context is precisely what learners find so rewarding about service-learning pedagogy in the language classroom.

Second language service-learning, when structured to support and challenge all members of the community who are engaged in it, provides learning opportunities in which the activity that students need to do determines what they need to know, as opposed to the traditional approach, in which knowledge determines what they do (Bragger & Rice, 2000). This builds on Wootton's (1997) statement that a learner's cognitive and social development is the result of the learner building up a store of social and cultural knowledge from which she draws as new situations arise. The learner develops new strategies for each situation based on her assessment of the situation's similarities to previous experiences. The L2 learner chooses grammar and vocabulary and makes interpretations of intonation, gestures, and facial expressions based on previous experiences and her knowledge of a community's cultural values. The interactions she has with individuals in a variety of community contexts, or discourses, influence the ways in which she chooses communicative strategies.

However, we do not know the extent of these influences, and an examination of these practices may reveal information not only about how FL activities vary in such a setting, but also perhaps information about activities that reveal themselves in the service-learning space. It is very possible that, as interactions and therefore relationships develop, participants on all sides reveal assumptions and perspectives that significantly affect the creation of language-based events.

Figure 3.1 illustrates the components of a service-learning space. While it incorporates many of the same elements of Nunan's (1999) concept map for speaking, it centralizes community interaction and includes both the community member and the language learner. Thus, it addresses the social and cultural elements of this pedagogy, as well as the role of all participants. Interaction, both

Figure 3.1. Service-Learning Concept Map

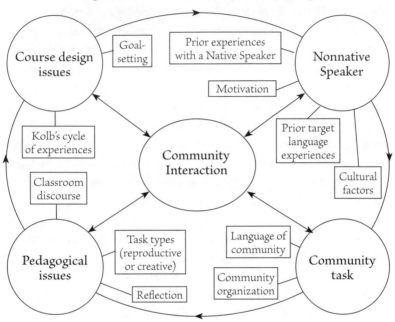

interpersonal and intrapersonal, moves in a number of directions in this map, and all of these offer opportunities for research. Hall's (1995) examination of classroom discourse reveals much about the nature of talk in a Spanish language classroom that at first might be characterized as linguistically and culturally rich based on the amount of Spanish that is spoken. It would be equally valuable to examine the instructional conversations and learner/learner and learner/community member talk that characterize the service-learning classroom.

Because service-learning pedagogy expands the concept of the traditional classroom to one in which the classroom and the community are inseparable, we must also conceptualize the nature of instructional conversations to include what occurs in the community context and what occurs in the classroom prior to, during, and after the community experience. What are the characteristics of these instructional conversations in these contexts? Do they share features? In what ways do they differ? What language activities in the classroom are used to support the learners outside of it, and how do learners choose to engage in those activities? How do native speakers who are involved in a service-learning project support and interact with nonnative speakers? What routines do novice and expert speakers develop as they establish strategies for conveying information and participating in social practices over the course of a semester or quarter? Does the nature of the teacher's language change as the learner's social and linguistic development progresses?

Additionally, research into a learner's private speech when engaged in service-learning experiences can be a source of information. For instance, it is likely that changes regarding cultural attitudes and perceptions regarding the role of the self and others in a "foreign" context can be best revealed through the analysis of private speech. Lantolf (2005) says that such research can reveal much about development that cannot be revealed through the study of performance alone. Private speech research sheds light on the transformational processes that cannot be seen simply through observation (Lantolf & Yáñez-Prieto, 2003; McCafferty, 1998; Saville-Troike, 1988).

■ Conclusions

Learning processes, whether they are examined in language classrooms or elsewhere, have individual, social, and cultural dimensions, and learners appropriate mediational tools for their learning based on the assistance of an expert. However, our understanding of human mediation is episodic, at best (Kozulin et al., 2003). The creation of service-learning language learning experiences acknowledges the scope of discourses and the ways that an individual's participation in one can lead to the transformation of knowledge as she enters another.

As Hall (1995) says, what learners learn to do in classroom practices depends on what is made available to those learners in those environments and the extended opportunities they have to develop their abilities. The most notable gap we have in the field of service-learning pedagogy in language classrooms is a glaring one: Little is known about how participants communicate with one another. While we have information about how students perceive their experiences in service-learning programs, we have yet to see extended discourse analysis that reveals the interactive practices in which novice language learners and experts engage when participating in a community discourse that is linked to a pedagogically structured setting. The surprise and satisfaction that students express when they have the opportunity to interact in authentic community discourses indicate that service-learning practices provide learners with opportunities that are often not available in other types of formal learning experiences. We do not know the extent to which learners who participate in these programs are given opportunities to build on their discursive knowledge when they return to their classrooms. This is a particularly important point, as it is only with these opportunities that learners will be able to transform their knowledge and create new practices. As noted earlier, when students do not have opportunities to build on those experiences, they experience frustration and boredom.

Because the learning space of service-learning pedagogy relies on the interaction of members of various communities as they create, examine, re-create, and transform experience, as well as on opportunities for the learner to engage in reflective moments that rely on private speech, analysis of the discursive practices in such a setting, as well as analysis of the private speech in which nonnative speakers engage during the service-learning cycle, is a potentially rich source of information. Given that the central tenets of sociocultural theory align with service-learning pedagogy, a close examination of the nature and impact of service-learning experiences for second language learners could lead to a greater understanding of the discursive practices that learners require in order to transform their understandings, and thus their practice, of the processes of discursive collaboration. The service-learning classroom acknowledges the power of the learner to participate in the creation of language-based learning experiences.

■ References

Barnes-Karol, G. (1995). Voices from beyond the classroom: Foreign language learners in non-traditional environments. In T. Dvorak (Ed.), *Voices from the field: Experiences and beliefs of our constituents* (pp. 33–76). Chicago, IL: National Textbook Company.

Bragger, J. D., & Rice, D. B. (2000). Foreign language materials: Yesterday, today, and tomorrow. In R. Terry (Ed.), *Agents of change in a changing world* (pp. 107–140). Lincolnwood, IL: National Textbook Company.

Calderon, J., & Farrell, B. (1996). Doing sociology: Connecting the classroom experience with a multi-ethnic school district. *Teaching Sociology, 24,* 46–63.

Cone, D., & Harris, S. (1996). Service-learning practice: Developing a theoretical framework. *Michigan Journal of Community Service Learning, 3,* 31–43.

Díaz-Rico, L. T. (2004).*Teaching English language learners: Strategies and methods.* Boston, MA: Allyn & Bacon.

Donato, R. (2000). Sociocultural contributions to understanding the foreign and second language classroom. In J. P. Lantolf (Ed.), *Sociocultural theory and second language learning* (pp. 27–50). Oxford, U.K.: Oxford University Press.

Eyler, J., & Giles, D. E., Jr. (1999). *Where's the learning in service-learning?* San Francisco, CA: Jossey-Bass.

Frawley, W., & Lantolf, J. (1985). Second language discourse: A Vygotskian perspective. *Second Language Learning, 6,* 19–44.

Gee, J. P. (1996). *Social linguistics and literacies: Ideology in discourses* (2nd ed.). London, U.K: Routledge Falmer.

Hale, A. (1999). Service-learning and Spanish: A missing link. In J. Hellebrandt & L. T. Varona (Eds.), *Construyendo puentes (building bridges): Concepts and models for service-learning in Spanish* (pp. 9–31). Washington, DC: American Association for Higher Education.

Hall, J. K. (1995). "Aw, man, where you goin'?": Classroom interaction and the development of L2 interactional competence. *Issues in Applied Linguistics, 6*(2), 37–62.

Hall, J. K. (1997). A consideration of SLA as a theory of practice. *Modern Language Journal, 81*(3), 301–306.

Hall, J. K., & Davis, J. (1995). Voices from the traditional classroom: Learner reflections. In T. Dvorak (Ed.), *Voices from the field: Experiences and beliefs of our constituents* (pp. 1–30). Chicago, IL: National Textbook Company.

Hall, J. K., Hendricks, S., & Orr, J. L. (2004). Dialogues in the "global village": NNS/NS collaboration in classroom interaction. *Critical Inquiry in Language Studies: An International Journal, 1*(2), 63–88.

Hopper, P. J. (1998). Emergent grammar. In M. Tomasello (Ed.), *The new psychology of language: Cognitive and functional approaches to language structure* (pp. 155–175). Mahwah, NJ: Lawrence Erlbaum Associates.

Kaplan, B., & Pérez-Gamboa, T. (2003). Stepping out of the classroom to increase Spanish language skills and cultural awareness. In C. M. Cherry (Ed.), *Models for excellence in second language education* (pp. 27–35). Valdosta, GA: Southern Conference on Language Teaching.

Kolb, D. (1984). *Experiential learning: Experience as the source of learning and development.* Englewood Cliffs, NJ: Prentice Hall.

Kozulin, A., Gindis, B., Ageyev, V. S., & Miller, S. M. (Eds.). (2003). *Vygotsky's educational theory in context.* Cambridge, U.K.: Cambridge University Press.

Lantolf, J. P. (Ed.). (2000). *Sociocultural theory and second language learning*. Oxford, U.K.: Oxford University Press.

Lantolf, J. P. (2005). Sociocultural and second language learning research: An exegesis. In E. Hinkel (Ed.), *Handbook of research in second language teaching and learning* (pp. 335–374) Mahwah, NJ: Lawrence Erlbaum Associates.

Lantolf, J. P., & Appel, G. (Eds.). (1994). *Vygotskian approaches to second language research*. Norwood, NJ: Ablex.

Lantolf, J. P., & Yáñez-Prieto, M. (2003). Talking into yourself in Spanish: Private speech and second language learning. *Hispania, 86,* 98–105.

Long, D. R. (2003). Spanish in the community: Students reflect on Hispanic cultures in the United States. *Foreign Language Annals, 36*(2), 223–232.

Marton, F., Runesson, U., & Tsui, A. B. M. (2004). The space of learning. In F. Marton & A. B. M. Tsui (Eds.), *Classroom discourse and the space of learning* (pp. 3–40). Mahwah, NJ: Lawrence Erlbaum Associates.

Maybach, C. (1996). Investigating urban community needs: Service-learning from a social-justice perspective. *Education and Urban Society, 28*(2), 224–236.

McCafferty, S. G. (1998). Nonverbal expression and L2 private speech. *Applied Linguistics, 19*(1), 73–96.

Morris, F. A. (2001). Serving the community and learning a foreign language: Evaluating a service-learning programme. *Language, Culture, and Curriculum, 14*(3), 244–255.

Mullaney, J. (1999). Service-learning and language-acquisition theory and practice. In J. Hellebrandt & L. T. Varona (Eds.), *Construyendo puentes (building bridges): Concepts and models for service-learning in Spanish* (pp. 49–60). Washington, DC: American Association for Higher Education.

National Standards for Foreign Language Education Project. (1999). *Standards for foreign language learning in the 21st century.* Lawrence, KS: Allen Press.

Nunan, D. (1999). *Second language teaching and learning.* Boston, MA: Heinle & Heinle.

Ohta, A. S. (2000). *Second language acquisition processes in the classroom: Learning Japanese.* Mahwah, NJ: Lawrence Erlbaum Associates.

Overfield, D. M. (1997). From the margins to the mainstream: Community-based learning. *Foreign Language Annals, 30,* 485–491.

Pica, T. (1987). Second-language acquisition, social interaction, and the classroom. *Applied Linguistics, 8*(1), 3–21.

Platt, E., & Brooks, F. (2002). Task engagement: A turning point in foreign language development. *Language Learning, 52*(2), 365–400.

Polansky, S. G. (2004). Tutoring for community outreach: A course model for language learning and bridge building between universities and public schools. *Foreign Language Annals, 37*(3), 367–373.

Rockquemore, K., & Shaffer, R. H. (2000). Toward a theory of engagement: A cognitive mapping of service-learning experiences. *Michigan Journal of Community Service Learning, 7,* 14-24.

Root, S. (1994). Service-learning in teacher education: A third rationale. *Michigan Journal of Community Service Learning, 1*(1), 94–97.

Saville-Troike, M. (1988). Private speech: Evidence for second language learning strategies during the "silent period." *Journal of Child Language, 15,* 567–590.

Sfard, A. (1998). On two metaphors for learning and the danger of choosing just one. *Educational Researcher, 27*(2), 4–13.

Shrum, J., & Glisan, E. (2004). *The teacher's handbook: Contextualized language instruction* (3rd ed.). Boston, MA: Heinle & Heinle.

Tsui, A. (2004). The shared space of learning. In F. Marton & A. B. Tsui (Eds.), *Classroom discourse and the space of learning* (pp. 165–186). Mahwah, NJ: Lawrence Erlbaum Associates.

Underwood, C., Welsh, M., Gauvain, M., & Duffy, S. (2000). Learning at the edges: Challenges to the sustainability of service learning in higher education. *Language and Learning Across the Disciplines, 4*(3), 7–26.

van Lier, L. (2000) From input to affordance: Social-interactive learning from an ecological perspective. In J. P. Lantolf (Ed.), *Sociocultural theory and second language learning* (pp. 245–259). Oxford, U.K.: Oxford University Press.

Vygotsky, L. (1978). *Mind in society*. Cambridge, MA: Harvard University Press.

Wells, G. (1999). *Dialogic inquiry: Toward a sociocultural practice and theory of education*. Cambridge: Cambridge University Press.

Wootton, A. J. (1997). *Interaction and the development of mind*. Cambridge, U.K.: Cambridge University Press.

4

Crossing Borders/Forging Identities: Echoes of Symbiosis Between Classroom and Community

Stuart Stewart

This chapter uses a framework of critical pedagogy (Freire, 1970/1993; Giroux, 1992; McLaren, 1989; Wink 2005) and sociocultural theory (e.g., Zone of Proximal Development and Principle of Continuous Access—Vygotsky, 1978 and 1986) to evaluate several interdisciplinary projects in the Department of Foreign Languages at Southeastern Louisiana University[1] (SLU) and to support the notion of service-learning. Critical pedagogy (CP), which draws on both progressive and experiential education, seeks to develop students' critical thinking skills, causes them to question the status quo, and invites them to offer creative solutions to problems they encounter within the real world. Sociocultural theory (SCT) is based on the tenet that the acquisition of knowledge (including language) comes from interactions with a learner's environment and others in it, all within the sociocultural norms of a particular society. Built on the notion of interaction and collaboration to achieve comprehension, SCT embraces the ideas of Vygotsky (1978, 1986) and other Soviet researchers who see language development as a social process and have identified a crucial link between thinking and speaking. These two theoretical approaches provide a solid basis for service-learning, especially in the foreign language curriculum.

■ Critical Pedagogy and Service-Learning

Critical pedagogy: Taken separately, the words "critical" and "pedagogy" invoke thoughts of criticism and teaching, respectively; combined, they have a much more profound significance. In tandem, critical refers to an ability to see below the surface, and pedagogy speaks to the creation of independent learners who are developing an awareness of identity, culture, and community. Since our most effective teaching is connected to everyday life, our teaching and learning should also be linked with our communities (Wink, 2005). And because "finding resources for teaching culture and language in an integrated fashion has been a challenge for language teachers over the years" (Omaggio Hadley, 2001, p. 359), what better way than through service-learning, which places students into the surrounding community with native speakers of Spanish?

Service-learning has adopted a number of ideas from John Dewey, a teacher, professor, philosopher, and social reformer. Dewey, who is considered by some to be the most influential of American philosophers, made major, albeit highly controversial, contributions to the field of education in the late 1800s and early 1900s. More than a century ago, Dewey defined education as "a process of living . . . not a preparation for future living" (Dewey, 1897, as cited in Gezi & Myers, 1968, p. 410). In discussing the subject matter of education, Dewey argued for language as a social instrument rather than as an expression of thought. To use language for anything other than the exchange of ideas and feelings, he concluded, is to lose the social motive and end to language, which undermines the study of literature and language.

Dewey and other progressive educators subscribed to the belief that the development of critical thinking skills was crucial since it promotes the ability to apply knowledge in new situations. From their perspectives, experiential learning, which involves learning by doing, seemed an excellent means for reaching that goal. Although their work was harshly criticized, progressive educators and their ideas were embraced in whole or in part by many of those in the field of critical pedagogy.

Freire, Giroux, and McLaren are names most often associated with critical pedagogy (CP). Paulo Freire started a national literacy campaign for peasants in Brazil that resulted in his being jailed and exiled. Although banished from his native country, Freire continued to speak out against the educational system in Brazil, which he labeled as oppressive and dehumanizing. In *Pedagogy of the Oppressed* (1970/1993), Freire draws the distinction between traditional education and problem-posing education.

In a traditional system, the teacher [dominant society] is an active, narrating subject, while their students [peasants] are passive listening objects who mechanically memorize the narrated concept. Freire invokes the "banking" concept of education to describe students [peasants] who receive, file, and store the deposits, and memorize and repeat information imparted by the teacher [dominant society]. At no time are students [peasants] invited to develop their own voice [become literate] in order to participate in the educational process [social reform]. Restricted by the banking concept of education, students [peasants] fail to develop the critical consciousness that would result from their intervention in the world. Such a fatalistic system ignores history and maintains the status quo by keeping the students [peasants] in their place and stifling their creativity [which might result in positive social change].

One of the basic tenets of problem-posing education is that teachers [members of the dominant society] must step back from their traditional role as dispensers of knowledge and allow students [peasants] to think (and act) for themselves. Students [peasants], who are seen as cognitive beings rather than empty receptacles, are encouraged to dialogue with the teacher [dominant society] to unveil reality and come to know it critically. The effect of such a humanistic partnership is the emergence of a consciousness that brings about new awareness and fosters legitimate social change.

A disciple of Freire, Henry Giroux is a leader in critical theory in education in the United States. His declaration that knowledge is produced, not received, supports Freire's (1970/1993) notion of education as an active, rather than a passive, experience. His view of CP as a form of cultural politics calls for educators to shape curricula from the lived experiences of students, challenging the status quo in order to move toward what is possible within individuals and society. He charges educators with linking learning to everyday life and with providing a living example of how to find ways to become involved, to make a difference, and to think globally while acting from specific contexts (Giroux, 1992; Williams, 2004).

These ideas coincide with many of those espoused by Peter McLaren, an educational activist, professor, and scholarly writer in the field of CP. McLaren (1989) calls for the development of an emancipatory curriculum that emphasizes student experiences and aids in identity formation. Instead of viewing learning as an "isolated product of meaning," he invites teachers to understand the different ways in which student identities are constructed and how the social world is experienced:

> The overall purpose of the critical educator is to reveal to students the forces behind their own interpretations, to call into question the ideological nature of their experiences, and to help students discover the interconnections between the community, culture and the larger social context: in short, to engage in the dialectic of self and society. (p. 237)

McLaren challenges teachers to be courageous moral leaders with a "teachable heart" who both encourage their students to actively engage and participate in society and help them to fashion a language of hope that works toward freedom and justice for all.

Wink (2005) adeptly synthesizes much of the above work and weaves it with many of her own ideas. For her, CP encompasses enlightenment, awakening, new awareness, questioning, reevaluating, reflecting, dialoging, opening up to new ideas, including going against the grain, and speaking one's truth. More than the sum of its parts, CP is essential to good teaching, because it allows us to see and know in new ways and leads us from silence to voice. CP results in the creation of lifelong learners who are responsible for their own learning and can generate and/or access new knowledge, critically reflect upon it, interpret it, and apply it in new ways, all of which are outcomes in line with the goals of service-learning.

■ Sociocultural Theory and Service-Learning

A sociocultural perspective on language teaching and learning is also situated in the belief that students are active participants in the learning process. A basic tenet of this theory is that humans learn language via cognitive and linguistic interactions with their material and social worlds. Through repeated participation in activities with more capable peers within a sociocultural environment, language learners acquire the linguistic, cultural, and other knowledge needed to function within a given society. This dovetails nicely with service-learning, which places students in the community interacting with native speakers of the target language. While an SCT approach to language teaching and learning certainly seems viable, it has met with some controversy over the years. To understand the obstacles that have faced teachers who are interested in using such an approach, a brief look at history is in order.

At least a quarter of a century ago, some foreign language educators were embracing the idea of progressive models of foreign language teaching (FLT) that paralleled Freire's model of problem-posing education (Grittner & Fearing, 1979; Jennings, 1979). They were acutely aware of the need for experiential learning that would ultimately carry into students' later lives. Jennings's (1979) argument for "community-based learning" called for students to be involved in "projects of real significance to them, projects that cause students to interact with people in the community" (p. 159ff) that result in some improvement in the lives of the students, the school, or the community. Such experiences create a more dynamic and effective educational experience for students while fostering self-discovery, problem-solving abilities, and expansion of career choices.[2]

Over the last 25 years, however, foreign language students have continued to learn much about the target language and culture but have had few opportunities to actually use the language or interact with those who speak it (unless they studied abroad or happened to make friends with a native speaker of the target language). Although various theories of language learning and teaching have been proposed over the years, students continue to complete several semesters of language study without being able to put together more than a couple of sentences, oftentimes with great difficulty.

This is because the focus on grammar persists, perhaps because students have come to expect it and teachers find it easier to manage. The reality is that the kinds of activities that teachers provide for their students shape the way students think about foreign language learning. "If the primary exercises of the classroom are written grammar exercises, students are likely to develop an understanding of the target language as grammar and language learning as doing exercises" (Hall, 2001, p. 40). However, language is much more than grammar, and learning a second language is much more than "learning forms of language to use someday in some possible situation; [rather it is about] learning to do the things you want to do with people who speak that language" (Rigg & Allen, 1989, p. ix).[3]

The role of interaction as a means of attaining competence in a second language (L2) is a recurrent topic in the second language acquisition (SLA) literature. Foreign language educators have devised numerous models of teaching and learning focused on interaction, including cooperative learning (Dörnyei, 1997; McGroarty, 1993; Oxford, 1997), collaborative learning (e.g., Aljaafreh & Lantolf, 1994; Di Pietro, 1987; Nyikos & Hashimoto, 1997), and interactive language teaching (Oxford, 1997; Rivers, 1997). Unfortunately, it is precisely the interactive facet of L2 learning that is most often neglected in a classroom environment:

> What is lacking, more often than not ... is classroom opportunity for the learner to speak in a social context where substantive communication takes place—where learners have a personal investment in the substance of the conversation and where meaning is "negotiated" through the give and take of verbal exchange. (Rutherford, 1987, p. 173)

It is the goal of SCT to contextualize the language learning experience so that negotiation of meaning can occur. Service-learning in FL shares this goal by moving students out of the classroom and into the community, because "learning and development occur as people participate in the sociocultural activities of their community, transforming their understanding, roles and responsibilities as they participate" (Rogoff, Matusov, & White, 1996, p. 390).

A sociocultural approach to language teaching and learning, which takes both thinking and speaking into account, has its orientation in Vygotskyan theory. Indeed Vygotsky's work (1978, 1986) and that of his disciples (Luria, 1981; Wertsch, 1981, 1985) contribute significantly to a better understanding of language use where linguistic and social acts are so closely entwined. Although originally proposed for child (first) language development, Vygotsky's ideas have been extrapolated to include second language learning as well (e.g., Darhower, 2004; Hall, 2001; Kinginger, 2001; Lantolf & Pavlenko, 1995). Acquisition of knowledge (including language) comes from a person's interactions with the environment and others in it, all within the sociocultural norms of a particular society.

As learners begin to interact socially, they become participants, or agents, in the learning process. As such, they are able to access the Zone of Proximal Development (ZPD), which is "the distance between [their] actual developmental level as determined by independent problem solving and the higher level of potential development as determined through problem solving under adult guidance or in collaboration with more capable peers" (Vygotsky, 1978, p. 86). In the case of the foreign language classroom, the teacher would be the adult guidance and the collaboration with more capable peers would come from more advanced language students; in a real-world setting, this guidance would come from native speakers. As learners gain more control over the L2, they are always able to employ what Vygotsky calls the principle of continuous access, which allows them to rely on those more capable peers for assistance in their spoken interactions.

The notion of human agency is an integral part of Wenger's (1998) communities of practice and the notion of learning as participation, which is based on engagement with the real world. Learning as participation 1) is experiential and social; 2) creates emergent structures; and 3) allows for the negotiation of meaning. Central to participation is practice, which Wenger defines as a process of meaningfully experiencing the world and (re)producing knowledge in new situations. Participation and practice involve conversation, which in turn entails the negotiation of meaning in the context of various communities.

Practice equates with learning in an ongoing, social, interactional process, and learning transforms who and what we are, allowing for the formation of an [L2] identity. This learning is not just about acquiring skills and information but also about implementing them to construct our identity and discover how and where "new ways of knowing can be realized" (Wenger, 1998,

p. 215). In fact, learning a language involves "acquiring a role [L2 identity] and knowing how to act according to that social definition" (Ogulnick, 2005, p. 254). This certainly cannot be accomplished if students are not active participants in the learning process. However, identity is subject to change over time, and the construction of an L2 identity comes only through repeated interactions with native speakers of the target language.

Service-learning presents students with a social and cultural context for L2 learning. It also provides more capable peers (in the form of native speakers) that students need to guide their learning. As learners actively participate in the process that Vygotsky and his associates so aptly identified, they come to see that language and culture are inseparable, that those things can be acquired only by engaging with members of the target community. In such interactions, students learn how to think on their feet as they use the L2 to verbalize their thoughts and their needs in a meaningful context. At the same time, they gain firsthand knowledge of how native speakers use the language they are attempting to acquire. Filling in the blanks with a correctly conjugated form of the verb gives way to filling in gaps in their conversations with live speakers of the language. Circumlocution, comprehension checks, and requests for additional information, which were occasionally mentioned during peer interactions in the classroom, stand to become an integral part of students' repertoires if they are to be successful in their interactions with community members, especially those who have limited English abilities.

Service-Learning in Humanities 400

My direct involvement began in spring 2003, when I responded to the SLU president's call for proposals for service-learning courses.[4] I offered a special topics course, Humanities 400 (in English) on "Hispanics in the US: Their language and culture" in the fall semester. The objectives of this class were to provide an overview of Hispanics in the U.S. and have students identify the various groups of

Hispanics in the U.S. and where they have settled in large numbers; understand immigration problems and migration patterns; learn about the educational problems facing U.S. Hispanics and their teachers; become familiar with some of the different varieties of Spanish spoken in the U.S.; discover the political and economic impact of U.S. Hispanics; learn about Hispanics in the media; become familiar with health issues facing U.S. Hispanics; read and discuss various short stories and poems written in English and in Spanish by U.S. Hispanics; and explore the Hispanic music scene in the U.S.—various styles and major works.

Seven Spanish majors enrolled in the course and rose to the challenge of performing ten hours of service with the local Hispanic population. A variety of projects arose from the class including an informal ESL class for workers at a local restaurant, tutoring for students in area public schools, and assistance at a local Head Start center. Each project took university students out of the classroom and put them in contact with native speakers of Spanish, giving them additional exposure to language and culture.

The informal ESL class sought to provide workers with English vocabulary they needed to perform their jobs more effectively and to provide a forum for conversational practice. University students used both English and Spanish during their sessions and exchanged information about their school and work lives. The public school tutoring project was designed to help the middle school children understand more of the content in their classes and to create a safe space for them to practice their English. University students were able to make the students feel more secure by helping them to understand directions, explaining words that they did not understand, and sharing their own stories of difficulties with learning a second language. Sessions at the Head Start center were designed as field hours for teacher-education students (although others were certainly welcome) that would provide small group and one-on-one work in a classroom setting. As the class had a mixture of students who were at varying stages of learning English, the university students were able to interact in both English and Spanish. Arrangements were made for university students to stay through the lunch hour (if their schedule permitted) in order to have further conversation in Spanish with the children.

ESL Class

One student inquired about the possibility of beginning weekly lessons for kitchen staff who had approached her about helping them to learn English. She found a time that was convenient for the workers, located a space on campus, recruited some help from another student, and began the process of amassing materials to use in her class. She consulted with the workers to see what they wanted to learn, then searched the web and went to the library to gather information. She and the other students spent several hours each week planning lessons and three hours on Sunday afternoons teaching their eight students. After she and her partner shared their experiences in class, two others decided to join them. The result was a resounding success: The Hispanics were able to improve their conversational English, and the university students acquired both language and culture. However, the class was unable to continue because the restaurant began staying open on Sundays and all the workers needed to be there to earn more money. They commented on this in class, and a discussion ensued regarding family values, economic hardships in the native country, and losses caused by immigration, bringing together several of the topics that we had been discussing in class.

Independence Middle School

Early in the fall 2003 semester I went to the Office of Migrant Education and explained that I had several students who were willing to give assistance to any public school students who might need help with English. The staff welcomed our assistance and identified several area schools that had students of limited English proficiency (LEP).[5] We decided on four schools: two elementary and two junior high. SLU students worked at each one, but they seemed to find their home at Independence Middle School. The principal welcomed us with open arms and has been very pleased with our efforts so far. The middle school students have become fond of my service-learning students, several of whom have continued in the program since its inception and others who join in as they learn about the opportunity. The project has been challenging because the middle school students are in various stages of learning—or not learning—English, which has made their educational experience different in each case. In addition, there are different levels of LEP students in the same public school classes.

SLU students' Spanish abilities have afforded them access to this population, which has forged a bond between the two groups that has been mutually beneficial to each. I have included comments from a number of the students regarding their experiences.

> C. O.: These are children of migrant workers, most of [whom] work in the strawberry fields. They know some English, but have some problems, especially with scientific words and terms. We over-simplify the words and work to help them understand the terms. The experience definitely helps me. It builds my vocabulary, makes me more fluent in the language, and helps me develop people skills and tolerance.

This student could not say enough about his experiences at the middle school. He encouraged others to join him there, and later he told me that this was the single best experience he had ever had in a Spanish class at the university.

> P. C.: I would hope to spend some more time with them, especially the one that cannot read English very well, to help her improve in her classes. I can understand her frustration because at one time I was there and felt helpless. It

is always good to have someone there by your side to help you understand the rules to follow in acquiring another language. I also spoke to one of the teachers there [who] encouraged me to continue my education and if possible apply for a job in there because they were in desperate need for an ESL teacher.

Working with these students was akin to an experience that this student, a Honduran immigrant, was all too familiar with. Being able to share what she had undergone when making the transition to the United States was invaluable to the middle school students who were in various stages of adjustment.

> C. L.: *Las mejicanas* all exhibit the same behavior inside the classroom. They mostly stay to themselves and barely participate in class activities (this has to do with the language barrier). They don't raise their hands to answer questions that the teachers ask them, nor ask questions back to the teacher. One of the girls feels like the other students make fun of her because they need extra help in understanding the material. A student from the United States in their math class shouted out loud, "Hey, I'm Spanish, can you help me?" I simply looked at her and turned my head without saying anything. This is one of the reasons why diversity in the classrooms and in schools should be integrated into the curriculum. I strongly believe that if these girls were participating in an ESL program, or an everyday tutoring program, they would excel academically.

This university student had moved from Puerto Rico to the mainland several years ago. Although she had studied English in school, she spoke only Spanish at home. She speaks very good English with little trace of an accent now, but she unashamedly admits that the language factor presented significant problems for her in the beginning.

Migrant Head Start

I was introduced to the director of the Regina Coeli Migrant Head Start Center by my colleague in nursing and obtained clearance for my students to work with the children there. They served as teacher's aides, helping out in the classrooms as needed. They read to the children in both Spanish and English and were able to practice their conversational Spanish skills with the children during lunch. For many, it was the first time the SLU students had ever had an extended interaction with a native speaker of Spanish. To be able to do so with a child, as opposed to an adult, was undoubtedly less intimidating to the university students.

Service-Learning in Spanish 303

Because the results from my Humanities 400 class were so positive, I wanted to continue them in a Spanish class. I had received a text in the mail that lent itself to doing so (Turner, Maisch, & Mendoza, 2004), and I proposed a new course (Spanish 303) that was quickly approved by the administration. Course objectives were the following: 1) to learn about the various groups of Latinos living in the United States; 2) to understand and appreciate many of the challenges facing U.S. Latinos; 3) to become familiar with different dialects of Spanish by listening to speakers from different parts of the Spanish-speaking world; 4) to learn new vocabulary and review grammatical concepts from prior courses; 5) to improve comprehension and production abilities by speaking, listening, reading, writing, and watching video; and 6) to gain additional exposure to language and culture by interacting with native speakers in the surrounding area.

Integration of a service-learning component into this course was supported by objective 6 in support of the following goals: to contextualize the language-learning experience by giving students a reason to speak Spanish; to afford firsthand knowledge of U.S. Latino culture by allowing them to meet and interact with some of the area's Spanish-speaking residents; to enhance their communicative abilities and improve their pronunciation in Spanish by increasing their exposure to the spoken language; and to allow them to offer a valuable service to the community.

I began teaching the course in fall 2004, offering service-learning placements at the middle school and at Migrant Head Start. Both sites provided valuable learning experiences for students, offering them not only language practice, but also direct exposure to U.S. Latino culture. In class, students were able to talk about how their experiences related to the material we were covering in class; in practice, students were able to use the material we were studying to facilitate their interactions within the community.

Early in spring 2005, I was contacted by the president of the senior nursing class, who was a former student of mine. Their class had selected the Migrant Head Start Center as the site for their capstone project, and they wanted some students from SLU's foreign language department to assist them on two days in March. I offered the opportunity to all of my Spanish classes, and several students volunteered—one from my fourth-semester class and several from two upper-division courses. Phase I of their capstone project was an afternoon for dissemination of information to parents regarding oral hygiene and childhood immunizations. Phase II was a morning of health screening for the children and cholesterol check for the first 25 parents. There were multiple opportunities for learners to work in conjunction with the nursing students and Head Start staff while practicing their spoken Spanish: to weigh and measure, to assist with vision screenings, and to assuage fears at various stations. All SLU students reported a great sense of accomplishment in being able to use their Spanish skills to perform a needed service:

> H. A.: I went to the Migrant Head Start to help with a health fair. This was the best experience for me this

semester because it concerned my major (Nursing) and my minor (Spanish). The children were so cute—some could speak fluent English while others spoke hardly any English. There were also parents there having cholesterol and blood pressure checked. I was able to explain to one parent who could not speak English about the two tests. It made me feel really good to be able to do that. These experiences have helped to broaden my concept on how culturally diverse our surrounding areas really are. Unless you get out into the community, you don't really know that they [the Spanish speakers] are there and need help. I can say that I truly appreciate this class for doing just that. I would recommend the class to anyone willing and able to learn of another culture and another language.

This student was very active at the health fair. She was unafraid to use her limited language skills, showing a side of herself that had been noticeably absent in the classroom, where she was shy and mostly unwilling to speak. Perhaps she felt less inhibited and less concerned about making mistakes because she was offering needed assistance and was working without pressure from a teacher.

Tutoring Project

In spring 2005, I encountered a Spanish-speaking mother who needed an advocate for her child at a local elementary school. She had been notified that her son was failing reading and would probably be retained in first grade in the coming year. Extremely upset at this possibility, she was anxious to talk to the teacher to see what could be done. However, her English skills were minimal, and she had failed in several prior attempts to have him placed with the school's resource teacher for extra help during the school year. Since I speak Spanish, I offered to accompany her to the school.

We met with the teacher and discussed what could be done to improve the child's reading skills. A plan was developed in which he would meet with the school's resource teacher for additional assistance in reading each day. I thought he might need additional assistance, so I asked the mother if she would be interested in after-school tutoring for her son. I was certain that I could find a couple of students who would be willing to work with him. She agreed to bring him to the university if I could supply the tutor(s).

At the next class meeting, I described the situation and immediately found three volunteers: One was a Spanish education major who had attended a summer study abroad program; the others were fifth-semester Spanish students who had no prior experience with native speakers. They were nervous, but they were willing. With a little help from me, the more advanced student was able to navigate her first-ever phone conversation in Spanish to set up their first session.

I attended the initial meeting to make sure that everyone got settled. The mother came with the boy and her other two children. Introductions were accomplished with lots of hesitations, questions, and puzzled looks. The students worked for about an hour with the boy and set up a second meeting two days later. Afterward they eagerly began to plan their next session. One had a son in first grade, so she had a good idea of what needed to be done; the others were willing to assist her in any way possible.

Over the course of the next several weeks, the students were faithful to their task. They brought books for the boy to read, worked on sounds and sound groups with materials they found on the Internet, and took him to the children's section of the library and allowed him to choose his own books (Dr. Seuss was his favorite). Each week they sent a list of what he had read to his teacher so that she could see that he was working hard. At each session, SLU students had to negotiate with one parent or the other about meeting times and places. Since the parents spoke no English, all of their interactions were in Spanish. This was challenging, but the students were able to navigate interactional obstacles and communicate.

There were several instances when the mother was late or failed to show up, which often ended in frustration:

> K. R.: I became frustrated during the tutoring experience by the fact that the family was always arriving 30 minutes late and never called, even if they decided not to come. This confirmed what we had learned about the different concept of time in Spanish-speaking countries. It is one thing to learn the language, but it is a totally different playing field when you get to learn the language and the culture and people that go along with it.

This student was able to experience a cultural difference and recognize that it was not sheer disregard for her or her partners but rather another way of organizing time. Although it did not quell her feelings, she accepted it for what it was and understood that this was part of the learning process.

> K. F.: The tutoring experience was frustrating for awhile when she [his mother] never called to say she couldn't come, but to watch his progress over the weeks was one of the most pleasant experiences I've ever had. In the beginning I was very nervous to talk to his Mom and his Dad, but when she saw how bad I struggled to speak, she became very patient. . . . This assignment made me realize that they [native Spanish speakers] are not as impatient with Americans trying to speak Spanish as we expect them to be, because they struggle to learn English just as much.

This student was able to see a good side of the situation. She obviously appreciated the acceptance on the part of the boy's parents for her willingness to continue to speak in spite of the difficulty.

Before the end of the term, the mother brought news that her son's reading had improved enough for him to be promoted to second grade. Everyone was excited, and the students explained to the mother that reading should continue over the summer. They told her about the summer program for children at the public library and encouraged her to take him there regularly.

These university students were able to utilize not only their Spanish, but also their critical thinking skills. With minimal knowledge of reading education practices, they were able to work collaboratively to devise a method that worked, and they achieved the desired results. As they learned to negotiate meaning in their interactions with the parents, they were more motivated to continue. And they were proud to recount their experiences to their classmates and to answer questions about how they were able to accomplish what they did.

New ESL Classes

In fall 2005 I learned about a neighborhood church that was beginning English lessons for interested adult members of their Hispanic congregation. I made it known to one of the members that I had students who might be interested in helping out, and they took me up on my offer. When I pitched the project to my class, a number of students showed interest immediately. We had been reading about and discussing some of the problems that face U.S. Hispanics who have limited English ability, and they saw an opportunity to engage with such a population. Since the second meeting, six of my students have come regularly to participate in this venture. Our goals are to work toward providing the adult learners with the vocabulary they need to more effectively do their jobs (or, in the case of one woman, develop a vocabulary sufficient to get a job). In their work at the church, the university students have been able to speak Spanish and get to know people from a variety of Spanish-speaking countries, as well as teach English to a group who is extremely interested in learning.

Also in fall 2005, other students taught English to Hispanics at an area learning center. Here the classes are more structured and the students are more consistent. The teacher allowed my students to assist her each week, and was willing to turn part of the class over to them completely. One of my students in particular became extremely interested in this group and was very dedicated to the project. Her reflections became increasingly sophisticated, and I know that she derived many benefits from her experience. She was also in my Spanish phonetics class, and she could see how the experience connected to that course content as well.

> J. M.: The teacher gave us some sheets with the short vowel sounds in English so each of us sat with a group of students and reviewed the worksheets. With these short vowels of course there were some consonant sounds, like b, v, etc. It was really cool because we are reviewing vowel sounds in the phonetics class, so we actually could compare and show them the differences in English and Spanish. We were able to use the things we learned in our classes to help them with Spanish and we helped to teach them things that they will use in the real world. [Next week] She [also] asked me some stuff that she would like to tell her boss. If she uses this vocabulary with her boss, maybe her job quality will be improved. This will help her in many ways, and it will also affect many people's lives around her. She was extremely excited about learning these practical things. I hope that this will make her feel more confident in all she does. I really feel that tonight I realized the connection between my service-learning world and the real world. I also feel that I am improving myself because I am getting to practice the Spanish language, my second language, while I am helping someone improve theirs.

■ Discussion

Standards-driven instruction "should allow all students to use Spanish to communicate outside the walls of the classroom [and] prepare students for successful real-life uses of Spanish [by enabling] them to interact appropriately with comfort and fluency [and] with intercultural appropriateness" (Met, 2000, p. 49). Service-learning projects in Spanish 303 speak to each of the goal areas of the 5 Cs, which comprise the framework of the national standards (National Standards for Foreign Language Education Project, 1999). Students use Spanish to communicate within a cultural context. In so doing, they are able to use the language with some autonomy (Ballman, 1998) and refine their use of communication strategies as they encounter real-time spoken Spanish with all of its demands. Afterward as students reflect on newly acquired linguistic, social, and cultural information and compare and contrast it with those of their classmates, they are able to confirm or refute textbook information and supplement or replace it with their own lived experiences. In so doing, they are able to connect to other academic and cultural content, to their peers, and to the community in an unprecedented way.

Service-learning removes the university from the "ivory tower" and puts students and faculty into the communities where they live and work (Carney, 2004). This increases the university's visibility in the community, while affording students and faculty the opportunity to work together in a way that would never be possible if they remained inside the classroom. Relationships between me and my students have deepened as they see me more involved in their learning process and in improving the lives of community members. The relationships we have established with administrative personnel at various sites have resulted in increased benefits for us and for the university.

The principal at Independence Middle School has written glowing letters of recommendation for two of my students who are in the Teacher Education Program. Receiving this appreciation for their efforts not only builds their self-esteem, but also adds a dimension to their professional portfolios. With such kind words from an administrator, they can feel more confident as they present themselves as prospective teachers.

Migrant Head Start personnel have become more inclusive of us in their activities. The interim director of the center asked me to bring two students to participate in a literacy workshop for parents during summer 2005. The students and I, in conjunction with two of the Head Start teachers, presented a short program on the importance of reading in early childhood development. Both students were nervous, but they were willing to participate. They helped distribute information in Spanish to the parents and then took turns reading a poem and a short story in Spanish to the parents so that they could see some of the materials that were available to their children in Spanish. Parents were appreciative of the information we provided, and the SLU students were asked to return and spend time reading to the children either in Spanish or English.

I was recently asked to provide translation services for parents who were to be a part of the committee that was interviewing candidates for the directorship of the Migrant Head Start Center. One of my students volunteered to spend the morning with them, and the result was a positive experience for them and a wonderful letter of recognition for her files. This symbiotic relationship that we are developing is proving fruitful for all concerned.

As a pedagogical tool, service-learning can create a stronger commitment to foreign language study (encouraging more majors and minors in the discipline) as students increase their linguistic and cultural knowledge during their field experiences. Reflection on service-learning experiences with teachers, other students, and community partners can foster the development of critical thinking skills (Arries, 1999; Eyler, Giles, & Schmiede, 1996; Varona, 1999), motivate career changes (Lesman, 2004; Olazagasti-Segovia, 2004), and positively impact the lives of language learners, as well as the populations they serve (Bennett, 2004; Cockerham, Nelson, & Anderson, 2004; Jorge, 2004; Varas, 1999).

The outcomes of the service-learning projects described in previous sections have certainly borne out several of these predictions. Students' evaluations of their service-learning experiences have become increasingly more positive as the projects have been refined over the course of several semesters. A recent graduate is now working full-time at the Migrant Head Start Center. At least two students in lower-level courses who were willing to participate in some aspect of community service last semester have been persuaded to minor or major in Spanish; another Spanish major who is about to graduate has made a commitment to the teaching profession, something that she had never considered before her involvement in the service-learning projects. Reflection papers indicate that some of the Spanish majors are doing what they had always dreamed of doing: interacting with a native speaker and having some measure of success. For many, it shows them how much practice they need and how important it is to seek conversational partners outside of the classroom.

■ Reflections and Future Plans

Reflection is the hyphen in service-learning (Eyler, 2001). For students, it is a process that improves the quality of their classroom experience while allowing them to do meaningful work in the community; that challenges attitudes, beliefs, assumptions, prejudices, and stereotypes; and that invites them to explore, understand, and question the status quo. For teachers, reflection provides a vehicle for deepening relationships with students, refining course content, and allowing for a continuing dialogue with community partners on how to improve the service-learning experience for both sides.

The following are some of my reflections on the projects in which my students are engaged.

Migrant Head Start. Although the language of classroom instruction is English, the staff at Migrant Head Start does much to preserve the linguistic and cultural heritage of their students. Several of their staff speak Spanish during the day, which reinforces the first language of the children. They provide bilingual materials that support dual language literacy skills for the children. In the summer of 2006 my students and I selected several monolingual Spanish and bilingual books that seemed appropriate for reading to the students. My plans are to have my nonnative students practice reading aloud with a native speaker so that they improve their pronunciation and reading skills before going out to share these with the children. Not only will they improve their pronunciation, but the reading process should foster self-confidence in them as they interact with the children at the center. As the children see that others appreciate their first language, they will likely feel additional pride in their linguistic and cultural heritage.

Independence Middle School. We have had three successful semesters of tutoring at Independence Middle School and are rapidly coming to the conclusion of a fourth. I met with the principal at the beginning of this semester to review what we had done and talk about what we might do to refine the experience for both sets of students. I believe that the changes we have made will result in an improved outcome for both parties. My goal for the coming academic year is not only to continue with this aspect of service-learning, but also to expand our efforts so that the Latino students will become more inclusive members of the school's population. I envision a collaborative project between them and the SLU students that highlights their Hispanic heritage and focuses on what they bring to the system as opposed to what they need from it, which is in line with Moll and Ruiz's (2002) notion of "educational sovereignty." As National Hispanic Heritage month is celebrated each year between September 15th and October 15th, the fall semester is an optimum time to capitalize on the cultural resources that these students embody. I am hopeful that the other middle school students will begin to embrace them and that the diversity they offer may begin to broaden the gap that necessarily exists in the absence of information and education.

ESL classes. My students' involvement in the English classes has introduced them to a population that they would never have met under traditional classroom circumstances. At the Learning Center, we have been afforded access to a population that we have wanted to approach (both in nursing and in Spanish) for several years. The classes there are well structured in the form of a teacher who is contracted to do testing, prepare lessons, and teach classes. This stands in stark contrast to the ESL classes at the church, where the atmosphere is much less informal and there is no teacher per se. My students have been working with the adults one on one (or two on one, depending on the numbers). I would like future classes to be more structured so that SLU students can approach the group with a plan each week that calls for more interaction between the ESL students. Role plays and jigsaw tasks (Brooks, 1992) are things that we have talked about doing for next semester. The two organizers of the group and I have spoken several times about what we might do to improve the quality of the instruction and encourage more adults to attend the classes. I hope that we can continue to assist in both places, and in the case of the learning center, I hope that we can partner with nursing to bring needed health care to this underserved population of workers.

■ Conclusion

We can clearly see the benefits of applying critical pedagogy and sociocultural theory to the Spanish curriculum. Critical pedagogy, which calls for moving from traditional education to problem-posing education, has allowed service-learning students in Spanish 303 to take an active part in the learning process by using their second language, taking risks, and making suggestions. In working with me and our community partners, they have created a more meaningful educational experience for themselves. Sociocultural theory, applied to the curriculum, offered students an alternative space in which to enhance their learning. Their interactions with community members have afforded them a greater level of linguistic and cultural knowledge than students who chose not to participate, and their lived experiences will remain with them forever.

With its obvious advantages for students of foreign languages, service-learning programs have critical implications for the academy as a whole that should be acknowledged by all institutions of higher learning that hope to provide a well-rounded education that shapes the character of its students. "Their [students'] values and conceptions of public life are formed and shaped through experience and dialogue. Higher education must assert a more powerful role in shaping experience and dialogue into a civic ethos" (Heffernan, 2002, p. 77).

Service-learning also addresses the lack of connectedness in higher education (Eyler & Giles, 1999), and speaks to the concerns that many employers have about graduates' abilities, including their unpreparedness to work as members of a team and their lack of knowledge in issues of diversity (Ehrlich, 1997, as cited in Eyler & Giles, 1999). As students synthesize information and begin to collaborate on ways in which the situations and/or lives of community members can be improved, they are perhaps creating a scenario in which they will continue their work long after their study of Spanish has ended. As Lesman (2004) reminds us, "If we are educators in the highest sense, we must in every way encourage our students to be fully developed, fully engaged citizens of our country" (p. 35). The service-learning opportunities in Spanish 303 are an attempt to do exactly that as they place students in a social environment and ask them to work together to identify and solve problems in a way that will positively impact the lives of community members. My students have risen to this challenge and have gained much in the process.

▪ Acknowledgments

Thanks to Nancy Joe Dyer, Dianna Laurent, Joey Sandrock, Billie Stewart, and to the editors of this volume for their thoughtful comments on earlier versions of the manuscript.

▪ Endnotes

1) Southeastern Louisiana University (SLU) is a regional state university located in Hammond, Louisiana, which lies at the intersection of I-12 and I-55, equidistant between New Orleans and Baton Rouge. The university is home to approximately 15,000 students who are enrolled in 65 undergraduate and graduate degree programs. Priority 4 of the university's strategic plan is:

> To strengthen collaboration and partnerships in internal and external communities. Southeastern embraces active partnerships that benefit faculty, students and the region we serve. Collaborative efforts are varied and dynamic; range from local to global; and encompass education, business, industry, and the public sector. (Southeastern Louisiana University, 2005)

SLU has long been committed to civic engagement in general and service-learning in particular. Although courses linking academic content with service in the community had been going on in a variety of disciplines for a number of years, coursework did not become identified as service-learning until the establishment of the Connections Program in spring of 1998. In 2000 service-learning was the focus of the Institute for Teaching and Professional Enhancement sponsored by the university's Center for Faculty Excellence. Subsequently, the university joined Campus Compact and Journey Towards

Democracy (Louisiana Campus Compact, 2005), both of which demonstrate a commitment to promote community service as a means of developing student citizenship skills and civic engagement. Subsequently, an office of service-learning has been established and a service-learning advisory committee has been created.

2) Although Jennings was writing within a context of the "alternative" school, his ideas can be easily extrapolated to a university setting.

3) Utterances may convey more than their literal meaning, so learning only the grammar is insufficient. The learners must have knowledge about which forms are right for which occasion, many of which require cultural knowledge that can only be acquired by participation in a community of speakers (Bialystok & Hakuta, 1994).

4) My initial exposure to the concept of service-learning came from several conversations with the director of the Connections Program in 2001 and 2002. After talking to him, I was certain that this could be a wonderful outlet for my students to gain exposure to language and culture. Since the North Shore of Louisiana is home to a growing population of Hispanics due to seasonal fieldwork, the establishment of several small industries in the area, and a few Mexican restaurants that employ mainly Spanish-speaking workers, integrating service-learning into Spanish courses seemed a natural progression.

5) Thanks to the Office of Migrant Education and Tangipahoa Public Schools for affording us a venue for our service-learning work.

■ References

Aljaafreh, A., & Lantolf, J. P. (1994). Negative feedback as regulation and second language learning in the zone of proximal development. *Modern Language Journal, 78*(4), 465–483.

Arries, J. F. (1999). Critical pedagogy and service-learning in Spanish: Crossing borders in the freshman seminar. In J. Hellebrandt & L. T. Varona (Eds.), *Construyendo puentes (building bridges): Concepts and models for service-learning in Spanish* (pp. 33–47). Washington, DC: American Association for Higher Education.

Ballman, T. (1998). From teacher-centered to learner-centered: Guidelines for sequencing and presenting the elements of a FL lesson. In J. Harper, M. G. Lively, & M. K. Williams (Eds.), *The coming of age of the profession: Issues and emerging ideas for the teaching of foreign languages* (pp. 97–112). Boston, MA: Heinle.

Bennett, C. H. (2004). The NDNU Community-Based Learning Project in Guadalajara, Mexico. In J. Hellebrandt, J. Arries, & L. Varona (Eds.), *Juntos: Community partnerships in Spanish and Portuguese* (pp. 62–68). Boston, MA: Heinle.

Bialystok, E., & Hakuta, K. (1994). *In other words: The science and psychology of second language acquisition.* New York, NY: Basic Books.

Brooks, F. (1992). Spanish III learners talking to one another through a jigsaw task. *Canadian Modern Language Review, 48*(4), 696–717.

Carney, T. (2004). Reaching beyond borders through service learning. *Journal of Latinos and Education, 3*(4), 267–271.

Cockerham, S., Nelson, A., & Anderson, M. K. (2004). It takes a holler: Appalachia goes Hispanic. In J. Hellebrandt, J. Arries, & L. T. Varona (Eds.), *Juntos: Community partnerships in Spanish and Portuguese* (pp. 83–99). Boston, MA: Heinle.

Darhower, M. (2004). Dialogue journals as mediators of L2 learning: A sociocultural account. *Hispania, 87*(2), 324–335.

Di Pietro, R. J. (1987). *Strategic interaction.* Cambridge, U.K.: Cambridge University Press.

Dörnyei, Z. (1997). Psychological processes in cooperative language learning: Group dynamics and motivation. *Modern Language Journal, 81*(4), 482–493.

Eyler, J. (2001). Creating your reflection map. *New Directions for Higher Education, 114,* 35–43.

Eyler, J., & Giles, D. E., Jr. (1999). *Where's the learning in service-learning?* San Francisco, CA: Jossey Bass.

Eyler, J., Giles, D., & Schmiede, A. (1996). *A practitioner's guide to reflection in service-learning.* Nashville, TN: Vanderbilt University.

Freire, P. (1993). *Pedagogy of the oppressed.* New York, NY: Continuum Publishing. (Original work published 1970).

Gezi, K. I., & Myers, J. E. (1968). *Teaching in American culture.* New York, NY: Holt, Rinehart & Winston.

Giroux, H. (1992). *Border crossings: Cultural workers and the politics of education.* New York, NY: Routledge.

Grittner, F. M., & Fearing, P. B. (1979). Futurism in foreign language teaching. In J. D. Arendt, D. L. Lange, & P. J. Myers (Eds.), *Foreign language learning, today and tomorrow* (pp. 1–12). New York, NY: Pergamon Press.

Hall, J. K. (2001). *Methods for teaching foreign languages: Creating a community of learners in the foreign language classroom.* Upper Saddle River, NJ: Prentice Hall.

Heffernan, K. (2002). Civic lessons. In J. Saltmarsh (Ed.), *The journal of public affairs: Volume VI. Supplemental Issue I—Civic engagement and higher education* (pp. 69–82). Providence, RI: Campus Compact.

Jennings, W. B. (1979). Alternatives in education. In J. D. Arendt, D. L. Lange, & P. J. Myers (Eds.), *Foreign language learning, today and tomorrow* (pp. 158–168). New York, NY: Pergamon Press.

Jorge, E. (2004). Dialogue and power: Collaborative language curriculum development. In J. Hellebrandt, J. Arries, & L. Varona (Eds.), *Juntos: Community partnerships in Spanish and Portuguese* (pp. 17–28). Boston, MA: Heinle.

Kinginger, C. (2001). Sociocultural approaches to teaching and teachers' research. In R. Z. Lavine (Ed.), *Beyond the boundaries: Changing contexts in language learning* (pp. 201–225). Boston, MA: McGraw-Hill.

Lantolf, J. P., & Pavlenko, A. (1995). Sociocultural theory and second language acquisition. *Annual Review of Applied Linguistics, 15,* 108–124.

Lesman, A. (2004). From service-learning to social activism: Growing the "soul of a citizen." In J. Hellebrandt, J. Arries, & L. Varona (Eds.), *Juntos: Community partnerships in Spanish and Portuguese* (pp. 29–35). Boston, MA: Heinle.

Louisiana Campus Compact (2005). *Service-learning programs and initiatives.* Retrieved October 4, 2006, from: www.selu.edu/Administration/President/lcc/programs.html

Luria, A. R. (1981). *Language and cognition.* New York, NY: Wiley.

McGroarty, M. (1993). Cooperative learning and second language acquisition. In D. Holt (Ed.), *Cooperative learning* (pp. 19–46). Washington, DC: Center for Applied Linguistics.

McLaren, P. (1989). *Life in schools: An introduction to critical pedagogy in the foundations of education.* New York, NY: Longman.

Met, M. (2000). Instruction: Linking curriculum and assessment to the standards. In G. Guntermann (Ed.), *Teaching Spanish is the five Cs: A blueprint for success* (pp. 49–69). Boston, MA: Thomson/Heinle.

Moll, L. C., & Ruiz, R. (2002). The schooling of Latino children. In M. Suárez-Orozco & M. Páez (Eds.), *Latinos: Remaking America* (pp. 262–274). Berkeley, CA: University of California Press.

National Standards in Foreign Language Education Project. (1999). *Standards for foreign language learning in the 21st century.* Lawrence, KS: Allen Press.

Nyikos, M., & Hashimoto, R. (1997). Constructivist theory applied to collaborative learning in teacher education: In search of ZPD. *Modern Language Journal, 81*(4), 506–517.

Ogulnick, K. (2005). Learning language / learning self. In S. Kiesling & C. Paulston (Eds.), *Intercultural discourse and communication: The essential readings* (pp. 250–254). Malden, MA: Blackwell.

Olazagasti-Segovia, E. (2004). Second language acquisition, academic service-learning and learners' transformation. In J. Hellebrandt, J. Arries, & L. Varona (Eds.), *Juntos: Community partnerships in Spanish and Portuguese* (pp. 5–16). Boston, MA: Heinle.

Omaggio Hadley, A. (2001). *Teaching language in context.* Boston, MA: Heinle.

Oxford, R. (1997). Cooperative learning, collaborative learning, and interaction: Three communicative strands in the language classroom. *Modern Language Journal, 81*(4), 443–456.

Rigg, P., & Allen, V. G. (Eds.). (1989). *When they don't all speak English.* Urbana, IL: National Council of Teachers of English.

Rivers, W. M. (Ed.). (1997). *Interactive language teaching.* Cambridge, MA: Harvard University Press.

Rogoff, B., Matusov, E., & White, C. (1996). Models of teaching and learning: Participation in a community of learners. In D. Olson & N. Torrance (Eds.), *The handbook of education and human development* (pp. 388–414). Oxford, U.K.: Blackwell.

Rutherford, W. (1987). *Second language grammar: Learning and teaching.* London, U.K.: Longman.

Southeastern Louisiana University. (2005). *Vision 2005.* Retrieved October 4, 2006, from: www.selu.edu/documents/docs/vision2005_strplan.pdf

Turner, J. F., Maisch, W. C., & Mendoza, H. D. (2004). *Somos vecinos: Intermediate Spanish through U. S. Latino culture.* Upper Saddle River, NJ: Pearson Prentice Hall.

Varas, P. (1999). Raising cultural awareness through service-learning in Spanish culture and conversation: Tutoring in the migrant education program in Salem. In J. Hellebrandt & L. T. Varona (Vol. Eds.), *Construyendo puentes (Building bridges): Concepts and models for service-learning in Spanish* (pp. 123–135). Washington, DC: American Association for Higher Education.

Varona, L. T. (1999). From instrumental to interactive to critical knowledge through service-learning in Spanish. In J. Hellebrandt & L. T. Varona (Eds.), *Construyendo puentes (building bridges): Concepts and models for service-learning in Spanish* (pp. 61–76). Washington, DC: American Association for Higher Education.

Vygotsky, L. S. (1978). *Mind in society: The development of higher psychological processes.* Cambridge, MA: Harvard University Press.

Vygotsky, L. S. (1986). *Thought and language.* Cambridge, MA: Harvard University Press. (Original work published 1934).

Wenger, E. (1998). *Communities of practice: Learning, meaning, and identity.* Cambridge, MA: University Press.

Wertsch, J. V. (1981). *The concept of activity in soviet psychology.* Armonk, NY: M. E. Sharpe.

Wertsch, J. V. (1985). *Vygotsky and the social formation of mind.* Cambridge, MA: Harvard University Press.

Williams, L. (2004). *Rage and hope.* Retrieved July 12, 2005, from: www.perfectfit.org/CT/giroux2.html

Wink, J. (2005). *Critical pedagogy: Notes from the real world* (3rd ed.). Boston, MA: Pearson/Prentice-Hall.

Section II

Domestic Service-Learning Efforts

The chapters in this section focus on service-learning programs and courses in the United States. Often referred to as the "land of immigrants," the United States has a long, though not always glorious, history of weaving culturally and linguistically diverse people into its social fabric. As we noted in the introductory chapter, during times of peak immigration in the U.S. there has historically been a concomitant decline in the acceptance of linguistic and cultural diversity. Weise and García (1998) suggest that increased immigration creates a feeling of instability, perhaps due to the unsettling aura of change, apparent job competition, or fear of an inability to communicate with immigrants. This feeling of instability often leads to fear of the unknown and an insistence on using the status quo language, English, creating a backlash against linguistic diversity. The authors in this section are united in their efforts to prevent xenophobia from unraveling America's social fabric; they describe innovative courses and programs that use service-learning to promote and prepare learners for educated and engaged citizenship in multilingual and multicultural settings in local and global arenas.

In Chapter 5 Ruth Spack describes how she gradually became aware of the sociopolitical dimensions of teaching English as a second language during the Vietnam War, and how today she seeks to help her own students understand better what language learning really entails. Serving as tutors of English to speakers of other languages (ESOL) in the community, and discussing movies and tales documenting the immigrant experience, her students reflect critically on a variety of language and literacy issues, ranging from the English-only versus bilingual education debate, to the role and impact of global English, and the availability and accessibility of ESL programs. In doing so, they gain a deeper appreciation of the diverse society they will enter as future business leaders and citizens of the world.

In Chapter 6 Jesse Kapper Moore collaboratively writes with selected students of an Introduction to TESOL (Teaching English to Speakers of Other Languages) course in which students apply classroom content to TESOL tutoring and curriculum development. Set in an area that, according to Census 2000 figures, saw the largest increase in Latino immigrants in the country, Kapper and her students provide practical insights for faculty and students planning service-learning projects in culturally and linguistically diverse (CLD) settings. The authors remind us of the critical importance of reflection in connecting community service and academic study while also illustrating how collaboration in service-learning, especially in CLD settings, is multidimensional.

In Chapter 7 Howard Grabois shifts the focus of the section from course-based initiatives to program design and administration. Describing a program-wide service-learning effort in which all undergraduate Spanish students have access to service-learning, the author argues that departments need to articulate service-learning goals with appropriate theories of second language acquisition to ensure meaningful student learning throughout the curriculum. Grabois describes how Spanish activity portfolios and seminars can help departments create the necessary infrastructure to draw large numbers of students to service-learning in Spanish. The *Ayuda y Aprende* program at Purdue University shows that with administrative support and careful articulation between second- and third-year Spanish, service-learning can permeate an entire undergraduate curriculum and further promote a department's civic engagement efforts.

In Chapter 8 José Centeno proposes a collaborative framework to train speech language students to work with bilingual minorities. Service-learning plays a key role in the program design due to its effectiveness in reducing negative stereotypes of the Other. When negative socially defined perceptions occur, they lead to biased assessments of minority individuals and their culture, including inappropriate categorization of their nonstandard linguistic forms as deficient linguistic systems. Carefully structured service-learning experiences in CLD communities can bring the experiences of minority populations in the United States to life for speech language pathology students, "bringing them to a new level of awareness and social justice."

■ Reference

Weise, A., & García, E. E. (1998). The Bilingual Education Act: Language minority students and equal educational opportunity. *Bilingual Research Journal, 22*(1), 1–18.

5

Teaching the Lived Experience of Language Learning

Ruth Spack

Iremember the moment when I realized that teaching English to speakers of other languages (ESOL) is not an innocent endeavor. It was in 1971, not long after I had received a master's degree in English and certification to teach ESOL. My husband, a pediatrician, was stationed at Andrews Air Force Base in Maryland, where I volunteered to teach English to other military wives, most of whom were Vietnamese brides of returning servicemen. What a wonderful opportunity, I thought. Armed with verb tenses and vocabulary, I could make use of my own basic training to help these women learn English and adapt to American culture. There was a war raging out there, and I could aid people who had suffered as a result of that very conflict.

At first things went just as I had hoped. But I soon came to understand that my work entailed more than simply teaching a new language and culture. In that classroom, I was compelled to engage with a perilous mix of race, class, gender, and colonialism. As the women learned more English and became more comfortable talking with me, I heard stories that revealed a deep pain that had been hidden while we were studying verb forms and idioms. I learned that it was common practice for their soldier husbands to have taught the women English during their stay in Vietnam but that these "lessons" included curse words whose meanings were not explained. The husbands would later roar with laughter, when, now living in the United States, their war brides would respond to their mothers-in-law's comments with such expressions as "No shit!" and "That's fucking unreal!" Such linguistically inappropriate language exacerbated already tenuous relationships, for several of the soldiers' mothers had trouble adjusting to the presence of their racially different daughters-in-law. Even the verb forms I had been teaching lost their innocence when I became aware of a dangerous link between language and social class identification: One woman suffered abuse when she corrected her husband's English, telling him he should say, "He doesn't," not "He don't."

As I reflect back on this teaching experience, I understand now that I entered the field rather naively, unaware of the colonialist mentality that may impinge on the teaching of English to speakers of other languages. I did sense that what Stephanie Vandrick (1999/2002) calls "a colonial shadow" (p. 411) had enveloped the minds of the U.S. servicemen who were teaching English to their spouses. However, I did not realize that it had also affected me: an ESOL instructor who mistakenly thought I was in the classroom to do good rather than to teach. In her rare and raw essay, titled "ESL [English as a second language] and the Colonial Legacy," Vandrick reflects back on her own past as a "missionary" kid, critiques her childhood behavior toward the children who lived in the village in India where her parents served as missionaries, and extrapolates from that experience to analyze her current teaching. In retrospect, Vandrick recognizes that she unwittingly saw herself in India as a miniature hostess in a foreign land, "graciously dispensing gifts, hand-me-downs, trinkets, wisdom, religion, and Western culture to the 'natives'" (p. 413). Wondering whether this attitude might have influenced her, years later, when she became an ESL instructor in a U.S. college, she asks herself whether she is now "graciously dispensing the gifts, prizes, and wisdom made available through the English language, 'American culture,' and academic skills for the American university" (p. 413).

Vandrick (1999/2002) extends this question to other ESOL instructors, asking whether the colonial shadow may have enveloped our unconscious behavior as well. Are we unintentionally infantilizing students by viewing ourselves as nurturers or saviors (as I once did) or by speaking loudly, making large gestures, or extending excessive or exaggerated praise? Are we unwittingly ignoring diversity if we set a particular Western standard of achievement or language (English) and measure students against that standard (as I once did)? Are we unconsciously positioning ourselves as superior if we predetermine the curriculum based on our perceptions of what students need—without consulting the students themselves—and then expect students to be grateful for all that we have done for them (as I once did)? Even if the answer to each of these questions is *no* for most of us, it is important to be aware that such attitudes persist and that multilingual students, if not always their instructors, may have a heightened sensitivity to these ways of thinking and behaving. It certainly is worthwhile, as Vandrick says, to grapple with this issue, not only as individual instructors but also within the ESOL profession.

I would like to be able to say that after my experience teaching Vietnamese wives of U.S. servicemen, I immediately and radically changed my teaching. However, in other settings, I continued to use materials that were state of the art but irrelevant to the particular group I was teaching or to create materials that were innovative but not meaningfully related to students' actual concerns or not sensitive enough to their racial, class, religious, cultural, or gender identity. I do not criticize myself for my own slow progress; I know that transformative teaching rarely follows a straightforward path. I also recognize that the environment I had created in the Air Force classroom, coupled with my willingness to stray from my preset curriculum, enabled the students' openness and in turn opened my eyes to the real contexts in which their language learning was taking place. And my Air Force volunteer effort laid the groundwork for a lifetime of reflection on teaching English to speakers of other languages. My own experience and research have shown me that the key to meaningful and appropriate language instruction does not lie solely in well intentioned teachers or inventive pedagogical strategies (see, for example, Spack, 2002).

I have often wondered how my own ESOL training might have been different so that I could have avoided a naive stance of neutrality toward language teaching and learning. Perhaps it could have been more like an undergraduate course I teach at Bentley College, titled "Language and Literacy: Theories into Practice." I was motivated to create the Language and Literacy course after I became aware that Bentley undergraduates were tutoring adult ESL learners through a service-learning program, with little or no training. I felt, first, that it was important for students to have a theoretical grounding for their tutoring. And because Bentley is a business university, I felt, too, that it was important for Bentley students to understand what the ESOL experience really entails, not only as citizens of the world but also as future business leaders who will interact with speakers of other languages, including the workers they hire to do skilled and unskilled labor. But most important, I wanted the students to gain a critical understanding of the underlying historical, social, political, and economic structures that inform the ESOL experience—information that had been missing from my own early training. I wanted them to understand why and how linguistic and geographical background, social and economic positioning, age and gender, and racial and religious identity affect English language learning. In short, I wanted them to be fully aware of the lived experience of English language learners.

■ Connecting Academic Study and Community Service

Within the context of the Language and Literacy course, all or most of the students tutor English language learners for approximately 20 hours during the semester. Bentley's Service-Learning Center makes the placements, and student project managers supervise the tutors on site. Students are assigned to tutor one-on-one or to assist in classrooms at local schools and agencies, including an emergency family shelter, whose ESL program was created by a Bentley student through a service-learning internship under my supervision. To fulfill the academic requirements of the course, students regularly write informal papers in response to assigned readings as well as formal essay or research assignments. The student tutors also write at least four three-part journal entries on their community service experience, which include a detailed non-evaluative description of what happened in a tutoring session, their reflections, insights, and questions, and connections to the course material. Class discussions, too, routinely link the course material and community service experience, allowing each to inform the other and opening unique possibilities for critical reflection, for example when an experience in the field raises questions about a theory studied in class, or vice versa. Final projects typically benefit the campus Service-Learning Center or community partners. For example, different classes have created ESL tutoring manuals and a video for the benefit of future tutors. Individual projects have included a funding plan for a community agency; translations of crucial documents; interviews with adult ESL learners that were integrated into the curriculum of their classes; and research on best practices that served as the foundation for a volunteer manual for an adult education program. Student tutors also write an end-of-semester service-learning reflection paper analyzing their entire tutorial experience and linking it to the course material.

In preparation for the tutoring, students examine their own language-learning experiences and draw from that experience to theorize about language and literacy acquisition, through the following exercise:

1) Describe in writing a language learning experience of your own. Where and how did it take place? Were you successful at learning the language? Why or why not?

2) Work in a small group to share the language learning experience you have just written about. Drawing on your combined experiences, make a list of conditions under which language learning is (a) successful or (b) unsuccessful.
3) Drawing from your lists, create a general statement (theory) to explain what makes language learning successful.

We then read theoretical articles so that students can compare their own findings to the published research on second language acquisition. And we read some pedagogical texts so that students can learn ways to apply the theory in practice.

The lessons on second language acquisition theory and pedagogy are timed to coincide with the start of students' tutoring, a few weeks after our class has begun. The course itself actually begins with historical studies of immigration and language policies so that students can learn how minority populations have been both welcomed and discriminated against, how the United States government has both fostered and restricted linguistic diversity, and how English became the medium of learning in U.S. schools, if not the official native language. And we examine such issues as the English-only versus bilingual education debate, the literacy crisis, and the lack of availability and accessibility of ESL programs designed for adult learners in the United States. Such issues take on new meaning after students become tutors of English language learners. For example, in the following excerpt from her service-learning reflection paper, Faith[1] reveals how her earlier belief that immigrant adults do not make enough effort to learn English was overturned by both her reading and her tutorial experience:

> So many of the issues brought up in "English Literacy in the U.S." by McKay and Weinstein-Shr that I could not fully understand before I started tutoring began to make sense. I think that before when I read the article and it said

that language minorities want to learn English, I believed it because I wanted to, not because I really did. After tutoring though I think I can honestly say that yes, they really do want to learn. Every week when they would come to class . . . it was written all over their faces and beyond that you could just tell they were eager to learn. Looking back on it, not only did tutoring give me a better understanding of this article but the article also gave me a better understanding of tutoring.

Another emphasis in the class is on the global impact of English—how it is spreading worldwide, how local conditions are spawning varieties of the language, how mastery of English establishes positions of power in government and commerce, and so on. We raise questions about the nature and dominance of standard English and the new linguistic colonialism that is taking root. And we read the Stephanie Vandrick (1999/2002) article I discussed earlier—"ESL and the Colonial Legacy"—so that students can address their own ethnocentric tendencies. Judy referenced the Vandrick reading when she wrote about her initial experience tutoring adult language learners:

> I can't imagine what it must be like for new immigrants who arrive here who have to raise children and work to learn English. I have much respect for the adults who take time out of their hectic lives to try to learn English. (When I wrote that sentence, I almost wrote that I respect the adults who are trying to *better* themselves by learning English. However, after reading [Vandrick's] article, it has made me more aware and more conscious of what would have been an unconscious attitude; it scream[ed] out at me.) As a tutor, I will to the best of my ability and consciousness try to not have a superior attitude when it comes to speaking English.

Because this is an undergraduate course—and an elective at that—I try to engage students with materials other than scholarly texts. To bring the course up to date, students find current news articles on language and literacy issues and take turns leading class discussions on their chosen topic. We also read poetry and personal narratives that focus on the themes of language and literacy. Such texts often have special resonance for students, especially if they are children of immigrants or immigrants themselves. Judy, whose parents emigrated from China and became U.S. citizens long before she was born, had a new appreciation of her own mother's second language acquisition after reading Amy Tan's (1990/2002) essay, "Mother Tongue":

> Amy Tan's passage hit very close to home. The experiences she shared with her mother and the English her mother speaks are similar in nature to some of the experiences my mother and I have shared. I wrote in my last journal about how the English my mother speaks sometimes does embarrass me and even nowadays I still wish that she was able to speak what I deem to be "proper" English. However, in reading this article I have realized that it is true that who is to say what is "proper" English. I can understand the English my mother speaks perfectly and she understands the English I speak. So who is to say that we are not able to communicate as effectively as anyone else?

In addition to analyzing scholarly articles, news reports, poetry, and personal essays, we analyze classroom scenes in films such as *Good Morning Vietnam* and *Lilies of the Field,* not for pedagogical purposes only but also to consider the colonialist context in which the movies' language lessons take place or the underlying assumptions about the primacy of standard English. So that students can grasp the larger political contexts in which new languages are taught and learned, we also view two films in their entirety: *Iron and Silk,* which features a U.S. college graduate who teaches English in China, and *El Norte,* which chronicles the harrowing journey to the United States of a brother and sister who escape certain death in Guatemala. Maureen's response to *El Norte* reveals the value of including a visual component in the course:

> This film was very enlightening for me. I never really looked at the reasons why people come to America. I have always oversimplified the idea that people come to flee oppression, but I have never had a visual image of what their journey, and cause of it, is really like. The scene where Rosa and Enrique climb through the Tijuana sewers was very disturbing, especially the part with the rats. I have been to Mexican border towns in Arizona, and have seen the poverty first hand, I just never thought about the ways that illegal immigrants enter the country aside from through the countryside.

But perhaps the most compelling materials I present in the class are works of fiction.[2] My experience has been that fictional works render the lived experience of language learning in a way that theoretical, pedagogical, and even autobiographical materials simply cannot capture. The stories we read contribute a unique aesthetic component, for the writers share a vibrant imagination, a striking gift for language and storytelling, and a compassionate ear. Together, the stories demonstrate that language learning processes are rarely smooth and often traumatic. In story after story we witness how illusions and dreams are shattered by real and imagined barriers, how moments of achievement are set back by incidents that bring shame and tragedy, and yet how it may be possible for fear or loss to be compensated by rich new opportunity, for frustration and embarrassment to give way to humor and joy. A major advantage of teaching through fiction is that the stories' imaginary constructs offer a distance that enables a frank and open conversation in the classroom. At the same time, ironically, the literary qualities of the stories, their poignancy, and the raw truths they reveal, draw students in, inviting them to reflect on their own experiences, practices, and expectations.

Among the most powerful stories are those that reveal the impact of English in such places as New Zealand, Hawai'i, and Native America, for they reflect the linguistic humiliation and cultural displacement that characterize colonial domination. In Patricia Grace's (1998) story, "Kura," we learn how Maori children in an English-only school were severely punished "for not speaking when they were spoken to" (p. 33), even though they did not understand the language, and how these children grew into traumatized adults who were silenced by memory. The young narrator of Lois-Ann Yamanaka's (1996) "Obituary" listens as her teacher in a Hawai'ian school explains that the students' "uneducated," "low-class" language will take them "nowhere in life" and that they must therefore "Speak Standard English" (p. 154). Having internalized this lesson in linguistic and cultural denigration, the narrator then thinks:

> how ashamed I am of pidgin English. . . . Sometimes I wish to be haole. That my name could be Betty Smith or Annie Anderson or Debbie Cole, wife of Dennis Cole who lives at 2222 Maple Street with a white station wagon with wood panel on the side, a dog named Spot, a cat named Kitty, and I wear white gloves. (Yamanaka, 1996, pp. 154–155)

Even as they portray the negative consequences of colonialist attitudes, the authors of such stories typically reveal the resistance and pride of colonized people. The narrator in Zitkala-Ša's (1900) "The School Days of an Indian Girl," educated in an English-only mission boarding school that denigrates Native American languages and cultures, ultimately learns enough English to rebel against authority. The narrator in Marie Hara's (1990) "Fourth Grade Ukus," placed in a Hawai'ian school for children who speak nonstandard English, is intimidated into silence by her teacher's disdain for the children's heritage language and culture. However, she also experiences joy when the supportive principal leads her to view Queen Kaahumanu as a model of accomplishment and power.

In the context of the course, students' responses to such stories move beyond outrage or pity as they consider ways to provide more compassionate educational experiences for language learners. For example, in her reaction to the Zitkala-Ša story, Nancy developed a teaching philosophy that calls for cross-cultural understanding and mutual respect:

> Absurd misunderstandings often brought unjustifiable trepidation and punishments into the young Native children's lives. Concepts that intrigued me the most was the fact that the paleface people often beat the children for not speaking or understanding English. Kind words and good examples to teach children right from wrong was the Indian way. How are the children supposed to learn anything if they don't understand the purpose to begin with? If they expected the Natives to conform to the English language and culture quickly, the teachers should have at least considered relating to the Indian ways first and not rely on beatings for reinforcement. Thus the source of communication is created and would have possibly made it easier for both cultures to understand and work with each other on the same level. Maybe then the young Dakota girl would be socioeconomically accepted in a paleface society and schooling system; her identity and dignity would remain alive and unharmed in her heart.

Stories that provide insight into the home experience lead student readers to understand the role language plays within the family, for example, when a child strives to learn language to fulfill parental expectations, when an adolescent's linguistic knowledge surpasses his parents' proficiency in English, when aging spouses struggle together to master a new tongue. Students are shocked to read about familial barriers to learning in Shauna Singh Baldwin's (1996) "English Lessons," as this excerpt from Margaret's response to the story illustrates:

> I feel bad for the narrator. Her boyfriend seems like he has total control over her. "I live like a worm avoiding the sunlight, and I wonder if he knows" (p. 376). I think he knows, but he likes it that way. . . . The passage that struck me most was [when he tells the ESL tutor], "I will not like it if you teach her more than I know. But just enough for her to get a good-paying job at Dunkin' Donuts or maybe the Holiday Inn. She will learn quickly, but you must not teach her too many American ideas" (p. 378). This really angered me. Who is he to say that? Is he afraid that she will get smart and leave him? I would hope that she does learn a lot of English and American ways so that she does leave him. He uses and abuses her. She isn't an object; she is a human being.

Such stories represent the complex realities of the learners' worlds and thus serve to underline for students the inextricable link between home life and language acquisition.

One of the effects of doing close readings of short stories is that students begin to observe classroom scenes with an attention to detail and level of analysis that they can apply to their own tutoring experiences. Here Isabel examines the role of the teacher in Lucy Honig's (1990/1992) story, "English as a Second Language":

> The teacher's role in this scene helps the students teach themselves. She is just there for support. The students seem to know words of the new language, they just need

to practice what they have learned. The teacher only inter-
cedes when none of the students know the proper way and
look for her help. This allows the students to correct each
other and learn from each other and teach each other
about their cultural differences as well. This is seen when
the student says "heat" when she meant "hit," the students
knew that her sentence did not make sense but they could
not figure out exactly what she meant. The teacher came
in the conversation and corrected them. The teacher was a
listener, a watcher, and therefore a teacher because the students seemed to be learning a great deal from each other.

By comparing a fictional and a real classroom, Cathy is able to analyze the inappropriate teaching used by a substitute teacher who
took over the adult ESL class to which she was assigned as a tutor:

"The English Lesson" by Nicholasa Mohr [1977/1991] has
a passage that I felt reflected part of my tutoring experience
this week: "Mrs. Hamma selected each student who was to
speak from a different part of the room, rather than in the
more conventional orderly fashion of row by row, or front to
back, or even alphabetical order. . . . Mrs. Hamma enjoyed
catching the uncertain looks on the faces of her students.
A feeling of control over the situation gave her a pleasing
thrill" (p. 24). In class on Monday, the substitute teacher
was randomly calling on the students to answer or ask different questions. I felt that because this was a very different
setting and because they were not used to being screamed
at during their lesson, none of them wanted to participate.
The teacher was correcting them on every single part of
their pronunciation and seemed to be confusing them more.
A few of the students will put an *e* in front of the words
they speak in Spanish so that their sentence would read: "I
espeak Espanish." Obviously, this is not correct, but I did not

feel that they needed to be called out every time they pronounced something incorrectly. Similar to Mrs. Hamma's class the students would almost slouch down and look away when the teacher was looking around the room to call on someone. They did not feel comfortable speaking with her.

The stories also allow student tutors to get inside the heads of adult ESL learners in ways that are not possible otherwise. In Honig's (1990/1992) "English as a Second Language," referenced earlier, we are taken to an award ceremony for adult ESL learners and hear what goes through the mind of a Guatemalan refugee as the mayor interrupts and ridicules her when she tries to tell one of the stories she collected for her class project. The awareness students gain from such a reading enables them to theorize about second language acquisition, as the following excerpt from Peggy's writing reveals:

> It is important to focus on the positive aspects of students' learning, not just to correct their mistakes. Students should not feel ashamed when they make mistakes, but learn from them instead. As Maria made a mistake [at the award ceremony] in Honig's story, she "realized she had not used the past tense and felt a deep, horrible stab of shame for herself, shame for her teacher. She was a disgrace!" (296). Maria should not have focused so much on her mistake as on the fact that she was able to get her main ideas across in English. It is of course easier to say this than to practice it, but if students are made comfortable while learning and learn from their mistakes, they should not be as embarrassed when making errors.

▪ Tutoring ESOL Learners

Because students regularly hand in journal entries describing and analyzing their tutoring, I am able to learn about their experiences and to provide feedback. At times I answer questions or provide advice, but mostly I offer support and praise for their efforts. I use marginal comments to respond, seen here in italics in response to Abigail's description of her work in an adult intermediate ESL class:

> When we arrived, the students were working in pairs, reading and answering questions from a workbook. The teacher let us walk around to observe and help if necessary. Several students asked us to help them right away. For instance, one student asked me how to say "drink" in the past. I told him the correct form was "drank," and he politely thanked me. Then I moved on to two women. One seemed to be in her 50s whereas the other was no more than 25. I asked "What are you working on?" and they looked at me confused. I then changed my question to "What are you doing?" and as I asked this, I pointed to their workbooks. [*Excellent strategy! You reworded the question to a form they could understand.*] They understood this and said they were asking each other questions. They continued, and the older woman asked the other what she did last weekend. The younger woman replied with "I went to saw my sister." She looked at me for approval, and since she communicated the general idea, I said it was good. [*Good for you! Letting her know she is speaking in a way that communicates her idea is so supportive.*]

Throughout the semester, students share their tutorial experiences in class and, in the process, help each other develop strategies for their tutoring. They struggle, for example, when they are convinced of the benefits of bilingual approaches but are placed at sites that require English-only instruction or when they understand the value of a participatory approach that allows learner input into the curriculum (Auerbach, 1992/2002) but then are handed a preset plan to teach. I facilitate these discussions but never fail to be amazed at how thoughtful, inventive, and appropriate the students' own solutions are. The following excerpt from a journal entry provides an example of how one student, Becky, negotiated seemingly conflicting agendas:

> [In my last] tutoring session, I tutored a male and a female from Peru. After they realized that they were both from Peru, they instantaneously created a bond with one another. During our initial conversation, they spoke a lot about Peru, and about how much they missed their country. Two of the topics that I had been assigned to teach the students included learning how to read [local] maps and learning about U.S. holidays. However, neither of the students [was] interested in reading maps of Waltham. Therefore, I had them draw a simple map of a city in Peru that they were familiar with. After the map was completed, and they . . . explained the city to me, I asked them various questions about how they would get to the post office, the doctor's office and the grocery store, and how many minutes it would take them to walk there. After we finished, we had a discussion on various U.S. holidays. However, I encouraged them to teach me about holidays that are celebrated in Peru. I realized that during these activities in which they spoke about Peru, their English was much more advanced.

Following a key precept of a participatory approach (Auerbach, 1992/2002), Becky assesses the students' interests and needs and adjusts the curriculum accordingly yet still fulfills the spirit of the curriculum by teaching its concepts if not its exact content. One thing that strikes me in this piece is that a natural conversation arises that leads Becky to begin to theorize about the session. She sees that by building upon the linguistic, cultural, and intellectual strengths that these adult learners bring to the classroom, she has created conditions for their second language to flourish. In analyzing her own tutoring, Jackie is engaged in the kind of critical reflection that leads to action, change, and growth—an ongoing process that is a model of transformative teaching.

Another student, Lynn, analyzed the cross-cultural tensions she observed in an adult conversation class in which students were asked to decide whether or not they would donate their organs when they died:

> Most of the answers were like this, "Yes, I would donate my organs because I will save a lot of people's lives." . . . I think the only reason the students wrote this is because one of the students was courageous enough to write his answer on the board. . . . I do not feel [that] a lot of the students would have answered the same way in their own languages. The reason I feel this way is because a lot of the Hispanic students have discussion in Spanish behind the teacher's back. Since I understand a lot of Spanish I realized they were talking about organ donating and how a lot of them would never do this because of their religious beliefs. . . . A lot of the Hispanic students who said no in Spanish were the same ones who said yes in English. I understand this may not be a real big issue in ESL, but . . . I found it to be really troubling. How good is learning another language if you [are] not really able to express YOURSELF completely in that language?

What strikes me about this excerpt is that Lynn has become an insightful observer and is raising a significant question as she reflects on her own observations. Her question echoes a principle of second language acquisition theory she has studied: the importance of promoting meaningful interaction in the language classroom (Krahnke & Christison, 1983/2002, p. 245). But that was not the end of Lynn's experience that evening. Lynn went on to work one-on-one with an adult learner from India who had enormous difficulty expressing herself. Lynn learned that the student had decided to answer "yes" to the teacher's question about organ donation even though she was not sure she would donate her organs, because "the teacher wanted a yes or no answer." With the help of Lynn's guiding questions, the tutee was able to think through her initial response. Lynn wrote,

> When I asked her why? she looked at me and laugh[ed]. She pointed to her eyes. Then I understood. She wanted to donate her eyes. I asked her questions to help me fully understand what she meant. She told me she would only want to donate her eyes because she would be interested to see . . . if after she dies would she be able to see through the eyes of other people. When I finally understood her answer I realized that she was fully expressing her feelings and thoughts in English. I was very happy for her because I saw that she was happy when I understood what she meant.

Here Lynn answers her own reflective question about the value of students' studying another language if they are not able to express themselves completely in that language. She wonders whether this is a "real big issue" in the ESOL field. After hearing her story, her classmates decided that it should be.

If students learn nothing else as a result of their tutoring, they know that, even under ideal conditions, the process of second language acquisition is long term and evolving because acquiring a new language entails much more than learning a new linguistic system. For one thing, it involves learning new ways of using words that are tied to different worldviews that may be disorienting. Furthermore, second language acquisition is dependent on personality and cognitive factors, and thus students' emotional responses and individual learning strategies figure prominently. Even the body is implicated, for students' relative physical comfort affects the learning process. Additionally, learners' history, family situation, socioeconomic position, linguistic background, cultural upbringing, racial identity, religion, and gender play a role in their educational lives, determining whether, when, how, and to what extent they learn a new language and adopt new ways of knowing. Precisely because acquiring another language is inextricably linked to learners' past experiences and issues of identity, students in Language and Literacy come to realize, tutors need to be responsive to language learners' sense of who they are and what they have already experienced and the complicated ways these identities and experiences are related to acquiring new ways with words.

■ Service-Learning in a Business University

Service-learning courses such as the one I have described enable students to keep their academic learning in constant dialogue with the world outside academia. It is possible to make similar connections in other courses, but I have found that many students' attitudes undergo remarkable changes precisely because they have become responsible for the education of English language learners and have, in turn, learned about these learners' real lives. Daniel's experience is one such example:

> With the completion of the service-learning program and my research paper about my student I understand the pressures immigrants face before and after immigrating to America. Before this semester I only thought of immigrants as cheap workers with no feelings. Now, I've come to see that these people have come from difficult lives and have found new challenges competing in a nation that relies on English to survive. Many Americans complain that if immigrants are living in our country then they

should know the language, but I say we must offer them the opportunity [rather than] discriminate against them.

Such a transformation would be striking in any setting. But in the context of a business university, the opportunity to link academic study with community service takes on special significance. As one student put it, "most courses at Bentley ultimately are about helping yourself or maybe a customer [but] our 'profits' come in the form of the feelings that we get from knowing that we helped out." Another student wrote of her new sense of civic responsibility: "Being involved in the community is not optional; it is the responsibility of everyone to contribute to make the community better." Yet another student extended that idea to the college itself: "Bentley is responsible to be connected with its surrounding communities in a responsible manner [in order to be] a well-respected, well-rounded institution of the community." That students willingly take advantage of the opportunity to move beyond their own self-interest in a business university—and that they desire to move the university beyond *its* own self-interest—is a testament to the value of service-learning.

■ Acknowledgments

A portion of this chapter appears in the Fall 2006 issue of *TESOL Quarterly*, 40(3).

■ Notes

1) All students' names are pseudonyms.
2) Several of the short stories I refer to in this chapter will be reprinted in *Language Lessons: Short Stories about Learners of English*, edited by Ruth Spack and Vivian Zamel (University of Michigan Press, in press).

■ References

Auerbach, E. (1992/2002). What is a participatory approach to curriculum development? In V. Zamel & R. Spack (Eds.), *Enriching ESOL pedagogy: Readings with activities for engagement, reflection, and inquiry* (pp. 269–293). Mahwah, NJ: Lawrence Erlbaum Associates.

Baldwin, S. S. (1996). English lessons. In S. S. Baldwin, *English lessons and other stories* (pp. 374–378). Fredericton, NB: Goose Lane.

Grace, P. (1998). Kura. In P. Grace, *Baby no-eyes* (pp. 29–39). Honolulu, HI: University of Hawai'i Press.

Hara, M. (1990). Fourth grade ukus. In M. Hara, *Bananaheart and other stories* (pp. 47–62). Honolulu, HI: Bamboo Ridge Press.

Honig, L. (1990/1992). English as a second language. In W. Abrahams (Ed.), *Prize stories 1992: The O'Henry awards* (pp. 60–74). New York, NY: Doubleday.

Krahnke, K. J., & Christison, M. A. (1983/2002). Recent language research and some language teaching principles. In V. Zamel & R. Spack (Eds.), *Enriching ESOL pedagogy: Readings with activities for engagement, reflection, and inquiry* (pp. 229–251). Mahwah, NJ: Lawrence Erlbaum Associates.

Mohr, N. (1977/1991). The English lesson. In W. Brown & A. Ling (Eds.), *Imagining America: Stories from the promised land* (pp. 21–33). New York, NY: Persea.

Spack, R. (2002). *America's second tongue: American Indian education and the ownership of English, 1860–1900.* Lincoln, NE: University of Nebraska Press.

Spack, R, & Zamel, V. (Eds.). (in press). *Language lessons: Short stories about learners of English.* Ann Arbor, MI: University of Michigan Press.

Tan, A. (1990/2002). Mother tongue. In V. Zamel & R. Spack (Eds.), *Enriching ESOL pedagogy: Readings with activities for engagement, reflection, and inquiry* (pp. 431–436). Mahwah, NJ: Erlbaum.

Vandrick, S. (1999/2002). ESL and the colonial legacy: A teacher faces her 'missionary kid' past. In V. Zamel & R. Spack (Eds.), *Enriching ESOL pedagogy: Readings with activities for engagement, reflection, and inquiry* (pp. 411–436). Mahwah, NJ: Lawrence Erlbaum Associates.

Yamanaka, L.-A. (1996). Obituary. In L.-A. Yamanaka, *Wild meat and the bully burgers* (pp. 154–163). New York, NY: Harcourt.

Zitkala-Ša. (1900, February). The school days of an Indian girl. *Atlantic Monthly, 85*(508), 185–194.

6

TESOL in Context: Student Perspectives on Service-Learning

Jessie Moore Kapper, Laura Clapp,
and Cindy Lefferts
With Missy Schwandt, Melissa Taylor,
and Nikki Wasikowski

▪ TESOL in Context: Student Perspectives on Service-Learning

Applied linguistics courses are a natural context for service-learning since this type of engaged learning activity can help students identify theory in practice. In an Introduction to Teaching English to Speakers of Other Languages (TESOL) course, for example, service-learning projects help students observe linguistics, education, and TESOL theories—to name a few—applied to classroom practice. Students can observe that, despite the array of disciplinary theories and best practices described in published scholarship, stakeholders in any given TESOL context will select only a subset of these theories and practices. As students work in partnership with these stakeholders, they can begin to identify the rationales (or lack of rationales) for these selections and see how TESOL scholarship plays out in a specific context.

Based on our experiences working in partnerships with local community agencies that provide resources for English language learners (ELLs), we are strong supporters of the use of service-learning in applied linguistics courses. In this chapter, we attempt to illustrate how service-learning projects in an Introduction to TESOL course gave us a context for the TESOL scholarship we

141

were reading and helped us identify connections between theories and practices.

■ Background and Context

We teach and study at Elon University, a small four-year university in the southeastern United States. Jessie is an assistant professor in the Department of English, and Cindy and Laura are undergraduate students majoring in Spanish and Spanish education, respectively.

Elon University emphasizes engaged learning and recruits faculty who value an interrelationship between teaching and research. As a result, students and faculty find extensive support for hands-on learning and innovative pedagogy. Available resources include a Service-Learning Scholars program that helps faculty examine ways to integrate service-learning into existing and new classes and a service-learning center that supports students, faculty, and community organizations who are interested in service-learning.

The university also attempts to expose students to international cultures and languages through study abroad opportunities, efforts to internationalize the campus, and community outreach. The larger community in which we live has experienced increasing linguistic and cultural variety in recent years, and Elon University students—especially education majors—are seeking more preparation for acknowledging and interacting with this diverse population. In the 2000 U.S. Census, 8% of the North Carolina population identified as speaking a language other than English at home, and percentages for Alamance and Guilford counties, where we work, learn, and volunteer, are similar (U.S. Census Bureau, 2000). The local Alamance-Burlington School System enrolls more than 3,100 English as a second language (ESL) students, up from only 192 ESL students in 1992 (Alamance-Burlington School System, 2005). Students in the nearby Guilford County School System speak 82 languages and dialects, demonstrating the diversity within this growing ESL population (Guilford County School System, 2004). Responding to student requests for more preparation to work with this population of learners, the Department of English developed an introduction to TESOL course to prepare Elon University graduates to teach in these types of linguistically and culturally diverse school systems, as well as to teach abroad.

The course has three primary goals. First, students completing the course are expected to acquire introductory knowledge of the current theories, research, and practices in the field of teaching English to speakers of other languages. Second, students should become familiar with national standards for teaching English as a second language and will consider how these standards might impact their future teaching. Finally, although a one-semester course cannot equip teachers with everything that they need to know about teaching ESL, by the end of the semester students will be better prepared to work with ESL students and to identify ESL resources. The first semester that she taught the course, Jessie worked toward these goals by emphasizing three course objectives: First, students will complete and discuss weekly readings intended to introduce them to current ESL theory, research, and practice; second, students will complete weekly writings/activities to assess their understanding of course materials and to consider applications for classroom teaching; and third, students will work collaboratively to examine and present an existing ESL curriculum in order to study ESL theory and research in action. This initial conception of the course introduced students to the locally diverse population, but it did little to foreground how teachers engaged the TESOL theories that students were learning, since students spent minimal time in ESL classrooms.

The next year, Jessie was determined to revise her Introduction to TESOL course so that her students had more opportunities to see TESOL theories in practice. Previously, she had required students to complete observations of ESL teaching in the local school system to inform their curriculum descriptions and to complete a Standards Project that built on activities described in TESOL, Inc's professional development manual for using the ESL standards (see Short, Gómez, Cloud, Katz, Gottlieb, & Malone, 2000). Yet students' limited time in these classrooms restricted the number of connections they could identify between their observations and class materials. Jessie wanted students to spend more time in settings with English language learners and to gain more awareness of the social and political influences on TESOL.

Jessie had previous experience incorporating service-learning in writing courses, where students could explore their potential to promote change through public writing, while contributing to local organizations. The course goals for Introduction to TESOL presented opportunities for similar student engagement, since the local community agencies working with English language learners welcomed Elon University students' participation as service-learners and could benefit from materials development that their own budgets and time constraints would not support. As a result, Jessie turned to service-learning as a way to further students' understanding of TESOL theories and practices and to contribute to the local community that was offering so much support for her students. Thus Jessie added a fourth objective: Students will develop ESL materials for which a local community agency has an expressed need. These materials also might benefit students in future teaching opportunities.

Jessie's redesigned introduction to TESOL course, as outlined in her syllabus, requires students to complete 15 hours of service at community organizations that work with English language learners. Throughout the semester-long course, students reflect on their service experiences in postings to a class discussion board in an online course management program, and they complete two major projects related to their service-learning partnership. For the first project, students work in groups to research and describe the curricula used by their community partners, and they present their descriptions to the class. These curriculum descriptions allow class members to see the vast array of English language learner programs in the local community and to explore how the programs intersect with or diverge from the theories and practices discussed in class. The second project requires students to consult with their community programs to identify real needs that the students then attempt to fill through materials development. Both of these projects are described in more detail below. Students still complete a Standards Project, but for some students, their service-learning components give them a chance to examine how these standards play out in an actual classroom setting on a weekly basis.

As a way to informally assess her revised curriculum and to reflect on the inclusion of service-learning, Jessie asked her students enrolled in the spring 2005 section of the course to help her evaluate the inclusion of service-learning in the Introduction to TESOL class. In the following pages, Jessie and two students, Cindy and Laura, trace our experiences during the semester and offer tips for incorporating service-learning in TESOL and other applied linguistics courses. Interspersed with our own accounts are the reflections of our classmates who agreed to lend their voices to this discussion.

First Impressions of Service-Learning in TESOL

Elon University offers strong support for service-learning through the campus's Kernodle Center for Service Learning. The center developed from service-learning initiatives during the 1990s and supports students, staff, and faculty initiating new service-learning courses or participating in existing service-learning opportunities. It is staffed primarily by students, although their efforts are guided by a director, an assistant director, an outreach coordinator and other staff members, as well as a faculty fellow. This supportive group worked with Jessie to identify community organizations that served English language learners in the local area and that were interested in partnering with students. On the second day of the spring course, a representative from the Kernodle Center visited the class to introduce students to the possible service-learning placements, to collect students' schedules, and to ask students to rank their preferences for their community partnerships. The Kernodle Center and Jessie had identified four possible partnerships for student placements: the central office for the system-wide ESL program in the local school system, an elementary-level ESL program at a specific school within the school system, an after-school enrichment program for children from at-risk families, and a community agency providing services to children up to five years old.

The representative returned the next week to give students information about their placements. Students then contacted their agencies, and most started their weekly visits by week three or four of the 15-week semester. Laura was placed at the community agency for young children; Cindy was placed at the after-school enrichment program. Our initial enthusiasm about our service-learning placements is evident in our first discussion board postings, despite some misgivings:

> I am excited that there is a service-learning component to the TESOL course. Service-learning is one of the best ways to learn because you learn by doing. I am looking forward to working with [the community agency]. I had never heard of this organization before. I have learned from their web site that they are highly involved with Head Start, a program that prepares children for kindergarten. I hope to learn more about what other programs they are involved in as well. I am a bit apprehensive because the organization requires fingerprinting and government testing and I have never worked with an organization that is this thorough in its screening of volunteers. This has caused some delay in beginning the program, so I have not had a chance to visit yet. (Laura, February 18, 2005)

Well, we went to [the after-school program] on Thursday. Much to my dismay, it wasn't anything like I expected. It was like an after-school day care in which we were to be the tutors. And there was only one ESL student there, for three people to tutor. And by the time we would get there, the kid would be done doing his/her homework for the day.... I am looking forward to actually interacting with people who can set an example of what to do, or what not to do, in an ESL setting. I want to see what I am learning in the classroom put into action. That way I will understand it better and it will become pounded into my head. My only apprehensiveness is that our group won't find anything to do. The [program] didn't turn out the way we expected ... I was looking forward to working with a larger array of students, whether they are high school or adult.... I hope that I will be placed in some other ESL program, because I really want to watch an ESL program being played out, to see what it's all about and how it works and if it's interesting and see if I can critically observe and pick out any of the methods. (Cindy, February 20, 2005)

Laura and Cindy's postings emphasize our enthusiasm for service-learning; we recognized service-learning as an exciting way to learn and to see TESOL theories and teaching approaches in action. To "learn by doing," though, Laura, Cindy, and several classmates would have to navigate some speed bumps. As we reassessed their placement options, Jessie realized that the after-school program now had fewer ESL students than the community partner had previously disclosed when Jessie and the Kernodle Center staff were identifying placements. In addition, although the program's hours were 2:30–5:30 P.M., the community partner was most in need of service-learning participants during the first 30 to 60 minutes, when Cindy was attending her own classes, including Introduction to TESOL.

Jessie also noted a mismatch with the community agency. Early discussions with the agency had emphasized interactions between the Elon University students and the agency's ESL students, as well as materials development for the agency; sometime between these discussions and the students' placements, however, the agency recognized that these interactions would require background and fingerprint testing, as well as tuberculosis testing for Laura and her classmates. As a result, the agency hoped the students would be interested in office-related, administrative duties, rather than classroom interactions. Unfortunately, Jessie was unaware of this change until Laura and her classmates submitted their first reflections.

Changes and Investments

In response to these miscommunications and changes, Cindy worked with Jessie to identify an alternate placement. She expressed her regrets to the after-school program and partnered with a local elementary school, where she worked with ESL students in a second-grade class. Two other students also shifted from the after-school program to local schools.

Laura and a classmate chose to remain partnered with the community agency. They navigated several weeks of tests and background checks, limiting their interaction with the students to a period of only a few weeks.

For Cindy, the change was positive, giving her lots of opportunities to practice TESOL theory and teaching methods:

> I'm going to help out a boy in [a] 2nd grade class. [The school] does not have as high an ESL population as [another school in the system], as far as I know, but every class still has quite a few Hispanic kids. [The second grader] is very, very quiet, but seems comfortable in the

atmosphere of the classroom. His native language is Spanish, and he is from Mexico. I do not know how long he has been in the States or how proficient he is in Spanish. I have to talk more to the teacher about him.

It is a whole lot easier working with an ESL student when you speak their language. I can speak Spanish pretty well, but a lot of the words I want to help translate for him I do not know. On Tuesday we read a book together. I think that is going to be our weekly ritual. He seems comfortable with me. He already knows his alphabet. He has trouble pronouncing the sound of letter B. He pronounces it with a "veh" sound, like how they do in Spanish.

So far I have just worked with him how the teacher has told me to. He reads the book aloud in English, and I correct the words he has trouble with. Then, on my own accord, I have been trying to make sure he can comprehend what is going on in the book. That is the hardest part I think. So at times I cheat and try to explain it in Spanish, because comprehension is important too. So what if he can pronounce the words if he can't read and understand them. On Tuesday the book we read was about outer space stuff, like comets and meteors. He learned what each of them were and what they were made of, though he mixed them all up a lot, so I'm not sure if he was just guessing.

I think it will be a lot of fun working with this boy, because it seems like he will make quick progress which is encouraging to me since I have little idea of what I'm doing. Since he stumbles with his pronunciation, even though I hate it, I figured I would try aspects of the Silent Method in terms of making the vowel long or short and the consonant hard or soft. I don't know how I'd do that, but it's something I will look into. This should be a nice challenge. (Cindy, February 24, 2005)

Cindy's reflection describes her attempts to use practices we discussed in class, including specific language teaching methods that we had examined. Her posting also identifies questions that she hopes to answer during her service with her community partner and her work for our class. Because her service-learning took her beyond merely observing the second graders to practicing TESOL teaching methods, Cindy became invested in learning more so that she could refine and enhance her contributions to the second grader's education.

Other students in the Introduction to TESOL class expressed similar commitments to their community partners:

> The students asked me to learn the body parts in Spanish for next week. I then challenged them to learn the body parts in English for next week. They are really excited! I need to get studying and hold up my end of the deal! (Missy, March 3, 2005)

> On Tuesday and Wednesday of this week, I visited [an ESL] class, and worked with a student on a worksheet that was teaching her about months of the year. She seemed to be very shy around me and I think was afraid of the language barrier, but I gave her a lot of encouragement and she eventually relaxed and became more confident. It was great to be able to work one-on-one with a student! (Melissa, May 5, 2005)

> I really think that a lot of the ways that [a high school ESL teacher] teaches resemble some of Desuggestopedia except that his room is virtually bare. He said he wanted it to be more friendly looking with posters hanging up, but he said he doesn't have too much of a creative side. So, I'm making posters for him to have a more Desuggestopedic class. (Nikki, April 18, 2005)

These reflections highlight students' interactions with ELL students and their enthusiasm for working with these learners and their teachers. Nikki, for instance, recognized that her community partner, a high school ESL teacher, used approaches that reminded her of a language teaching approach we had discussed in class, and her commitment to this teacher and his students extends to wanting to provide him with materials to make his approach more successful.

Despite the class's overall positive experiences, not all of the partnerships resulted in these opportunities for engaged learning. Laura, who had remained partnered with the community agency, was often frustrated by her sessions at the organization.

> Unfortunately, there has not been much connection between these [class] topics and my observations. In each class at [the community agency], there are about two to four children who are English language learners and they seem to have mastered the amount of English they should know at their age. Also, their day is very unstructured. They spend most of their time either on the playground or having free play at various stations in the classroom. The few connections I have seen are the use of visual aids in learning and objects in the classroom being labeled in Spanish (though this is mainly to help students when they have first arrived in the country). (Laura, April 18, 2005)

While Laura enjoyed her interactions with all the children at the community agency, she felt shortchanged when she compared her experiences to those of her classmates. She had minimal interaction with ESL students at the agency, and unlike her classmates, she did not have an opportunity to interact with experienced ESL teachers.

Midpoint Reflections: Curriculum Descriptions

These experiences are reflected in our midsemester curriculum descriptions. This collaborative project required us to describe the ESL curriculum or program used by the community agency with whom we were working. The primary goal of the project was to enable us to examine how the ideas that we were discussing in class are put into action by local agencies working with ESL learners. A secondary goal of the project was to describe the community agencies to our classmates so that we could gain a stronger awareness of other local contexts for ESL learning.

Students in our course prepared both class presentations and written descriptions, describing the community agencies and their curricula or materials and making connections between these pedagogical materials and the readings we had discussed in class. In the written descriptions, Jessie wanted to read detailed descriptions of the community partners and the materials and curricula that they use. She also wanted student analysis of how the materials enact or relate to the theory and research we read and discussed during the first half of the semester. Jessie encouraged students to consider:

- Physical and social contexts in which the agencies operate
- ESL learners with whom the agencies work
- Teaching approach(es) most identifiable in the agencies' materials/activities
- The agencies' instruction in listening, speaking, reading, and writing
- Agencies' stakeholders
- Agencies' felt or expressed needs for materials or other resources

Jessie noted that although students were still learning about TESOL, these curriculum descriptions included several attempts to connect theory to practice. Cindy, Laura, and our classmates incorporated a range of practices that reminded us of approaches we had discussed or theories about skills instruction. These descriptions convinced Jessie that, despite some initial mismatches in the service-learning placements, we and our classmates were engaged in what we were learning and were identifying more connections between theory and practice than Jessie's previous students had made when she only required them to observe ESL classes.

Fulfilling Our Partnerships

In response to these curriculum descriptions, we spent the second half of the semester developing materials that responded to the agencies' expressed needs. For our final assignment, the class created materials for our agencies, based on their real needs. We therefore needed to consult with the teachers and program directors with whom we were working to negotiate what type of materials would be helpful for them that students could realistically produce over a five-week period. Jessie suggested possible materials:

- Supplemental lesson plan materials for ESL students in a mainstream setting
- Self-study resources for ESL students
- Activities for ESL students focused on acquiring a specific skill (reading, writing, speaking, or listening)
- Classroom materials (posters, bulletin boards, etc.) to make the classroom setting more inviting for ESL students
- Take-home materials for ESL students and their parents
- A proposal recommending the purchase of specific ESL resources
- A review of ESL textbooks or resources that the agency is considering purchasing
- Other materials that the agency contact has expressed an interest in or need for

To complete the project, Laura, Cindy, and our classmates often had to conduct additional research to learn more about ESL instruction strategies and theories related to these projects. For instance, if students intended to create materials for ESL students focused on improving their reading, they needed to learn more about TESOL research on reading.

Since these materials development projects were a graded requirement for the Introduction to TESOL course, we negotiated the grading criteria for our individual projects. All the students in our class were assessed on three common criteria: First, how well did the materials fulfill the agency's expressed needs? Second, were the materials well organized and did they include clear directions so that the agencies could implement use of the materials on their own? Third, were the materials edited and polished for public use? Students identified five additional criteria specific to their individual projects and collaborated with Jessie on the phrasing of each. This assessment approach allowed Jessie to demonstrate that students in our class were completing comparable projects, even though we all had different goals and outcomes, and it allowed her to tailor her assessment to each project. Furthermore, the process of negotiating criteria gave us and our classmates additional insight into assessment practices.

To supplement the projects and to assist Jessie with her assessment of them, students also prepared and submitted reflective self-assessments. This supporting assignment gave us a chance to acknowledge the additional reading or research conducted, but Jessie also encouraged students to answer the following questions:

- How well do your materials meet your expectations and your agency's expectations?
- What additional research did you have to do to develop your materials?
- What process did you follow as you developed the materials?
- What decisions did you make about the materials? (For example, if you had multiple options for a feature of your materials, why did you choose the option that you did?)

- How did TESOL theory and/or research influence your materials development? How would you justify the choices you made about your materials?
- How did you obtain feedback on early versions of your materials, and how did you use that feedback to revise?
- Given the criteria that we've negotiated for your project, how would you assess your materials?

Responses to these questions helped Jessie assess how well the class understood the course material and whether they could apply class discussions and readings to actual teaching situations. The questions also encouraged connections between service and our course material, further solidifying the service-learning outcomes.

These common expectations and requirements still allowed students in our class to produce a variety of projects that met their agencies' individual needs. Laura and a partner created flash cards and other teaching materials that would help English language learners at the community agency, but that also would appeal to the broader student body. Using strategies reminiscent of the Language Experience Approach (Rigg, 1989), Cindy worked with second-grade students to write and illustrate a story that the students narrated. The teacher with whom she partnered then published the story using a self-publishing site. Our class projects included:

- A book highlighting people, places, and things on each continent
- Self-study resources for ESL students in a middle-grades math class
- A vocabulary bingo game
- An American holiday bingo game
- A classroom management board for an ESL classroom
- Games and activities for a traveling ESL classroom
- Classroom posters featuring English grammar, with examples that were requested by students in the class

All these materials allowed students to try out the TESOL theories and practices we had discussed in class while tailoring work to the ELL students in the community agencies. We fulfilled our partnerships with the community organizations while demonstrating that students had acquired an introductory knowledge of TESOL. Students further clarified the connections they had made in reflective self-assessments that described how they had applied TESOL theories and practices to materials development.

As a final step in solidifying the service-learning connection, we as a class presented our projects to our classmates and to other professors at our university. This public presentation gave us one more opportunity to articulate the connections we saw between the course content and the experiences we had with and the materials we created for our community partners. What's more, the presentations allowed students to practice expressing the connections to an audience who did not have the background in TESOL that they had acquired.

Overall, then, the service-learning component of the class was successful. As Jessie had hoped, our service-learning projects helped students connect TESOL scholarship to teaching practices used by the community partners. We also were able to use our class discussions to inform students' development of TESOL materials designed for our partner organizations. Our ups and downs along the way, though, have inspired us to share several tips for teachers and students involved in future service-learning projects.

■ Recommendations for Instructors Conducting Service-Learning Projects

To faculty incorporating service-learning in TESOL and other applied linguistics courses, we recommend advertising the service-learning component of the course when students prepare to register for the semester and investigating each community organization's policies and requirements before the class starts. Once students enter the course, we encourage faculty to arrange tours of service-learning locations. We also believe that the success of the service-learning project hinges on faculty adjusting their time and workload expectations to accommodate the service-learning and incorporating readings related to the local ELL populations with which students will work.

Course descriptions and advertisements should highlight the service-learning component so that students are aware of the service-learning requirements before they enroll. Some students will decide not to enroll; others will look forward to the opportunity and will appreciate the chance to adjust their class and work schedules accordingly.

Instructors also should fully investigate the entry procedures for each site (background checks, introductory sessions, etc.) so that they can evaluate the appropriateness of potential community partners. If students will need to complete several weeks of entry procedures, or if students will incur an unexpected financial burden, the site might not be appropriate for the project, even if students otherwise would benefit from the partnership. The community agency with which Laura partnered could be an exciting site for service learning, but the time and financial commitments for entering the site will discourage Jessie from partnering with the agency in the future, since they create a lack of balance between the students' and the agency's commitments to the partnership. As service-learning projects evolve, faculty should establish criteria for selecting community partners in an effort to achieve a balance between these commitments. In addition to analyzing these types of entry procedures, faculty should consider the range of placements that support the content of the course, the time commitment required to meet learning goals within possible partnerships, and the potential for service activities to spark students' identification of connections between the service and their course content (Howard, 1993/2003).

If students have a choice among several possible community partnerships, students might need more information about placement locations than what faculty can provide in brief written descriptions. Touring possible locations helps students identify the placements that most appeal to their interests, helping build their enthusiasm for the service-learning projects. In our course, touring the sites also would have enabled Jessie to identify potential mismatches before students started working with the community partners.

In addition to conducting this pre-course and pre-partnership planning, instructors should adjust their use of class time and their coursework expectations to account for the time commitment of a service-learning project. Students and instructors will be overwhelmed if the service-learning project is added to an already full schedule without something else being cut. Jessie assigned less reading than she had in her non-service-learning course, correctly anticipating that the service-learning experiences would provide the basis for many of the class discussions in which she wanted students to engage. In future semesters, she will look for ways to reduce the number of minor class assignments so that students can spend more time writing their reflections on their service-learning experiences. These types of adjustments do not decrease the rigor of the course; instead, they may actually increase the rigor as students look for connections between their service-learning experiences and the course content (Howard, 1993/2003).

By planning class discussions and readings related to the ELL populations with whom students will work, instructors help their students identify theories in practice and make these connections. If students do not see their community partners represented in class discussions, they may have a more difficult time making connections between course content and their experiences in their service-learning interactions. Reflecting on the semester's readings and discussions, Jessie identified a gap between her students' coursework and their service-learning. Although several of the students were working with pre-kindergarten English language learners, this age group was not represented in the class readings. As a result,

Jessie is adjusting her reading selections for future semesters and plans to leave more flexibility for adjusting the class's reading list.

■ Tips for Students

Based on our own experiences, Laura and Cindy also offer the following tips for other students enrolled in service-learning courses. For faculty planning service-learning projects, we elaborate on these tips below.

- Research your community partner to identify their goals and policies.
- Visit your placement as soon as possible.
- Keep reflections on your interactions with your community partner.
- Look for connections between your community involvement and your coursework.
- Decide what you want to gain from your service-learning experience.
- Participate actively when you visit your organization.
- Prepare to work hard.
- Maintain a relationship with your community partner.

Knowing more about their community partners helps students assess the appropriateness of the partnership for their service-learning projects. If students conduct research on the organizations early, they are more likely to avoid poor fits—for the students and the organizations. This research allows students to collaborate with faculty to cultivate strong, ongoing partnerships that benefit both the students and the community partners (Holland & Gelmon, 2003). Even if students learn that an organization is not a good partner for a service-learning project, researching the organizations might help students identify places where they still would like to volunteer on their own. Researching the community partners' goals and policies also helps students prepare for their visits to the organizations.

Visiting the community organizations early helps students assess the appropriateness of the placement and gives them a jump start on their service-learning projects. Community organizations and the populations they serve can change over time, so what seemed like a good placement a year ago, or even a month ago, might not be a good fit now. Both the organization and the student should benefit from the service-learning experience. If students are concerned that the placement is not ideal, they should have opportunities to speak with their instructor about alternative placements. Both the students and the organizations benefit from taking the time to find the best fit.

Writing reflections after each visit or interaction helps students piece together what they are learning about their community partners and the course content. Keeping these reflections up to date helps students discuss the connections that they observe with their classmates and instructor. These reflections also help students identify questions they want to ask or research they want to conduct to learn more about their partner organization or the course content. Bringle and Hatcher (1999/2003) describe several types of reflective activities, including key phrase journals, double-entry journals, critical incident journals, three-part journals, experiential research papers, and case studies. Our reflections closely resemble their three-part journal, which describes an event that happened at the community site, analyzes how it relates to course content, and applies the experience and analysis to personal learning goals. Maintaining our reflections on an electronic discussion board, though, made it easier to keep our reflections up to date and to compare our experiences to those of our classmates.

Completing these reflections also helped us identify differences between our service-learning experiences and our course content. Sometimes coursework does not connect directly with what happens in a service-learning placement. Talking about discrepancies (and building some flexibility for these discussions into lesson plans) helps students explore the variety of contexts in which English language learners study and the array of strategies that ELL teachers employ. When activities in the service-learning site do match course content and discussions, students need time and space to identify and explore these connections.

As we have emphasized repeatedly, service-learning provides an opportunity to see theory in practice, but students will gain more from their experiences if they set personal goals for their interactions with their organizations. Including an early activity that requires students to identify their goals for the experience can help students understand their role in determining the success of the service-learning project. Some students prefer only observing at their organization, but practice is better. Students should negotiate their roles with their community partners in relation to their personal learning goals, but the more actively involved students are in their organizations' activities, the more connections they will make to course content.

Finally, students should be willing to work diligently with their partner organization. Both students and organizations benefit when the students commit fully to their service-learning projects. This dedication to the mutual success of both the student and the community partner creates a foundation for a long-term relationship. If students keep in touch with their organizations after completing their service-learning projects, they have opportunities to continue their education about TESOL and English language learners. They also might be able to request references or explore future job opportunities.

■ Conclusion

We continue to believe that service-learning is one of the best ways to learn. Our own experiences demonstrate how partnering with community agencies can benefit both the community organizations and the students. Our partners benefited from extra volunteers in their classrooms and from our materials that were tailored to their needs. Students benefited from working with experienced ELL teachers and from seeing TESOL theories in practice. Jessie benefited from the ability to expose students to TESOL practice not accessible in texts and from the relationships she formed with our community partners. While we strongly encourage instructors to consider incorporating service-learning in other applied linguistics classes, we hope that our experiences have demonstrated the need for careful planning.

■ References

Alamance-Burlington School System. (2005). *ABSS Fact Book—2005: English as a Second Language.* Retrieved October 4, 2006, from: www.abss.k12.nc.us/modules/cms/pages.phtml?pageid=2377&sessionid=b74183738edf5317ea779ced3e5516ab&sessionid=b74183738edf5317ea779ced3e5516ab

Bringle, R. G., & Hatcher, J. A. (2003). Reflection in service learning: Making meaning of experience. In Campus Compact, *Introduction to service-learning toolkit: Readings and resources for faculty* (2nd ed., pp. 83–89). Providence, RI: Author. (Reprinted from *Educational Horizons*, pp. 179–185, Summer 1999)

Guilford County School System. (2004). *Working together for success: Guilford County schools, 2003–2004 annual report* [Brochure]. Greensboro, NC: Author.

Holland, B. A., & Gelmon, S. B. (2003). The state of the "engaged campus": What have we learned about building and sustaining university-community partnerships? In Campus Compact, *Introduction to service-learning toolkit: Readings and resources for faculty* (2nd ed., pp. 195–198). Providence, RI: Author. (Reprinted from *AAHE Bulletin*, pp. 3–6, October 1998)

Howard, J. (2003). Community service learning in the curriculum. In Campus Compact, *Introduction to service-learning toolkit: Readings and resources for faculty* (2nd ed., pp. 101–104). Providence, RI: Author.

(Reprinted from *Praxis I: A faculty casebook on community service-learning*, by J. Howard, Ed., 1993, Ann Arbor, MI: OCSL Press)

Rigg, P. (1989). Language experience approach: Reading naturally. In P. Rigg & V. G. Allen (Eds.), *When they don't all speak English: Integrating the ESL student into the regular classroom* (pp. 65–76). Urbana, IL: National Council of Teachers of English.

Short, D. J., Gómez, E. L., Cloud, N., Katz, A., Gottlieb, M., & Malone, M. (2000). *Training others to use the ESL Standards: A professional development manual.* Alexandria, VA: TESOL, Inc.

U.S. Census Bureau. (2000). *Census 2000 demographic profile highlights: North Carolina.* Retrieved October 4, 2006, from: http://factfinder.census.gov/home/saff/main.html?_lang=en

7

Service-Learning Throughout the Spanish Curriculum: An Inclusive and Expansive Theory-Driven Model

Howard Grabois

S ervice-learning as a pedagogical tool has grown a great deal over the last two decades and in recent years has received ever-increasing attention by educational institutions at all levels. The integration of service-learning into language courses, and particularly Spanish, has been particularly significant. Given the social and demographic developments related to Spanish in the United States, it is not surprising that service-learning is perceived as a highly satisfying and enriching experience for students of the language, at the same time that it allows students to participate in addressing real needs of people who are struggling to become integrated into educational, social, and economic institutions. This is reflected in the large number of service-learning programs being offered in Spanish courses throughout the country, and the attention that Spanish service-learning has received in recent years in scholarly publications (Hellebrandt, Arries, & Varona, 2004; Hellebrandt & Varona, 1999; Kaplan & Perez Gamboa, 2003; Plann, 2002; Weldon & Trautmann, 2003). While Spanish service-learning courses are offered in a variety of formats both in terms of how learning is structured for the students, and in terms of interaction with community groups, they are typically organized in relation to other specific courses or sections.

The model offered in this chapter is a more inclusive and expansive one, designed to be open to students in a wide variety of courses, levels and contexts. This allows Spanish service-learning to become part of the fabric of the undergraduate learning experience, rather than being limited to participants in specific courses. It allows us to invite virtually all students of Spanish to have a service-learning experience and for service-learning to become intertwined with the overall Spanish curriculum.

Despite the increasing popularity of service-learning, most articles on the subject are primarily concerned with some combination of the mechanics of its implementation, evidence and descriptions of the positive influence it has on learners, or documentation concerning the positive influence it has on participating community partners or members of the broader community. This sort of documentation is certainly important, not only as a way of validating the service-learning enterprise, but also to provide practical models for those who wish to engage in this pedagogy.

One research area that has received less attention has been that of service-learning in relation to theories of second language acquisition. Perhaps this is because service-learning is such a powerful pedagogy that its value is self-evident, and there is no compelling need to contextualize or justify it within a theoretical framework. However, a central interest of applied linguistics, a field which is to a very large extent theory driven, is in attempting to better understand the cognitive and social processes related to language learning. While service-learning may not require justification from theory in order to establish its value to learners and the community, the analysis of service-learning from a theoretical perspective may help us to better understand service-learning as a pedagogy, and the language learning process itself.

A significant theoretical orientation that was used to inform the organization of the courses described in this chapter is sociocultural theory (SCT), which is largely derived from the thinking of Vygotsky (1978, 1986). It is important to note that SCT is not a theory of language learning per se, but rather represents a much broader vision of human cognition and learning. It has proved of interest to researchers and theorists not only in applied linguistics, but also to those in psychology, cognitive studies, education, and communications. Within the area of language pedagogy there are some methodologies that are clearly informed by SCT (e.g., collaborative learning) and others that, while not immediately informed by SCT, are highly consistent with it (e.g., task-based learning, content-based learning, reflective language learning, and issues related to learner autonomy).

One of the more basic concepts within SCT is that cognition and learning need to be understood not as something that occurs primarily within the head of the individual (as in many cognitivist theories) but rather as something that occurs in the interaction between individuals, and with the mediation of cultural artifacts (Cole, 1996; Wertsch, 1998). This seems intuitively germane to service-learning as a pedagogy, and an analysis of service-learning in relation to this theoretical orientation may be of use in allowing us to better document the powerful influence service-learning has on students and community stakeholders, to better understand why it is such a compelling pedagogy, and perhaps even to enhance other areas of the language learning curriculum.

■ The Articulation of Service-Learning With Other Parts of the Curriculum

The model that has been developed at Purdue University is based on the idea of providing an infrastructure for service-learning that students from different courses and sections can take advantage of. In effect, the service-learning program *Ayuda y Aprende* draws on students from the second-year sequence (201/202), the third-year sequence (301/302), as well as students who receive one credit toward their fourth-year requirements (419). Students from virtually any section in 201/202 (as many as 50 sections per semester) or 301/302 (approximately 20 sections per semester) can participate. In terms of numbers of students, this provides us with a pool of 1,500–1,800 second-year students, approximately 300 third-year students, and a small number of students who choose to participate in 419 (as many as 12 per semester.)

In terms of its implementation, *Ayuda y Aprende* is very closely articulated with two specific structures that are used in our second- and third-year courses. In both courses a substantial part of the student's grade (well over 10%) is based on Spanish activity portfolios. Currently third-year students turn in three portfolios per semester with a value of 45 points each, while second-year students turn in five portfolios per semester with a value of 40 points each. Although the second-year point total is higher, it also includes workbook exercises that are evaluated separately in the third-year course, so that in practice the list of portfolio activities and their values is very similar in both courses. (For a discussion of the use of similar tasks for different learners, see Coughlan and Duff, 1994.) The basic idea behind the portfolio tasks is to encourage students to explore Spanish texts and Hispanic cultural artifacts and communities according to their own particular interests. Portfolio options include seeing films, reading, engaging in online chats, participating in local Hispanic activities, and guided reflections on language learning, and are open ended in nature. They are designed so that students have a great deal of control over not only the activities that they engage in, but also the number of points that they receive, to be determined by the number of activities in which they engage. For students who participate in *Ayuda y Aprende* the portfolios are significant in two ways. First, participation in the program is worth a substantial number of points (20 per portfolio for 201/202 students, 35 per portfolio for 301/302 students), and may account for a large proportion of total portfolio points over the course of the semester. Furthermore, students who participate in *Ayuda y Aprende* are also eligible to receive extra-credit points

(50 per semester in 201/202, 45 per semester in 301/302). This is at once a way of rewarding those students who choose service-learning, as it does represent a substantial commitment, and a way to encourage service-learning students to explore other portfolio options during the course of the semester.

The other structure that is closely articulated with service-learning is the seminar system for the third-year course, which itself is somewhat unique. The semester is divided into seven blocks of approximately two weeks each, alternating between tutorials and seminars. The four tutorial periods use a content-driven intermediate course book, *Noticias* (Bell & Schwartz, 2002), and the seminar is not radically different from more conventional language-focused courses. The seminar periods do represent a more radical departure, in that the higher-level goal is clearly learning about content, with language serving as an embedded goal, and as a tool to accomplish the higher-level goal. Furthermore, a great deal of autonomy is provided to both teachers and students. Before each seminar period, instructors think of seminar topics that they find personally interesting. These vary widely, including topics relating to literature, linguistics, contemporary social and political issues, art and music, to name but a few. The instructors provide abstracts for each seminar, and these are made available to the students. The students in turn choose those seminars that they find most compelling. All students are free to choose from any seminar offered. In order to bring the content of the seminars back to a language focus, students write at least two drafts of compositions relating to their seminar topics. In practice this system has proven to be extremely popular among teachers and students alike. For third-year students who participate in *Ayuda y Aprende*, the service-learning experience counts as one of their seminars and is the topic for a composition.

The reflective component of service-learning is accomplished in a variety of ways, for some of which there is also articulation between *Ayuda y Aprende* and the broader curriculum. Service-learning requirements beyond those related to portfolios and seminars include participation in a discussion group, organized separately from the courses, as well as six guided reflections on topics related to service-learning. The concept of guided reflections is already integrated into the general course structure, as students can write guided reflections on language learning as an option for their portfolios, an option that the vast majority of students choose on a regular basis. Beyond this there is a reflective component for reporting portfolio activities, where students are expected to comment on language aspects of the activity, and how engaging in the activity helped them to learn. In this way reflective learning (Richards & Lockhardt, 1996) is already an established part of the broader curriculum. Between the discussion groups, guided reflections, and (in the case of 301/302 students) compositions, there is particular emphasis on the reflective aspect of service-learning in a variety of complementary ways.

■ A Brief History of *Ayuda y Aprende*

Before assuming direction of Spanish 201/202 and 301/302, I attended a service-learning workshop offered by John Pomery, a highly recognized leader in service-learning at Purdue University. I was immediately impressed by the possibilities that this pedagogy could offer to learners of Spanish, particularly in a community with a burgeoning Hispanic population. Greater Lafayette, like many areas of the country without a historically significant Hispanic population, has seen tremendous growth in this population in the past 10 to 15 years. Service-learning also seemed very consistent with ideas associated with SCT that inform much of my thinking about second language learning, and service-learning would combine well with other structures that I was contemplating instituting.

With the support of my department head, Paul Dixon; the collaboration of a graduate student, Teresa Nunes; and the assistance of Purdue's director of community relations, Mike Piggott, we organized our first service-learning partnership at a local elementary school three years ago. We had about 25 students participating two hours per week in the program. The second year of the program, when I had the collaboration of another graduate student, Heidi Herron-Johnson, we were quickly overwhelmed as the popularity of the program exploded. We began to offer the service-learning option to 200-level students at the same time that interest in SL multiplied among 300-level students. Other schools and organizations in the community began to seek us out, and we were forced to scramble to accommodate new partnerships and greatly increased enrollments at the same time. Enrollment in the program stabilized at nearly 150 students per semester, representing nearly 300 hours per semester of engagement with the community. Since then we have been working toward finding more efficient ways to administer the program and enhance communication among students and all course instructors regarding service-learning. At the same time we have taken on new partnerships and are seeking ways to further increase student participation.

A Variety of Partnerships

Because of the large number of students who enroll in *Ayuda y Aprende,* no single partnership has enough demand to place all of our students. In addition, by having an assortment of partnerships we are able to offer students a variety of schedules, as well as the ability to participate in different environments and with different age groups, according to the individual student's interests. A further advantage to having multiple partnerships, even with similar institutions, is that it allows us to try different models and to work with the individual institutions to best meet their needs. In greater Lafayette the schools in particular are struggling to find ways to best integrate Hispanic children into the educational system, often with very limited resources. A brief description of these partnerships and some of the particular needs and challenges associated with each one can be seen in Table 7.1.

Table 7.1. Service-Learning Partnerships

Partnership	Student Interaction
Glen Acres Elementary School	
This was our initial service-learning partnership, with a school that has a Hispanic population of approximately 30%. The participation of Purdue students is widely recognized by the institution as having a significant influence on the children's academic performance. We are now in the fourth year of this partnership.	Purdue students work with Hispanic children four days a week in an after-school program, providing help with homework and tutoring in English, as well as engaging in interactive activities and reading in Spanish. This program is oriented toward students in grades 1–5 with limited English.
Murdock Elementary School	
This school has a smaller percentage of Hispanic children than Glen Acres, and also has a significant federal grant to fund after-school programs. We are now in the third year of this partnership.	As compared to Glen Acres, greater emphasis is placed on developing Spanish literacy, rather than help with homework.[1] As this school offers a wide variety of after-school programs, the participation of Purdue students is limited to two days per week.
Klondike Middle School	
Purdue students work with Hispanic children with limited English throughout the school day. We are now in the second year of this partnership.	Purdue students' participation is a combination of attending class with the children, as well as providing individual tutoring during study hall.
McCutcheon High School	
This is a rural high school with a small number of Hispanic students (10–14, depending on the semester) with very limited English. Due to limited resources a comprehensive bilingual education program is not feasible. We are now in the third year of this partnership.	Purdue students at McCutcheon attend class with the Hispanic students, helping them to better understand and learn course content and to improve their English. Purdue students represent a significant resource for these high school students, both academically and affectively, and often come to be academic role models.

Table 7.1. Service-Learning Partnerships (*continued*)

Harrison High School	
This is a new partnership that came about when the school lost the bilingual assistant they had planned on as a primary resource for Hispanic students. The school has 14 Hispanic students with limited English. We are now in the first year of this partnership.	Purdue students provide assistance for these students four days a week, primarily in a bilingual study hall for Hispanic students.
Girl Scouts of America	
A small number of very committed service-learning students have helped to set up and participate in Girl Scout troops in Hispanic neighborhoods. We are now in the second year of this partnership.	It is rare for Hispanics to participate in the Girl Scouts, partly because of transportation issues, and partly because it is a cultural activity with which Hispanic families are unfamiliar. Purdue students participate as group leaders.
Lafayette Adult Resource Academy	
LARA is a nonprofit organization that is heavily involved in adult education for those in the community who speak limited or no English. We are now in the second year of this partnership.	Purdue students help to tutor adult Hispanic students, or assist in child care by working with the children of Spanish-speaking clients (LARA provides free child care for their students while they are in class).
Lafayette Neighborhood Housing Services	
A small number of students work with LNHS, a nonprofit organization that assists those with limited resources in regard to housing needs. We are now in the second year of this partnership.	Purdue students assist in facilitating communication with Hispanic families about a variety of issues relating to home purchase and personal finance. Students participate at regularly scheduled times in the afternoon, and LNHS encourages their Hispanic clients to come at those times.

Challenges

The organization of *Ayuda y Aprende* allows for large numbers of students from different courses and sections to participate in the program, and also allows for multiple and diverse partnerships in the community. There are, however, a series of challenges that this sort of program presents that may not be present in a more conventional service-learning course, where all students enrolled in a particular course will participate with a limited number of community partners.

The first thing to take into account is administrative staffing. This is a large and somewhat complex program that requires a time commitment well beyond that which a single faculty member can provide. Departmental support is extremely important to make such a program work, and our department head has been extremely supportive of our service-learning initiative from its inception. The department currently provides one course release per semester for a graduate student or lecturer to take on much of the work related to the day-to-day running of the program. Without the efforts and commitment of those who have served in this position the development and administration of this program would not have been possible. In addition, because enrollment in *Ayuda y Aprende* creates a significantly reduced student population in the last seminar period of the third-year course, we are able to provide partial course release to some teaching assistants as a way of enrolling their support. Finally, we are currently experimenting with the use of an undergraduate work-study student to take on some tasks. Nonetheless, there are limited resources for the administration of the program, and we face continuing issues regarding ways to operate more efficiently and to best marshal the resources that we have.

Perhaps the single most time-consuming aspect of *Ayuda y Aprende* is the enrollment of students in the program, including their assignment to a community partner and to a discussion group. In the past we tried various manners of doing this, ranging from having the students sign up individually, by email, or by using an application form online. All of these methods proved extremely time consuming and messy, as students would often sign up without being fully informed about the nature of the program, which would result in extremely large numbers of emails, office hour visits, and assignment changes. In the current semester we have instituted a system of scheduling multiple orientation/sign-up sessions, with instructions that students may sign up only at these sessions. This was accompanied by the distribution of a recruitment/information handout, which included the schedule of sessions. While the sign-up system still needs refinement, we have been able to enroll more students than in previous semesters.

Another area that requires attention is communication. Communication with students, both to enroll them in the program and to keep them informed, is of obvious importance. It is also important, however, to establish and maintain communication about service-learning with the entire cohort of instructors, as they are the primary point of contact for most students in relation to their Spanish course. In the past we have attempted to maintain communication with students and instructors primarily through announcements on WebCT (used in all courses) and through email, with information provided to instructors during their orientation. In addition, service-learning ambassadors have visited some classes. Overall, these measures have not been sufficient. Current plans to enhance communication (beyond the handouts) include the development of informational videos that can by played in all sections where students are eligible to participate. This is being pursued with the use of a grant from Indiana Campus Compact. In addition, there is a clear need for a web site dedicated exclusively to *Ayuda y Aprende*. We hope to accomplish this in the near future through the collaboration of another faculty member involved in service-learning, Alka Harriger. She regularly teaches a course in dynamic web design, for which the primary student project involves forming a team that will build a web site in support of a campus service-learning project, or a community organization. Having a campus-wide service-learning culture can certainly be of great assistance.

A final area that requires some comment is the relationships with our community partners. Given the large number of partnerships that we have this is of particular importance. The interaction with these partners, while invariably extremely positive, has also provided some challenges. This is partly because we have often been in the position of establishing new partnerships at the beginning of semesters, as needs have arisen. Furthermore, the person responsible for collaborating with *Ayuda y Aprende* in any given partnership may change from year to year, and so there may be limited institutional memory. Clear communication and advance planning is thus extremely important.

There are a variety of challenges that may present themselves in the design and administration of such a diffuse program. None of them are overwhelming, but they do need to be taken into account by anyone wishing to engage in this sort of undertaking.

■ Sociocultural Theory and Service-Learning

SCT has its origins in the writing of Lev Vygotsky during the early years of the Soviet Union. His intention was to create a way for understanding human cognition in a way that differed from Western models that saw cognition primarily as something that takes place within the individual (Vygotsky, 1978, 1986; Wertsch, 1998). Vygotsky was particularly interested in the relationship between thought and language (Vygotsky, 1986), and saw the word as the basic unit of analysis for an understanding of higher-level cognition, as well as the primary semiotic system for the transmission of culture and the social construction of mind. He was particularly interested in language as a psychological tool (Newman & Holzman, 1993), maintaining that psychological processes take place on two levels: first on an interpsychological plane between members of a culture (typically one more expert than the other), and then on an intrapsychological plane, as an internalization of the first process. In this way the notion of inner speech (with a series of its own unique qualities) becomes central to his understanding of human consciousness. Many scholars see this as similar to Bakhtin's ideas concerning ventriloquation (Holquist, 1990; Wertsch, 1998), or the appropriation of other voices into one's own, an idea that Wertsch succinctly summarizes as "voices of the mind" (Wertsch, 1991). Central to virtually all thought in the Vygotskian tradition is the idea that higher-level cognition is mediated in some way by language, cultural artifacts, interaction with others, or goal-oriented activity. Perhaps most significantly to language learning, it sees meaning not as a set of definitions or feature matrices, but rather as a process of constant negotiation and the construction of meaning in relation to a particular culture (Grabois, 1999).

While an in-depth analysis of sociocultural theory is beyond the scope of this chapter, there are a series of concepts associated with it, and related theories of language learning, that are of particular relevance. The first among these is Vygotsky's notion of the Zone of Proximal Development (ZPD, Vygotsky, 1978, 1986). This is the area where the child or learner is not yet capable of doing a task on her own, but is capable of doing so with the assistance of someone more expert. In language learning, for example, the learners may not be able to find the word or structure that they need to fulfill their communicative goals on their own, but may be able to do so with assistance. Not everything the learner can't do, however, is within the ZPD, as there may be things that they can't do even with assistance. The ZPD is in constant flux, and may vary widely among individuals. More than a metaphor for learning, it is a description of what learning may actually be. Within the education and pedagogy communities, the notion of scaffolding (first introduced by Wood, Bruner, & Ross, 1976; see also Donato & McCormick, 1994; McCormick & Donato, 2000, for further discussion of scaffolding in relation to the ZPD), while not equivalent to the ZPD, does provide a set of useful guidelines about how to facilitate learning that is extremely compatible with a Vygotskian orientation. These include recruitment, reduction of degrees of freedom, maintaining direction, marking critical features, controlling frustration, and modeling expected behavior. While engaged in service-learning, students are able to progress organically within their own ZPDs according to the interactive needs of each context. A system of mutual scaffolding is often constructed to facilitate the coconstruction of meaning between all participants.

Activity theory, first introduced by Leont'ev (1978) and highly influential among leading contemporary researchers in the Vygotskian tradition (Cole, 1996; Cole & Engeström, 1993; Wertsch, 1998) varies from Vygotsky's emphasis on semiotic mediation by positing cultural artifacts as the basic unit of analysis for higher-level human cognition. It emphasizes cognitive processes as related to goal-directed activity and their relation to communities of practice. With its analysis of operations embedded within actions, which are in turn embedded in activity, it falls more clearly within the materialistic tradition of Marxism, and it is more explicit in its analysis of cognition as a distributed process, not just in terms of ontogenesis (i.e., in relation to individual development within a cultural, historical, and institutional environment) but also in terms of microgenesis (i.e., in relation to the particular action or activity). This allows us to better understand the full extent to which cognition may be understood as distributed rather than individual (Salomon, 1993). Service-learning provides an interesting model for distributed cognition as linguistic ability and cultural knowledge reside in varying ways within all participants.

Closely associated with activity theory, and clearly informed by the Vygotskian tradition, is apprenticeship theory (Lave & Wenger, 1991; Rogoff, 1995). This orientation sees learning essentially as a sort of apprenticeship, as the learner moves closer to the center of a community of practice. The learner begins from a position of what Lave and Wenger term legitimate peripheral participation, and through engagement with a group or representative of that group, gains in expertise. While we often think of medieval trade guilds in relation to apprenticeship, Lave and Wenger provide a series of contemporary examples, ranging from West African tailors to midshipmen to supermarket butchers to members of Alcoholics

Anonymous. While there is not a single model for apprenticeship, all share the notion of movement toward the center of a community of practice, and hence expertise, as central to the process of learning. Service-learning provides a unique opportunity for students to become legitimately engaged with a community of native speakers of the language they are studying.

Collaborative learning, elaborated by Bruffee (1999), is another concept that is at least partially informed by Vygotskian thought, and which articulates with it in significant ways. It is highly consistent with concepts like the ZPD and distributed cognition. It allows us to see learning, not in terms of a container metaphor (where the mind is filled up with information, perhaps to the point where a student might talk about it coming out of her ears) but rather as a collaborative and distributed process. A process, not where the mind is filled, but rather where it formed. While collaborative learning is typically elaborated in relation to students working toward common goals, service-learning provides a model where participants strive toward complementary goals, with different types of knowledge and expertise.

Content-based learning and task-based learning (Ellis, 2003; van Lier, 1996), while not specific to SCT, are in fact highly consistent with it. The basic idea behind both methodologies is to engage students in such a way that the higher-level goal is not language learning itself, but rather the accomplishment of a task or engagement with content. In this way language learning may become an embedded goal or a tool to accomplish higher-level tasks. While these methodologies don't abandon language learning objectives, typically emphasizing a post-task focus on language, they do provide a framework for a pedagogy that is based much more on what students do than on what teachers do to them. They also provide a framework where the exploration of cultures and use of cultural artifacts for the mediation of learning can become more central to second language pedagogy, where learning is less focused on individual linguistic competence and more on what students can do

in authentic interactions. It is difficult to think of another educational context where language learning objectives are as clearly
embedded in meaningful activity as in service-learning.

The notion of learner autonomy is one that has been discussed
in the literature independently of sociocultural theory (Benson
& Voller, 1997). At times frameworks for learner autonomy are
motivated as much by questions of economy as by issues relating to effective learning. This is particularly so for a language like
Spanish, in which more than half of university language students
are enrolled, at times raising serious questions about staffing and
course delivery. However, independently of economic concerns
and more closely associated with questions of motivation, learner
autonomy can also be conceptualized in terms of providing frameworks where students can make choices about the content and
nature of the activities they engage in. In fact, there is an accepted
notion of the importance of a student-centered classroom (seeing
the teacher not as *sage on stage*, but rather as a *guide on the side*).
Taking this idea one step further to the notion of student-centered
learning, the classroom itself may cease to be the place of learning
and instead become one of several. This does articulate with SCT
in the sense that properly structured autonomy for students promotes learning not as a treatment to be received in the classroom
(a medical metaphor more consistent with notions of learning and
cognition as a primarily individual process), but rather encourages
students to be active participants whose intentions, goals, interests,
and affective orientations can come into play. Service-learning students' desire to contribute and engage less privileged members of
society in a positive way transforms language learning from a simple acquisition of knowledge and ability to something situated in
relation to personal and meaningful activity.

SCT can provide a significant framework not only for understanding learning in general and language learning specifically, but
also for the construction of environments that will allow students
to engage in learning in productive ways. This may be less specific

in determining methodology than other approaches. For example the audiolingual method, which, being derived from behaviorist principles, sees language learning as habit formation, bases its pedagogy on a narrow interpretation of learning as habit formation. Input processing approaches, which see language acquisition primarily in terms of comprehensible input, base their pedagogy to a large extent on one aspect of cognition. Swain (2000) in her discussion of output provides an interesting contrast between SCT and input theories. While input theories prescribe a specific type of methodology predicated on a narrow interpretation of cognition, a sociocultural orientation can inform pedagogy in other ways. It does so by presenting culture and content not as peripheral to language learning, but rather as a starting point (Kramsch, 1993). It provides a framework for understanding language learning as a process that students need to engage in rather than as something that is done to them. SCT emphasizes language and learning not as individual possessions, but rather in terms of activities that involve the participation of others; it constructs language learning not simply in terms of breaking a code, but rather in terms of moving closer to the center of a community (or communities) of practice.

SCT in many ways informs the structures of the courses that *Ayuda y Aprende* is articulated with in the Spanish curriculum described above. The use of portfolios, for example, encourages students to pursue their own interests and goals, and to engage in learning within their individual ZPDs. It places emphasis on the use of cultural artifacts for the mediation of learning, presents language as a tool for the accomplishment of higher-level goals, and emphasizes learner autonomy. The seminar system empowers students to pursue their own interests, putting culture and content at the center of learning, and provides a structure where students are engaged with a community of practitioners instead of a single teacher. They are not expected to learn the idiolect of one person, but instead are provided with the legitimacy to move toward the center of a community of practice.

Service-learning, particularly in relation to language learning, is also extremely consistent with a SCT approach, and framing it in those terms may help us to better understand why and how it is such a powerful pedagogy. While the seminar system may allow students to move closer to the center of an academic community, service-learning puts the students in contact with a broader community of language speakers, and in such a way that their participation has tremendous legitimacy. It engages students in a way that there is constant negotiation in terms of language and meaning, such that the role of tutor and pupil is often obscured, and learning takes place among all participants. There is truly a distribution of expertise: University students help Hispanics to learn English and become better acculturated within the local community, while those whom they tutor help the students to better understand Hispanic cultures and to become more skilled at communicating in Spanish. Students have the opportunity to engage in an activity that they understand has importance well beyond their course grade or typical course content, and where the use of linguistic tools is central to their ability to carry out those higher level goals. It diminishes the classroom as the primary place of learning, and establishes an environment where authentic interaction is not a pedagogical goal, but rather social reality. It allows students to engage with communities and learn about them in a way that may prove to be far more enduring than their ability to conjugate irregular verbs in the imperfect subjunctive (although perhaps through service-learning interactions they will come to recognize the importance of knowing how to use the imperfect subjunctive). It provides us with a much broader perspective of collaborative learning: Students strive in collaboration with those learning the same material, and in close contact with those striving to learn complementary material. Students have personal contact with Hispanic voices and experiences in a way that can only be approximated in the classroom, and they engage in language learning in a way that is not separate from, and even helps them to establish, their linguistic identities (Kramsch, 2000; Pavlenko & Lantolf, 2000). Service-learning puts students into a significant social environment where they can recontextualize and draw upon their other language learning experiences.

Student Reflections

One of the joys of directing *Ayuda y Aprende* has been to see the influence that the service-learning experience has had on students in so many ways: their increased openness to and interest in Hispanic culture, the enormous sense of satisfaction they feel at having a positive influence on the life of another human being, their desire to remain involved in community service as a lifelong venture, the increased awareness they attain of complex social issues and their own civic responsibilities. These are all highly significant outcomes and important reasons in their own right to promote service-learning in Spanish and throughout the university curriculum. Furthermore, from a SCT perspective, these affective aspects are not simply factors that contribute to language learning, but are inseparably part of what a successful language learning experience is for these students.

One of the guided reflection questions given to *Ayuda y Aprende* students was: "How has engaging in service-learning influenced your learning of Spanish?" In their responses, many students talked about how it influenced their motivation to learn Spanish:

> For one thing, it has given me more motivation to learn the language better, so I can speak more fluently with the children I work with. I want them to see that I am interested in the language too, and that is important to me that I learn it well.

Also, knowing that I am able to help those people who speak Spanish natively, I am now very motivated to learn more Spanish so I am able to help more and more people, especially in the future when I work in a hospital.

Since I have participated in service-learning, I have become more serious about learning Spanish. It's one thing for me to know that there are a lot of Spanish speakers in our country, but it's entirely different to immerse myself in the Hispanic community of Lafayette, IN.

Others talk about the increased confidence to engage in authentic conversation that participating in service-learning gives them.

Before participating with Ayuda y Aprende, I was not the most confident in my Spanish speaking capabilities. . . . This experience gave me the most real life communication with another person of Hispanic race, and it made me have to practice my speaking with her. Now, I feel that I am a little more confident, the most I have ever been, with my speaking capabilities, and I have this service-learning experience and the little girl I worked with to thank for that.

I was worried at first because I didn't think I knew enough Spanish to teach someone, and I didn't think that they would understand me when I tried to speak to them, but now I don't worry so much, and I have more confidence when speaking to them, or speaking in class.

I find that my confidence in my use of Spanish has increased, thanks to the acceptance and willingness of the children to help me as well. Especially after I worked with a few girls who spoke very little English, I was challenged to use what I knew, and learned that I really did know things.

Another common theme is the extent to which the service-learning experience helps students to become more fluent and communicative.

> I have become more comfortable talking in Spanish with them and the experience is amazing. I am so grateful that I have the opportunity to converse with them for over an hour per week. It has really influenced and improved my Spanish speaking skills. Although I have much more to learn I can't think of a better way to improve my learning of Spanish while doing community service.
>
> My learning of Spanish has been greatly influenced by service-learning because it has shifted the entire focus of my work. My learning has now been much more geared toward being able to interact with people in the real world instead of learning vocabulary and focusing on interacting with people on selected subjects in a much more guided manner.
>
> I have learned more conversational Spanish through talking to the girls than I ever have in class. Just talking to them helps me to really pick up on the language and has made me nearly fluent.

Some students even talk about how the service-learning experience helps them to better understand the structure and grammar of Spanish.

> When I teach them English, I see the mistakes they make in English and it helps me to better understand the mistakes that I make in Spanish.
>
> I have also improved my own speaking skills greatly. I often have to think quickly to translate directions into Spanish or explain exercises to students. Both my vocabulary and grammar skills have improved. Overall, the

Ayuda y Aprende program has helped me a great deal with my knowledge of the Spanish language.

When I am there, I notice that I talk more fluidly in Spanish, I am quicker to process ideas, and I make less gramatical mistakes [sic] compared to situations in the classroom.

Many students explicitly mention the reciprocity of the service-learning experience, and that they are in a position of being teachers and students at the same time.

I feel as though, even though I'm supposed to be helping the students learn English, that they've done a better job of teaching me Spanish than I have done teaching them.

Especially after I worked with a few girls who spoke very little English, I was challenged to use what I knew, and learned that I really did know things. And even if I didn't, they and the other students were very helpful and kind to make sure I would not make the same mistake again.

Participating in service-learning has not only greatly increased my understanding of the Spanish language, but it has also increased my reading, writing and speaking abilities as well. I was forced into a situation where I had to speak Spanish or the adults I was working with would not understand me. So as I helped them learn English they helped me speak better Spanish!

The overall impression given by students is that engaging in service-learning is in many ways a transformative experience. Students came in close contact with another culture, had a satisfying experience helping others in the community, and developed a heightened sense of civic awareness. Moreover, and very much in relation to these other aspects, they significantly improved their Spanish. The transformative effect that service-learning often has on language learning cannot be fully explained by models of mind that emphasize cognition and learning as easily isolated, primarily individual, or modular activities. It appears instead that concepts like the ZPD, collaborative learning, legitimate peripheral participation, and distributed cognition can provide a principled framework for understanding why service-learning is such a powerful pedagogy.

■ Conclusion

We have examined a model for service-learning that is both expansive (in the sense of being able to grow to accommodate new partnerships and increasing student participation) and inclusive (in that it does not limit the service-learning experience to any particular section, course, or schedule). *Ayuda y Aprende* is articulated with and complements other course structures that are in place. SCT and associated theoretical orientations to second language learning have been discussed—in relation to service-learning and in relation to various course structures that *Ayuda y Aprende* articulates with. Given the overwhelming success of service-learning programs, no specific theoretical framework is necessary as a means of validating service-learning (though theory is certainly useful as a way of informing it). However, the vision of second language learning that SCT provides may help us conceptualize service-learning within a broader curricular framework. In addition, a sociocultural analysis of why service-learning is so successful can help us better understand second language learning and construct other frameworks that could facilitate this process.

■ Endnote

1) Interestingly, studies that were carried out in the 1980s (Torres, 1990) but are probably still relevant indicate that while Anglo students perceive learning Spanish as empowering, Latinos often view being bilingual as marginalizing. Introduc-

ing children at an early age to Spanish as a language of literacy, and not just as the home language, may help them to view use of a heritage language as empowering as they grow up.

■ References

Bell, A., & Schwartz, A. M. (2002). *Noticias.* Columbus, OH: McGraw-Hill.

Benson, P., & Voller, P. (Eds.). (1997). *Autonomy and independence in language learning.* New York, NY: Longman.

Bruffee, K. (1999). *Collaborative learning: Higher education, interdependence, and the authority of knowledge.* Baltimore, MD: Johns Hopkins University Press.

Cole, M. (1996). *Cultural psychology: A once and future discipline.* Cambridge, MA: Harvard University Press.

Cole, M., & Engeström, Y. (1993). A cultural-historical approach to distributed cognition. In G. Salomon (Ed.), *Distributed cognitions: Psychological and educational considerations* (pp. 1–43). New York, NY: Cambridge University Press.

Coughlan, P., & Duff, P. (1994). Same task, different activities: Analysis of SLA task from an activity theory perspective. In J. P. Lantolf & G. Appel (Eds.), *Vygotskian approaches to second language research* (pp. 173–193). Norwood, NJ: Ablex Publishing.

Donato, R., & McCormick, D. (1994). A sociocultural perspective on language learning strategies: The role of mediation. *The Modern Language Journal, 78*(4), 453–464.

Ellis, R. (2003). *Task-based language learning and teaching.* New York, NY: Oxford University Press.

Grabois, H. (1999). The convergence of sociocultural theory and cognitive linguistics: Lexical semantics and the L2 acquisition of love, fear, and happiness. In G. Palmer & D. Occhi (Eds.), *Languages of sentiment: Cultural constructions of emotional substrates* (pp. 201–236). Philadelphia, PA: John Benjamins Publishing.

Hellebrandt, J., & Varona, T. L. (Eds.). (1999). *Construyendo puentes (building bridges): Concepts and models for service-learning in Spanish.* Washington, DC: American Association for Higher Education.

Hellebrandt, J., Arries, J., & Varona, L. (Eds.). (2004). *Juntos: Community partnerships in Spanish and Portuguese.* Boston, MA: Heinle.

Holquist, M. (1990). *Dialogism: Bakhtin and his world.* New York, NY: Routledge.

Kaplan, B., & Perez Gamboa, T. (2004). Más allá del salón de clase: Una experiencia de integración de aprendizaje de español y servicio comunitario en UGA. *Hispania, 87*(1), 137–38.

Kramsch, C. (1993). *Context and culture in language learning.* New York, NY: Oxford University Press.

Kramsch, C. (2000). Social discursive constructions of self in L2 learning. In J. P. Lantolf (Ed.), *Sociocultural theory and second language learning* (pp. 133–153). New York, NY: Oxford University Press.

Lave, J., & Wenger, E. (1991). *Situated learning: Legitimate peripheral participation.* New York, NY: Cambridge University Press.

Leont'ev, A. N. (1978). *Activity, consciousness, and personality* (M. J. Hall, Trans.). Englewood Cliffs, NJ: Prentice-Hall.

McCormick, D., & Donato, R. (2000). Teacher questions as scaffolded assistance in an ESL classroom. In J. K. Hall & L. S. Verplaetse (Eds.), *Second and foreign language learning through classroom interaction* (pp. 183–202). Mahwah, NJ: Lawrence Erlbaum Associates.

Newman, F., & Holzman, L. (1993). *Lev Vygotsky: Revolutionary scientist.* New York, NY: Routledge.

Pavlenko, A., & Lantolf, J. P. (2000). Second language learning as participation and the (re)construction of selves. In J. P. Lantolf (Ed.), *Sociocultural theory and second language learning* (pp. 155–177). New York, NY: Oxford University Press.

Plann, S. J. (2002). Latinos and literacy: An upper-division Spanish course with service learning. *Hispania, 85*(2), 330–38.

Richards, J., & Lockhardt, C. (1996). *Reflective teaching in second language classrooms.* New York, NY: Cambridge University Press.

Rogoff, B. (1995). Observing sociocultural activity on three planes: Participatory appropriation, guided participation, and apprenticeship. In J. V. Wertsch, P. del Río, & A. Alvarez (Eds.), *Sociocultural studies of mind* (pp. 130–164). New York, NY: Cambridge University Press.

Salomon, G. (Ed.). (1993). *Distributed cognitions: Psychological and educational considerations.* New York, NY: Cambridge University Press.

Swain, M. (2000). The output hypothesis and beyond: Mediating acquisition through collaborative discourse. In J. P. Lantolf (Ed.), *Sociocultural theory and second language learning* (pp. 97–114). New York, NY: Oxford University Press.

Torres, L. (1990). Spanish in the United States: The struggle for legitimacy. In J. J. Bergen (Ed.), *Spanish in the United States: Sociolinguistic issues* (pp.142–151). Washington, DC: Georgetown University Press.

van Lier, L. (1996). *Interaction in the language curriculum: Awareness, autonomy, and authenticity.* New York, NY: Longman.

Vygotsky, L. (1978). *Mind in society* (M. Cole & V. John-Stiener, S. Scribner, & E. Souberman, Eds.). Cambridge, MA: Harvard University Press.

Vygotsky, L. (1986). *Thought and language* (A. Kozulin, Ed.). Cambridge, MA: MIT Press.

Weldon, A., & Trautmann, G. (2003). Spanish and service-learning: Pedagogy and praxis. *Hispania, 86*(3), 574–585.

Wertsch, J. (1991). *Voices of the mind.* London, U.K.: Wheatsheaf.

Wertsch, J. (1998). *Mind as action.* Oxford, U.K.: Oxford University Press.

Wood, D., Bruner, J. S., & Ross, G. (1976). The role of tutoring in problem solving. *The Journal of Child Psychology and Psychiatry, 17,* 89–100.

8

From Theory to Realistic Praxis: Service-Learning as a Teaching Method to Enhance Speech-Language Pathology Services With Minority Populations

José G. Centeno

Speech-language pathologists (SLPs) diagnose and treat communication impairments in speech production, such as vocal problems, stuttering, and unintelligible speech, and impairments in language comprehension and expression, such as expressive delays in children and difficulties understanding or using vocabulary/sentences after a stroke. SLPs rely on both formal and informal testing procedures (i.e., standardized tests and conversational observations, respectively) as well as background interviews to collect a broad base of diagnostic information that can realistically inform treatment methods. Steady demographic trends in the country impose challenges in the training of SLPs to implement the above clinical services. The United States increasingly has become culturally and linguistically diverse (CLD) in the last century. Approximately 83 million (30%) of the population belongs to a racial or ethnic minority group. Also, almost 47 million (17.9%) individuals in the U.S. speak a language other than English at home, an increase of 15 million people since 1990 (U.S. Census Bureau, 2002, 2003). Such prominent growth in the U.S. cultural and linguistic landscape suggests that SLPs will increasingly provide services to members of minority groups who speak a language other than English.

Working with members of minority populations in CLD contexts often challenges the training and attitudes of many speech-language pathologists. Minority individuals often represent life experiences, including social, cultural, educational, and linguistic backgrounds that may be unfamiliar to speech-language trainees. Additionally, a large number of minority individuals develop in bilingual environments involving the use of two languages in different communication contexts and for different purposes. Though such experiential backgrounds have important consequences in clinical services with bilingual minority speakers, this body of information is not often discussed comprehensively nor are relevant clinical experiences sufficiently provided in professional training programs in speech-language pathology. SLPs working with bilingual speakers in the U.S. continue to experience limitations in the knowledge base and clinical tools necessary to implement realistic clinical services with these clients (American Speech-Language-Hearing Association, 2003, 2005; Kohnert, Kennedy, Glaze, Kan, & Carney, 2003; Roseberry-McKibbin, Brice, & O'Hanlon, 2005). Such limitations, however, represent theoretical and technical weaknesses. Because beliefs and attitudes of professionals working with minority individuals play a crucial role in service delivery (Gonzalez, Brusca-Vega, & Yawkey, 1997), it also is important to include practitioners' personality as part of the areas to address for appropriate case management in CLD contexts.

The purpose of this chapter is to provide a framework for the training of speech-language students to work with bilingual minority individuals, in which bilingualism theory, cultural awareness, and realistic clinical procedures closely interact. A key component of this approach is service-learning. In this framework, service-learning, when incorporated in clinical training, serves as an important teaching tool to link theoretical descriptions of bilingualism with their clinical applications in a socially conscious manner. Ultimately, both accuracy and sensitivity in service implementation should be enhanced. Similar to other collaboration-based service-learning approaches (e.g., Keene & Colligan, 2004), this framework envisions service-learning as a collaborative partnership between students and clients who, under faculty supervision, join in communication and mutual discovery, leading to intercultural awareness and, in turn, trust, understanding, and validation. Very importantly, service-learning experiences would expose speech-language students to the cultural and social dimensions of minority clients' realities, not often obtained through classroom discussions or mandated clinical internships.

Service-learning experiences have not traditionally been employed in the training of speech-language clinicians to work in CLD environments. Typically, the collection of detailed ethnographic observations is emphasized to enhance cultural sensitivity with CLD children and adults in clinical trainees and licensed practitioners (e.g., Brice, 2002; Kayser, 1995; Wallace, 1997). Although ethnographic data can provide descriptive information on the individual and the community with critical clinical relevance, well designed service-learning activities can widen and deepen students' cultural knowledge of and sensitivity to CLD communities and their members. The overall objective is to stimulate students' socially conscious integration of theoretical bases, clinical practices, and sociocultural knowledge to distinguish communication differences from genuine communication impairments. The former results from life experiences in environments different from a mainstream culture while the latter is caused by true language-learning disabilities. Additionally, by heightening trainees' awareness of the special life circumstances present in many minority individuals, service-learning can empower future practitioners to communicate this knowledge as they later collaborate with other practitioners working with minority individuals.

Clinical management of bilingual minority clients provides a rich context to illustrate the proposed service-learning-based teaching framework in CLD contexts. Bilingualism, generally viewed as a linguistic behavior, is in fact a complex sociolinguistic phenomenon in which the interaction between society and language use must be understood at both micro-personal and macro-societal levels operating in the life of bilingual minority individuals. What is crucial to the accuracy and sensitivity of the clinical process in CLD environments is the realistic separation between identifiable objective factors from deeper, socially defined subjective elements. The former refer to those overt elements and processes determining actual language performance that can be identified by observations or personal reports, whereas the latter involve covert, less identifiable, and often unspoken beliefs and attitudes in the clinician resulting from misinformation on and personal biases toward minority groups. Service-learning can be a powerful teaching method to distinguish objective from subjective elements, foster intercultural understanding, remediate possible biases, and in turn facilitate clinical management that is theoretically and socially grounded.

Discussing all the intrinsic linguistic and sociocultural dynamics of each minority group in the U.S. with an impact on speech-language services is beyond the scope of this chapter. Throughout our discussion, Hispanic individuals in the U.S. will be used as a case illustration for various reasons. Hispanics represent both the largest minority group and the group with the most prominent demographic growth in the country (National Alliance for Hispanic Health, 2004; U.S. Census Bureau, 2002). They similarly constitute the most common ethnic group in speech-language caseloads, as suggested by pediatric contexts (Roseberry-McKibbin et al., 2005). Also, Hispanics in the U.S. are a heterogeneous group whose intrinsic diversity will serve to highlight similar internal phenomena in other minority groups in the country. Principles based on Hispanics discussed in this chapter are expected to be adapted to the particular circumstances of other bilingual minority groups in the U.S.

The proposed framework will be discussed in the following manner. First, because it is important to understand that there is intrinsic diversity within each minority group in our diverse society, we start by setting the scenario for subsequent discussions with a description of the heterogeneous backgrounds of Hispanics living in the United States. We then define bilingualism, which represents personal and societal factors operating in the life of bilingual minority individuals. There follows a description of the objective factors that interact in bilingual development and individual language proficiency. Next, societal variables acting on bilingual minority communities are discussed to highlight the possible impact of subjective elements on case management decisions. Finally, based on suggestions for student training, we conclude with a framework for service-learning experiences linking theoretical principles of bilingualism, cultural awareness, and realistic speech-language praxis with bilingual minority individuals.

■ Diversity Within Diversity: The Case of Hispanics in the U.S.

Hispanic individuals in the U.S., also identified as Latinos(as), are a heterogeneous group. Hispanics constitute about 42 million people (14%) of the total U.S. population, exceeding the size of other minority groups, such as African-American, Asian American, or Native American groups. Among Hispanics, Mexican-Americans (66.9%) constitute the largest group followed by Central Americans and South Americans (14.3%), Puerto Ricans (8.6%), Cubans (3.7%), and other Hispanics (6.5%; U.S. Census Bureau, 2002). Hispanics are projected to be one in four persons (25%) of the U.S. population by the year 2050 (National Alliance for Hispanic Health, 2004; U.S. Census Bureau, 2002). Similar to other CLD groups, Hispanics represent varied levels of schooling, life experiences, and socioeconomic circumstances that have an impact on their clinical services (Centeno, 2005b). Hispanics' language skills also reflect different dialectal varieties of Spanish consistent with their countries of ancestry, and, like all bilingual populations in the U.S., exhibit varying degrees of bilingualism with a wide range of receptive and expressive skills in their first (L1) and second (L2) languages (Spanish and English, respectively) (Centeno, 2005a; Centeno & Obler, 2001; Iglesias, 2002).

Such heterogeneity in Hispanics in the U.S. needs to be examined within the complex process of acculturation. Latino(as) in the country have different degrees of cultural identification to the Hispanic and American cultures and their norms. In general, understanding the relationships, challenges, and outcomes in the interaction between ethnic identity formation and cultural allegiance is complex and so is beyond the scope of this chapter (see Marín, Organista, & Chun, 2003; Phinney, 2003; Smart & Smart, 1995). Regarding Hispanics, research has shown that both individual and societal factors need to be assessed, and that cultural acceptance/rejection may vary according to gender, generation, urban versus rural locations, socioeconomic circumstances, and length of residence in the U.S. (Hidalgo, 1993; Torres, 1997; Zentella, 1997a, 1997b).

The demographic and sociocultural trends summarized above underscore the need to develop approaches that foster cultural awareness for appropriate and respectful case management of the communicatively impaired Latino(a) client. Hispanic diversity in the U.S. suggests the need to examine each client's background (Centeno, 2005b; Rodriguez & Olswang, 2002; Salas-Provance, Erickson, & Reed, 2002). However, this intra-group diversity is not unique to Hispanics and should similarly be examined in the other minority groups in the U.S. receiving speech-language services (Battle, 2002; Roberts, 2001). Next, keeping in mind the diversity aspects highlighted in this section, we discuss bilingualism and the individual and societal sociolinguistic factors leading to bilingual heterogeneity in minority groups.

Linguistic Heterogeneity in Minority Groups: Toward a Definition of Bilingualism

Understanding language skills in members of racial minority groups is complex. On the one hand, there are individuals who mostly know and use the group's language of ancestry (e.g., Spanish in the U.S. Hispanic community) and have minimal skills in the language of the majority (e.g., English in the U.S.). On the other hand, there are individuals who know and use both languages considerably (e.g., Spanish and English). In terms of language proficiency, the former speakers can be considered monolingual in the minority language whereas the latter are considered bilingual users of both minority and majority languages. Yet, understanding the reasons why both groups exhibit different language profiles requires the examination of micro-personal and macro-societal sociolinguistic factors determining bilingual development. Before we address those factors in subsequent sections of this chapter, we define *bilingual*.

Defining *bilingual* is a challenge. Bilingual speakers are a linguistically heterogeneous group because they generally use their two languages differently. Their communication routines in L1 and L2 may call for contrasting usage practices across language modalities (i.e., reading, listening, writing, and speaking), linguistic skills (e.g., vocabulary, sentence comprehension and production, etc.), and communication contexts (i.e., formal [e.g., academic purposes] versus informal [e.g., conversation]; Centeno & Obler, 2001). Hence, when defining *bilingual,* it is important to specify how proficiency in each language was assessed in terms of three dimensions: language modality, linguistic level, and linguistic context. The degree of ability in the assessed areas will place performance in L1 and L2 along a continuum ranging from minimal to native or near-native proficiency (Centeno & Obler, 2001).

Definitions of bilingualism have attempted to capture such linguistic diversity in bilingual speakers. Though earlier definitions narrowly described bilingualism as the alternate use of two languages by the same individual (Mackey, 1962; Weinreich, 1953), later labels aimed to identify specific proficiency or acquisition patterns. Regarding proficiency, for instance, Fishman, Cooper, and Ma (1971) argue that identifying a bilingual speaker as *balanced* is unrealistic since rarely will anyone be equally competent in all communicative environments. Fishman (1965) argues that most bilingual individuals use their two languages for different purposes and functions. For instance, as frequently observed in bilingual communities, both adult and young bilinguals use one language at home and another one at work or school. Further, some bilingual speakers have been considered to be *semilingual* in both languages when their language skills in each language, such as vocabulary repertory and correctness of language use, are not comparable to those of monolingual speakers of each language (Skutnabb-Kangas, 1981). However, this label must be used with caution because limitations in either of a bilingual's languages may be the result of a lack of stimulation in L1, unavailable in their new country to the same extent as in their country of origin, and socioeconomic circumstances isolating the bilingual immigrant group from an intensive exposure to L2 in their new country (Baetens Beardsmore, 1986).

In educational contexts, proficiency labels describe bilingual students as *limited English proficient* (LEP) or *English language learners* (ELLs) to identify those students who come to bilingual schools with considerable difficulty in all or some of the linguistic modalities in English (García, 1999; Gonzalez et al., 1997). Regarding reading and writing skills, when discussing the extent of attainment in overall linguistic performance in bilinguals, we need to look into the level of *biliteracy* in bilingual speakers to explore if reading and writing in their two languages have been equally stimulated and developed (Baetens Beardsmore, 1986).

In terms of acquisition, bilingualism often is divided into two general categories, namely, *simultaneous* or *sequential* learning of the two languages. Simultaneous bilingualism is used in the case of young children regularly exposed to both L1 and L2 before age three whereas sequential bilingualism identifies the initiation of L2 experiences after age three (McLaughlin, 1978). Simultaneous bilingualism was later identified as *bilingualism as a first language* to specify that there are two languages regularly present in the child's life from birth (De Houwer, 1990). Similarly, successive bilingualism has been broken down into more specific categories. For instance, *early successive bilingualism* refers to the onset of L2 experiences after some years of L1 acquisition but "before the age of 8–10" (Hamers & Blanc, 2000, p. 131) whereas *preschool or school-age successive bilingualism* refers to the initiation of L2 exposure upon entering school at age three to four or after age five, respectively (Kayser, 2002).

The number of definitions to identify bilingual speakers' specific language learning contexts and extent of proficiency in L1 and L2 is extensive. Describing them is beyond the scope of this chapter. The examples given above underscore the linguistic heterogeneity in bilingual speakers. The reader is advised to refer to comprehensive reviews on the measurement of bilingual skills and the difficulty of defining bilingual performance (e.g., Baetens Beardsmore, 1986; Hamers & Blanc, 2000). In the following sections, we address the possible individual and societal factors responsible for bilinguals' linguistic diversity.

Language Development and Use in Bilingual Speakers as an Objective Process

It is not always possible to make a clear separation between bilingualism as an individual and a societal phenomenon. The reasons why a person becomes bilingual or makes conscious decisions regarding language use interfaces with the sociopolitical factors acting on the bilingual person's racial group (Duncan, 1989; Romaine, 1995). Hence, I have classified the variables participating in bilingual speakers' linguistic development and use into objective and subjective factors. As mentioned earlier, the former refer to those overt elements and processes determining actual language performance that can be identified by observations or personal reports whereas the latter involve covert, less identifiable, and often unspoken beliefs and attitudes in the clinician resulting from socially defined judgments on minority groups. We discuss objective variables in this section and continue with subjective variables in the subsequent section. The reader will notice that, in fact, some phenomena may be difficult to categorize as either individual or societal and are more interactive in nature.

Acquisitional considerations. Individual factors in bilingual development involve the specific circumstances shaping each bilingual learner's experiences in each language. These circumstances basically refer to the interaction among sociolinguistic patterns and contexts of language use, socioeconomic circumstances of the language-learning environment, motivational elements, and the person's age at the time of language exposure (Centeno, 2005a; Centeno & Eng, 2005).

Sociolinguistic patterns and environments of language use affect the amount, frequency, and nature of language practice. Patterns of language use in the home, the school, work, and the community will condition when, to what extent, and for how long a person will be bilingual (Grosjean, 1982; Manuel-Dupont, Ardila, Rosselli, & Puente, 1992). The number of times, the amount, and the specific environments of exposure for each language throughout the day may differentially be reflected in the receptive and expressive skills exhibited by bilingual speakers (Hoffmann, 1985; Manuel-Dupont et al., 1992; Oller & Pearson, 2002; Pearson, Fernandez, Lewedeg, & Oller, 1997). For instance, bilingual students raised in Spanish-English homes using Spanish only for conversational purposes and educated in monolingual English classrooms tend to exhibit a stronger performance in English than in Spanish in literate language areas (Kayser, 2004).

In addition to the amount and frequency of L1-L2 input, the specific linguistic functions and demands of each acquisitional environment on the bilingual learner must be examined. Cummins

(1984) identifies variability in linguistic demands by distinguishing between informal (conversational) and formal (academic) communication environments of language use. Cummins argues that basic interpersonal communication skills (BICS) develop in informal, cognitively unchallenging situations (e.g., talking to friends) whereas cognitive/academic language proficiency skills (CALPS) are demanded in situations in which there is a need to integrate and process information (e.g., writing an essay). Similarly, Bialystok (2001) suggests that language proficiency involves increasing levels of complexity, including oral (speaking), literate (reading and writing), and metalinguistic levels (language analysis), with different linguistic and cognitive demands.

Hence, varying formal and informal use of L1 and L2 would lead to differences in how language modalities are experienced, which can be reflected in bilingual speakers' strategies and overall performance during language assessment. For example, Snow, Cancino, De Temple, & Schley (1991) reported that bilingual students show a stronger ability to provide definitions, an academic task, in the language of instruction, thus supporting that differences in oral (informal)-literate (academic) language uses can have an impact in language testing.

Socioeconomic factors similarly have a tremendous effect on the nature of language experiences. In general, growing up in contexts of limited learning opportunities can present several challenges for children, particularly because children in such social environments may not experience language or literacy in ways that are commensurate with the expectations of mainstream schools or formal tests (Roseberry-McKibbin, 2001). Translated to bilingual minority speakers, language experiences may occur for many of these individuals in economically stringent contexts, a fact that, when ignored, leads many educational and clinical practitioners to equate bilingualism with language restrictions (Baker, 2001). There are a number of societal factors such as poverty, deprivation, and unemployment, which cluster together to make underachievement and difficulties in learning a reality for many linguistic minority learners (Baker, 2001; Duncan, 1989). It is therefore critical to use alternative assessment procedures that would accommodate the different learning experiences and lack of educational opportunity in children from CLD backgrounds (Gutierrez-Clellen & Peña, 2001).

Finally, personal factors, such as attitudinal disposition to each language and age of onset of L2 experiences, similarly shape language skills and proficiency. Regarding individual attitudes, language is the main indicator of how much a person identifies with a culture and the language of that culture (Marín et al., 2003). However, as mentioned earlier, ethnic or cultural identification must be seen within the complex process of acculturation through which individuals form psychological relationships and affective bonds with elements of a particular culture—that is, values, routines, behaviors, symbols, and language (Phinney, 2003). This interaction among cultural identification, language, and emotional elements must be analyzed at both individual and group levels because it varies among members of a bilingual minority and it can also reflect the social challenges imposed on the minority community by the majority society. The latter aspect of minority-majority interactions will be addressed in the next section.

At the individual level, cultural adaptation involves emotional and psychological challenges as the person adjusts to new lifestyles, including a new language and values, and responds to the attitudes of two sets of often conflicting human environments: members of the new L2 culture, who react to the newcomer, and members of the original L1 culture, who react to the person's adapted behaviors (Smart & Smart, 1995). Cultural identity can play an important role in bilingualism because the extent of a bilingual individual's cultural affinity has an impact on his/her motivations for either L1 or L2 with implications in linguistic gains or losses in each language (Hamers & Blanc, 2000; Hidalgo, 1993). Torres (1997) reports that the majority of Puerto Rican bilingual students in

Brentwood, New York, though supporting the use of Spanish for affective reasons toward their family and culture, rated English as their best language and did not identify Spanish "as the language or even a language of the United States" (p. 29). Hence, one could suggest that the bilingual speakers' attitude to both languages during bilingual acquisition can be a regulator of the amount of linguistic exposure, since highly motivated individuals are likely to seek out a greater amount of language input than those less motivated (Cummins, 1991). However, motivational factors at the personal level may interact with social perceptions of minority groups. Pavlenko (2000) argues that interactional possibilities between L2 learners and native L2 speakers may be limited when native L2 individuals refuse to interact with minority individuals, who are perceived as incompetent or illegitimate L2 users. This phenomenon will be discussed further in the next section when we describe societal variables in bilingualism.

Regarding the role of age in L1 and L2 proficiency differences, age-related constraints in bilingual development refer to a time-restricted "critical period" for language development from birth to puberty reflecting progressive maturation of cerebral language areas (Centeno, 2005a). However, understanding the role of age in second language acquisition is complex and requires the examination of interacting factors, particularly differences between rate of learning and final language gains, and the learner's personality variables (e.g., motivation, talent to learn a second language, etc.). Though there are exceptional adult L2 learners who can speak like native L2 individuals (Novoa, Fein, & Obler, 1988), those people exposed to L2 earlier in life tend to do better. Krashen, Long, and Scarcella (1979) argue that older learners may acquire L2 skills faster but, in the long run, younger learners become more proficient. While adult L2 learners may bring more mature and experienced linguistic and cognitive skills and strategies to the presented experimental tasks, evidence irrefutably confirms that child L2 learners' final attainments tend to be more complete (Centeno, 2005a.)

Oral expressive features. Understanding the origins of the expressive features in bilingual discourse is also crucial. Bilingual speakers' expressive routines represent typical patterns in sociolinguistic situations of language contact that need to be understood to avoid the inaccurate or biased labeling of routine expressive behaviors as clinical deficits or inferior communication patterns (Centeno, 2005b; Zentella, 1997b). Bilingual speakers frequently travel in both monolingual and bilingual communication environments in which the cross-linguistic effects between the two languages are inevitable. Depending on their bilingual or monolingual communication modes, bilingual individuals may use both languages in an utterance (code-mixing or code-switching), employ particular vocabulary items from one language when speaking in the other language (borrowing), or show L1 or L2 syntactic patterns when speaking in the other language (transfer). They may also exhibit L1 limitations, such as a reliance on simple verb tenses rather than complex verb structures, due to loss of L1 mastery (attrition), pronounce sounds in one language under the influence from the other (phonetic transfer), or use linguistic features of another speech community, such as African-American English (AAE), in their utterances (dialectal influences) (Centeno, 2005a, 2005b; Zentella, 1997a).

Hence, a Spanish-English bilingual who says, "The girl was getting ready *porque su boyfriend la estaba esperando*" [the girl was getting ready because her boyfriend was waiting for her] and "You *was* here yesterday" [you were here yesterday] is using appropriate expressions reflecting his/her daily linguistic routines. In the first utterance, both languages are mixed in one utterance following the grammatical rules of each language, whereas in the second the bilingual speaker has produced an utterance resulting from frequent interactions with AAE-speaking neighbors. Expressions of this sort are not "deficient" or "inferior." They represent rule-governed grammatical structures, cumulatively developed over time from cross-linguistic influences in a community, and, in turn, constitute typical linguistic forms in the expressive repertory of individuals from that sociolinguistic environment (Romaine, 1995; Wolfram, 1997).

■ Language Use by Bilingual Speakers as a Subjective Process

Nonstandard language and speech patterns evoke value judgments and racial stereotypes resulting from a socially constructed hierarchy of prestige based on political, socioeconomic, and racial factors (Hamers & Blanc, 2000; Nero, 2001; Zentella, 1997b). Both languages and dialectal varieties of a language are under constant societal assessment that assigns social values to certain groups in society and their culture, including their forms of linguistic expression. Prestigious linguistic forms are positively valued through their association with high-status social groups whereas socially stigmatized linguistic variants carry a stigma through their association with low-status groups. No language or dialect is "superior" or "inferior." These socially constructed perceptions are perpetuated by the agents of standardization in society—language academies, teachers, the media, and other institutional authorities setting the standards of behavior (Nero, 2001; Wolfram, 1997; Zentella, 1997b).

Sociopsychological processes within intergroup relations can be explained using Giles, Bourhis, and Taylor's (1977) *ethnolinguistic vitality* model. In this framework, the survival of a minority group as a distinctive community with its culture (ethno) and language (linguistic) relative to those of a majority group is defined by a combination of three main factors: status and its demographic and institutional support. In brief, status refers to the overall power of a group and reflects an interaction of the group's social, political, and economic strength in the society at large. Because bilingualism often occurs in interracial social contexts involving communities of unequal political and economic power, this model suggests that a high socioeconomic status in a minority ethnolinguistic group translates into power, prestige, and, in turn, acceptance of its culture and language by the majority community. In the opposite scenarios, in which a minority group is perceived to have a low socioeconomic standing, its culture and language members will be negatively judged and stigmatized. Similarly, the vitality of the group and its culture depends on the support received by the group's demographic representation and geographic distribution. The larger the number of individuals belonging to the group and living in close proximity, the better the group's chances for survival. Finally, the institutional support provided to the group and its culture by the government—as in education programs or in official acts, and by mass media, such as newspapers and radio—can provide imprimatur and impetus to the group's ethnolinguistic strength.

A minority group's social standing is linked to its perception by the majority society and the approval of its culture. Lack of support and pressure from the majority group has an impact on the minority group members' self-perceptions and adherence to their own culture and language. In fact, some members of the group will likely tend to shift to the majority language since the minority language is seen as lacking prestige and is not associated with academic achievement and economic progress (Appel & Muysken, 1987; Grosjean, 1982). They may also encourage their young to emphasize learning the majority language to protect them from the negative experiences they had as immigrants and to prevent the young members of the group from being stigmatized later in life (Giles et al., 1977; Grosjean, 1982). Also, children of a stigmatized minority may decide not to use their native language so as not to be differentiated from the children of the majority group (Grosjean, 1982). Finally, as mentioned above, negative social judgments on minority groups can hinder interactional possibilities between L2 learners and native L2 speakers when native L2 individuals refuse to interact with minority individuals, perceived as incompetent or illegitimate L2 users (Pavlenko, 2000).

Hence judgments, based on negative stereotypes, prejudices, and biases, have implications for intergroup relations, the life of minority individuals, and the education of their children (Hamers & Blanc, 2000). It is worth pointing out that such phenomena do not uniformly affect all members of a minority group. As suggested by Hispanics in the U.S., minority communities are intrinsically diverse with varied educational, economic, cultural, and social backgrounds, and extent of bilingualism (Zentella, 1997b). Obviously, individual examination of each minority person's history is mandated. Yet when negative socially defined perceptions occur, they lead to biased assessments of minority individuals and their culture, including inappropriate categorization of their nonstandard linguistic forms as deficient linguistic systems. In clinical and academic settings, understanding these forces is critical. A lack of attention to sociopolitical factors in the life of minority individuals and their possible influence on practitioners' approaches with these individuals can result in misinformed, biased, and unfair diagnostic and intervention decisions on behalf of bilingual minority persons (Duncan, 1989; García, 1999; Gonzalez et al., 1997; Kayser, 1995; Verhoeven, 1997). In the next section, we examine how individual and societal variables in bilingualism can be realistically addressed in speech-language training programs using a service-learning component in the curriculum.

■ A Training Framework for Speech-Language Pathology Services in Minority Bilingual Contexts

The preceding discussion underscores the need to have a sound theoretical understanding of bilingualism, and its associated social components, in order to implement realistic speech-language services with bilingual minority individuals. Sociolinguistic factors at both micro-individual and macro-societal levels have repercussions on the linguistic abilities in bilingual speakers that are treated by SLPs. However, sociolinguistic circumstances vary across individuals in a bilingual group, which results in great linguistic diversity among members of the group. Further, as exemplified by Hispanics in the U.S., diversity in each minority group in our CLD society goes beyond linguistic skills. Additional individual differences exist in terms of life experiences, educational and socioeconomic factors, and acculturation. Our discussion similarly highlights the crucial role of clinicians' self-assessment during clinical management. Because SLPs working with minority individuals also live in the same sociopolitical environments assigning social judgments to minority individuals, speech-language clinicians need to evaluate their own attitudes toward minority groups and their realities.

Standard clinical practices in speech-language pathology require clinicians to employ a broad base of formal (tests) and informal assessment methods (conversational tasks) as well as comprehensive background interviews to collect realistic diagnostic data to inform therapy. In CLD environments, both an in-depth theoretical knowledge of bilingualism and a positive attitude to cultural minorities are required for the above clinical steps to be accurate and effective. One does not work without the other. A realistic distinction between a language difference and a language disorder may not be possible when there is an incomplete understanding of acquisitional and expressive factors in bilinguals or when personal subjectivity clouds the fair assessment of the language, behavior, and overall performance exhibited by a bilingual minority person.

Poor theoretical knowledge or biased attitudes can have pernicious effects in speech-language services with bilingual minority individuals. Regarding formal testing, a lack of understanding of the acquisitional and routine communication experiences in minority individuals can create a mismatch between the language used in the formal test and the language used by the bilingual minority person (Centeno, 2003; Centeno & Eng, 2005; Verhoeven, 1997). Similarly, in the analysis of informal conversational samples, clinicians' expectations, if based on standard communication skills or a lack of knowledge of typical bilingual expression, are very likely to encourage the analysis of a bilingual minority speaker's mixed-language utterances (code-mixing/-switching), L1 accent in L2 speech (phonetic transfer), or L1-influenced grammatical structures in L2 utterances (syntactic transfer) through the prism of negative stereotypes. Finally, behavioral disposition during testing, such as sustained attention during structured tasks, may not be a familiar routine for a minority immigrant with different educational experiences in the country of origin (Centeno, 2005b).

There are instances when language or speech skills exhibited by bilingual speakers may constitute real clinical issues. However, a differential diagnosis between bilingualism-related features and genuine impairments can only be possible when typical experiential and linguistic routines in the life of bilingual individuals are fully understood, and negative subjective beliefs are removed from the clinical process. Indeed, as suggested regarding educational evaluators (Gonzalez et al., 1997), the most important tool for clinical communication assessment of minority individuals is the evaluator's own personality.

Service-learning can be an effective teaching tool to facilitate the connection between theory, praxis, and self-analysis in speech-language students. In addition to mandated clinical internships and classroom discussions, the incorporation of service-learning activities in CLD situations would foster a realistic, respectful, and empowering understanding of minority groups. Because educational and clinical services with minority individuals call for an in-depth understanding of the individuals' ethnic identity, emotions, and life experiences beyond theoretical constructs (Altarriba & Bauer, 1998; Mio, 2003; Nero, 2005), an approach based on service-learning in speech-language training would involve experiences within the context of the clinical process that would expose the student to the social and cultural realities of minority individuals, including family dynamics, community, cultural norms, and individual characteristics. In a sense, the speech-language trainee would simultaneously act as an ethnographer, learner, clinician, and social facilitator. The student clinician, under the watchful eyes of an experienced faculty member, would observe and collect direct evidence on minority individuals, engage the client (and family) in communication and mutual discovery, and convey both therapeutic and intergroup knowledge.

The proposed service-learning framework is based on collaborative partnerships guided by faculty supervision. Collaborative approaches provide socially conscious service-learning experiences in which both the student clinician and the client are active participants (see Keene & Colligan, 2004). This approach would extend the student's analysis of information beyond ethnographic approaches typically recommended in multicultural speech-language service delivery. Because of the reciprocity between service and learning, clinical trainees would collect, analyze, revise, and apply gathered information on a dynamic and ongoing basis involving trainee-client communication throughout the clinical process. Since direct and local observations provide the best and richest evidential information in CLD contexts (Díaz-Rico & Weed, 2002), collaborative clinician-client engagement would allow the student to gain background information on the client not realistically or comprehensively addressed in textbooks or classroom lectures. Yet the partnership works both ways toward mutual discovery. The student obtains knowledge from the client while simultaneously sharing his/her own history. Differences in life experiences are discussed informally as ways to gain intercultural insights, understand different perspectives, and pursue the clinical process as a joint effort. The client's family and community are also part of the student's informative sources in the partnership. Though personal "shields" in the form of attitudes and prior experiences might make both student and client hesitant (see Gonzalez et al., 1997, for relevant discussion), faculty assistance would be helpful to address concerns and enhance engagement and communication.

Similar to other service-learning programs in health care professions (e.g., Lamsam, 1999), service-learning activities in multicultural speech-language pathology would be based on a well-designed plan with goals closely tied to class content. While students implement procedures consistent with the goals, they also maintain journal records of their experiences for class discussion and a final term paper, consolidating the client's (and his/her relatives') responses to the presented activities as well as students' own reflective thinking and learning from the experiences. For example, because testing of bilingual clients often is a challenging process, the student may be given the goal to devise assessment procedures based on class discussions on bilingualism and testing of bilingual clients and commensurate with the bilingual client's life experiences. Upon approval by the class instructor, students implement the plan, particularly engaging the client and his/her family to communicate their reactions to the clinical procedures and how such activities reflect their lives. Simultaneously, students provide feedback, explain the rationale behind each testing step, and describe the complexity and challenges of language acquisition in bilingual speakers, especially within a larger majority culture. After the session, students assess their own attitudes and reactions to the process as they reflect on these episodes in their journals for class discussion and a later term paper.

When used throughout the various diagnostic and therapeutic steps of the clinical program, such systematic plans of student-client engagement and reflection should lead to mutual personal realizations, understanding, and trust. It should also empower both the client and the student clinician. Regarding the client, this new awareness is expected to encourage a sense of empowerment and validation as the client learns about the integrity of his/her group within the society at large and ways to challenge inequalities in the system. This empowerment should similarly result in trust that enhances participation during the clinical program. For the student, the outcome should be an invaluable wealth of knowledge that would facilitate a revised interpretation of the minority client's life experiences and their effect on current performance. Likewise, this new cultural awareness and sensitivity should also empower the student to communicate a similar message to colleagues working with minority individuals, hence bringing them to a new level of awareness and social justice.

Implemented in this manner, service-learning experiences are expected to facilitate the integration of theory, praxis, and a well-informed understanding of the complex interplay of sociocultural, societal, and linguistic dimensions in minority individuals. As in other disciplines in the social sciences (e.g., Keene & Colligan, 2004), the goals of speech-language pathology and the philosophy of service-learning help each other. While speech-language pathology (and its reliance on applied linguistics) brings theoretical bases to the clinical procedures with minority individuals, service-learning enhances the application of that theory for a holistic understanding and management of minority clients as individuals functioning within a large social world extending beyond the therapy room. Future efforts targeting CLD clients in speech-language training programs should include the development of approaches to incorporate service-learning in CLD contexts, the applications of research in communication disorders (and related aspects from applied linguistics) to CLD groups through service-learning-based experiences, and the emphasis of the ongoing benefits of service-learning for both clinician and CLD client throughout clinical practice. Efforts of this nature are imperative given the steady increases in cultural and linguistic diversity in the country. Further, such socially conscious application of classroom knowledge is consistent with proposals suggesting that community service-learning can be an effective approach to bring our teaching, our research, and our citizenship into meaningful, socially grounded synergy (Keene & Colligan, 2004).

■ **References**

Altarriba, J., & Bauer, L. M. (1998). Counseling the Hispanic client: Cuban Americans, Mexican Americans, and Puerto Ricans. *Journal of Counseling and Development, 76,* 389–395.

American Speech-Language-Hearing Association. (2003). *2003 Omnibus survey caseload report: SLP.* Rockville, MD: Author.

American Speech-Language-Hearing Association. (2005). *Background information and standards and implementation for the certificate of clinical competence in speech language pathology.* Retrieved October 5, 2006, from: www.asha.org/about/membership-certification/handbooks/slp/slp_standards_new.htm

Appel, R., & Muysken, P. (1987). *Language contact and bilingualism.* London, U.K.: Edward Arnold.

Baetens Beardsmore, H. (1986). *Bilingualism: Basic principles* (2nd ed.). San Diego, CA: College-Hill.

Baker, C. (2001). *Foundations of bilingual education and bilingualism* (3rd ed.). Clevedon, U.K.: Multilingual Matters.

Battle, D. (Ed.) (2002). *Communication disorders in multicultural populations* (3rd ed.). Boston, MA: Butterworth-Heinemann.

Bialystok, E. (2001). *Bilingualism in development: Language, literacy, and cognition.* Cambridge, U.K.: Cambridge University Press.

Brice, A. (2002). *The Hispanic child: Speech, language, culture, and education.* Boston, MA: Allyn & Bacon.

Centeno, J. G. (2003). Evaluating communication skills in bilingual students: Important considerations on the role of the speech-language pathologist. In E. Atkins (Ed.), *The ELL companion to reducing bias in special education.* Minneapolis, MN: Department of Education.

Centeno, J. G. (2005a). *Bilingual development and communication: Dynamics and implications in clinical language studies.* Manuscript submitted for publication.

Centeno, J. G. (2005b, March). Working with bilingual individuals with aphasia: The case of a Spanish-English bilingual client. *American*

Speech-Language-Hearing Association Division 14—Perspectives on Communication Disorders and Sciences in Culturally and Linguistically Diverse Populations, 12, 2–7.

Centeno, J. G., & Eng, N. (2005). *Clinical use of sociolinguistic reports on bilingual students.* Manuscript in preparation.

Centeno, J. G., & Obler, L. K. (2001). Principles of bilingualism. In M. Pontón & J. L. Carrión (Eds.), *Neuropsychology and the Hispanic patient: A clinical handbook* (pp.75–86). Mahwah, NJ: Lawrence Erlbaum Associates.

Cummins, J. (1984). *Bilingualism and special education: Issues in assessment and pedagogy.* San Diego, CA: College-Hill.

Cummins, J. (1991). Interdependence of first- and second-language proficiency in bilingual children. In H. Bialystok (Ed.), *Language processing in bilingual children* (pp. 70–89). Cambridge, U.K.: Cambridge University Press.

De Houwer, A. (1990). *The acquisition of two languages: A case study.* Cambridge, U.K.: Cambridge University Press.

Díaz-Rico, L. T., & Weed, K. Z. (2002). *The crosscultural, language, and academic development handbook* (2nd ed.). Boston, MA: Allyn & Bacon.

Duncan, D. (Ed.). (1989). *Working with bilingual language disability.* London, U.K.: Chapman & Hall.

Fishman, J. A. (1965). Who speaks what to whom and when? *Linguistics, 2,* 67–88.

Fishman, J. A., Cooper, R., & Ma, R. (Eds.). (1971). *Bilingualism in the Barrio.* Bloomington, IN: Indiana University.

García, E. (1999). *Student cultural diversity: Understanding and meeting the challenge* (2nd ed.). Boston, MA: Houghton Mifflin.

Giles, H., Bourhis, R. Y., & Taylor, D. M. (1977). Toward a theory of language in ethnic relations. In H. Giles (Ed.), *Language, ethnicity, and intergroup relations.* London, U.K.: Academic.

Gonzalez, V., Brusca-Vega, R., & Yawkey, T. (1997). *Assessment and instruction of culturally and linguistically diverse students with or at-risk of learning.* Boston, MA: Allyn & Bacon.

Grosjean, F. (1982). *Life with two languages: An introduction to bilingualism.* Cambridge, MA: Harvard University Press.

Gutierrez-Clellen, V. F., & Peña, E. (2001). Dynamic assessment of diverse children: A tutorial. *Language, Speech, and Hearing Services in Schools, 32,* 212–224.

Hamers, J. F., & Blanc, M. H. A. (2000). *Bilinguality and bilingualism* (2nd ed.). Cambridge, U.K.: Cambridge University Press.

Hidalgo, M. (1993). The dialectics of Spanish language royalty and maintenance on the U.S.–Mexico border: A two-generation study. In A. Roca & J. M. Lipsky (Eds.), *Spanish in the United States: Linguistic contact and diversity* (pp. 47–74). Berlin, Germany: Mouton de Gruyter.

Hoffmann, C. (1985). Language acquisition in two trilingual children. *Journal of Multilingual and Multicultural Development, 6,* 479–496.

Iglesias, A. (2002). Latino culture. In D. Battle (Ed.), *Communication disorders in multicultural populations* (3rd ed., pp. 179–202). Boston, MA: Butterworth-Heinemann.

Kayser, H. R. (1995). Assessment of speech and language impairments in bilingual children. In H. Kayser (Ed.), *Bilingual speech-language pathology: A Hispanic focus* (pp. 243–264). San Diego, CA: Singular.

Kayser, H. R. (2002). Bilingual language development and language disorders. In D. Battle (Ed.), *Communication disorders in multicultural populations* (3rd ed., pp. 205–232). Boston, MA: Butterworth-Heinemann.

Kayser, H. R. (2004). Biliteracy and second language learners. *The ASHA Leader, 9,* 4–29.

Keene, A. S., & Colligan, S. (2004). Service-learning and anthropology. *Michigan Journal of Community Service Learning, 10*(3).

Kohnert, K., Kennedy, M. R. T., Glaze, L., Kan, P. F., & Carney, E. (2003). Breadth and depth of diversity in Minnesota: Challenges to clinical service competency. *American Journal of Speech-Language Pathology, 12,* 259–272.

Krashen, S., Long, M., & Scarcella, R. (1979). Age, rate, and eventual attainment in second language acquisition. *TESOL Quarterly, 13*, 573–582.

Lamsam, G. D. (1999). Development of a service-learning program. *American Journal of Pharmaceutical Education, 63*, 41–45.

Mackey, W. F. (1962). The description of bilingualism. *Canadian Journal of Linguistics, 7*, 51–85.

Manuel-Dupont, S., Ardila, A., Rosselli, M., & Puente, A. (1992). Bilingualism. In A. E. Puente & R. J. McCaffrey (Eds.), *Handbook of neuropsychological assessment: A biopsychosocial perspective* (pp. 193–212). New York, NY: Plenum Press.

Marín, G., Organista, P. B., & Chun, R. M. (2003). Acculturation research: Current issues and findings. In G. Bernal, J. E. Trimble, A. K. Burlew, & F. T. L. Leong (Eds.), *Handbook of racial and ethnic minority psychology* (pp. 208–219). Thousand Oaks, CA: Sage.

McLaughlin, B. (1978). *Second-language acquisition in childhood*. Hillsdale, NJ: Lawrence Erlbaum Associates.

Mio, J. S. (2003). On teaching multiculturalism: History, models, and content. In G. Bernal, J. E. Trimble, A. K. Burlew, & F. T. L. Leong (Eds.), *Handbook of racial and ethnic minority psychology* (pp. 119–146). Thousand Oaks, CA: Sage.

National Alliance for Hispanic Health. (2004). *Delivering health care to Hispanics: A manual for providers*. Washington, DC: Estrella Press.

Nero, S. (2001). *Englishes in contact: Anglophone Caribbean students in an urban college*. Cresskill, NJ: Hampton Press.

Nero, S. (2005). Language, identities, and ESL pedagogy. *Language and Education, 19*, 194–211.

Novoa, L., Fein, D., & Obler, L. K. (1988). Talent in foreign languages: A case study. In L. K. Obler & D. Fein (Eds.), *The exceptional brain: Neuropsychology of talent and special abilities* (pp. 294–303). New York, NY: Guilford.

Oller, D. K., & Pearson, B. Z. (2002). Assessing the effects of bilingualism: A background. In D. K. Oller & R. E. Eilers, *Language and literacy in bilingual children* (pp. 3–40). Clevedon, U.K.: Multilingual Matters.

Pavlenko, A. (2000). Access to linguistic resources: Key variables in second language learning. *Estudios de Sociolingüística, 1,* 85–106.

Pearson, B., Fernandez, S., Lewedeg, V., & Oller, K. (1997). The relation of input factors to lexical learning by bilingual infants. *Applied Psycholinguistics, 18,* 41–58.

Phinney, J. S. (2003). Ethnic identity and acculturation. In K. M. Chun, P. B. Organista, & G. Marin (Eds.), *Acculturation: Advances in theory, measurement, and applied research* (pp. 63–82). Washington, DC: American Psychological Association.

Roberts, P. M. (2001). Aphasia assessment and treatment for bilingual and culturally diverse clients. In R. Chapey (Ed.), *Language intervention strategies in adult aphasia* (4th ed., pp. 208–234). Baltimore, MD: Williams & Wilkins.

Rodriguez, B., & Olswang, L. B. (2002). Cultural diversity is more than group differences: An example from the Mexican American community. *Contemporary Issues in Communication Science and Disorders, 29,* 154–164.

Romaine, S. (1995). *Bilingualism* (2nd ed.). Oxford, U.K.: Blackwell.

Roseberry-McKibbin, C. (2001). Serving children from the culture of poverty: Practical strategies for speech-language pathologists. *ASHA Leader, 6,* 4–16.

Roseberry-McKibbin, C., Brice, A., & O'Hanlon, L. (2005). Serving English language learners in school settings: A national survey. *Language, Speech, and Hearing Services in Schools, 36,* 48–61.

Salas-Provance, M. B., Erickson, J. G., & Reed, J. (2002). Disabilities as viewed by four generations of one Hispanic family. *American Journal of Speech-Language Pathology, 11,* 151–162.

Skutnabb-Kangas, T. (1981). *Bilingualism or not: The education of minorities.* Clevedon, U.K.: Multilingual Matters.

Smart, J. F., & Smart, D. W. (1995). Acculturative stress of Hispanics: Loss and challenge. *Journal of Counseling and Development, 73,* 390–396.

Snow, C. E., Cancino, H., De Temple, J., & Schley, S. (1991). Giving formal definitions: A linguistic or metalinguistic skill? In H. Bialystok (Ed.),

Language processing in bilingual children (pp. 90–112). Cambridge, U.K.: Cambridge University Press.

Torres, L. (1997). *Puerto Rican discourse: A sociolinguistic study of a New York suburb*. Mahwah, NJ: Lawrence Erlbaum Associates.

U.S. Census Bureau. (2002). *Annual demographic supplement to the March 2002 current population survey*. Washington, DC: Author.

U.S. Census Bureau. (2003). Nearly 1-in-5 speak a foreign language at home. *U.S. Census Bureau News* (Rep. No. CB03–157). Washington, DC: Author.

Verhoeven, L. (1997). Sociolinguistics and education. In F. Coulmas (Ed.), *The handbook of sociolinguistics* (pp. 389–404). Oxford, U.K.: Blackwell Publishers.

Wallace, G. L. (1997). Treatment of individuals from diverse backgrounds. In G. J. Wallace (Ed.), *Multicultural neurogenics* (pp. 103–114). San Antonio, TX: Communication Skill Builders.

Weinreich, U. (1953). *Languages in contact*. The Hague, Netherlands: Mouton.

Wolfram, W. (1997). Dialect in society. In F. Coulmas (Ed.), *The handbook of sociolinguistics* (pp. 107–126). Oxford, U.K.: Blackwell.

Zentella, A. C. (1997a). *Growing up bilingual*. Malden, MA: Blackwell.

Zentella, A. C. (1997b). Spanish in New York. In O. Garcia & J. A. Fishman (Eds.), *The multilingual apple* (pp.167–202). Berlin, Germany: Mouton de Gruyter.

Section III

International Service-Learning

International service-learning has been gaining momentum among proponents of international education. Not surprisingly, an increasing number of students and educators consider international service-learning a meaningful alternative to what *The Wall Street Journal* calls "The Deluxe Semester Abroad" (Bernstein, 2003). As Waldbaum (2003) writes in "International Service Learning and Student Values: Seeking Higher Ground," service-learning abroad "guides students away from self-interest, diversion, and the embellishments of Grand Tour, toward a commitment to serve others." Drawing on their service-learning projects in Guatemala, Japan, and the Philippines, the authors in this section strongly affirm Waldbaum's argument that "education abroad with a service-learning component builds humanitarian values and affects students' propensity for engaged world citizenship, civic commitment and social responsibility and guides them into a life dedicated to the public good."

In Chapter 9 Darci Strother and Rosario Díaz-Greenberg describe an international service-learning partnership in which university students in the United States worked with bilingual Mayan/Spanish communities in Guatemala. As part of an interdisciplinary collaboration with students in education and world languages courses, prospective teachers and Spanish students

219

learned about the plight of refugees from Guatemala, prepared school backpacks, and then traveled to a rural Mayan area to deliver their supplies. The authors reflect on how their international service-learning project has benefited their own faculty collaboration and how it has helped their students to better connect theory and practice.

Chapter 10 focuses on service-learning projects with Deaf people in Japan. Amy Szarkowski describes how students in her Sign Language and Deaf Culture class organized school events for Deaf students and a lecture in Sign Language for a Deaf professional. The results of her study showed that students benefited in three areas: their perception of the Deaf, personal growth, and civic engagement. As the title of her contribution, "Talking Hands: Sharing in the Lives of Deaf People" illustrates, with service-learning signed language students can accomplish much more than simply talking with their hands.

In Chapter 11 James Perren informs us about second language use and intercultural communication in a multilingual community-based workplace in the Philippines. Using critical theory and poststructuralism to illuminate issues of power and ideology characteristic of second language use bypassed in traditional applied linguistics, Perren then applies conversational analysis to interpret the nuances of multilingual communication. The results show that bilingual or multilingual speakers used different languages depending on the task at hand rather than Standard English. Perren's research suggests that the preparation of participants for international and intercultural community-based work needs to include the study of country-specific languages as well as exposing learners of English to varieties beyond the British and American standards.

References

Bernstein, E. (2003, February 7). The deluxe semester abroad. *The Wall Street Journal*, pp. W1, W6.

Waldbaum, R. (2003). *International service learning and student values: Seeking higher ground*. Retrieved October 5, 2006, from: www.college values.org/proceedings.cfm?ID=59

9

Harnessing the Potential of International Service-Learning: An Example Working With a Bilingual Mayan/Spanish Community

Darci L. Strother, Rosario Díaz-Greenberg

■ International Service-Learning

Taking service-learning beyond our local communities and into our "global village" is an increasingly popular way to expose students to all that is positive about service-learning. If properly designed and executed, an international service-learning experience can offer students the best of both worlds: an exciting study abroad opportunity, enriched with the added service-learning component that can expand students' horizons in ways that ordinary study abroad programs might not. This chapter will introduce the reader to some existing international service-learning programs, explore how international service-learning can be an especially effective mode of instruction for language students and teachers-in-training, and describe specifically the fruitful collaboration between colleagues from two different fields but with similar goals for student learning.

One of the best known advocates of such student opportunities is the International Partnership for Service-Learning and Leadership, a worldwide association of universities, colleges and nongovernmental organizations. They have been in existence since 1982 and have a comprehensive network of service-learning programs that spans the globe. Students may take service-learning courses in countries such as Ecuador, France, India, Russia, Philippines, Thailand, and many more. In addition, they offer an innovative master's degree program in International Service, wherein students spend a year engaged in travel, academic study, and community service in London, New York, and either Jamaica or Mexico. Moreover, this organization coordinates an annual conference, and offers other resources for interested students and faculty.[1]

Amizade-Global Service Learning Consortium is another organization dedicated to enhancing students' learning through community-based projects around the world. Students can enroll in academic courses in disciplines such as education, film studies, political science, journalism, history, and anthropology, and engage in course-specific service-learning activities throughout the globe. Most courses garner academic credit through the University of Pittsburgh, although other universities that join the consortium may offer their own credit.[2]

A third example of the growing number of organizations that recognize the value of offering service-learning experiences abroad is the Center for International Service Learning for the Academic Community. Based in Kansas City, Missouri, this organization serves students from more than 65 U.S. colleges and universities and has programs in Costa Rica, Nicaragua, Belize, Mexico, and Tanzania. A number of general program options are offered, along with specific programs for health students and education majors.[3]

The aforementioned organizations all provide the opportunity for students from the U.S. to interact actively and purposefully with their international host country communities. At the same time, it is important to note that U.S. educational institutions do not hold the monopoly on service-learning and that students throughout the world have opportunities to engage in community-based learning. Silcox and Leek (1997) write:

> Because of America's isolationist tendencies, few practitioners have reflected on the impact that this methodology

might be having throughout the world. We at the Institute for Service Learning had no idea how widespread the service-learning movement was internationally until we received invitations to attend annual conferences of the European Council of Independent Schools. . . . We originally thought that we were expected to be the experts on service learning who were bringing American ideas to Europe. In fact, we were just one part of a worldwide network of service advocates who are sharing ideas and experiences. (p. 1)

Eberly (1997) has found examples of service-learning practices throughout the world, although he notes that the term service-learning is not universally employed. He points out some specific examples in two Spanish-speaking countries, Mexico and Costa Rica:

Mexico made a bold advance with service learning in 1937 when it began requiring medical students to serve for six months in areas lacking medical services. The students sent weekly reports describing the general conditions as well as the state of sanitation and disease rates. The program, known as Servicio Social, made such an impact that the federal government doubled expenditures on public health. In 1947, Servicio Social became mandatory for all students in higher education. . . . A high degree of integration between service and learning is found in Costa Rica's Trabajo Comunal Universitario (TCU). The typical TCU project finds two dozen students and a couple of professors putting their academic learning to practice on a village project. The projects encompass such areas as public health, teacher training, technical assistance to small farmers and manufacturers, and educational programs that help preserve traditional values. (Eberly, 1997, p. 24)

Something we have found with our own students is that those new to service-learning sometimes perceive it initially to be an act of noblesse oblige, rather than the development of a true partnership with the community members/organization as equals. This misconception can become even more pronounced when students go abroad. Students from service-learning programs in the U.S. who travel to lesser-developed countries with lower gross domestic products still need to understand that their role is to learn just as much as it is to serve and that it is very likely that university students native to their host country could also be engaged in similar activities. Providing students with examples such as those of Mexico and Costa Rica goes a long way toward helping service-learning students understand their role as a member of a diverse and complex international educational community.

Regardless of what it is called or where it is practiced, educators throughout the globe are becoming increasingly aware of the value of service-learning as a vehicle to enhance student learning. In *Encounters with Difference: Student Perceptions of the Role of Out-of-Class Experiences in Education Abroad,* Laubscher (1994) studies the impact of the experiences students gain outside the classroom on their overall learning when enrolled in a study abroad program. According to Laubscher's study, the out-of-class experiences that were most effective in helping students meet their educational objectives fell into three major categories: "participant observation, personal interaction, and travel" (p. 110). Drawing from his data, Laubscher makes the following recommendations for study abroad programs:

> Once students have been provided with the opportunities for experiential learning, the skills to take advantage of those opportunities, and the cognitive frame of reference on which to base the application of those skills, they will need a pedagogical mechanism to facilitate their efforts to bring all three components together in a productive

fashion. The key to reflective observation as a step toward abstract conceptualization is the ability to think critically and to analyze the newly acquired data within the context of the preexisting "furniture" of the mind. If such a mechanism is not made an integral part of the education abroad program, students will tend not to take the time to exercise their critical skills. (Laubscher, 1994, p. 112)

Although Laubscher does not specifically mention service-learning in his study, many of his recommendations for improving study abroad programs share common ground with the tenets of service-learning. Students enrolled in a study abroad program benefit tremendously from out-of-class opportunities to engage actively with the host community, and to reflect, in a guided and systematic way, upon their experiences. At the same time, Laubscher cautions against creating situations in which too much of students' out-of-class time is highly structured, since "[s]ome of the most significant learning experiences recounted by the informants for this study were the product of chance occurrences, unplanned activities, and unexpected events" (p. 110).

It is clear that students from virtually all the disciplines can benefit from a chance to study abroad and to engage in out-of-class activities that put them in close contact with host country natives. The focus of this study, however, will be on foreign/second language students and student teachers who intend to teach a foreign/second language. These are two groups of students who share a number of learning goals and who can be particularly well served by an international service-learning opportunity.

■ Combining Foreign Language Study and International Study

Published in 1999, the *Standards for Foreign Language Learning in the 21st Century* outline what the community of scholars and teachers of foreign languages generally agrees to be "best practice" when creating learning opportunities for students. Goal Five, "Community," is an essential area of the standards, and the area where service-learning comes into play most directly. Goal Five asks that students "participate in communities at home and around the world," and provides as an example: "Students participate in internship programs in Spanish-speaking countries" (National Standards for Foreign Language Education Project, 1999) Abundant throughout the "best practice" examples offered in the standards are cases of students making active use of the target language, making connections between their classroom learning and the real world, developing cultural competence alongside their communicative competence, and developing a proactive approach to obtaining new knowledge.

At the same time, a quick glance at the required curricula for most U.S. university foreign language majors reveals that courses in literature are still predominant in many undergraduate degree programs. While there is certainly nothing inherently wrong with using literary works as important sources of input for students of language, the manner in which students engage with the literary texts is of utmost importance in determining whether or not they will finish their degree programs with the sorts of skills exalted in the standards. A word of caution comes from Parkinson and Reid Thomas (2000), in *Teaching Literature in a Second Language*:

> Especially when working with older literature, the teacher often has a mass of information—biographical, historical, cultural, linguistic—and the learner has almost none, so the teacher feels almost forced into "lecture mode," simply telling the learners what they should know and even think, perhaps even translating parts of the text. This may sometimes be the only way to get learners through exams, but it clearly conflicts with one of the first principles of communicative methodology, that learners should talk about themselves and what they think. (p. 12)

It seems clear that if foreign/second language educators are to meet the goals laid out in the standards, we must either rethink how we teach literature, or reexamine the central role given to literature in many of our degree programs (or both).

Many of the types of teaching practices embraced in the standards find support in the tenets of the Learning Pyramid. There are several variations of the Learning Pyramid, and we have included an example of one in Figure 9.1. But all versions seem to agree that we retain the least amount of material when it is presented to us via lecture or reading, and the most when we are engaged in direct, purposeful experiences. Linking cognitive

Figure 9.1. Sample Learning Pyramid

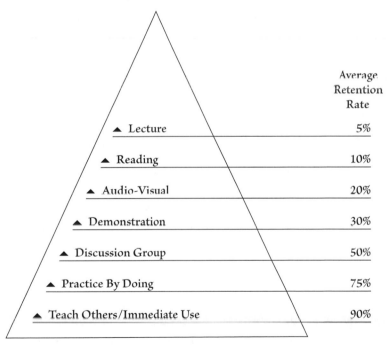

	Average Retention Rate
▲ Lecture	5%
▲ Reading	10%
▲ Audio-Visual	20%
▲ Demonstration	30%
▲ Discussion Group	50%
▲ Practice By Doing	75%
▲ Teach Others/Immediate Use	90%

Source: NTL Institute for Applied Behavioral Science, 300 N. Lee Street, Suite 300, Alexandria, VA, 1-800-777-5227. Reprinted with permission.

activity with physical activity, theory with personal experience, and creating an overt purpose for the learning all seem to stimulate and enhance retention of information. At lower levels of language learning, Asher's (2000) "Total Physical Response" technique, well known to language teachers for linking physical movement to language acquisition, is often used as an effective classroom activity. At more advanced levels of study, such as in advanced-level language classes, students engaged in dramatic performances, students who participate in service-learning activities, students who tutor others in the class material, etc., would all be expected to retain far more than students enrolled in a more traditionally structured course.

Service-learning activities would most routinely fall within the 75%–90% retention range, according to this Learning Pyramid, and can therefore be seen as extremely effective in getting students to remember what they have learned and experienced. An international service-learning experience gives students the additional advantage of broadening their exposure to and understanding of the diverse global community of target-language speakers and their cultures. Students at the undergraduate level whose primary goal is to perfect their communicative and cultural competence in the target language can benefit from an international service-learning experience for all the reasons we have mentioned. Post-baccalaureate students enrolled in teacher credential programs have the added advantage of having at their disposal an effective pedagogical model, which they would then be well prepared to emulate in their own future classes.

Harvard University Professor R. Light's (2001) *Making the Most of College—Students Speak their Minds*, a 10-year study of thousands of undergraduate students, reported the following:

From the interviews a fascinating observation emerges about certain faculty members whom students identify as having had an especially powerful influence on their thinking, and on their lives. The faculty members who had an especially big impact are those who helped students make connections between a serious curriculum, on the one hand, and the students' personal lives, values, and experiences, on the other. (p. 110)

Therefore, apart from the issue of retention of course materials, those faculty members who engage their students in the sorts of experiences inherent in well-designed international service-learning programs can expect that they will have a powerful impact on the students' overall education, and perhaps on their lives.

■ Faculty Collaboration

We now turn to a specific example of an international service-learning initiative that we carried out. Dr. Rosario Díaz-Greenberg is associate professor of multicultural studies in the College of Education at California State University–San Marcos. Dr. Darci Strother teaches at the same institution and is professor of Spanish in the College of Arts and Sciences. Díaz-Greenberg has for many years been personally involved in efforts to support the educational systems in several Latin American countries, through direct on-site teacher training in impoverished schools, collection and distribution of school supplies, and advocacy efforts with individuals within communities who have the capacity to make a difference. She began involving her education students in these efforts in 2003, as she describes here:

In the fall of 2003, I was asked to teach a course on education and cultural diversity to a group of juniors who were enrolled in the Integrated Teacher Credential Program. At the onset of the course I explained to the class that, in the past, my students had collectively worked in service-learning projects, on a voluntary basis, in order to connect theory and practice. I shared pictures and videos of previous projects with the class. The students were very excited by the pictures and videos and began asking about different types of projects that they could do. This course entails learning how to develop a community of learners. As part of this process and in order to get to know each other, students share their own autobiographies as well as family trees. These activities help initiate an internal dialogue and promote a better understanding of the similarities existing between them, regardless of such factors as ethnicity, race, and creed. One of the members of the class was a young refugee from the highlands of Guatemala, a country torn by internal war and violence. Coincidentally, I had just begun working in a pilot project training bilingual Mayan teachers in Guatemala and was making several trips a year to develop it. When Juan told the class about how he came from Guatemala fleeing persecution, about the plight his village had experienced during the 31 years of internal war, and how his sisters were still there, the students decided to organize a school supply drive to help his community.

Throughout the semester the students discussed the different aspects of the project and brainstormed about how to carry it out. After looking at different options, they decided to get the supplies and make a small package for each teacher and child in Juan's village. Toward the end of the semester the class gathered together and began assembling packages of school supplies. Using small zip-lock type bags they filled them up with pencils, pens, erasers, sharpeners, stickers, and hand-written notes. One student volunteered to videotape the activity so that the students in Guatemala could see who had prepared the bags for them. Upon seeing the video a student commented: "When we were able to watch the video, excitement flowed through my soul knowing the students in Guatemala [would see] the same video. I know the students in Guatemala [will feel] the same way." After three hours the class had prepared more than 300 bags and 12 teacher packets. The bags were placed in suitcases, and later on they were transported to Guatemala as part of my luggage, where Juan's family collected and distributed them.

Juan showed his classmates the pictures and letters that the children in the village had sent him to give to the class: The students were very moved and vowed to continue helping his community in the future. One of them said:

> As a student in the [Integrated Teacher Credential Program] I would have no problem being involved further in this program, or offering any support I can give to help this program to become permanent. I would even be willing to go to Guatemala if a trip was ever put together. Thanks for giving me this opportunity.

Juan and I did a presentation for more than 100 students in the College of Education, and many of Juan's classmates shared their personal testimony with the audience: "The Project intensified the classroom community-building process in a foundational teacher-preparation course."

Each member of the class was enriched by this humanitarian experience. "It still stands as one of the brightest moments of my educational career." The students' response to this project serves as proof that connecting theory and practice can easily be done by providing the students with opportunities to collaborate together in hands-on ventures that they can actually conceptualize, plan, and implement.

Such feelings were summarized by a participant who said:

> As future teachers we often read about how it is important to teach our students to think globally and connect what we teach in the classroom with the outside community. The Guatemala project was our way to experience the impact of such a task first hand. By connecting with students and teachers in another country, our ICP group

came together as a community. We were able to put aside any other differences we may have had and work together to create something positive. The Guatemala project not only benefited the students in Guatemala but it also helped us as future educators to see that we have the capacity to make a difference in the world (at a global level) and in our classroom (at a local level).

In spring 2004, Strother learned of these efforts, and was at the same time preparing a course reader for her fall 2004 upper-division Spanish students who would be taking a community service-learning course. After coincidentally stumbling upon an article coauthored by Díaz-Greenberg (Baldwin, Díaz-Greenberg, & Keating, 1999), "Service Learning With Bilingual Communities and the Struggle for Change," Strother decided to include the article in the course reader, and asked Díaz-Greenberg to give a guest lecture to the class. Díaz-Greenberg's presentation sparked a fire in the students who heard it, and many were energized to want to do more. Below are two examples of student comments submitted to the class listserv following her visit, presented verbatim:

Student 1:
    Hola clase, yo sólo quería comentar sobre la presentación de hoy. Creo que los 50 minutos en esta clase fueron tan valiosos como nuestro servicio comunitario, el leer el artículo de Rosario fue algo magnífico que nos abrió los ojos a un servicio eficaz, sin embargo siento que el haber escuchado a la autora de este artículo no solo nos abrió los ojos sino que nos transmitió el deseo y necesidad de ayudar a la gente que necesita de nosotros, y lo que más me gustó fue que nos hizo ver que no necesitamos tener dinero para ayudar, todos podemos ayudar con nuestro espíritu y nuestra solidaridad.

Translation:

Hello class, I just wanted to make some comments about today's presentation. I think that this 50-minute class was as valuable as our service-learning. Reading Rosario's article was something magnificent that opened our eyes to effective service; however, I feel that having listened to the author of this article not only opened our eyes but transmitted to us the desire and necessity to help those who need us, and what I liked most was that she made us see that we don't need money to be able to help, we can all help with our spirit and with our solidarity.

Student 2:

Realmente creo que la "guest speaker" de Hoy fue la mas inspiradora para mi. Que lindo mensaje nos dio LA ayuda se encuentra en todas partes sin importar la situacion economica. Creo que por medio de esta clase todos pueden hacer esa connecion de dar lo que uno sabe para ayudar a otros en la comunidad. Esto me recuerda a lo que ensene ayer en mi sitito a un padre de los ninos que van al Centro de Aprendizaje en los Apartamentos Turnagain Arms en Fallbrook me dice "oiga senorita no me ensena eso del internet y como funciona" El explicar el inmenso mundo de la red no fue facil pero la idea de por comunicarse a traves de la comutadora con alguien en China le parecio realmente emocionante. Me dio mucha alegria que los padres tambien utilisen el centro para aprender. Bueno fue algo muy bonito ver como el poco conocimiento mio de la computadora fue una ensenanza grande para este padre. Creanme que yo no pude explicar a fondo como es que la persona en China recibi el email pero ise lo que pude. Uno debe de apreciar lo que sabe y compartir su conocimientos con otros.

Translation:

I really think that today's guest speaker was the most inspirational for me. What a beautiful message she gave us. One can find help all over, without regard to the economic situation. I think that via this class everyone can make that connection of giving out what we know in order to help others in the community. This reminds me of what I taught yesterday in my placement site to a father with children who go to the Learning Center at the Turnagain Arms Apartments in Fallbrook. He says to me "Listen, Miss, won't you teach me about the Internet and how it works?" Explaining the immense world of the web wasn't easy but the idea of being able to communicate with someone in China by using the computer was truly very exciting for him. I was very glad to see the parents also using the center to learn. Well, it was something really wonderful to see how my little understanding of the computer was a great teaching for this father. Believe me, I couldn't explain in detail how the person in China would get the e-mail, but I did what I could. People should appreciate what they know, and share that knowledge with others.

Díaz-Greenberg also gave a presentation about Guatemalan culture to Strother's intermediate-level Spanish language class that semester, and included in her presentation information about the efforts to reach out to Guatemalan schoolchildren. As a result of this information, Strother's students decided to participate by creating backpacks full of supplies and gifts for those students who were "graduating" from their elementary-level studies, in order to encourage them to continue their schooling at the next level (something which is not common, since most are put to work by their families to increase the families' meager economic base). Intermediate-level Spanish students were given the option, in lieu of a more academic-style composition, to write a letter in Spanish congratulating the backpack's recipient on his or her achievements and touting the value of continued education (plus whatever other personal remarks the writer wished to include). Everyone in the class chose the letter-writing option, and students worked on these letters with a level of dedication and excitement unmatched in any other writing assignment of the semester. What made this particular activity unique was that Díaz-Greenberg was able to hand-deliver the supplies during the course of the semester and bring back for the Spanish students the photos of children receiving the backpacks, along with their thanks and other feedback.

Many students of Spanish typically hit a roadblock around the intermediate level, when they realize that Spanish is not as easy as they may have thought, and that despite studying for what seems to them like a long time, they are still not fluent in Spanish. This project, however, gave these intermediate students a much-needed boost, as it showed them that they could indeed do something very valuable as Spanish students (writing a letter that was comprehensible enough for someone with no knowledge of English to read it), and as human beings (encourage others to continue their education, provide much-needed school supplies, etc.). The fact that their letters and school supplies were destined for children in a bilingual community, in which Spanish was also a second language for many of the Mayan speakers, was an added bonus for the U.S. Spanish students. They increased their cultural knowledge (most had not been aware of the tremendous linguistic diversity present in Latin America), and they also felt less threatened as writers and more comfortable expressing themselves and writing beyond their traditional comfort zone. An anonymous end-of-term evaluation of the activity revealed that students had just one complaint: They wished the class had done more for the Guatemalan schoolchildren over the course of the semester, rather than simply making a one-time effort.

Díaz-Greenberg has named her project "Solidarity, not Charity," and this spirit is essential to combat the potential noblesse oblige attitude among students. As part of her dealings with Guatemalan counterparts, Díaz-Greenberg explores ways to help Guatemalans (and particularly Guatemalan women) help themselves. Donations of restored sewing machines, for example, are accompanied by sewing lessons. The recipients in turn produce items that can be sold locally and internationally, and they are then in a position themselves to teach others this money-making skill. Díaz-Greenberg regularly returns from Guatemala with products that are the result of this collaboration and incorporates them into class lessons. Students are introduced not only to surface-level aspects of Guatemalan culture (e.g., food, geography, etc.), but through this project they learn about real-world problems faced by a rural population, the in-country organizations set up to help ameliorate the difficulties associated with abject poverty, the grassroots efforts within communities to help themselves, and how they, the students, can play a part in helping support education and economic development. Through this activity the students of Spanish and of education typically "gain" far more in knowledge, understanding, and a sense of camaraderie, than the economic value of the letters, school supplies, and other items they send to Guatemala in exchange. This truly becomes a two-way street, in which both parties (the students and rural Guatemalans) have something essential to offer, and both parties have something important to gain.

Working as a team in such a venture, both professors were able to find new commonalities in their approach to service-learning. Their understanding of what service-learning entails was transformed, and their desire to help communities in need led them to find future forms of collaboration. As a result, Strother accompanied Díaz-Greenberg and her students on a trip to Guatemala, where students and teachers were directly involved in giving out supplies, exchanging views with local teachers, and gaining a better understanding of education in indigenous Mayan rural areas.

Upon returning from Guatemala, both professors began to explore new ways of collaborating and their joint ventures helped them forge a new type of relationship. Díaz-Greenberg commented:

> I was thrilled to have Darci go to Guatemala with us. I know that the trip provided her with a new understanding of the needs faced by Mayan rural teachers and students. It also gave her an opportunity to see the type of work that I do outside of the university setting. Almost no one knows this side of my work since they only hear about it. In Darci's case, she had an opportunity not just to see it but to live it side by side. Furthermore, traveling together allowed me to get to know her better, trust her, and approach her for advice and guidance. I doubt that we would have developed such friendship and understanding of each other without going on this trip.

Likewise, the trip had a significant impact on Strother, who stated:

> Participating in this service-learning trip with Rosario and her students was a transformative experience. Not only did I personally benefit from the opportunity to meet and work with members of rural Mayan communities, but through this trip I came to recognize and deeply appreciate both the humanitarian value of Rosario's work, and the tremendous pedagogical value to her students. I was able to witness students making the sorts of discoveries, connections, cognitive leaps, and linguistic progress that I cannot imagine them making in any other type of program. Students typically return from study abroad programs with a broadened worldview and a deeper knowledge of their host country's culture. However, much like the guest at a restaurant who enjoys a delicious meal but then "forgets" to leave a tip, most students enrolled in traditional study abroad programs spend weeks or months as guests

in the host country, but leave little behind once they are gone. Rosario's students, however, returned from Guatemala knowing that they had made a lasting impact on the children and teachers whose lives they had touched during their stay, and committed to continuing to support the developing communities they visited. The students' active level of engagement, their ability to reflect deeply on complex issues surrounding social justice and education, and their progress in using the target language (Spanish) in a relatively short amount of time all convince me that this is a concept worth pursuing and further developing.

In working together, we became aware of the fact that we share similar ideas about the true meaning of education and the need to connect theory with practice. Despite the fact that we come from different backgrounds and different disciplines, we agreed that our approach to teaching was in tandem with Phelan's (1990) words:

> Making connections is at the heart of real education. Of what use are an author's ideas if we cannot make our own meaning from them, test the ideas against our experience, and see how they relate to our picture of the world? (p. 1)

Furthermore, we discovered that we share a common belief in what good teaching is supposed to be, as stated by Palmer (1998): "Good teaching cannot be reduced to technique; good teaching comes from the identity and integrity of the teacher" (p. 10). Moreover:

> Bad teachers distance themselves from the subject they are teaching—and in the process, from their students. Good teachers join self and subject and students in the fabric of life. Good teachers possess a capacity for connectedness.... The connections made by good teachers are held not in their methods but in their hearts—mean-

ing heart in the ancient sense, as the place where intellect and emotion and spirit will converge in the human self. (p. 11)

Regardless of the methods we choose to employ, then, we must find ways to break down the wall that might separate us from our students and their life experiences, and consider such experiences and consequent emotions as valid and valued in our classes.

Taking into consideration the students' experiences and valuing their emotions after their service-learning activities has helped us bridge the gap between teacher and learner, or what Freire (1970) has referred to as reconciling both poles of the contradiction. Giving the students the opportunity to become involved in service-learning by what seemed to be a simple exercise in writing, Strother was able not just to connect theory with practice, but also to have the students develop a personal connection with Mayan children overseas. In doing this activity, Strother was able to promote what distinguished scholar John Ruskin determines to be central to the teaching/learning process:

> The entire object of education [is] to make people not merely do the right things, but enjoy the right things; not merely learned, but to love knowledge; not merely pure, but to love purity; not merely just, but to hunger and thirst after justice. (as cited in Goble & Brooks, 1983, p. 11)

Díaz-Greenberg's international service-learning project and her humanitarian efforts on behalf of the children in Guatemala resulted in the students developing a sense of caring for those who are in need, and it helped debunk a conceptual problem as exemplified by Carr (1991):

> In an educational climate currently unconducive to the airing of any sort of difficult theoretical or conceptual

problems about the purpose and conduct of education, it would appear that the college training of many student teachers has been focused well nigh exclusively on the procedural or mechanical aspects of teaching to the virtual neglect of any considerations concerning the ethical or moral dimensions of the teacher's role. (p. 10)

Admittedly, there are a number of challenges inherent in the development of international service-learning projects, not the least of which revolve around logistical, administrative, and risk-management issues. Much of the experience presented here hinged upon the personal contacts Díaz-Greenberg had developed over a number of years, which are not always available to those who wish to develop new programs. Fortunately, as explained at the beginning of this chapter, there are increasing numbers of organizations that offer international service-learning options for academic credit, and tapping into their existing programs can sometimes be an attractive alternative for faculty wishing to provide these experiences for their students. We continue to work together toward overcoming obstacles and developing experiences for students at our university that take into account the common ground we have found exists between our two disciplines. Such work is certainly time and labor intensive, but it is truly a labor of love, since we have seen the many benefits that our students accrue.

■ Conclusion

Service-learning, when properly implemented, can help students become effective agents of change not just in their own local communities but also at the global level. It can help them connect theory with practice, and it can help develop a more just society. For learners and preservice teachers of languages, an international service-learning experience offers the added component of exposing them to real-world use of language, and allowing them to make use of their emerging language skills that require them to engage in contexts that are purposeful, meaningful, and at times even life altering.

■ Endnotes

1) More information about this organization and the programs it sponsors is available at www.ipsl.org
2) More information about Amizade-Global Service-learning Consortium is available at www.globalservicelearning.org
3) The Center for International Service Learning for the Academic Community provides information about its programs at www.islonline.org

■ References

Asher, J. J. (2000). *Learning another language through actions* (6th ed.). Los Gatos, CA: Sky Oaks Productions.

Baldwin, M., Díaz-Greenberg, R., & Keating, J. (1999) Service learning with bilingual communities and the struggle for change: A critical approach. In J. Hellebrandt & L. T. Varona (Eds.), *Construyendo puentes (building bridges): Concepts and models for service-learning in Spanish* (pp. 77–94). Washington, DC: American Association for Higher Education.

Carr, D. (1991). *Educating the virtues—An essay on the philosophical psychology of moral development and education.* London, U.K.: Routledge.

Eberly, D. J. (1997). An international perspective on service learning. In J. Schine (Ed.), *Service-learning: Ninety-sixth yearbook of the national society for the study of education* (pp. 19–31). Chicago, IL: University of Chicago Press.

Freire, P. (1970). *Pedagogy of the oppressed.* New York, NY: Continuum Press.

Goble, F. G., & Brooks, D. B. (1983). *The case for character education.* Ottawa, IL: Green Hill Publishers.

Laubscher, M. R. (1994). *Encounters with difference. Student perceptions of the role of out-of-class experiences in education abroad.* Westport, CT: Greenwood Press.

Light, R. L. (2001). *Making the most of college: Students speak their minds.* Cambridge, MA: Harvard University Press.

National Standards for Foreign Language Education Project (1999). *Standards for foreign language learning in the 21st century.* Lawrence, KS: Allen Press.

Palmer, P. J. (1998). *The courage to teach: Exploring the inner landscape of a teacher's life.* San Francisco, CA: Jossey-Bass.

Parkinson, B. & Reid Thomas, H. (2000). *Teaching literature in a second language.* Edinburgh, U.K.: Edinburgh University Press.

Phelan, P. (1990). *Literature and life: Making connections in the classroom.* Urbana, IL: National Council of Teachers of English.

Silcox, H. C., & Leek, T. E. (1997, April). International service learning. *Phi Delta Kappan, 78*(8), 615–618.

10

Talking Hands: Sharing in the Lives of Deaf People

Amy Szarkowski

To many people who have not had the opportunity to meet or interact with deaf people, deafness is perceived as a handicap, a disability. People often assume that a deaf person lives in silence (Padden & Humphries, 1998). They believe that by "missing one of the senses" a deaf person is in some way broken. This perspective influences the ways in which people typically respond to those who are deaf.

This chapter will explore the impact of exposure to Deaf Culture on students who studied a Signed Language. The students participated in a service-learning project that allowed them the chance to interact with Deaf people. The argument is made that learning about Deaf Culture while simultaneously acquiring knowledge about Sign Language is important for understanding the lives of Deaf individuals. Service-learning projects that grant students the opportunity to interact and work with the Deaf are a vital component to increasing their awareness of the challenges, issues, concerns, and causes for celebration among these unique individuals.

▪ Deaf Communities/Deaf Culture

No introduction to deafness would be complete without a brief overview of the concept of Deaf Culture. To those who consider

245

themselves Deaf, their hearing loss and the resultant use of a Signed Language to communicate are factors that form a unique identity and culture (Woll & Ladd, 2003). Members of Deaf communities are often involved in Deaf-related activities or clubs and they typically develop relationships with other Deaf people.

Consistent with the literature in the field, this chapter will use the capitalized word *Deaf* to denote individuals with a hearing loss who use a Signed Language to communicate and view themselves as a part of Deaf Culture, first proposed by Woodward in 1972 (Woll & Ladd, 2003). Traditionally, Deaf also referred to those who attended residential schools for the deaf or specialized training that excluded hearing children (Padden & Humphries, 1998; Armstrong & Wilcox, 2003). That may or may not be the case today, given the many ways that Deaf children are now being educated. The use of *deaf* will refer to the status of being unable to hear. Individuals who consider themselves deaf are likely to not use Sign Language as a means to communicate. They are more likely to rely on assistive technology to enhance any residual hearing they might have. They generally do not participate in Deaf Culture activities and do not perceive of themselves as outside the majority (hearing) culture. The use of *d/Deaf* will refer to those who do not hear, whether they consider themselves a part of Deaf Culture or not. Individuals who have some hearing loss are referred to as *hard-of-hearing*.

For a number of years, there has been a struggle among d/Deaf people regarding their involvement with those with disabilities (Bienvenu, 2001). Some feel that joining forces with those with other disabilities provides more political clout, better resources, and more visibility in society. Other Deaf individuals, however, tend to prefer to distance themselves from "other disabilities" (Corker, 2002). They generally view their language and their culture as a part of themselves, not as a disability, but rather as a different way of experiencing the world. Whereas much work in the field of disabilities focuses on prevention, for example, Deaf people might ask questions such as, "What do you mean when you talk about prevention, cure, and early intervention?" or "Do you want to eliminate people like us from the face of the earth?" (Bienvenu, 2001, p. 319).

The number of Deaf people who consider themselves to be a part of a distinct cultural group with its own beliefs, customs, and language is growing (Munoz-Baell & Ruiz, 2000). The idea of "pathology" is less appealing to Deaf people, who prefer instead to focus on the aspects of themselves that are unique, not on those aspects that are "broken." In an effort to empower this minority group, there are several strategies that have been identified as a means of altering public perception from "disabled" to "diversity of language and culture." These include providing necessary information to the public and to persons with hearing loss, improving legislation regarding communication barriers, and improving health care provided to deaf persons.

It is surprising to many hearing people that Deaf individuals would, in fact, prefer to have Deaf children (Fletcher, 2002). While some critics might consider this abusive, such as not wanting everything possible for one's child, Deaf people argue that they can be better parents to children with whom they can most easily communicate and relate (Bienvenu, 2001). In 2002 the *Washington Post Magazine* did a feature article on two women, Deaf lesbians, living in the Washington, DC, area. These two women were seeking a sperm donor in order to have a child together (as cited in Fletcher, 2002). They wanted a genetically deaf man to be the donor, thus increasing their chances of having a deaf child. In his critique of the ethics of this situation, Fletcher, a professor emeritus of bioethics, considered several reasons that might be given for wanting a deaf child (Fletcher, 2002). The two women indicated that they would be happy to have a hearing child as well. They had no plans to abort a hearing fetus or do any harm that would cause an otherwise hearing child to become deaf. However, they hoped for a deaf child.

Many researchers have looked at disability from the standpoint of culture. In their seminal work on the topic, McDermott

& Varenne (1995) provide a number of examples in which the culture itself determines what disability is. They demonstrate that the culture view of *differently abled* has significant impacts on the lives of those within each culture: "Disabilities are less the property of persons than they are the moments in a cultural focus. Everyone in any culture is subject to being labeled and disabled" (p. 323).

There have been many reports in history of cultures where "disability" becomes the norm for a variety of reasons. One famous example is that of Martha's Vineyard in the United States (McDermott & Varenne, 1995). Individuals living on Martha's Vineyard, a small island off the coast of Cape Cod, Massachusetts, previously had a high rate of genetically inherited deafness. As a result, the majority of the community learned to use Sign Language to communicate. Since the community lived on an island and there were jobs that needed to be accomplished, it mattered little whether the person doing the task was hearing or not. Interestingly, when Martha's Vineyard was discovered by reporters from the East Coast, they interviewed people regarding their experiences of interacting with the Deaf on the island. The older generation had a difficult time recalling which of their neighbors had been hearing and which had been deaf. They indicated that they used Sign Language to communicate, but were unsure whether the other person they were communicating with was also hearing. From this example, along with many other examples in the world in which deaf people have been incorporated into the larger society, we can think critically about the influence of the culture on our perceptions of disability. McDermott and Varenne state, "A disability may be a better display board for the weaknesses of a cultural system than it is an account of real persons" (p. 326).

It should be noted that being Deaf is not the same the world over. While much of the research cited in the present chapter focuses on Deaf communities in the U.S. and Europe, it does not attempt to describe Deaf communities elsewhere. While the author does not claim to be an expert in Japanese Deaf Culture, having lived in

Japan and been working within the community here, some significant differences have been noted. For example, in Japan, there is no equivalent of the Americans with Disabilities Act, which ensures that persons with disabilities are not discriminated against. In Japan colleges and universities are not required to pay for interpreting services for Deaf individuals, which has had a significant influence on the number of Deaf people in Japan who have attended college.

■ The Study

How does learning Sign Language affect the learner's perspective of Deafness? How does increasing communication skills in a non-verbal language impact student growth? How will student conceptions of the world change as a result of learning a Sign Language? What will be the impact on the perceptions of Sign Language students as they gain communication skills? These questions formed the basis for the inquiry of the present study on service-learning and Sign Language acquisition.

The present study utilized information from a group of Sign Language students to attempt to answer the aforementioned questions. Initially, students enrolled in a Sign Language and Deaf Culture class served as the participants for the present research. Those students were asked three open-ended questions in an attempt to explore how, as a result of their involvement in service-learning projects with Deaf individuals, their own perceptions of Deafness and disability had changed. Those students were also encouraged to reflect upon the changes they experienced in themselves as a result of having had the experience of learning this new communication method. Lastly, the students considered the impact of learning Sign Language on their level of civic engagement.

Participants

The participants in the present study were made up of students at a small liberal arts college in Japan. The class was a volunteer effort, with no credit given. It covered one semester, during which time students learned some basic American Sign Language and were introduced to Japanese Sign Language. Guest speakers to the class included two Deaf Japanese individuals, both professionals and accomplished in their careers. While not technically service-learning projects, these guest lectures did introduce students to Deaf people and gave them the chance to interact with them and ask questions. This provided some real-life context for their continued learning of Sign Language. Additionally, students were asked to participate in two service-learning projects. The first involved working with a school for the Deaf to organize an all-school event. The second project entailed organizing a lecture, to be conducted in Sign Language, by a Deaf professional. The number of students who completed the Sign Language course was small, just five people. As a result of class conflicts, part-time jobs, and job hunting, five students who began the course were unable to complete it.

Methods

Qualitative methodology was utilized to analyze the impact on the students of having participated in service-learning projects related to the local Deaf community. Students were asked to keep reflection journals throughout the course. At the completion of the course, they were asked to answer the following three questions in writing:

1) How have your perceptions or ideas about Deafness changed as a result of learning Sign Language and being involved with the Deaf community?
2) How have you changed or grown personally by being involved with this project?
3) Has this experience influenced your desire to be involved in the wider community (civic engagement)? Why or why not?

Students involved in the project were also asked, in person, for their thoughts regarding these topics immediately following each of the service-learning activities in the course. These informal interviews were noted and included in the analysis. Additionally, members of the Deaf community were asked about the involvement of the Sign Language students following each encounter with them. They shared their perceptions and insights as well. On occasion, students informed the Deaf individuals of changes in perception that they failed to note in their writing. In these cases, the researcher noted the changes in perception they described. This information was used to substantiate the information gathered directly from the students.

Written responses to the questions were coded and analyzed for emergent themes. The researcher notes from class discussions, the reflective journals from the semester, and the written comments from the Deaf community members with whom the class interacted were also analyzed in this manner. When the researcher was unclear about the written work from the students, the researcher asked follow-up questions. At the close of the course, students were shown their collective responses to the questions posed. They were allowed an opportunity to correct any information that may have been incorrect in representing their "voices." The sharing of the group responses led to a discussion about personal growth and change as a result of learning Sign Language and being involved with the Deaf community. This final meeting served the purpose of solidifying for the class the collective gains they had achieved and the growth they had experienced as individuals and as a group.

■ Results

Perceptions of the Deaf: Not Knowing
What They Did Not Know

Students wrote repeatedly throughout the course that they were constantly amazed at what they did not know about Deaf people.

In Japan, until quite recently, children with any type of disability were sent to special schools. Mainstreaming or interacting with children with special needs rarely occurred. Students signed up for the course because it seemed interesting, and they admittedly knew little about Deaf Culture from the beginning. Every student remarked that he or she was surprised to find out there was a culture they were unaware of in Japan:

> I am embarrassed to say I did not know anything about Deaf Culture before I started the Sign Language class. I did not know, when I was child, that people who were "different" even existed. They were separated from us and sent to other schools. Now that I have met some Deaf people, I can't believe that I didn't know anything about them before.

Four of the five students had never met a d/Deaf person prior to taking the course. The fifth person had a deaf relative. This student reported that the deaf cousin was "a mystery" to her. No one in her family talked about the cousin for fear of being shamed. For this student, in particular, meeting empowered Deaf individuals and being involved in service-learning projects seemed to be particularly rewarding.

> I have never understood my cousin, because she could not speak. We could gesture and get along OK at family gatherings, but I did not feel close to her. Now that I know more about Deaf Culture, I have so much respect for the things that she has gone through. I feel like my life has changed. I want to do volunteer work, I want to improve my (Sign Language) skills, and I want to make a difference.

Sign Language Is Not Just Gestures

All of the students remarked that they were surprised to learn that anything that can be communicated in an oral language can also be communicated in Sign Language. They entered the class with the assumption that the Sign Language would be a simplified version of a "normal language." When they met college-educated Deaf individuals and had an opportunity to ask about what they studied, the students were admittedly amazed that the Deaf people they encountered had a repertoire not only of language skills, but of general and specific knowledge within their own fields as well.

> I thought Sign Language would be easy, with lots of words left out. I thought you could point to things to help a Deaf person understand what you were talking about. When I met Ken, I couldn't believe how smart he was! He signed so fast, and he knew so much! I realized that Sign Language is not just gestures, it is really a language.

■ Personal Growth

Learning Is Mutual

The students wrote, at the beginning of the class, that they would like to help Deaf people. They believed that, if they learned Sign Language, they could help by serving as interpreters or assisting Deaf people in their daily lives. One theme that was prominent in their writing was the strong impression they had gained that learning was mutual. After their first service-learning encounter, the students wrote about their changing attitude toward helping "the poor deaf people." They realized that they have a lot to learn from Deaf people. They could not learn Sign Language and "go in and help" without acknowledging the skills and knowledge held by those in the Deaf Community. Deaf people had a lot to teach these students.

> When I started Sign Language, I thought I could learn it and then help them. I thought, "They are disabled, so

they probably need help." Now, after meeting Yuko, I am embarrassed that I thought I could just help them like that. She is not a dumb person who needs sympathy. She is smarter than me! When I saw her signing, I was so amazed. I have only studied Sign Language for a short time. I realize now that I do not need to teach Deaf people, I need to let them teach me about their culture.

Owning One's Biases

The students wrote about their personal growth in terms of understanding their own biases. They reported that, although they had a desire to help Deaf people, they had some initial hesitation about actually meeting people who were different. They expressed concern about being "looked at" in public if they were signing with a Deaf person.

> I realized the other day, when I saw two people signing together, that I would probably be embarrassed if people were watching me sign with Deaf people. I would not want them to stare. I know I shouldn't care, but I would not want that attention. Even though I say that I want to help Deaf people, I realize that part of me would be embarrassed by it. I have to get over that. I realize now that I am biased.

Finding One's Strengths

Students were surprised to find that they could learn Sign Language and that some of them could do so quickly. One of the participants, a self-reported "bad student," excelled at Sign Language. For this student in particular, but all of the other students as well, learning Sign Language was doable. The students expressed a feeling of success when they were able to use the signs they had learned to communicate with Deaf people they met. This feeling of empowerment seemed to be the primary motivator for students in the remainder of the course.

> I feel like I finally found something I am good at! When I started this class, I just thought it would be fun. Now, I think it is actually important because Deaf people need hearing people to communicate with them. I know now that I can learn, that I am not just a "bad student." Maybe I just had to find something I liked to learn. I feel good about myself now.

Civic Engagement: Being More Involved With Their Community

Students were surprised to learn that, very near the college they attend, there is a school for handicapped children. Students reported a desire to be engaged with their community, to learn more about the issues, and to be more involved citizens.

Continuing With Sign Language

Each of the students who completed the course reported wanting to continue learning more about Deafness, Sign Language, Deaf Culture, and issues of concern in the Deaf Community. They reported feeling the duty as well as the desire to be involved, having learned more about the treatment of some deaf persons and the difficulties with which some deaf individuals live in the hearing world.

> I used to think that things like the Barrier-Free movement had nothing to do with me, because I am not handicapped. Now, I know that I cannot wait for deaf people to make the changes themselves. I want to continue to learn more sign language so I can be involved and help the Deaf Community. Even if I am not handicapped, I must be involved.

People with handicaps need people without handicaps to help them get laws and services. I want to learn more and help more.

■ Discussion

The Impact of Service-Learning

The participants in the present study reported significant personal growth and changes in their way of thinking regarding Deafness specifically and disabilities more broadly. They expressed their amazement at the things they did not know prior to beginning the course. The students also shared their desire to learn more and stay involved with the Deaf community.

At the onset of the course, the reasons given for enrolling included "It seems like fun" and "I want to learn how to use sign language with songs." The reasons given at the end of the course reflect a deeper desire to be involved with Deaf people. Each of the participants cited their first encounter with a Deaf person as "the turning point" in which their motivations for learning Sign Language changed. Involvement in service-learning, in this context, seemed the pivotal point in changing the focus of the students from one of casual interest to a more committed level of involvement in the Deaf Community. Students were widely impressed with the Deaf people they encountered, suggesting that their impressions of the Deaf, prior to meeting them, were somewhat less than complimentary. However, after being introduced to Deaf people, those perceptions seemed to change remarkably.

By having to implement what they had learned in a real-life situation and conversing with Deaf people, the students in the present study became more aware of their own limitations. Whereas they initially believed that Sign Language was easy, they readily changed their perceptions when they witnessed fluent signers communicating with each other. While, for this set of students, learning the basics in Sign Language was relatively easy, they acknowledged that the basics would not be enough for them to fully communicate with the Deaf. The students in the present study all reported that they would like to remain involved with the Deaf Community and hope to continue improving their Sign Language skills. At the time of this writing, each of the participants has continued his/her involvement in this area.

The literature suggested several areas of improvement often seen in students involved in service-learning projects (Astin, Vogelgesang, Ikeda, & Yee, 2000). While academic and writing skills were among the positive benefits of service-learning, because of the nature of learning Signed Language, these benefits were not noted in the students. However, some typical outcomes of service-learning were noted in this group of Sign Language learners, notably a reported and observed increase in activism, and the development of interpersonal skills. Additionally, three of the five students who completed the study indicated they would like to incorporate working with the Deaf into their work life, whether as paid interpreters, or volunteer interpreters at events. Thus, it seems that service-learning does have the capacity to alter student career perceptions and plans.

The current literature also considered positive outcomes that students tend to identify as a result of their involvement in service-learning (Astin et al., 2000). The students in the present study, similar to those in the Astin et al. study, reported greater awareness of the world and an increased awareness of their own values. Greater involvement in the classroom, a characteristic reported by many students in the previous study, was not mentioned in the present case. This is likely because the course was voluntary and comprised of a small group of people. Students self-selected to be involved with the group and were thus already highly involved.

While it is possible that service-learning activities can create volunteers who then take the jobs of paid professionals, as Dahlquist, White, and Humphers-Ginther (2003) have cautioned, such is not the case with the Deaf community in Japan.

There are relatively few people working in the field of deafness, and nondeaf people with no personal connection to deafness (e.g., family history) working in this field are even more rare. The students involved in this service-learning project were not, in any way, displacing permanent workers.

As Eyler (2000) has noted, the true impact of service-learning can be difficult to measure. Measuring moral development, for example, is certainly more difficult than measuring the amount of information a student can memorize for an exam in a particular discipline. Using traditional methods to measure this type of growth does not make sense. Yet, if alternative methods are used to tap the process of change that occurs with involvement in service-learning, notable and significant learning can be found. When a student proclaims that she never knew of the existence of Deaf people, and then voluntarily reports, orally and in her journals, that her entire worldview has changed as a result of her exposure to Deaf people, it is difficult to deny that some learning has taken place.

It is important to remember the influence that teachers have on students' perceptions when designing service-learning projects. The way in which a teacher frames any experience certainly influences the learning of those in the classroom. If students are required to take a political science class, for example, and are asked to do a service-learning project with a particular political party, the ramifications of such a required service-learning project would need to be considered, as it may be unethical to involve students in such a project. When the learning that is taking place, however, is voluntary, such as was the case with the Sign Language course, students theoretically are more in line with teacher beliefs about the importance of a topic. In the Sign Language class, the teacher presented herself from the onset as an advocate for Deaf individuals and an activist within the Deaf Community. Students were also free to discontinue the course at any time without penalty, had they not wanted to be involved with the service-learning activity.

Teachers should be aware, however, of the strong influence they can have on students, and the expectations of the service-learning projects should be made explicit so as not to unfairly take advantage of the power differential in the teacher-student relationship.

It is relevant to note that "development of a civic identity" is one of the positive outcomes cited by Astin et al. (2000). The relationship between the development of a civic identity and increased civic engagement, one of the outcomes noted in the present study, was not overtly stated by the students in their reflection journals. Yet it is likely that there is a relationship between feeling more like a citizen within a community and an enhanced desire to be involved with that community. The evidence in this study does not support the statement that service-learning leads to the development of a civic identity that then leads to civic engagement. The question of the relationship between these two phenomena is a good one and requires further inquiry.

Limitations

The participants were Japanese students, completing their education in an English-language environment. Their first language was not English, though they were asked to write their reflective journals and their reactions to the service-learning projects in English. For some students, this may have limited the extent to which they could fully express themselves. Although the students were given the option of writing their responses in Japanese and having them translated, no students took advantage of that opportunity. Since follow-up questions and member checking were used, it is believed that the written work of these students did a fair job of capturing their experiences.

The students who initially began the course but were unable to finish (an additional five students) were asked their perceptions as well. Their responses, although similar to the cohort who completed the course regarding the changes in their own perceptions, did not address the latter two questions because they were not involved in the service-learning projects. Their responses were not included in the analysis.

The number of students who completed the Sign Language and Deaf Culture class was only five students. This is a limited sample size and as such, the results are not generalizable to the wider population. However, as an initial qualitative inquiry, this number of participants is adequate. The influence on students of learning Sign Language and participating in service-learning projects with the Deaf community warrants further investigation.

■ Implications

This small project—looking at the impact of involvement on students' growth and perceptions as a result of learning Sign Language and being involved in the Deaf community—suggests that the service-learning component, as well as the introduction of Deaf persons to the students, was quite significant. The reasons for taking the class changed for each of the students. What was initially a passing interest in talking with their hands became something much greater. The students reported a change in their paradigms regarding Deaf persons. By being introduced to intelligent and accomplished Deaf people, they became aware that the Deaf, generally, are not in need of sympathy, nor are they in need of nondeaf people "helping them" with everything.

The results of the present study imply that service-learning projects are an important component of learning a Signed Language. Some academic subjects might seem irrelevant to students, including the study of Sign Language, if students do not perceive the subject as valuable or meaningful in their own lives. As such, the need for education about Deaf Culture, not just Sign Language, is paramount. The inclusion of Deaf persons in the course is highly important. Since students reported meeting Deaf people as the turning point in their perception of Deafness and their desire to learn Sign Language, this inclusion should be a part of Sign Language courses. The service-learning portion of the class forced the students to take what they had learned outside the classroom and apply it in life, as best they could. As a result, the students became more aware of their own communication limitations. Seeing the needs of Deaf people, including Deaf children, was highly motivating for these students. While the students initially wrote of "wanting to help the Deaf," they did so in what could be considered a condescending manner, in which they seemed to believe that Deaf people could do little for themselves. Although their desire to assist the Deaf community reportedly increased, the manner in which they assumed they might assist changed. The students were better able to see the role that hearing people can have within the Deaf Community, though they also saw that Deaf people do not need "saving." The inclusion of service-learning in applying what students learn in a Sign Language course gave students a realistic view of their abilities and provided motivation for their continued learning of the language and participation within the Deaf Community.

■ References

Armstrong, D. F., & Wilcox, S. (2003). Origins of sign language. In M. Marschark & P. E. Spencer (Eds.), *Oxford handbook of deaf studies, language, and education* (pp. 305–18). Oxford, U.K.: Oxford University Press.

Astin, A. W., Vogelgesang, L. J., Ikeda, E. K., & Yee, J. A. (2000). *How service-learning affects students*. Los Angeles, CA: Higher Education Research Institute.

Bienvenu, M. (2001). Can deaf people survive "deafness"? In L. Bragg (Ed.), *Deaf world: A historical reader and primary sourcebook* (pp. 315–23). New York, NY: New York University Press.

Corker, M. (2002). *Deafness/disability—problematising notions of identity, culture and structure*. Retrieved October 5, 2006, from: www.leeds.ac.uk/disability-studies/archiveuk/Corker/Deafness.pdf

Dahlquist, J. P., White, D., & Humphers-Ginther, S. (2003). *Toward a sociology of service-learning.* Paper presented at the meeting of the Midwest Sociological Society, Chicago, IL.

Eyler, J. S. (2000). What do we most need to know about the impact of service-learning on students? *Michigan Journal of Community Service-learning* [Special Issue], 11–17.

Fletcher, J. C. (2002). Deaf like us: The Duchesneau-McCullough case. *L'Observatoire de la genetique-Cadrages, 5.* Retrieved October 13, 2006, from: www.ircm.qc.ca/bioethique/obsgenetique/cadrages/cadr2002/c_no5_02/cai_no5_02_1.html

McDermott, R., & Varenne, H. (1995). Culture as disability. *Anthropology and Education Quarterly, 26,* 323–348.

Munoz-Baell, I. R., & Ruiz, M. T. (2000). Empowering the deaf: Let the deaf be deaf. *Journal of Epidemiological Community Health, 54*(1), 40–44.

Padden, C., & Humphries, T. (1998). *Deaf in America: Voices from a culture.* Cambridge, MA: Harvard University Press.

Woll, B., & Ladd, P. (2003). Deaf communities. In M. Marschark & P. E. Spencer (Eds.), *Oxford handbook of deaf studies, language and education* (pp. 151–163). Oxford, U.K.: Oxford University Press.

11

International Service-Learning in the Philippines: Community Building Through Intercultural Communication and Second Language Use

James Michael Perren

Sometimes I stop to think about why I am here,
and I face my powerless self and wonder.
Bayanihan taught me to go forward,
even if others around me do nothing.
In order to succeed at least I must do something,
but not in competition.

The song verse above was written by students from a Japanese university during a trip to the Philippines. They participated in a service-learning project with an organization that builds affordable houses. The students originally wrote the song in Japanese and we translated it to English together one evening after dinner while reflecting on the activities of the day. In line three the word *bayanihan* is used to mean "working together" in the official language of the Philippines, Tagalog. This lexical item integrated into a song written in Japanese is an example of second language (L2) use about a community-based work experience in the Philippines. It presents one type of accomplishment made through intercultural communication (IC) and additional language use. The symbolism of this Tagalog word appearing in this expressive song is important because it illustrates different elements of the students' learning experience. The enormity of this accomplishment is that students participated actively and effectively using multiple languages in a service-learning project while in a country where the local citizens do not speak their first language (L1) as a primary means of communication.

This study examines language use between people from different cultures in the Philippines. The chapter is a pilot study with the purpose of exploring a community-based workplace (CBW) context in which significant levels of communicative complexity exist that influence the flow of information. One factor that determined whether understanding was achieved involved participants having differing viewpoints on what was the most appropriate language to use for communication in various situations.

■ Theoretical Framework

A poststructural approach with a critical lens guides this study and assists in documenting multiple language use during the development of social relations. In a general sense, poststructuralism is a means of critically investigating and theorizing how social relations are constructed and reproduced with language and how the processes of additional language learning are influenced by social dynamics (Pavlenko, 2002, p. 282). This framework is advantageous for examining multilingual contexts of CBW communication because a poststructural approach:

> allows us to examine how linguistic, social, cultural, gender, and ethnic identities of L2 users, on the one hand, structure access to linguistic resources and interactional opportunities and, on the other, are constituted and reconstituted in the process of L2 learning and use. (p. 283)

Examining this study from a poststructural orientation permits a view of how participants position themselves in a service-learning context. They do this through agency in social relations using multiple languages as part of the process of community building. The way participants assert themselves actively on their behalf to solve communication dilemmas is referred to in this research as "agency." A key feature of this study was to examine participants using languages other than their L1; their previous experiences using different languages in other contexts structured their opinions of appropriate communication. Of particular significance in this study was whether participants thought communication should be carried out in a standard or variety of English, in a local Filipino language or dialect, in Japanese, or in Korean. Weedon (1987) maintains that different forms of poststructural theory share fundamental assumptions strengthening the theory and relating to language, subjectivity, and meaning (p. 20). Pavlenko posits that poststructural theory in second language acquisition (SLA) yields novel perspectives of how different identities of L2 users configure access to linguistic resources and interactional opportunities and the way they are constituted and reconstituted during L2 learning and use (p. 283). Language is viewed by poststructural scholars as the site of symbolic capital and identity construction (Bourdieu, 1991; Pavlenko, 2002; Weedon, 1987), learning as language socialization (Scheiffelin & Ochs, 1986), and L2 users as agents who have dynamic and multiple identities (McKay & Wong, 1996; Norton Peirce, 1995).

A number of advantages of poststructural approaches in SLA are highlighted in Pavlenko (2002). Several of the key points mentioned by Pavlenko provide a way to theorize L2 learning and use sensitized to the contexts in which they take place:

> examining L2 users as legitimate speakers rather than failed native speakers; acknowledging multicultural communities with coexisting language users; considering a global application of language learning contexts; supporting the notion of multicompetence instead of a native speaker outcome. (pp. 295–298)

The poststructural theoretical framework is valuable for service-learning practitioners because it places an emphasis on L2 use in connection with social relationships. Strategically positioning issues of L2 use at the forefront of a comprehensive and critical service-learning research agenda provides answers to important questions of language and communication rather than relegating these issues or completely overlooking them as unnecessary constituents. The undeniable connection between language, communication, and relationship building directly relates to the educational concept of service-learning.

One practical application of critical theory (specifically poststructural theory) to service-learning is to problematize taken-for-granted assumptions. For example, a closer examination of service-learning literature reveals a troubling reality. Several popular service-learning textbooks provide little or no discussion of language issues (Claus & Ogden, 1999; Eyler & Giles, 1999; Rhoads, 1997; Stanton, Giles, & Cruz, 1999; Wade, 1997). Moreover, additional popular service-learning texts promoting the integration of service-learning and multicultural education (Boyle-Baise, 2002; O'Grady, 2000) provide only brief overviews of language as a peripheral issue. It is clear that a proportion of service-learning literature does not present language as a significant enough topic to be treated as a focal point. On the contrary, language, communication, and L2 use are crucial elements in the *relationship-building process,* which is overwhelmingly reported on as one of the primary components of the service-learning educational concept. Fortunately, a small proportion of service-learning literature provides accounts of the intersection of L2 learning and use and service-learning (Griffith, 2002; Hara & Corbin-Mullikin, 2002; Heuser, 2000; Minor, 2001, 2002). This limited number of action research reports is pioneering and useful for examining the interdisciplinary overlap between service-learning and applied linguistics. However, service-learning practitioners will have significantly greater explanations of the language dynamics in an international or multicultural setting by applying a poststructural and critical approach using qualitative and ethnographic methodology.

▣ Intercultural Communication: Definition, Background, and Theory

Jandt (1998) maintains that intercultural communication is "face-to-face interactions among people of diverse cultures" (p. 36). The definition goes beyond unidirectional characterizations in IC literature by describing IC as a dynamic process. A brief historical background provides further understanding of its designation and corresponds to Pennycook's (2001) statement that critical applied linguistics (CAL) needs to be centered "on an historical under-standing of how social relations came to be the way they are" (p. 6). The development of current IC theory originated around the end of World War II as a result of the United States having one of the few intact economies after the devastation of the war (Damon, 2003; Gudykunst, 2003; Jandt, 1998). Advancements in transportation and technology have allowed people from diverse cultures all over the world to interact on a routine basis, thus increasing the need for learning about different ways of communicating and understanding each other (Kumaravadivelu, 2003; Porter & Samovar, 1991).

An exhausting number of traditional IC theories exist today (Gudykunst, 2003). One major weakness of traditional IC theories is that they overlook the overarching theme of power in relationships between dominant and minority groups. In addition, IC theories often avoid the topic of the subservient status that varieties of English are relegated to as well as the phenomenon of multilingualism. Many scholars propose new directions in IC research (Chen & Starosta, 1998; Nakayama & Martin, 1999; Orbe, 1998; Rodriguez, 2002). The methodologies and ideological frameworks suggested by these scholars contrast with traditional IC viewpoints that attempt to maintain long-standing Western hegemonic positions of authority and power. A number of scholars call for IC investigations conducted within the critical theory domain synthesizing postcolonial, poststructural, and postmodern influences (Blasco, 2003; Chuang, 2003; Hibler, 1997).

Intercultural Communication and Varieties of English

A second main component of the study was to explore connections between the process of IC and the attitudes toward varieties of English used by participants in this context. Related to this was my interest in English as an international language. I scrutinize how participants' perspectives differ from each other and document those features in relation to the concept of how a global English standard shaped participants' attitudes. English standards are not necessarily declining, rather, other standards are being elevated. Fishman (1992) remarks, "English is spreading, but its spread is being controlled and counterbalanced by the sponsored, protected spread of national and subnational languages" (p. 23). These historical factors fuse with political issues in the broader contexts of sociopolitical choices of norms and standards. This is where a strong connection is made between Japan and the Philippines.

Language choice and use in the Philippines are pivotal to this pilot study because as Sridhar (1996) reports there are a number of successful movements in parts of the world aimed at gaining recognition and status for indigenous languages that have been sidelined or repressed by dominance and colonialism, for example, in Malaysia, the Philippines, Ecuador, Bolivia, and Peru. The functions that English serves depends on, among other factors, the history of English use in the country and the range and depth of its use. In the Philippines, English is used by a variety of people at different levels of society. Generally, in large urban centers where education in English is prevalent, English use is more common among members of wealthier socioeconomic classes. In rural areas (with modest financial resources) characteristic of less access to formal education in English, it is more common to see an increased use of local languages (Visayan, Cebuano, etc.), the Filipino national language (Tagalog), or a mix of any of these languages with English in various configurations. A brief discussion of English and English language teaching in Japan is presented next since these languages are spoken between Filipinos and Japanese university students in this study.

Why does Japan need English? English has become the main language of international communication. An editorial in *The Daily Yomiuri* of Japan warned:

> With the rapid proliferation of the Internet and progress in international exchanges, it appears inevitable that English will become the common global language. Japanese [people] will not be able to play certain kinds of roles in the international community if they do not have a good command of the [English] language. ("Acquiring English," 2000, p. 6)

Before Japan can even realize its English language education goals, it needs to think more specifically about new roles of English in the world. McArthur (1998) points out that since English is now an international language, "everyone who uses English (native or foreign) has to negotiate its standard forms at an international level" (p. 205). What do Japanese learners of English need to know? In an interview in *The Daily Yomiuri* newspaper, Professor Shigeru Matsumoto of Tokai University's Research Institute of Educational Development states:

> If a native speaker of English says "We say that this way," you may say, "Not necessarily. It's used in different ways in other parts of the world." This kind of thing could happen and, in fact, it's only natural because this is what it means for a language to become an international language. (Kobayashi, 1998, p. 14)

In other words, there are now several different, but similar, varieties of English. Using English does not mean becoming American, British, Australian, or Filipino for that matter. Japanese people need to make English their own to express themselves to the world, as Keio University's Professor Takao Suzuki observes (Sugiyama, 1997). This empowers language users, for "you are proficient in a language to the extent that you possess it, make it your own, bend it to your will, assert yourself through it rather than simply submit to the dictates of its form" (Widdowson, 1994, p. 384). With all of the considerations above guiding this pilot study, the research questions developed were:

1) What purposes do various languages serve in an international community-based project?
2) What are participants' opinions of the role of English as a standard for intercultural communication?
3) What communication challenges do participants experience?

■ Methodology

The settings for this research are affordable-housing construction sites in the Philippines sponsored by a nonprofit organization dedicated to eliminating substandard housing around the world. I made three different excursions in 1998, 1999, and 2001 to three separate locations, performing multiple duties and roles as a community-based home builder, participant-observer, and doctoral student investigating intercultural communication. I also accomplished the task of chaperoning groups of students on international community-building events. The participants of this research include university students of Japanese descent, American university instructors/advisors, other members of the international community such as individuals from Korean medical teams, and Filipino citizens.

I took on the role of participant-as-observer while I interacted with the participants as I became familiar and comfortable with them in the actual environment (LeCompte & Preissle, 1993). This role allowed me to get familiar with their language use, in which case I acted as an "insider" (Brown & Rodgers, 2002). I tried to maintain as much distance as possible from my participants, to maintain impartiality in the analysis (Hammersley & Atkinson, 1995; Lofland & Lofland, 1995).

Data Analysis

Data set one: Field notes and observations. The first data analysis involves reflecting on my field note/journal as a participant-observer and provides preliminary answers to the first and third research questions. I made general field note/journal observations corresponding to IC during the three separate trips, with the first beginning in August 1998. I wrote the second set of notes in March 1999 and completed the entire set during August 2001. I was especially interested in recording notes about any intercultural communication occurring near me that I could observe in detail. I was also interested in how a language (whether Japanese, Tagalog, English, or any other) was used or not used in those particular instances. I also made observations about how participants communicated with each other in the area where the community-based work occurred.

I followed Silverman's (2001) guidance for interpretation while recording field observations in order to establish preliminary categorical descriptions (p. 64). Information from the journal entries was examined using grounded theory (GT) for text analysis (Titscher, Meyer, Wodak, & Vetter, 2000). GT is relevant for analyzing field notes, allowing for scientific decoding into a sociological interpretation. I classified and separated the codes by condition, interaction, strategy, or consequence related to the concept required in the axial coding phase (Table 11.1). The role and identity that I took as an insider/outsider and participant/researcher in this linguistically complex environment emerged as the central story.

Table 11.1. Axial Coding of Data Set One

Journal Excerpts	Key Code Concept	Key Code Classification	Relationship Link(s)
1	detached social control	strategy	link to social control (5)
2	emotional authority	interaction	link to detached social control (1), social control (5), and role tension (3)
3	role tension	consequence	link to role change (8)
4	linguistic complexity	condition	link to role tension (3) and constraints (6)
5	social control	strategy	link to detached social control (1) and emotional authority (2)
6	constraints	condition	link to role tension (3) and linguistic complexity (4)
7	self-image	consequence	link to role change (8), linguistic role change (9), and role tension (3)
8	role change	strategy	link to role tension (3), self-image (7), and linguistic role change (9)
9	linguistic role change	strategy	link to role tension (3), linguistic complexity (4)
10	detachment	consequence	link to detached social control (1), social control (5), role change (8), and linguistic role change (9)

As a participant, I was partially involved in interacting with the other participants in a number of contexts using a variety of languages. Analysis of several key excerpts from my field note/journal exposed the most striking feature, the range of language issues emanating from different roles:

The JU [Japanese university] student was unable to understand the word "suggestion" that the local guy used about what he had thought would be productive for this meeting. I intervened and tried to let the Japanese student know that it was only a suggestion and that they could use that as a place to start. (Field note/Journal Entry, August 5, 1998)

I acted as the translator for the students as they looked at the food menu in English and realized that they would need to speak in English to get food. (Field note/Journal Entry, August 10, 2001).

These two quotes suggest the difficulties with the competing roles I was assigned at various times in these environments. On the one hand, I was trying to be as helpful as possible to the students by assisting them with any language problem-solving needs they had such as ordering food or communicating with English speakers. On the other hand, I was attempting to stand back and let the students approach these problems with their own solutions. This was a difficult balancing act because I had also established problem-free relationships with community members on the work sites. Even though I was building solidarity with Filipino homeowner/community leaders I needed to maintain my position as an advocate for multilingual language users.

These next two excerpts show different types of challenges balancing the different roles. In the first one I was listening to a homeowner's comments about language skills of Korean medical team members. "Our host family's mother, Jenny, went to the airport to pick them up and made a comment to me that it was difficult to communicate with them in English" (Field note/Journal Entry, August 11, 1998). The next quote from my field notes/journal is a contradicting aspect of being isolated from the majority language group. I observed, "The group solidarity and language exclusion is found when Japanese are speaking at the group level about topics that concern them only" (Field note/Journal Entry, August 14, 2001). I was negotiating the conflicting roles of advocating for a group from which (at times) I simultaneously felt excluded.

Not all of the observations I made related to tension were unfavorable. In these final two excerpts it is clear that some of the tension I experienced related to learning and having fun in this context. I documented, "I think some of the fun things to learn at the site are working with the skilled laborers and they teach some words in local language and then give short sentence orders in English" (Field note/Journal Entry, August 12, 2001). My notes also demonstrate the skilled Filipino laborers' multi-competence as in this excerpt: "On the job site I also feel that when discussing the main components of the house construction, the carpenters and homepartners use Visayan and communicate with themselves. When working with the Japanese volunteers, they use English" (Field note/Journal Entry, August 13, 2001). The Filipino workers seldom used Japanese language with the students.

It was clear that to manage those roles and identities led to tension, whether I facilitated a communication gap between members of different groups, translated for the students I was chaperoning, learned from the skilled Filipino laborers, or tried to understand the reasons for using a particular language. The central story in this subset of data is of conflicting roles and multiple identities with additional language use at the center. These results provide answers to research question three; a number of participants in this multilingual setting have personal and often conflicting linguistic experiences. This point is especially relevant considering the recurring notion of "role" and how that fits into the social structure of the groups with which I was affiliated. These data also provides answers for research question one. Groups tend to use their L1 when interacting with a homogeneous membership, in this case Japanese, Visayan and Cebuano, or Tagalog. Multiple languages tend to be used by some people when working with group members from multiple language backgrounds depending on the purpose and the people involved. Communication challenges surface when multiple languages (or language varieties) are used at the same time. Difficulties are magnified when one or more members of that group are not familiar or comfortable with different pronunciation patterns and have different ability levels than their interlocutors in the language being utilized. A practical application is for teachers and service-learning practitioners to prepare their students for these experiences far in advance. Students may not be aware of the complexities of interacting with members of other cultures in service-learning contexts. Planning for these occurrences and for the demands of negotiating various roles (which at many times may be in conflict) using different languages will serve a meaningful purpose. Teachers can explain to their students the potential ramifications for being an outsider in a homogeneous language group and possible ways to manage the difficulties. Role playing can be implemented for students to practice these types of multilingual circumstances.

Data set two: Survey interviews. The second data type involved a survey-interview protocol. This analysis led to partial answers to the three research questions. This survey was administered during the final three days of the first project. It included three sections: 1) general information about the interviewee; 2) aspects of IC in social contexts; and 3) issues on the work site. I administered the survey in interview format to as diverse a population as possible. There were 8 females and 17 males. Four nationalities were represented consisting of three Americans, seven Filipinos, five Koreans, and 11 Japanese. The participants' age range was between 18 and 57 years old. There were no problems interviewing people with a wide variety of ages, nationalities, project roles, socioeconomic status, and language backgrounds. A language consultant/research partner translated and interpreted words and phrases into Tagalog and Cebuano; my Japanese language skills were developed enough to interview with little difficulty. I sought information from participants with various project roles in order to collect as broad a

Table 11.2. Participant Responses of Best/Easiest
Intercultural Communication

Social Contexts		Work Site Issues	
Language and Culture	5	Instructions	6
Kindness & Hospitality	5	Talking With Skilled Workers	4
Greetings	4	Culture	4
Conversation	4	Introductions and Greetings	2
Requesting	2	Playing With Children	2
Sports	2		

range of input as to how people feel about the two types of communication mentioned: social and work issues.

After reviewing these data following the steps outlined for content analysis in Silverman (2001), I separated comments into two groups: best or easiest communication and least-liked or difficult communication. A summary of participants' opinions of IC is provided (Table 11.2). I made six general groups for the best social context communication and indicated the total number of times mentioned in each group. The large number of responses about language and culture indicates that the participants enjoyed learning and using another language.

I also categorized the work site issues into five broad groups. The majority of comments centered on discussing issues related to building houses. I recorded one comment specifically targeting multiple language use as a benefit. The participant stated, "Sometimes English sometimes Tagalog, deep communication between Japanese work campers." The deep communication mentioned highlights an interesting point. The participant is making note of Japanese students using two additional languages for the purpose of relationship building or home construction. These data reflect the utility of Cook's (1991) notion of multicompetence in several languages depending on the purpose. In addition, there is an overlap between social contexts and work site issues with another cat-

Table 11.3. Summary of Participant Perceptions
of Difficult Intercultural Communication

Social Contexts		Work Site Issues	
Challenging Communication	10	Instruction and Clarification	6
Health Issues	5	Challenging Communication	4
Uncomfortable Topics	3	Communicative Problem Solving	3
Conversation Length	3	Project Role/Language Concern	2
Imposing	2	Extending Work Operation Hours	2

egory of communication, greetings. Comments participants made about the best-liked communication such as "Greetings in English" and "Greeting, Filipino words" demonstrate that small talk can be useful for additional language users. Other comments made by participants include references about being taught elements of a particular language, as in this remark, "Talked with carpenters, taught Japanese to them and they taught me some Cebuano." Other comments such as, "Easy to use English with Americans" pertained to the ability to communicate with some language users.

I then repeated the same procedure for categorizing the comments given by participants related to difficult communication (Table 11.3). Five broad groups for these comments emerged for both the social contexts and the work site issues. The large number of comments in the challenging communication category contrasts with the number of comments received about positive communication. Two comments provide some insight into the self-image some participants have of their language abilities as well as opinions about why communication is difficult on the work site. One skilled laborer stated, "For me it is easy to talk with work campers. But other masons and carpenters are ashamed to talk because education is not high." Another skilled laborer claimed that "Some carpenters don't understand English: Information incorrect and because of this communication is difficult."

Table 11.4. Challenging Social Communication

Comments Made by Participants
• Host family couldn't understand English and I also, so communication was difficult.
• Communication to each other is hard because of languages, Korean language, Japanese language, Filipino and American. So we need to improve our English language.
• Their English was very fast so I could not understand.
• The dialect of English was difficult and different.
• Accent of Japanese and Koreans is difficult for communication between skilled laborer and volunteers.
• I couldn't understand Tagalog or Cebuano.

The participants also provided a significant number of comments about the challenges of social communication in this context (Table 11.4). The difficulties in communications are attributed to factors such as level of ability, pacing of communication, similarity of dialects and languages, and unfamiliarity with a language. These comments highlight the intricacy of a multilingual environment. Several statements direct the dilemma away from themselves while other participants accept responsibility for the communication difficulty. Two unique comments worth mentioning provided alternatives to the challenging communication with some insight about problem solving. One participant frankly stated, "Language is always a problem, but sometimes serves to increase communication rather than limit it. Mistakes can be funny and attitude is all important." Another participant expressed the belief that more than verbal communication encompasses the ability to achieve understanding. He indicated, "Even though it has no way, there was a language problem. As you know, however, we overcame that with mixing body language."

I reread each interview response to confirm that the broad themes were accurate, relevant, and useful. The answers provide some insight into the participants' struggles to discover an appropriate standard English or any language to use. This accumulates additional preliminary answers to research questions two and three. Many comments about the lack of English ability or the need to learn English point to a common theme that participants believe English is needed for intercultural communication. Responses concerning the difficulty in understanding accents, speed of talking, unfamiliar languages, contribute to answering research question number three. A partial answer to research question one is that L1s can also be used by participants in this context to build relationships and foster a sense of trust and kindness in people from different ethnic and linguistic backgrounds.

A best practice suggested after considering the results is again related to preparing students for what to expect in an international setting specifically related to languages used for particular purposes. In this case, since English was only one common language used in this context and the perception among numerous participants was that English was needed, it would be advantageous to educate participants about those types of (mis)perceptions beforehand and that other languages would be equally relied upon depending on the circumstance.

Data set three: Naturally occurring spoken interaction. The third data set required investigating transcripts of naturally occurring spoken interaction drawing from ten Have's (1999) general strategy for conversation analysis. Answers to research questions one and three emerged from this analysis. I examined the naturally occurring data by working through the transcript in terms of a restricted set of organizations: turn taking, sequence, repair, and turn construction/design. Interesting or relevant findings were analyzed within the framework of the four organizations (ten Have, 1999). A guideline for transcription conventions is available in the Appendix at the end of this chapter.

The first interaction involves a group of student workers providing a skilled laborer with buckets of cement as he is pouring them into a portion of a wall for reinforcement. Sometimes the cement dries too much in the heat of the sun and the skilled laborer requests water to mix into the cement making it easier to work with. This process is rather hectic and must be done in a timely fashion; therefore, the communication to get the supplies to the desired area is critical and takes place rapidly. Prior to this interaction the students had been carrying heavy buckets of cement and water up to a laborer upon request. It is nearly impossible for a student worker to predict what type of material will be needed since the skilled laborer (SL), often working in tandem with another, is two meters up above the ground on scaffolding with a view of the construction process.

One interesting component of this sequence is that male student worker number three (MSW3) displays multicompetence (Cook, 1991) by using the Tagalog word *tubig* (water). He also directs a question in English at the skilled laborer on the scaffold. After several turn changes this fourth request for an answer obligates the listener to respond.

Interaction 1: Water or Cement?

Line	Speaker	Utterance
1	MSW2:	Water? (.5)
2	FSW:	Water? (.2)
3	MSW3:	[*Tubig*?
4	MSW2:	[Huh? (.5)
5	MSW1:	Excuse me? (.)
6	SL:	Yeah? (.)
7	MSW1:	Do you need wa water? (.)
8	SL:	No. (.) no.
9	MSW3:	No.=
10	MSW1:	=No?
11	MSW2:	No.(.2)
12	SL:	Cement cement (.5)
13	MSW1:	Ok (.) Cement? (.)
14	SL:	Ok

The second naturally occurring interaction comes from a video recording collected near a building site. In this interaction, an American university professor was communicating with two female student workers and several other young Filipino children playing near the two students. The two students were located away from the construction process. They were sitting in the shade of a dining area and folding 10-inch pieces of long thin wire into a U shape to be used for ties in the support system of a steel and concrete house foundation. The interaction begins with the professor (P) self-selecting his turn (1) with the first part of a question-answer adjacency pair.

Interaction 2: How many?

Line	Speaker	Utterance
1	P:	How many have you made? (3.0)
2	FSW1:	Naturaru *chotto* (.5) please
3	FSW2:	How many? (1.5)
4	FSW1:	Uh? (.)
5	P:	How many? (.5)
6	FSW1:	How (1.5) how many? (.4)
7	P:	*Nan mai?* (.5)
8	FSW2:	Ahhhh!=
9	P:	=*Nan pun?*=
10	FSW1:	=Oh (.) [very
11	FSW2:	[MANY. (.5) >many many many< (2.0)
12	P:	Oh very many (3.0) oh let's see (2.0) Ahhhhh (5.0)
13	FSW2:	Camera=
14	FSW1:	=Video (.)
15	P:	Video.
16	FSW1:	(.5) Video (.2) video (.2) children very cute (.) CUTE CUTE (.) all of them very handsome

What emerges as salient in the analysis of the naturally occurring data is that participants are able to use additional languages to perform various communicative functions necessary to complete work tasks. In the first interaction, one of the participants uses a vocabulary item in a local language, but gets a minimal response from the recipient. Given the pressure that the participants are under in this example they demonstrate exceptional ease of L2 use. In both examples, members of the same group assist each other in communication while working with people from other cultural backgrounds. They take turns and attempt to repair potential gaps in understanding while maintaining focus on the job at hand. The successful communication in these interactions revolves around work tasks. However, successful additional language use is also cultivated through rapport building and small talk as in the closing remarks of interaction two. The insight gained from these findings is important for service-learning practitioners so they can prepare students for community-based work in multilingual settings. Part of this preparation can include education about multilingualism, multicompetence, and the realities of modern-day global language use that may differ from what students learn and understand in potentially limiting monolingual L1 environments. One component of this education could incorporate comparing transcripts from authentic data captured in a study such as this with the perceptions about language use collected in data set two. This provides a contrast between perceptions and realities of L2 use in particular settings. Another important component of student preparation is educating students about the importance of small talk and managing a limited number of useful expressions for on-the-job tasks and social setting small-talk encounters.

◾ Results and Discussion

To complete the analysis I use an approach outlined in Lofland and Lofland (1995) as part of "working at" an open-ended analysis as it emerges from the data (p. 181). I then examined the field notes, interviews, and spoken data cumulatively in order to cross-reference similar themes. This is a means of triangulating the data to achieve what Lincoln and Guba (1985) term *credibility*. Results from the study provide an account of intercultural communication that confirms what is suggested about the myth of a standard English (Lippi-Green, 1997; Tollefson, 1999). Examining these data provided information about participants' attitudes and opinions regarding IC. This information provides cohesion with the other data sets in that the complexity of the multilingual environment inevitably leads to challenging communication. This fact is compounded when considered in tandem with physically and mentally demanding work-related tasks. A review of the questions is provided next.

The first research question about the purposes various languages serve in an international community-based project yielded several tentative answers when all data sources were considered cumulatively. Various languages are used by different individuals at different times depending on the task. Participants exercised agency in this multilingual community with either their bilingual or multilingual ability and evidence of this appears in all three data sets. Stated earlier, groups use an L1 when interacting within their own group. When working with members from multiple language backgrounds, multiple languages are required, but with varying degrees of competence and effective outcome. The American professor exercised agency by using Japanese to build rapport; English was used by the students to communicate about work topics and small talk while applying their agency. L1s can also be used for relationship building and developing trust. These are key elements for service-learning practitioners to take note of, because teaching students to display kindness in any language toward people from different ethnic and linguistic backgrounds will assist in completing important tasks for the benefit of others. It will also foster multicompetence.

Limited and contradictory information appears with respect to the second research question related to participants' opinions of the role of English as a standard for intercultural communication. At least two of the participants found other languages beneficial for intercultural communication. English-language ability is what some participants believe to be a determinant to success in interaction with people from other cultures. The field note and naturally occurring spoken data offer opposing indications of this.

The numerous communicative challenges listed in responses from data set two (survey/interviews) concerning difficulty in understanding accents, speed of talking, and unfamiliar languages contribute answering research to question number three concerning communication challenges. This provides a contrast to data set three, in which the problems for the participants in the first interaction were deciding which language to speak and who should actually ask questions about necessary construction materials. The combined data used to answer this question provided more new questions than answers. Should the study of context-specific languages such as Tagalog be a key issue? What do people need to know about code mixing/switching? Is it an important to discuss/educate students about the "failed native speaker" perspective? Do non-Western forms of communication need to be integrated into English foreign language curricula? How do we solve the communication challenges described in these interview responses?

One consistent finding that appears in all three data sets is the agency exercised by participants in the face of challenging communication. This point is critical for going beyond the failed native speaker frame of reference of L2 use that has influenced many L2 users. The data reflect that favorable outcomes in complex communication can be reached when L2 users interact with individuals with similar goals regardless of their language proficiency. Even modest results are possible when limited amounts of preparation are coupled with a good attitude.

■ Limitations and Implications

From an educator's orientation, more preparation is needed by participants and service-learning practitioners for a better understanding of how languages are used during community-based projects. Teachers and researchers have the responsibility to raise awareness of linguistic varieties and the discourses of power that are associated with political and cultural relationships often found in economics, history, and language. This includes teaching university students about Filipino and Japanese English, and about the linguistic rights of cultures that are in the process of identifying and constructing their own meaning. McGroarty (1996) writes about a related theme and states, "history, geography, and political and commercial relationships all help to determine appropriate choices and models for teaching" (p. 27). But the historical events that led to the perceived binary split between British and American English standards have been shadowed by other global events that have influenced the rapid increase in national and international varieties of English. It is wise to instruct students about the changes in English language use that will come in the future. Japanese English learners need to be aware of differences between how English is used in Japanese and how it is used in standard varieties. Students also need to know about the current situation of English in the world as well as having their awareness raised about world Englishes (Matsuda, 1998).

Furthermore, organizations responsible for bringing diverse groups of people together should evaluate the effectiveness of their written materials and training for communication and interaction. This suggestion is based directly on the observations made of how people in authority positions, regardless of what culture they are from, work for equal representation of their local languages. A reasonable presentation of useful expressions is needed by participants to complete work tasks and build meaningful relationships with people from other cultures.

To address some of the communicative challenges presented in this pilot study and to provide multilingual individuals with additional means to exercise agency, I argue that some of the guidelines for communicating effectively in Scollon and Scollon (1980) can benefit intercultural service-learning projects. They include listening until the other person is finished, allowing extra time, talking openly about communication, seeking help, and learning to expect and appreciate difference. Implementing these items into an educational program would require a structured amount of integration into an existing curriculum or it can be developed from a needs analysis.

It would be favorable to conduct similar studies in other contexts so that similar issues addressed in this pilot study could be explored. Supplementary studies of communicative interactions would allow a researcher to arrive at more complete understandings of the purposes and relationships between the participants involved. From a researcher's standpoint, I was not able to provide as wide an account of a critical research as I had hoped for in this study. Although conversation analysis is relevant from a methodological perspective, to be truly critical it must involve collecting judgments from research participants in a follow-up interview about the meaning of recorded utterances that would be elicited by playing tapes back to them. I did not perform this playback phase to my data collection. This would be one step toward developing the interdisciplinary approach advocated in Bremer, Roberts, Vasseur, Simonot, and Broeder (1996) that would allow the voices of the participants to come forth.

I have presented a unique account of intercultural communication in a community-based workplace that gives a clear understanding of the meaning of *bayanihan*. Providing future participants with a means to communicate more effectively during projects like the ones represented in this research would definitely be one goal of this chapter. This would allow them to go even further forward with their social cause regardless of the surrounding indifference. The students who wrote the song verse that opened this chapter have demonstrated that through their multilingualism and active social participation they are, in fact (although they believe the opposite to be true), powerful.

■ Appendix

Transcription Conventions

[	C2: quite a [while Mo: [yea	Left brackets indicate the point at which a current speaker's talk is overlapped by another's talk.
=	W: that I'm aware of = C: = Yes. Would you confirm that?	Equals signs, one at the end of a line and one at the beginning, indicate no gap between the two lines.
(0.4)	Yes (0.2) yeah	Numbers in parentheses indicate elapsed time in silence in tenths of a second.
(.)	to get (.) treatment	A dot in parentheses indicates a tiny gap, probably no more than one-tenth of a second
_	What's_up?	Underscoring indicates some form of stress, via pitch and/or amplitude.
::	O:kay?	Colons indicate prolongation of the immediately prior sound. The length of the row of colons indicates the length of the prolongation.
WORD	I'VE GOT ENOUGH TO WORRY ABOUT	Capitals except at the beginnings of lines, indicate especially loud sounds relative to the surrounding talk.
.hhh	I felt that (0.2) .hhh	A row of "h"s prefixed by a dot indicates an inbreath; without a dot, an outbreath. The length of the row of "h"s indicates the length of the inbreath or outbreath.

( )	future risks and ( ) and life ( )	Empty parentheses indicate the transcriber's inability to hear what was said.
(word)	Would you see (there) anything positive	Parenthesized words are possible hearings.
(( ))	confirm that ((continues))	Double parentheses contain author's descriptions rather than transcriptions.
.	That's that.	Indicates a stopping fall in tone
,	one, too,	Indicates a continuing intonation
><	>so that's it<	Shows talk that is noticeably faster than surrounding talk
?	What do you think?	Indicates a rising intonation

Adapted from: Silverman, 2001.

◾ References

Acquiring English-language skills. (2000, February 7). *The Daily Yomiuri* [Editorial], p. 6.

Blasco, M. (2003). *Stranger to us than the birds in our garden? Reflections on hermeneutics, intercultural understanding and the management of difference* (Working Paper No. 72). Frederiksberg, Denmark: Copenhagen Business School, Department of Intercultural Communication and Management.

Bourdieu, P. (1991). *Language and symbolic power.* Cambridge, U.K.: Polity Press.

Boyle-Baise, M. (2002). *Multicultural service learning: Educating teachers in diverse communities.* New York, NY: Teachers College Press.

Bremer, K., Roberts, C., Vasseur, M. T., Simonot, M., & Broeder, P. (1996). *Achieving understanding: Discourse in intercultural encounters.* London, U.K.: Longman.

Brown, J. D., & Rodgers, T. S. (2002). *Doing second language research.* Oxford, U.K.: Oxford University Press.

Chen, G., & Starosta, W. J. (1998). *Foundations of intercultural communication.* Needham Heights, MA: Allyn & Bacon.

Chuang, R. (2003). A postmodern critique of cross-cultural and intercultural communication research. In W. J. Starosta and G. M. Chen (Eds.), *Ferment in the intercultural field: Axiology/value/praxis* (pp. 24–56). Thousand Oaks, CA: Sage Publications.

Claus, J., & Ogden, C. (1999). *Service learning for youth empowerment and social change.* New York, NY: Peter Lang.

Cook, V. (1991). The poverty of the stimulus argument and multicompetence. *Second language research, 7*(2), 103–117.

Damon, L. (2003). Closing the language and culture gap: An intercultural-communication perspective. In D. L. Lange & R. M. Paige (Eds.), *Culture as the core* (pp. 71-88). Greenwich, CT: Information Age Publishing.

Eyler, J., & Giles, D. E., Jr. (1999). *Where's the learning in service-learning?* San Francisco, CA: Jossey-Bass.

Fishman, J. (1992). Sociology of English as an additional language. In B. Kachru (Ed.), *The other tongue: English across cultures* (pp. 19–26). Urbana, IL: University of Illinois Press.

Griffith, L. (2002). *English as a second language courses.* Mesa, AZ: Campus Compact National Center for Community Colleges.

Gudykunst, W. B. (2003). *Cross-cultural and intercultural communication.* Thousand Oaks, CA: Sage Publications.

Hammersley, M., & Atkinson, P. (1995). *Ethnography: Principles and practice.* New York, NY: Routledge.

Hara, M., & Corbin-Mullikin, L. (2002). *Service-learning and reading instruction.* Mesa, AZ: Campus Compact National Center for Community Colleges.

Heuser, L. (2000). Service-learning as a pedagogy to promote the content, cross-cultural, and language-learning of ESL students. *TESL Canada Journal, 17*, 1.

Hibler, K. (1997). Inter/cultural communication and the challenge of postcolonial theory. *The Edge: The E-Journal of Intercultural Relations, 1*(3). Retrieved October 6, 2006, from: www.interculturalrelations .com/v1i2Spring1998/sp98hibler.htm

Jandt, F. (1998). *Intercultural communication.* Thousand Oaks, CA: Sage Publications.

Kobayashi, G. (1998, November 2). Separating language from culture. *The Daily Yomiuri,* p. 14.

Kumaravadivelu, B. (2003). *Beyond methods: Macrostrategies for language teaching.* New Haven, CT: Yale University Press.

LeCompte, M., & Preissle, J. (1993). *Ethnography and qualitative design in educational research.* San Diego, CA: Academic Press.

Lincoln, Y. S., & Guba, E. G. (1985). *Naturalistic inquiry.* Beverly Hills, CA: Sage Publications.

Lippi-Green, R. (1997). *English with an accent: Language, ideology, and discrimination in the United States.* New York, NY: Routledge.

Lofland, J., & Lofland, L. H. (1995). *Analyzing social settings: A guide to qualitative data.* London, U.K.: Wadsworth.

Matsuda, A. (1998, March). *World Englishes in English textbooks in Japan.* Paper presented at the 32nd Annual TESOL Convention, Seattle, WA.

McArthur, T. (1998). *Living words: Language, lexicography and the knowledge revolution.* Exeter, U.K.: University of Exeter Press.

McGroarty. M. (1996). Language attitudes, motivations, and standards. In S. L. McKay & N. H. Hornberger (Eds.), *Sociolinguistics and language teaching* (pp. 3–46). Cambridge, U.K.: Cambridge University Press.

McKay, S., & Wong, S. (1996). Multiple discourses, multiple identities: Investment and agency in second-language learning among Chinese adolescent immigrant students. *Harvard Educational Review 66*(3), 577–603.

Minor, J. L. (2001). *Using service-learning as part of an ESL program.* Retrieved October 6, 2006, from: http://iteslj.org/Techniques/ Minor-ServiceLearning.html

Minor, J. L. (2002). Incorporating service learning into ESOL programs. *TESOL Journal, 11*(4), 10–14.

Nakayama, T. K., & Martin, J. N. (1999). *Whiteness: The communication of social identity.* Thousand Oaks, CA: Sage Publications.

Norton Peirce, B. (1995). Social identity, investment, and language learning. *TESOL Quarterly, 29*(1), 9–31.

O'Grady, C. R. (2000). Integrating service learning and multicultural education: An overview. In C. R. O'Grady (Ed.), *Integrating service learning and multicultural education in colleges and universities* (pp. 1–19). Mahwah, NJ: Lawrence Erlbaum Associates.

Orbe, M. P. (1998). *Constructing co-cultural theory: An explication of culture, power, and communication.* Thousand Oaks, CA: Sage Publications.

Pavlenko, A. (2002). Poststructuralist approaches to the study of social factors in second language learning and use. In V. Cook (Ed.), *Portraits of the L2 user* (pp. 275–302). Clevedon, U.K.: Multilingual Matters.

Pennycook, A. (2001). *Critical applied linguistics: A critical introduction.* Mahwah, NJ: Lawrence Erlbaum Associates.

Porter, R. E., & Samovar, L. A. (1991). Basic principles of intercultural communication. In L. A. Samovar & R. E. Porter (Eds.), *Intercultural communication: A reader* (6th ed., pp. 5–21). Belmont, CA: Wadsworth Inc.

Rhoads, R. A. (1997). *Community service and higher learning: Explorations of the caring self.* Albany, NY: State University of New York Press.

Rodriguez, A. (2002, April). Culture to culturing: Re-imaging our understanding of intercultural relations. *Journal of Intercultural Communication, 5.* Retrieved October 6, 2006, from: www.immi.se/intercultural

Scheiffelin, D., & Ochs, E. (1986). Language and socialization. *Annual Review of Anthropology, 15,* 163–191.

Scollon R., & Scollon, B. (1980). *Interethnic communication.* Fairbanks, AK: Alaskan Native Language Center.

Silverman, D. (2001). *Interpreting qualitative data: Methods for analysing talk, text, and interaction.* Thousand Oaks, CA: Sage Publications.

Sridhar, K. (1996). Societal multilingualism. In S. L. McKay & N. H. Hornberger (Eds.), *Sociolinguistics and language teaching* (pp. 47–70). Cambridge, U.K.: Cambridge University Press.

Stanton, T. K., Giles, D. E., Jr., & Cruz, N. I. (1999). *Service-learning: A movement's pioneers reflect on its origins, practice, and future.* San Francisco, CA: Jossey-Bass.

Sugiyama, C. (1997, August 4). English in all its varieties. *The Daily Yomiuri,* p. 15.

ten Have, P. (1999). *Doing conversation analysis.* Thousand Oaks, CA: Sage Publications.

Titscher, S., Meyer, M., Wodak, R., & Vetter, R. (2000). *Methods of text and discourse analysis* (B. Jenner, Trans.). London, U.K.: Sage Publications.

Tollefson, J. (1999, October). *Language ideology and language education.* Paper presented at the Fourth International Conference on Language and Development, Hanoi, Vietnam.

Wade, R. C. (1997). *Community service-learning: A guide to including service in the public school curriculum.* Albany, NY: State University of New York Press.

Weedon, C. (1987). *Feminist practice and poststructuralist theory.* New York, NY: Basil Blackwell.

Widdowson, H. (1994). The ownership of English. *TESOL Quarterly, 28*(2), 377–388.

Section IV

Service-Learning Research Reports

The call for carefully designed research studies in service-learning has been raised repeatedly over the last decade by experts in the field who believe that documenting student-learning outcomes is essential to ensure broader acceptance for service-learning among educational and political leaders (Eyler & Giles, 1999; Gelmon, Furco, Holland, & Bringle, 2005; Zlotkowski, 1996). Despite this concerted effort to improve the state of service-learning research, most published studies are limited in scope and design. A recent meta-analysis of research on service-learning in English studies found, for example, that while 90% of the articles reviewed included critical analysis of practice and course or program description, the majority (54%) did not use empirical research methods to support their claims (Bacon, Deans, Dubinsky, Roswell, & Wurr, 2005).

Together with the other empirically based research studies included in this anthology, the chapters in this section help document some of the research findings from the field. Given the challenges inherent in service-learning research, these studies, while still limited to the boundaries of a single course or program, are commendable in their efforts to document the impact of service-learning on students, faculty, and community partners in carefully

293

designed studies that move beyond anecdote and teacher testimony to empirical, classroom-based research.

In Chapter 12 Gresilda Tilley-Lubbs draws on two and a half years of ethnographic research to document the emerging relationships between Spanish university students and members of the Latino community in southwest Virginia as they cross socially constructed boundaries of ethnic groups, educational levels, and socioeconomic status. Through numerous observations, interviews, and reflection papers, the author concluded that both groups benefited from their service-learning partnership in enhanced understanding of and appreciation for diversity in second language acquisition and learning, and in building cross-cultural friendships.

In Chapter 13 Mary C. Hutchinson grounds her study in a college composition course. Working with basic writers on research projects involving service-learning, and using pre- and post-course surveys, written assignments, and progress reports as data sources, she corroborates the findings of earlier research by Deans and Meyers-Goncalves (1998) in noting how, "for the first time, students realize that reading and writing are more than a packet of skills. They come to see literacy not only as a way of succeeding in the academy, but as acting in the world" (p. 15). While noting that the results were not uniformly positive, Hutchinson concludes that overall the service-learning experience not only had a positive impact on the development of the students' writing skills, but also helped them to change their own perceptions of the community and their abilities as writers in an academic environment.

In Chapter 15 Fu-An Lin investigates the effectiveness of a TESOL teacher training program with a service-learning component. Allowing findings to emerge from her data, and then confirming inferences through triangulation, Lin notes how language awareness and advocacy issues surface along the blurry boundary defining native and nonnative speakers of English, as most of the teacher trainers were international students and the service recipients immigrants. Yet Lin concludes the program's success and ultimate sustainability rests in large measure on the teacher trainer's professional dedication and enthusiasm for the teaching experience offered through service-learning, as well as the support from the university.

In Chapter 15 Erin Whittig and Aileen Hale examine an ESL-designated section of first-year composition where service-learning was the primary pedagogy. Using qualitative research and case studies to foreground their students' voices, and student writing and interviews as data sources, the authors find affective outcomes including increased self-confidence and awareness of ability to contribute as significant results of ESL students' involvement in service-learning projects. Adding a new wrinkle to the blurry NS/NNS boundary, the authors describe the "varying degrees of refugee status" that apply to one student as he more fully assimilates into American society.

In Chapter 16 Robin Glenn Walker considers how immigrants assimilate into mainstream American society and focuses in particular on a group of older Montagnard, Russian, and Vietnamese immigrants in the Southeast. In her roles as teacher-researcher and cultural mediator, Walker conducts an ethnographic study using qualitative assessment as a methodology to blend classroom observation, interviews in the local language community, and intergenerational dialogue into her study. Highlighting how the professional identities of elderly immigrants as well as the teacher's affect their perceptions of a casual conversation class, Walker finds that understanding the students' perceptions of their identities is necessary to an effective and equitable classroom where older adults feel connected to their learning.

■ References

Bacon, N., Deans, T., Dubinsky, J., Roswell, B., & Wurr, A. (2005). *Community-based and service-learning writing initiatives: A survey of scholarship and agenda for research.* Unpublished CCCC research report prepared for the National Council of Teachers of English.

Deans, T., & Meyers-Goncalves, Z. (1998). Service-learning projects in composition and beyond. *College Teaching, 46,* 12–15.

Eyler, J., & Giles, D. E., Jr. (1999). *Where's the learning in service-learning?* San Francisco, CA: Jossey-Bass.

Gelmon, S., Furco, A., Holland, B., & Bringle, R. (2005, November). *Beyond anecdote: Further challenges in bringing rigor to service-learning research.* Paper presented at the 5th Annual International Conference on Service-Learning Research, East Lansing, MI.

Zlotkowski, E. (1996, January/February). Linking service-learning and the academy: A new voice at the table? *Change, 28*(1), 20–27.

12

The Intersection of the Academy and the Community: Researching Relationships Through Community-Based Education

Gresilda Tilley-Lubbs

As this semester is winding down, and I will be moving to Chapel Hill in May, I am unsure if I will see Berta[1] again, however, I am going to keep calling and calling until she finally answers ☺. But I will always know that we did, and in my mind still do have, a wonderful bond, that crossed cultural barriers and differing circumstances. One of my expectations from my first reflections, is definitely pertinent in this situation, and has definitely come true, "My greatest expectation is to come out of this experience learning first hand through a cross-cultural *indefinable* relationship, *that although our circumstances may be different,* the inherent human spirit rises above all cultural borders." (Jane, Transformation Paper, May 5, 2003)[2]

Jane's words are typical of those that I encounter each semester in the final transformation papers written by students attempting to sum up their semester-long journeys in Crossing the Border Through Service-Learning, a course that partners university students with a Latino family in the local community for the purpose of exchanging language and culture. In this paper I share the findings of a qualitative study whose overarching objective was to examine the nexus of the relationships that emerged between the students and Latino families paired through this service-learning course, which was situated in a Department of Foreign Languages and Literatures at Virginia Polytechnic Institute and State University (Virginia Tech). The relationships crossed socially constructed boundaries of ethnic groups, language, educational levels, and socioeconomic status, exploring the intersection of community service, scholarship, and teaching-and-learning. The initial pilot study sought to investigate linguistic gain and deepened cultural knowledge as students spent their required 50 hours per semester in the partner homes. However, the emergent data presented findings that indicated changes of perspective in both the students and the families with resultant reciprocal relationships previously suspected but not documented.

The time frame for the entire study as presented encompasses a period of two and a half years, but the narrative begins with my initial immersion in the Latino community in July 1999, and traces the final intensive data collection period with the resultant analysis and presentation of findings in August 2003. In this narrative, I first present the history and development of the course, which provided the context and participants for the study. Next, I describe the methodology that guided the qualitative research. Then I present the findings that emerged from the study, followed by the summary and discussion. Although the nature of qualitative research does not lend itself easily to generalizations, I hope to provide information that will help the reader to make an informed decision about the efficacy of incorporating service-learning as part of a Spanish curriculum.

▪ Background

In summer 1999 my journey into service-learning began when I received a phone call from the Roanoke Office for Refugees and Immigration asking me to interpret for young Mexican and Honduran female clients at the Prenatal and the Family Planning Clinics at the health department. I'd be a substitute for the regular interpreter who was on vacation. Contrary to what I had expected, the "clinics" were times in the day when only women with specific needs were seen, and the "Hispanic clinic" simply referred to a time within that framework when a Latina was scheduled, whether for prenatal care or family planning. There were few Latinas so they were included with other English-speaking women; consequently, I spent countless hours in the waiting room with the women and their children, forging friendships that continue to this day.

For many of the women, I was their only personal contact with the Anglo world. I routinely began to hand them my business card, so they could call me for help in navigating the baffling culture in which they found themselves living. By fall 2000, I was overwhelmed as my hours at the Health Department increased while at the same time I continued teaching full-time at the university and pursuing doctoral studies.

I mentioned to my department head in Foreign Languages and Literatures that I wished my Spanish students could be in the community with the Latinos, not only for the benefit of the Latinos, but also for the benefit of the students who would be able to learn more about Latino culture as they practiced their Spanish. She suggested that I design a course that would provide the opportunity for the students and Latino families to interact, and from there emerged the course, Crossing the Border Through Service-Learning (CTB).

As I developed the course, the director of the service-learning center (SLC) provided invaluable guidance and information, helping me understand the concept of service-learning as opposed to community service, which provides opportunities for people to perform a service in the community, such as working on a Habitat for Humanity house or serving in a soup kitchen. However, service-learning combines community action, academic knowledge, and reflection, the precepts upon which I developed the course.

The university approved the course, and the first class became a reality in spring 2001. The justification for the course was to provide an immersion experience in the Latino community, giving students the opportunity to interact in a personal way with members of the community, thereby enriching their understanding of the culture and the language. Although the class was primarily designed for Spanish majors and minors, a variety of other students enrolled in the class, citing "wanting to know more about Hispanics" or wanting to "help the less fortunate" as primary reasons for their interest in the class.

The class represented the intersection of academia, community, and teaching-learning. Students read the literature dealing with issues of service-learning, Latino immigration, and social justice. They visited with their partner families twice a week, during which times they taught ESL, tutored and mentored the children in the families, helped with transportation to and interpretation at medical and social service appointments, translated documents, made phone calls, and served as cultural mediators as needed. Many of the students found themselves supporting their families in situations as diverse as negotiating rental contracts or registering children for the Salvation Army Christmas gift program.

Each week the students posted a journal reflection to Blackboard, the online school portal at Virginia Tech, relating the readings for the week to the experiences and conversations they were having with their families. At the end of the semester, they wrote a transformation paper to reflect on the journeys they had made during the semester, revisiting their expectations at the beginning of the course and examining whether their perspectives and perceptions had changed during the semester as they read the literature, participated in class discussions, and partnered with Latino families in the community.

■ The Study

From the first class in spring 2001 until the end of the third class in spring 2002, I collected and analyzed data, seeking evidence of linguistic acquisition and cultural knowledge. However, the data that emerged from this initial pilot study led me to believe that the true importance of the study lay in the relationships described by both students and community participants. Therefore, I designed a research project that would examine the relationships that occurred within the boundaries of a service-learning course that linked Spanish university students with the Latino community, highlighting the formation and development of the relationship between these two disparate groups.

The nature of this research necessitated the use of qualitative research methods. In conducting this study, my objective was to understand the meaning participants constructed of their interactions. True to qualitative research, I present the findings in a narrative format relying heavily on description, stories, and citations from the participants.

Theoretical Framework

This study is informed by critical theory, service-learning pedagogy, and sociocultural theory, all of which provide a background for investigating the research question. Critical theory was defined by the Frankfurt School in the 1920s as scholars generated theory and practice grounded in the understanding of contemporary social and political issues with a resulting unification of theory and praxis, or self-creating action informed by theoretical considerations (Jay, 1996). Building on this foundation, I have chosen to challenge societal hierarchical limits imposed by class, ethnicity, language, and education, applying expanded connections of ideas that transcend social codes in an attempt to analyze a setting in which diverse people can regard their commonalities as well as learn to appreciate their differences.

Critical theory also informs critical pedagogy as transformative education (Freire, 1970). Freire's precept that dialogue, or interaction with the world, and praxis, referring to the acts that shape and change the world, are fundamental aspects of education involving the learners as stakeholders in the formation of curriculum. Dewey's (1897/1997) belief in experiential education also challenges traditional university educational practices regarding the community as central in providing the pragmatic element in education, one of the tenets of service-learning.

Service-learning pedagogy (Giles & Eyler, 1998; Sigmon, 1979; Stanton, Giles, & Cruz, 1999) also provided a framework for the study. Service-learning places together people whose paths might never have crossed, allowing for the possibility of genuine dialogue that Freire defines as the indivisible solidarity between humans and their world (Crotty, 1998). Such dialogue crosses societal barriers, allowing humans to regard one another as people who share common interests and concerns. Normally, middle-class students who attend university tend to mingle with others whose ethnic group, language, educational level, socioeconomic status, religion, and academic level are similar to their own (Harro, 2000). In this case, I sought to examine the relationships that developed between middle-class university students and recent immigrants, similar to the work done by Jorge (2004) and Olazagasti-Segovia (2004), both of whose work positioned students and families in a similar fashion. By placing middle-class students in the homes of Latino immigrants, the possibilities exist for nurturing an appreciation of the funds of knowledge that all people bring to their relationships (Greenberg & Moll, 1990).

Sociocultural theory framed the study as well. Strategies including apprenticeship (Rogoff, 1990) and scaffolding (Vygotsky, 1978) provided a means of examining the relationships as the students and community members interacted and learned from/with each other. Sociocultural approaches to language learning (Krashen, 1982; Shrum & Glisan, 2000) and cultural mediation (Wertsch, 1991) presented a lens to examine language acquisition and cultural knowledge in the study, which, based on the pilot study, seemed to play a role in shaping the reciprocal relationships.

Methodology

Research Design

As stated earlier, the overarching question that shaped the study sought to understand the formation and development of the relationships between these two disparate groups. I wanted to investigate the expectations of each person involved in the relationship and how these changed over the course of the semester. I wanted to examine the salient issues that factor into a mutually beneficial relationship between students and community families, and lastly, I wanted to confirm the role the service-learning course played in the development of that relationship.

An appropriate qualitative methodology for this study was a case study using ethnographic data collecting techniques, relying on the examination of a single subject or event (Merriam, 1998) to focus on a particular culture through an "intensive, holistic description and analysis of a single unit or bounded system" (p. 12). Creswell (1998) expands this definition by stating that this system "is bounded by time and place" (p. 61).

This case study examines the meeting of two disparate cultural communities: university students and Latino community members. In using the case study method to examine the nexus of the relationship of these groups who interacted within the bounds of a service-learning class, this microsocial order (Sjoberg, Williams, Vaughan, & Sjoberg, 1991, p. 26) could be viewed in rich detail. The setting of the service-learning course presented the opportunity to observe the interactions of the students and the families by means of studying the written materials, the interviews, and the discussions generated by the participants.

The social situation of the project had three components: the place, the actors, and the activities (Ary, Jacobs, & Razavich, 1996). The service-learning program itself was the place. The participants in the case studies were the actors functioning within the integrated system (Stake, 1995) of the service-learning program. The activities were the interactions among the students and the community participants as generated in the data.

Data Collection

I spent one and a half years as an interpreter/participatory member in the Latino community prior to beginning the research study. I collected data for this study for two additional years, examining the backgrounds of the participants, their perspectives toward their partners, and the role of service-learning in the development of relationships between these two disparate groups. I conducted 46 formal, taped, transcribed interviews with students and community members. I interviewed each student during the first two weeks of class to establish background, but I depended on documents generated through the class to collect additional information relating to the research questions. I interviewed the community participants during the first three weeks of class, then again in the middle of the semester, and a final time after the semester ended. Between January 2001 and December 2002, I collected over 2,500 reflection papers, 100 transformation papers, and 25 PowerPoint presentations from students; approximately 25% of these documents represented the semester when I also conducted the interviews. During the four semesters, I wrote up field notes in a journal, reflecting on the data collected through informal conversations and classes. To triangulate data collected through interviews with the Latino community members, I also referred to journals in which I had kept field notes for a previous study, conducted during the first year and a half I spent immersed in the community as an interpreter (Tilley-Lubbs, 2000).

Due to the time I had spent in the community prior to the commencement of data collection, entry into the community was not an issue. Because I had been to the homes of these young Latina women countless times, I was familiar with the actual community geographically and socially. In addition, since they had all faced pregnancy and motherhood far from their close-knit families who would have provided support and advice throughout the process, they had turned to me as a mother figure who filled in for their own distant mothers. Also, my family and I had attended baptisms and birthday parties, so I was already part of the community, albeit as an outsider/insider, since no amount of contact and time spent in the community could change the fact that I am a white, middle-class, middle-aged university professor whose ethnicity, socioeconomic class, and educational status more closely resembled the students than the Latinos; my age was vastly different from that of any of the participants.

Throughout the study, my role changed to fit the time and place, ranging from spectator to collaborative partner (Merriam, 1998). At times, I sat on the sidelines and observed the action; for example when attending birthday parties, I tend to sit and observe, much as I do when in large group settings of any kind for which I have no responsibility. At other times, I was part of the action as a participant, such as when I served as interpreter at clinic appointments or met with the class and the community members for our biweekly meetings. Often, I was a collaborative partner with the students or community partners as we discussed and planned the research. At all times, I checked my interpretations of the data with the participants, using member checking as a means of triangulating data (Merriam, 1998).

Data Analysis

What had begun as a hunch during the course's first three semesters was confirmed as I systematically analyzed the data I collected through interviews, documents, and field notes in fall 2002. Bogdan and Biklen (1998) define data analysis as "the process of systematically searching and arranging the interview transcripts, field notes, and other materials that you accumulate to increase your own understanding of them and to enable you to present what you have discovered to others" (p. 157), which accurately describes the process of my data analysis.

Following Merriam's (1998) advice about conveying an understanding of the analysis of data in case studies, I was searching for patterns or significance through direct interpretation. I was trying to find consistency within certain conditions, and trying to understand behavior, issues, and contexts. I reviewed the data constantly and repeatedly, reflecting and looking for triangulation.

I interpreted the data by generalizing patterns in the descriptive data gathered from the students and the families (Erickson, 1986). Uttech (1999) refers to this analytic procedure as seeking to "find emerging themes, patterns, or concepts that cut across the data. This step facilitates the procedure of uncovering the relationships among the themes winnowed" (p. 96). These units of data, or bits of information, were organized into categories. Each category reflected the purpose of the research. Uttech (1999) says the emerging patterns and relationships must be comprehensive, and "because they stem directly from data, they become grounded" (p. 95).

Description of the Setting and the Participants

This research was primarily conducted in two locations: a classroom at Virginia Tech, a Research I university situated in Blacksburg, a medium-sized town of some 40,000 permanent inhabitants, located in the Blue Ridge Mountains in southwest Virginia, and in the homes of the certain Latino families now living in the Roanoke Valley, a medium-sized metropolitan area also located in the mountains. Virginia Tech was comprised of approximately 25,000 undergraduate and 4,000 graduate students at the time this study was conducted. The Roanoke Valley encompasses Roanoke City and the surrounding area for a total of about 200,000 inhabitants. Due to the fact it is the largest city in southwest Virginia, Roanoke serves as a commercial hub, making it seem larger than its size would indicate. It is situated approximately 40 miles from Blacksburg, but because of the mountains, the trip from Tech to Roanoke takes close to an hour, a fact that automatically eliminates students not intensely interested in an immersion experience.

The students have represented a number of regions, states, and countries, but they have been primarily from the mid-Atlantic region of the United States, with the majority Virginia residents. In spring 2003, the semester of intense data collection, there were 17 students, all native speakers of English. Although one student was Indonesian-American, her first language was still English. The students also represented a variety of levels of Spanish language proficiency, ranging from novice-low through intermediate-low to mid based on the Proficiency Guidelines developed by the American Council on the Teaching of Foreign Languages (ACTFL). The majority hovered between novice-high and intermediate-low.[3]

Their educational levels varied only in that some were undergraduates, ranging from freshmen through seniors, and others were graduate students pursuing a master's degree. The university students who participated in the study represented some disparity, but still all were members of a privileged class as can be evidenced by their attendance at the university.

Although all the community participants are referred to as Latinos for the purpose of this study, in fact they classified themselves as either Mexican or Honduran. Despite shared commonalities, the Mexicans and Hondurans perceived themselves as differing significantly from each other. Some spoke Spanish as a second language, having first spoken an indigenous language. The Latinos were still learning the basics of communicating in English, and had it been possible to formally assess their English skills using a measurement similar to the ACTFL (1998) Oral Proficiency Guidelines, I suspect they would have all placed at the novice-low range, with the exception of two Hondurans, one who might have placed at the novice-mid range, and another whose spoken English probably would have been novice-high.

The Latinos represented a variety of educational levels, ranging from those who had graduated from high school, to others from la prepa, preparing them to work as teachers, social workers, secretaries, etc. Others had quit school following ninth or tenth grade, either due to economic necessity or lack of interest; in their home countries, they were able to work as receptionists or in other types of office work. Among these participants, completion of sixth or ninth grade was typical for those who were unable to finish high school. Those who completed sixth grade often worked as sales clerks or restaurant workers in the home country. One woman had been a maquiladora, or factory worker, in a border town prior to immigrating. Some of the Latinos had completed second grade, and performed jobs commensurate with the lack of education.

In their home countries, the Latinos had represented a slightly more varied group, but here in the United States they all worked at jobs that depended on physical labor, whether in factories, meat-packing plants, bakeries, or restaurants, to name a few of their occupations. They all lived in marginalized conditions as members of the low socioeconomic class. Despite the fact that they lived in conditions that were considerably different from those of the students, they all considered their economic situations here in this country superior to the ones they left in their native countries.

■ Findings

The salient emergent theme was that reciprocal relationships developed between the students and the families who participated in the course. The data demonstrated that both students and Latino community members developed an appreciation for and understanding of diversity, resulting in an exchange of linguistic and cultural knowledge situated in cross-cultural friendships. The

students began to position themselves in solidarity against perceived injustices toward their Latino partner families. The course
emerged as a catalyst for linking the academy to the community
in a way that made the appreciation of diversity a lived experience
rather than a studied theory.

Formation and Development of Relationships: Reasons and Expectations for Participation in Crossing the Border

In the interviews and the documents, the students talked at length
about their motives for participating in the program. In their early
reflections, they talked about "becoming more fluent in Spanish" and "helping the less fortunate." Many of the students were
motivated by the desire to help Latino immigrants adapt to an
English-speaking society and new environment. By the final transformation papers, however, they wrote about how much they had
learned from their families; many expressed a belief that they had
learned far more from their families than their families had learned
from them. For the most part, they had ceased to speak of "helping
them" and "volunteering." They had reached an understanding of
the possibilities inherent in collaboration as opposed to charitable
acts. The underlying attitude changed from one of "othering" to
one of friendship and relationship:

> They will continue to be my amigos for a long time, and in
> some cases "mi familia." As Isaias told me the other night
> "Te quiero como si fueras mi hermano" [I love you like
> a brother]. (Mike, Transformation Paper, December 1,
> 2003)

Bill said even more eloquently:

> Often there isn't proper social justification for behaving in
> ways that we want to behave. Our class *Crossing the Bor-
> der* is a perfect example. It has allowed complete strangers

with common interests to justify opening their homes and hearts to each other. The beauty of this class is that it takes advantage of this subtle social force and uses it to bring people closer together, to open themselves and offer themselves in a way that without its "social justification" would be awkward or impossible. (Transformation Paper, December 17, 2002)

Similarly, in the first interviews conducted with the families, the Latinas expressed a desire to learn English and to have help in navigating society. In the final interviews, however, they spoke of the friendships they had developed and the ways they had been able to help the students with learning Spanish; they were also proud at having been able to share their culture with the students. Both groups spoke of the exchange of information, language, and life experiences while developing a personal, reciprocal relationship. To quote Isabel, one of the women who participated the first semester, and who is still with us in the tenth semester of the program:

Yo quiero participar porque eh, uno, quiere tratar de entender mucho el inglés. A mí me gusta, pero yo creo no tengo mucha comunicación con personas que lo hablan y por eso no logro entenderlo bien pero, eh, esa es una y otra porque encuentra uno mucha amistad, muchos ami-gos, este, eh, invitación, o sea, son muchas cosas mezcladas entonces, sí, sí me gustaría, sí me gustaría y sí con esto pues ayudo a las demás personas pues mejor, mucho mejor.

Translation:
I want to participate because, well, you try to understand a lot of English. I like it, but I think I don't have much communication with people who speak it and so I don't manage to understand it very well. But that's one [reason],

and another is that you find so much friendship, many friends, this, uhm, invitation, that is, it's a lot of things mixed together, then yes, I would like to [participate] and if by doing so then I can help other people, well, that's better, much better. (I. García, personal communication, January 15, 2003)

And echoing Isabel's statement, John sums up his feelings about teaching English:

In crossing the border through Service Learning, we do more than just teach English, we try to provide the Latino community with the tools to operate within an English-dominated society. In working together, we realize it is more than just helping the families, but rather it is a mutually beneficial relationship. (J. Worland, public speech, May 5, 2003)

Appreciation for and Understanding of Diversity

Both groups exhibited an appreciation for and understanding of diversity in terms of exchanging linguistic and cultural knowledge and forming cross-cultural friendships.

Mark says:

I have gained an appreciation and understanding of so many different ways of thinking and living, and I haven even uncovered a new fascination with how a world so different can be so much alike. (Transformation Paper, December 17, 2002)

John, who continually referred to the crossing of barriers and the tearing down of walls between people, said:

Things started slowly. It was hard to see the common ground between our two worlds. Language and age difference stood like a wall between us. I had never taught English before. I was somewhat overwhelmed trying to teach in a way that was comfortable and not a burden for them. After a few sessions their openness and sense of humor relaxed the atmosphere. Communication began to flow between us, creating gaps in the wall. Light shone through the wall of us and them, illuminating submerged truths of commonality. . . . I enjoyed looking at my world through another's eyes. . . Most importantly I learned that language and societal labels are only obstacles between people and not fundamental. (J. Worland, public speech, May 5, 2003)

Throughout the course students and families alluded to their discovery of commonalities, whereas before they had concentrated on differences.

Language Acquisition

In their comments about language acquisition, the participants described high motivation coupled with lower anxiety, reminiscent of Krashen's (1982, 2005) theory that meaningful interaction leading to natural communication in low-anxiety situations with native speakers results in increased comprehensible input. The students referred to the power of using language in vital life experiences, rather than in a classroom, in essence affirming that contextualized language learning became automatic and reciprocal (Shrum & Glisan, 2000). Similarly the Latinos spoke of lowered anxiety when speaking with students who were struggling to learn Spanish, and both groups spoke of working together, describing collaborative apprenticeships that led to natural learning at the side of an experienced expert (Rogoff, 1990). Being involved in reciprocal language learning also allowed the learners to be in control of their learning as they mediated and provided tools and signs for each other, echoing Wertsch's (1991) theory of mediated learning. Being involved in service-learning in a grassroots project gave language learning a meaningfulness not possible in the sterile atmosphere of the classroom, similar to the experience of Mullaney's (1999) students who participated in a similar service-learning class.

Karen articulates her feelings:

> Like most of the other students, I too was nervous upon first meeting my family. I wasn't too sure of what to expect. Most of all, I was worried about how the communication would be and if my Spanish was good enough. Also, I was worried about what my family would think of me and how they would feel about me since I wasn't too confident about my Spanish abilities. . . . Upon meeting my family, all my communication worries went away as we just started conversing. From then, I became very excited to start working. (K. Rogers, public speech, May 5, 2003)

Karen's feelings are representative of the lower anxiety and the contextualized use of language that many students echoed.

Similarly, the Latinos commented on learning English from the students. In this instance, Isabel is positioning herself as Kathy's teacher of how to teach English, commenting on Kathy's inexperience as a teacher, recalling both Rogoff's (1990) theory of apprenticeship and Vygotsky's theory regarding the efficacy of scaffolding in which the experienced peer coaches the less experienced peer in the learning process:

> Kathy no tiene todavía una idea de cómo enseñarme y yo la entiendo porque ella nunca ha enseñado y entonces yo más o menos le explico mis necesidades y ella me enseña pero me ha ayudado bastante incluso con los biles, bueno

es una latera con esos biles y me han ayudado mucho también en eso. Ellas hablan con usted y ya usted las guía como debemos hacer las cosas, pero si yo les estoy agradecida, porque me ha ayudado mucho.

Translation:
Kathy still has no idea how to teach me and I understand because she has never taught and then I more or less explain my needs to her and she teaches me, but she has helped me enough even with the bills; she is a friend with the bills and she has helped me a lot with them. They talk to you and you guide them about how to do things, but I am grateful to them, because they have helped me a lot. (personal communication, October 31, 2002)

The interesting aspect of Isabel's comment is her description of how she takes ownership for her learning, guiding Kathy to teach her what she needs to know.

Cross-Cultural Friendships and the Role of the Service-Learning Class

Both groups of participants moved into a sense of mutual friendship, with varying degrees of closeness. The relationships resulted from an artificially contrived placement at the beginning of the semester; as the instructor, I arbitrarily placed students in the Latino community, basing the choices on my knowledge of the participants' needs, personalities, and schedules. Out of these serendipitous placements, relationships grew, some casual and others seemingly deep, and very few resulting in unsuccessful pairings.

At the beginning of the semester, the students saw themselves as teachers working with students, mirroring the Latinas' perceptions about CTB. Although the Latinas spoke of helping the students with their language, and sharing their culture, most regarded the students as the teachers and themselves as the students at the beginning of the semester. However, by the end of the semester, both the Latinas and the students realized how much the community members had to offer the students, and they spoke of each other as "teachers." Karen expresses her feelings about spending time with Esmeralda:

> My relationship with my family has changed through out each visit. At first, everything was "structured"—I came to "teach" and we would start right away. However as we got to know each other better, things changed and we became more like friends. The teacher/student role not only reversed many times, but began to dissolve and we just became friends helping each other out and having a good time. (K. Rogers, public speech, May 5, 2003)

Depending on the circumstances, the roles reversed, and the teachers and learners were indistinguishable, expressing reciprocity. The students and Latino families spoke consistently of the reciprocal relationships they had developed over the course of the semester, and of the fact they would never have known each other without benefit of the class.

Standing in Solidarity

As an example of the solidarity the students frequently wrote about, Kathy acted as an interpreter at a parent-teacher conference at an elementary school. In writing about the experience, Kathy expressed frustration at the way the teacher described Janeth, the second-grade student with whom she worked, as having a learning disability, perhaps the result of the language barrier. Kathy states, "I think she does not understand what a BARRIER a language 'barrier' can really be" (Reflection 11, November 11, 2002). Continuing, Kathy expressed her feelings about the teacher's attitude toward Janeth's mother: "I was frustrated and hyper aware of the way this woman looked at and spoke to Isabel [the mother]. It is just that I do not understand why [I was] given more respect than she. In the perspective of the teacher, I think, she sees this business of dealing with other cultures and languages a hassle that was not in her planning book when she applied for the job" (Reflection 11, November 11, 2002). Throughout this journal, Kathy positions herself in solidarity with her friend Isabel, who is suffering discrimination from a member of Kathy's own culture.

Another student, Liz, partnered with a pregnant Honduran woman who had been diagnosed with gestational diabetes. Due to her inability to communicate, María did not understand how to check her blood with a glucometer, nor did she understand how to obtain the necessary strips to do the testing. Most confusing of all was the diet the nurses gave her to follow. Liz stepped in as her advocate and located a source for getting the strips free of charge. She also helped María make sense of the diet information. Her loyalty to María continued when the baby was born and Liz went to the hospital to take the new mother and baby home since María's husband could not leave work. Liz's anger and articulateness helped her to advocate for María's rights as a prenatal patient when María's language skills did not allow her voice to be heard.

Experiencing the End of the Semester

Many of the students spoke of the sadness they felt at ending the semester, realizing that with their hectic schedules it would be difficult to maintain the close relationships they had enjoyed during the semester. Some students developed close, ongoing relationships with their families; others enjoyed the experience for a semester, but had no intention of continuing the relationship beyond the confines of that period. There have been occasional placements that have not been successful, and students have had to change to another family. The reasons have included changes in work schedules and incompatibility or differences in expectations, but for the most part the relationships have been successful, some to a greater and some to a lesser degree.

The transitory nature of the relationships was especially trou-
blesome to some of the Latinas. In the final interview, it became
apparent that some students were accustomed to experiencing
short-term relationships while Latino culture places more value
on lasting relationships that may persist for a lifetime. Becoming
cognizant of this information has caused me to make changes in
the way the course is presented; from the beginning, I make both
groups of participants aware of the nature of the course and the
resultant relationships, which seems to have resolved some of the
issues related to the end of the semester.

The power of the course lies in the cross-cultural experiences
that involve both majority and minority students in the Latino
community. Through experiential education as espoused by Dewey
(1897/1997), students are able to put into practice the theory they
learn in the classroom, whether learning Spanish or learning about
immigration and social justice. They have the opportunity to take
the classroom into the community; the community becomes the
classroom. To quote Tom:

> I chose this service-learning class for many reasons. First
> of all, I have realized in the last year or so (even before I
> had a sneaking suspicion) that my education transcends
> the walls of a classroom. In fact, I realized that the major-
> ity of what I have learned in this life has come from the
> direct interaction with other people, listening to their sto-
> ries and attempting to soak up all the wisdom contained
> within. I think we are all teachers and until we understand
> that, we will never learn. Secondly, I simply find no reward
> in everyday college life; I have a desire to be productive,
> cultivate good, and am not satisfied by the age-old mantra
> that "real life" is something that eludes you until gradua-
> tion. As this semester draws to a close, it is hard to look
> back at our time with the Martínez's [sic] as a completed
> project or something that could be assessed as a success

or failure. These words will have different definitions and connotations depending on each group and their families. What did we want to get out of this experience, what did we think they would get out of it? I know what I expected, but I don't know how to compare that with what happened, to tell the truth. My Spanish speaking ability sky-rocketed, my understanding and compassion for the Hispanic population living in the United States has been truly born because for the first time I have been truly exposed to it. What I am trying to say I suppose, is that this experience did what any good learning experience should, it transcended the world of classrooms, standardized testing, levels and degrees of performance, the usually stale and dry relationship between student and teacher, and replaced it all with a living adventure that can not be categorized or evaluated with a check in a box. I'm not sure if that came out coherently but this class will not end at the end of the semester, nor will its benefit end after the last test when most college kids forget why they were supposed to learn whatever was being taught to begin with. None of this will happen, because this is not a class, at least not the way we define it now, it is community, people, emotion, frustration, life; true education that can't be separated from anything else. (Transformation Paper, May 8, 2001)

■ Discussion

In framing the study in critical theory and critical pedagogy, I sought to investigate whether students experienced a change in perspective through their experiences in the community. When I provided the guiding questions for the transformation paper at the end of each semester, I included a question that asked them to revisit their journal reflections to see if they had changed in perspective, and most stated that they had. Some expressed a feeling of embarrassment at the selfish motives that had led them to take the class, including sentiments such as "wanting to improve my Spanish" or wanting to "help the less fortunate." They described transformations that caused them to regard their partner families as friends, and not as class projects. On the other hand, some students indicated there had been no change in perspective, whether due to the fact they had previously experienced positive interactions in the Latino community or because they had not become close to the partner families.

The participants developed relationships at different levels, some resulting in friendships that will probably continue for some time; others shared respect and concern for each other only during the placement. A few unsuccessful partnerships had to be changed. The data illustrated the possibility for satisfying reciprocal relationships in which students and families emerged united in solidarity against a society they deemed unjust. With the exception of the relationships that were unsatisfactory, both students and Latino families spoke of the reciprocal relationships they had developed over the course of the semester, and of the fact they would never have known each other without benefit of the class. Student and community voices presented an appreciation for the partner's language and culture. The data reinforced my initial hunch that a service-learning class situated in an immigrant community provides a space for disparate groups to come together and form relationships that would otherwise never take place.

In regard to sociocultural theory, which positions language learning as a social activity, the data confirmed that many students felt their ability to communicate in Spanish improved, but the information was anecdotal and not based on formal assessment. They definitely confirmed that lowered anxiety allowed them to speak more freely, but once again, the data were anecdotal and not based on results from formal measurement instruments. My assertions regarding language acquisition are based solely on the students' own narrative evaluations of their progress. The Latinos made similar statements about improving in English, but they continued to feel inadequate in their ability to communicate. A future study to measure language acquisition using an instrument such as the ACTFL Oral Proficiency Interview (OPI) would provide useful information for instructors interested in service-learning as a means of giving students mini-immersion experiences in a Latino community with the purpose of improving language acquisition.

■ Conclusions

This paper seeks to provide information for educators considering whether to implement service-learning programs in their own curricula by examining a course that provides opportunities for interaction between university students and community members. Through the participants' voices, the reader can explore the integration of academic learning with learning lived in the community.

Finally, this paper submits general proposals for the inclusion of service-learning programs in foreign language programs as a means of nurturing paradigm shifts in student attitudes toward members of other cultures as well as paradigm shifts in the Latinos' attitudes toward their new culture, suggesting possible deeper societal transformation as the academy and the community become agents of change through service-learning situated in the university and the Latino community.

The goals of the course can best be summed up in the words of John:

> We have been faced with the socially constructed border between cultures for our entire lives. Through this class, we have been given the experience of crossing this border. We cross it only to find that the people on the other side are the same as us. (J. Worland, public speech, May 2, 2003)

The implications for community-based education focus on partnering students in higher education with members of immigrant communities as a means for fostering social change in a post-9/11 world in which global communication and understanding are more crucial than ever.

■ Endnotes

1) The names used are pseudonyms to protect the privacy of both the student and the Latino community member.
2) All quotes from student and Latino community member papers or interviews are cited exactly as they appeared in print or as they were transcribed from the audiotapes. There has been no alteration in spelling, grammar, or stylistics. Any italics or other markings are reproductions from the original documents.
3) These assessments are informal, based on the speaking I heard in the classroom and the papers that some wrote in Spanish. In addition, I taught all but two of the students in an Intermediate Spanish class, either the semester prior to spring 2003 or concurrently that same semester.

■ References

American Council on the Teaching of Foreign Languages. (1998). *Proficiency guidelines*. Retrieved October 6, 2006, from: www.actfl.org/files/public/Guidelinesspeak.pdf

Ary, D., Jacobs, L. C., & Razavich, A. (1996). *Introduction to research in education*. Fort Worth, TX: Harcourt Brace.

Bogdan, R. C., & Biklen, S. K. (1998). *Qualitative research for education: An introduction to theory and methods*. Boston, MA: Allyn & Bacon.

Creswell, J. W. (1998). *Qualitative inquiry and research design: Choosing among five traditions*. Thousand Oaks, CA: Sage.

Crotty, M. (1998). *The foundations of social research: Meaning and perspective in the research process.* Thousand Oaks, CA: Sage.

Dewey, J. (1997). My pedagogic creed. In D. J. Flinders & S. J. Thornton (Eds.), *The curriculum studies reader* (pp. 17–23). New York, NY: Routledge. (Original work published 1897)

Erickson, F. (1986). Qualitative methods in research on teaching. In M. C. Whittrock (Ed.), *Handbook of research on teaching* (3rd ed.). Old Tappan, NJ: Macmillan.

Freire, P. (1970). *Pedagogy of the oppressed* (M. Bergman Ramos, Trans). New York, NY: Continuum Publishing.

Giles, D. E., Jr., & Eyler, J. (1998). A service-learning research agenda for the next five years. In R. A. Rhoads & J. P. F. Howard (Eds.), *Academic service-learning: A pedagogy of action and reflection. New directions for teaching and learning* (pp. 65–72). San Francisco, CA: Jossey-Bass.

Greenberg, J., & Moll, L. C. (1990). Creating zones of possibilities: Combining social contexts for instruction. In L. C. Moll, (Ed.), *Vygotsky and education: Instructional implications and applications of sociohistorical psychology* (pp. 319–348). Cambridge, U.K.: Cambridge University Press.

Harro, B. (2000). The cycle of socialization. In M. Adams, W. J. Blumenfeld, R. Castañeda, H. W. Hackman, M. L. Peters, & X. Zúñiga (Eds.), *Readings for social diversity and social justice: An anthology on racism, anti-Semitism, sexism, heterosexism, ableism, and classism* (pp. 15–20). New York, NY: Routledge.

Jay, M. (1996). *The dialectical imagination and the Frankfort School and the Institute of Social Research, 1923–1950.* Berkeley, CA: University of California.

Jorge, E. (2004). Dialogue and power: Collaborative language curriculum development. In J. Hellebrandt, J. Arries, & L. T. Varona (Eds.), *Juntos: Community partnerships in Spanish and Portuguese* (pp. 17–28). Boston, MA: Heinle.

Krashen, S. (1982). *Principles and practices in second language acquisition.* Oxford, U.K.: Pergamon.

Krashen, S. (2005). *Stephen Krashen's theory of second language acquisition.* Retrieved October 6, 2006, from: www.sk.com.br/sk-krash.html

Merriam, S. B. (1998). *Qualitative research and case study applications in education* (2nd ed.). San Francisco, CA: Jossey-Bass.

Mullaney, J. (1999). Service-learning and language acquisition In J. Hellebrandt & L. T. Varona (Eds.), *Construyendo puentes (building bridges): Concepts and models for service-learning in Spanish* (pp. 49–60). Washington, DC: American Association for Higher Education.

Olazagasti-Segovia, E. (2004). Second language acquisition, academic service-learning, and learners' transformation. In J. Hellebrandt, J. Arries, & L. T. Varona (Eds.), *Juntos: Community partnerships in Spanish and Portuguese* (pp. 5–16). Boston, MA: Heinle.

Rogoff, B. (1990). *Apprenticeship in thinking: Cognitive development in social context.* New York, NY: Oxford University Press.

Shrum, J. L., & Glisan, E. W. (2000). *Teacher's handbook: Contextualizing language instruction* (2nd ed.). Boston, MA: Heinle & Heinle.

Sigmon, R. L. (1979). Service-learning: Three principles. *Synergist, 8*(1), 9–10.

Sjoberg, G., Williams, N., Vaughan, T. R., & Sjoberg, A. F. (1991). The case study approach in social research. In M. Orum & G. Sjoberg. (Eds.), *A case for the case study* (pp. 1–26). Chapel Hill, NC: University of North Carolina.

Stake, R. E. (1995). *The art of case study research.* Thousand Oaks, CA: Sage.

Stanton, T. K., Giles, D. E., Jr., & Cruz, N. I. (1999). *Service-learning: A movement's pioneers reflect on its origins, practice, and future.* San Francisco, CA: Jossey-Bass.

Tilley-Lubbs, G. A. (2000). *Somos una: Understanding across borders* (Unpublished manuscript). Blacksburg, VA: Virginia Polytechnic Institute and State University.

Uttech, M. R. (1999). *Education and migration in rural Mexico: An ethnographic view of local experience* (Unpublished doctoral dissertation). Tucson, AZ: University of Arizona.

Vygotsky, L. S. (1978). *Mind in society.* Cambridge, MA: Harvard University Press.

Wertsch, J. V. (1991). *Voices of the mind: A sociocultural approach to mediated action.* Cambridge, MA: Harvard University Press.

13

Service-Learning and Academic Literacy: Linking Writing Students, Research, and the Community

Mary C. Hutchinson

We are led to imagine our basic writing courses as intellectually engaged immersions in the real writing practices
of people learning new ways of expressing their ideas, their
delight, and their critical inquiry, for new audiences. To
demand less of our curriculum, of ourselves as teachers,
and of our students is to sell ourselves short, and our work
with it. (Collins, 2002)

If I were asked to define myself as a professional, I would say I
am a teacher of basic writers. Of course, I teach other courses
for my university; however, the most rewarding, frustrating, and
happiest moments of my now two-decade career have been as a
teacher of basic writers. I love this part of my job and I am not sure
why. Perhaps it is because most basic writing students come into
my course with that sometimes unalterable mix of enthusiasm
and fear, and the pure conviction that they hate writing. For some
odd reason, I find that totally exhilarating.

Those of us involved in the development of a basic writing
curriculum are fully aware of the challenges it presents. But difficulties aside, I truly believe faculty work hard to create courses
that "intellectually engage" students and immerse them in literate

practices that provide them with opportunities to grow and develop as learners. Service-learning adds another dimension to this exchange by also allowing students to interact with others outside of the institution and experience new ways of thinking and being that many of them have never encountered before. In addition, I feel that service-learning, perhaps more than any other type of pedagogical strategy, can be transformative and can positively influence students' connections to the university and the community, which could ultimately have an impact on retention and academic success.

Over the last decade or so, a number of scholars have examined the influence of service-learning on the personal and academic development of college undergraduates (Astin & Sax, 1998; Eyler & Giles, 1999; Sax & Astin, 1997). One of the more comprehensive assessments of the impact of service-learning was conducted by the Higher Education Research Institute in January 2000. Among the significant findings of this study is "that service learning is effective in part because it facilitates four types of outcomes: an increased sense of personal efficacy, an increased awareness of the world, an increased awareness of one's personal values, and increased engagement in the classroom experience" (Astin, Vogelgesang, Ikeda, & Yee, 2000, p. iv). In fact, the "benefits associated with course-based service were strongest for the academic outcomes, especially writing skills" (Astin et al., 2000, p. ii).

In my own research, I am concerned with examining the theoretical implications of service-learning in particular and the intersections between academic discourse and social action that affect the development of writing skills. The general goals for the basic writing course are for students to recognize the value of writing as a form of communication and to understand the fundamental principles and attitudes concerning both the process and practice of effective writing. Recently, I implemented a service-learning research project (I refer to it as *ServiSearch*) in my basic writing course that provides students with opportunities to contribute to the community in an area of their choosing and to write research papers about a topic related to this contribution. Students self-select agencies and programs and participate in projects throughout the semester. In class, we examine service-learning and civic engagement and explore opportunities to connect with the community. We do address some of the societal issues that arise from their service (social policy and philosophy), but the focus is more on having them relate their experiences to the material they encounter as they research various topics related to their service. And although this consciousness-raising is valuable, Herzberg (1997) states, "writing personal responses to community service experiences is an important part of processing the experience, but it is not sufficient to raise critical or cultural consciousness" (p. 59). In fact, in response to Herzberg, Adler-Kassner (1995) asserts that "issues about social structures, ideology, and social justice...should be raised but not serve as its primary emphasis" (p. 554). Adler-Kassner believes that "a course like this [basic writing] should concentrate on developing students' acumen with academic writing" and that it "is a good place to start helping underprepared writers frame their ideas in a form that is more acceptable in the academy" (p. 554).

This focus on strengthening and solidifying the students' academic writing abilities, although controversial, is crucial, particularly to a group of students who view themselves as weak and incapable of thriving in an educational setting. Through the *Servi-Search* project, students come to see writing and research as very relevant to their own lives. Rosemary L. Arca (1997) emphasizes this transformation:

> One of the fascinating outcomes of using community service writing in a basic skills class is the synergistic effect it has on the writers, their texts, and their communities. Although historically service-learning has not been a part of most developmental writing programs, perhaps because

of the perceived disparity of student writing skills and
community agency standards, I would argue that community service writing can be a powerful agent for change
in basic writers' thinking, writing, and interactions with
their communities. (p. 133)

Arca is not alone in her conviction that service-learning can have a
profound impact on writers, particularly on the very essential academic and personal growth skills they will need to flourish in higher
education. Wurr (2002), in a study of first-year college students,
found that "incorporating service-learning in college composition
improves student writing, improves understanding of the course
content, and improves student satisfaction with the course" (p. 119).
Gates (2001), in a study of how service-learning in a basic writing
classroom affected students thinking about and understanding of
literacy, sees service-learning "as a springboard for writing" and as
"a way to talk about writing as an essential component of college
literacy" (p. 4). This transformation for basic writers is invaluable.

■ Basic Writers Defined

As William DeGenaro and Edward M. White (2002) state in
their introduction of *Assessment and the Basic Writer*, there is no
one definition for the term *basic writer*; instead the designation is
more of a "social construction" that generally refers to students
"assigned to a writing course that exists below (at least in terms
of course number) a first-semester composition course." This is
undoubtedly true in my course. Of the 16 students (6 female,
10 male) in this particular study, 31% (n=5) were either in pro-
visional status—that is, they had not met the basic entry-level
requirements for degree status at the institution—or had not
been formally admitted into a specific college. In addition, more
than a third of the class (41%; n=7) were from minority backgrounds and the majority of this group (31%, n=5) were English

as a second language (ESL) learners. All of the students had low scores on their English placement test (a common assessment given to students prior to their first semester to determine writing ability), which indicated a need for remediation.[1] This remedial designation is not without controversy and often sets up the conditions for how the students see themselves as being academically unprepared for university-level work. Shaughnessy (1997) underscores this perception, stating that "basic writing, alias remedial, developmental, pre-baccalaureate, or even handicapped English, is commonly thought of as a writing course for young men and women who have many things wrong with them" (p. 289). With these conditions as a backdrop, a teacher of basic writing is put in the unenviable position of designing a course that addresses these "deficiencies" for students who, at best, are challenged by writing, and at worst, are scared to death that they will not succeed.

■ Service-Learning Defined

A review of the literature reveals that there is no shortage of definitions for the term *service-learning*, nor is there a scarcity of synonyms either. As a form of experiential education, service-learning is often compared to internships or volunteer work, though there are important distinctions between these. Sax and Astin (1997) underscore this point:

> The basic idea behind service learning is to use a community or public service experience to enhance the meaning and impact of traditional course content. Connecting service directly with academic courses makes it quite different from "volunteer" work that is performed in the community. Service learning also involves more than simply sending a class of students into communities for additional course credit. Properly designed service learning courses relate the community service experience to the

course material and require that students reflect on their experiences through writings, discussions, or class presentations. (p. 25)

This was certainly the case for this basic writing course. Students were introduced to the concept of service-learning at the beginning of the course, were immersed in hands-on experiences throughout the semester, and were asked to reflect on these experiences periodically, both orally as well as in writing. The focus was to help them see the relevance of writing, particularly as it is applied in an academic setting. Arca (1997) asserts that students writing about their community service "are engaged in analysis and expression that engages and challenges them in their real world" (p. 135). The inspiration of immersing students in an experience and having them write about it is not novel, although the majority of basic writing students in my classes have had limited exposure and practice in academic research writing.

■ Effectiveness of Service-Learning in Composition

The literature is replete with examples of service-learning in the composition classroom. As Thomas Deans and Nora Bacon (2002) state in their introduction, "Composition, as a discipline has been an 'early adopter' of service-learning" (p. 125). Evidence of the proliferation of service-learning in the composition classroom can be seen in Deans's book, *Writing Partnerships* (2000), which lists more than 60 college and university courses and programs involved in service-learning activities. In fact, service-learning in composition has been studied for well over a decade, although very little has been done to examine the impact of this pedagogy on basic writers (Gates, 2001; Lu & Horner, 2000). The reasons for this shortage are unclear; it could be tied to the divisions within the academy about the appropriateness of service-learning students with this developmental population. Arca (1997) hints at the arguments when she states that "some teachers have questioned the wisdom of involving basic writers in community service writing, arguing that writing for the public requires a strong grasp of grammar fundamentals and unified coherent prose" (p. 135). Bartholomae (1997) maintains that basic writers are expected to enter into the language of the university, but "it is very hard for them to take on the role—the voice, the persona—of an authority whose authority is rooted in scholarship, analysis, or research" (p. 591). Although this is true, service-learning has the potential to connect students to a broader community and to aid in the development of writing skills—benefits that can help basic writers in their quest to formally grow in the academy. As Heilker (1997) states:

> Students need to experience an urgency to enter and master a particular code, to write from a position of true authority in a real community, and to use language to recreate the worlds they live in and the people they are. (p. 72).

Service-learning can provide basic writers with that experience.

On the Teaching Basic Writing faculty listserv, Kathleen Baca (2002) outlined four specific reasons for integrating service-learning into the basic writing curriculum:

1) Basic writers, as they practice real writing that has real impact on their community, can see the value of writing and the need for competence in that writing.
2) Basic writing faculty have built-in audiences and rhetorical needs in every service learning assignment. Classroom assessment takes on a different feel when students are faced with their work being judged by those in the community—their community.
3) Institutions that offer basic writing can showcase the talents of basic writers while demonstrating the need for and value of basic writing courses.

4) Community members benefit from the services provided and from the connection to the college or university community.

The concept of connecting students' community immersion encounter with research writing skills is important because, as Gerri McNenny (2002) states, the more that writing assignments relate to students' experiences, "the chances of their being motivated to respond to that assignment dramatically increase." Arca (1997) also makes the case for service-learning and basic writers:

> First of all, a community service writing class is predicated on the notion that our students are already knowers and thinkers, capable of responding to a call to serve. Second, a community service writing curriculum challenges our students beyond paragraph and sentence-level exercises and gives them opportunities to be makers of meaning and agents for change. Such a curriculum provides more "nourishing food for thought" for the students, welcoming them into the academy, acknowledging their diverse voices, and re-creating them as "authorities" in all senses of that word. (p. 134)

An examination of their reflection artifacts collected during the course (pre- and post-service surveys, progress reports, writing assignments) indicates that this service-learning initiative had a positive impact on not only most students' writing skills, but more importantly on the way they viewed themselves and their abilities as writers.

■ Results of the Study

The purpose of this study was to examine the impact of academic service-learning on basic writers, particularly on the development of their academic writing skills and their perceptions of themselves as writers. To explore this effect systematically from a variety of angles, data were gathered through an assortment of mechanisms, particularly since I was relying primarily on students' self-perceptions in addition to my own observations. Although there are problems inherent in collecting this type of qualitative data, I knew that it was only through the students' feedback as well as my own evaluation of their skills that I could assess attitude awareness and change, as well as change in writing ability. Gates (2001) asserts that "by looking at individual experiences with literacy, and by observing basic writers in action as they struggle with the difficulties of literacy work, we can more fully understand the process of students' thinking about and understanding literacy" (p. 33).

Baseline data about students' writing skills and attitudes toward writing were gathered at the beginning of the course, including a diagnostic essay and writer's survey. From this point on, detailed records were kept about students' writing skills in five main areas (idea/content development, organization, sentence fluency, expression, and mechanics), which corresponded to the primary assessment traits used to evaluate their assignments. There are a number of factors that can impact a writer's ability, so in many ways it is difficult to isolate service-learning as the sole variable influencing the development of skills. Wurr (2002) alludes to this challenge:

> Establishing a relationship between improved learning of traditional school subjects as a result of service-learning participation has proven difficult for researchers because of pedagogical differences in how the service component is structured in different courses and institutions. (p. 106)

However, through the examination of these data in conjunction with students' perceptions about the *ServiSearch* assignment, general inferences can be made about the impact of this service-learning initiative on these basic writers' perceptions and performance of academic writing skills.

The students were given a variety of writing assignments throughout the semester, and all but a few initial ones (a self-profile, personal story, and reflective essay) were related to service-learning. Hence, a majority of the students' time was devoted to the *ServiSearch* project. The purpose of this assignment was for them to discover, through active participation and an exhaustive research process, information about an area of personal interest that would meet a particular community need. For example, if students wanted to work with young children to develop literacy skills, they might become involved in the America Reads program and work with learners in a local elementary school. The research aspect might be about literacy in general or America Reads in particular, or perhaps about the field of second language acquisition for children who are from different cultures. Early in the semester, students identified a service project, made contact with the staff at that particular agency, and began their work. This self-selection process was predicated on Heilker's belief that allowing students to choose their own agencies "increases students' enthusiasm for doing a good job" (1997, p. 76).

There were no set hours, per se, for these projects; the students needed to spend enough time to be able to write about the project and its connection to their research. I also was conscious of the trade-off that Astin and Sax (1998) discuss between duration of service and impact on academic development: "Devoting much time to service activities does not necessarily impede academic development, but a heavy involvement in service activities may frequently reduce the time available for students to devote specifically to formal academic pursuits" (p. 260). Indeed, in their feedback both before and during the service-learning projects, many of the students expressed concerns about being able to devote the time to this type of assignment with all the other activities in their lives. In fact, more than two-thirds of the students in this study

(69%; n=11) held part-time jobs in addition to their full-time academic studies.

The students were responsible not only for participating in a community service project, but for finding a variety of information resources, including interviewing someone from the agency. This integrated research process combining community service-learning with academic inquiry had a tremendous impact on the students. Heilker (1997) discusses various versions of service-learning integrated into composition courses. The focus for this basic writing course was on the second type—"the experience of doing community work as *research*—research to be used as a work consulted or work cited for a term paper or as a basis for criticizing an author's treatment of a given topic" (p. 74). In addition, the approach emphasized was the one promoted by Adler-Kassner (1995) that focuses on developing students' academic discourse skills.

During the semester, students submitted periodic progress reports, which helped them keep track of their service experience and reflect on their thoughts and feelings about this engagement. These updates provided an opportunity for me to oversee the process and make specific suggestions about their service projects as well as their research. Students worked with a variety of organizations, such as Habitat for Humanity, American Cancer Society, America Reads, Big Brothers/Big Sisters, 4-H Program, and various local hospitals, rehabilitation clinics, retirement homes, soup kitchens, and other social service agencies. Their research projects focused on poverty, homelessness, volunteerism, childhood disabilities, endangered species, literacy, community-based service agencies, conservation, and tutoring—to name a few.

Pre-Service Data

At the beginning of the course, students were asked to complete two surveys (Appendix A): one to assess their perceptions and attitudes about writing and one to provide feedback about the upcoming service-learning project. The level of interest in writing varied among the 16 students. On a scale of 1 (low) to 10 (high), the average response was 6.1, but the range of responses was from 1–10. This wide disparity of interest in writing was clarified in their responses to their feelings about writing in general. Most students had mixed emotions about the subject, revealed in such comments as "I would enjoy writing more if it was not always for a grade" and "I feel I can write but am lacking in most writing skills." For most students, their perceptions of the qualities of good academic writing centered around two primary traits: organization of ideas and grammatically correct sentence structures. Indeed, when asked what the easiest part of writing was for them, 50% (n=8) indicated that structuring and organizing essays and reports were strengths. The hardest part of writing for the majority of these students (63%, n=10) was knowledge and application of grammar. On the whole, the students expressed expectations of learning how to write better by learning how to develop ideas and improve their grammar and sentence structures.

The pre-service-learning survey revealed the students' attitudes toward the upcoming experience. Of the 16 students in the study, none had taken an academic service-learning course before, although almost two-thirds of the students (63%, n=10) had prior community volunteering experience and indicated a positive attitude toward the service-learning project. When asked whether they felt service-learning would positively impact their writing skills, 69% (n=11) responded that it would and 56% (n=9) felt that the experience would help them to define their personal strengths and weaknesses.

Overall, the data collected at the beginning of the semester revealed that the students were interested in learning more about writing and improving their skills and were interested in participating in the service-learning experience.

Mid-Semester Progress Reports

The students were asked to submit two progress reports about their service-learning project—one approximately four weeks into the experience and one about three weeks later (or approximately two weeks prior to the due date for the paper). The first report had them specify their community organization, their related research topic, the work they had accomplished to date (both for the service and for the writing assignment), and their overall thoughts and feelings about the project.[2] Although some students were still deciding which agency to contact and expressed nervousness related to this new experience, the main concern for most students was finding a viable research topic and enough information to complete the paper.

The second progress report had the students list the specific research information they had obtained (books, articles, pamphlets, etc.), who they would interview, the number of pages written, and their concerns for completing the assignment by the due date. Although a couple of students at this point had not identified any research materials, the majority had found several sources of information and had written more than half the paper. More than two-thirds of the students felt that they did not have any concerns about the assignment, and the remaining students felt they might not have enough material to write about the topic they had selected.

In addition to the progress reports, the students completed an anonymous evaluation about different aspects of the course. The first evaluation was given six weeks into the semester. On a scale of 1 (low) to 10 (high), the average student rating for the appropriate experiences and practice in writing was 7.1, the value and effectiveness of the service-learning project was 6.0, and the impact of the course on the development of writing skills was 7.7. The same evaluation was given again four weeks later. There was an increase in the average in one area only: appropriate experiences and practice in writing was 7.7. The remaining areas showed a slight decrease in the average rating: The value and effectiveness of the service-learning project was 5.8, and the impact of the course on the development of writing skills was 7.3. Although the *ServiSearch* assignment at this point was not due for another five weeks, 46% of the students felt that the service-learning project was the one aspect of the course that they liked the least. However, when asked for specific suggestions to improve the course, only 15% of the students stated that they would like to get rid of the service-learning assignment.

Post-Service Data

An examination of the *ServiSearch* assignment revealed some improvement in most students' academic writing abilities. And although, as stated earlier, it is difficult to correlate these advances to this specific assignment, because the majority of time and writing activities were devoted to service-learning, a case can be made that this concentrated effort had an impact on their writing skills. Initial writing samples taken during the first week revealed typical errors in basic writing skills—lack of a strong thesis, undeveloped support and organization, and mistakes in sentence structure and grammar. By the end of the semester, many students had made progress in these areas, particularly in their ability to develop and support a thesis, and their ability to develop coherent and grammatically correct prose. Several students commented on this growth:

- "[The service-learning project] made me more aware of the fluency a research paper should have, instead of jotting down information in random order."
- "I was able to utilize skills, such as researching, paragraph formation, and statistics."
- "[The service-learning project] helped me find my weaknesses, such as citing information. But overall, I learned different ways to write papers than what was taught in high school."

At the end of the course, students also were asked to complete a post-service survey and answer specific questions related to their participation in a service-learning course. When asked whether the service-learning experience helped them to develop writing and research skills, 71% (n=10) agreed that it had, and this same percentage of students felt that it had enhanced their ability to communicate ideas in a real-world context. In addition, most students (57%, n=8) believed that their work in the community helped them to define their personal strengths and weaknesses (14% were unsure, and 29% felt that it did not), and 64% (n=9) felt the work helped them learn how to plan and complete a project. As one student stated:

> I think this is the best research paper that I have written because I was involved myself, and it meant more to me than just writing about a general topic. It was more important for me to get my point across because I actually took part in the issue.

Other students also commented on how the service-learning experience helped them to develop their skills. One student stated that the service-learning project gave her "a different view to write about instead of just facts from books," and another specifically stated how the experience helped her overall:

> I think that [the service-learning project] made me a better writer because getting involved made it easier to understand what I was going to be writing about, and in turn it made my paper better. Being able to be hands-on is so much better than just looking up everything. It is easier to write when you have a firsthand view of things.

Finally, when asked to comment about a course where learning takes place in a community setting, a number of students expressed the desire to see service-learning in other classes:

- "This was my only official service-learning class. It was a really good experience and I feel that I would encourage others to take part in them too. It helps you understand the course at a real worldly level."

- "I think this was one of the best English classes I have taken. There have only been two classes I really could walk away with 'personal growth.' This was one."
- "It should be a requirement for every college student."
- "I think this was a great idea . . . I learned a whole lot, not only about myself but about other people."

The impact of the service-learning on the students' perceptions and performance of academic writing skills was evident, although the complex nature of this assignment was daunting for some of them. Engaging in a project in the community and reflecting on the experience, gathering research information, reading critically and writing about an issue, interviewing stakeholders, and weaving all this information together into a multipage research paper was challenging. Students who worked diligently on the process throughout the semester reaped noteworthy rewards, not only in their understanding about the community, but in their awareness of how much their writing had improved throughout the endeavor. But this was not the case for all students, unfortunately. Along the way, I encountered resistance, lack of preparation, denial, and avoidance from students who felt resentful of the assignment and overwhelmed by the work involved. (Two students did not complete the assignment.) This is not surprising, as basic writers "are often stuck in a cycle of powerlessness that shapes the students' thinking about what they can do and what they can be" (Arca, 1997, p. 137). This was certainly the case for a couple of students in the course who seemed immobilized by their own negative perceptions about the lack of ability to accomplish this task.

■ Implications for Basic Writers

The results of this preliminary study indicate that service-learning in the basic writing classroom can impact students in a number of positive ways. First and foremost, the data convinced me, yet again, of the power of experiential learning. In my two decades of teaching basic writers, I have seen a powerful transformation in the quality of research papers students write when they are intimately connected with the topic. As Deans and Meyers-Gon-calves (1998) state:

> Service learning provides students a new way to think about writing. Perhaps for the first time, students realize that reading and writing are more than a packet of skills. They come to see literacy not only as a way of succeeding in the academy, but as acting in the world. Moving learning beyond the boundaries of the classroom is the best way that we have discovered concurrently to meet the needs of community agencies with limited resources, provide a context for significant learning, and encourage critical social awareness. (p. 15)

I, too, have witnessed the significant learning that takes place when students become active participants in their own literacy development and learning. This "new" view of their skills allows them to see the community through different eyes as well as see their own potential as students who can be successful in the academic environment.

■ Appendix A

Writer's Survey
1) Gender
   ☐ Female
   ☐ Male

2) Age Group
   ☐ Under 21
   ☐ 21–30

☐ 31–40
☐ 41–50
☐ Over 51

3) Ethnic Background
☐ African American
☐ Asian
☐ Caucasian/White
☐ Hispanic
☐ Indian
☐ Middle Eastern
☐ Native American
☐ Other

4) How do you feel about writing in general? Why?

5) How much writing did you do in high school?
☐ Very little
☐ Some
☐ A lot

6) What kinds of writing did you do in high school? Please check all that apply.
☐ Personal journals
☐ Articles for the school newspaper or newsletter
☐ Personal essays
☐ Essay test questions
☐ Short stories
☐ Poetry
☐ Research papers
☐ Other

7) If you listed "other" in the previous question, please explain.

8) On a scale of 1 (low) to 10 (high), indicate your level of interest in writing.
   □ 1
   □ 2
   □ 3
   □ 4
   □ 5
   □ 6
   □ 7
   □ 8
   □ 9
   □ 10

9) What do you think are the qualities of good writing?

10) What is the easiest part of writing for you? What do you do well?

11) What is the hardest part of writing for you? What do you think you need to work on?

12) What do you expect to learn in this writing course?

■ Appendix B

Pre-Service-Learning Survey

1) I currently have a job(s) that requires me to work
   □ 1–10 hours per week
   □ 11–20 hours per week
   □ 21–30 hours per week
   □ 31–40 hours per week
   □ 41+ hours per week
   □ I do not have a job.

2) Prior participation in an academic service-learning experience
   ☐ I have participated in an academic service-learning experience before
   ☐ I have never participated in an academic service-learning experience

3) If you have participated in a service-learning course before, please describe.

4) Prior community volunteering experience
   ☐ I have served as a volunteer in the community before
   ☐ I have never served as a volunteer in the community

5) If you have volunteered before, please describe your experience(s) below.

6) Did you write about your volunteer work at all?
   ☐ Yes
   ☐ No
   ☐ Not applicable (No previous volunteer work)

7) If you did write about your volunteer experience, please describe.

8) Describe the thoughts/feelings you have about the academic service-learning project we will do in this course.

9) Do you feel that your work in the community will have a positive impact on your writing skills?
   ☐ Yes
   ☐ No

10) Do you think that your work in the community will help you to define your personal strengths and weaknesses?
☐ Yes
☐ No

▪ Endnotes

1) Although the issues of marginalization of basic writing students and the way in which they are defined within the particular institutions will not be discussed in this paper, it is important to note that these concerns have an impact on the curriculum and the way students are viewed and placed within the larger institution as a whole.

2) At this point, two students had dropped the course.

▪ References

Adler Kassner, L. (1995). Digging the groundwork for writing: Under prepared students and community service courses. *College Composition and Communication*, 46(4), 552–555.

Arca, R. L. (1997). Systems thinking, symbiosis, and service: The road to authority for basic writers. In L. Adler-Kassner, R. Crooks, & A. Watters (Eds.), *Writing the community: Concepts and models for service-learning in composition* (pp. 133–141). Washington, DC: American Association for Higher Education/National Council of Teachers of English.

Astin, A. W., & Sax, L. J. (1998). How undergraduates are affected by service participation. *Journal of College Student Development*, 39(3), 251–264.

Astin, A. W., Vogelgesang, J. K, Ikeda, E. J., & Yee, J. A. (2000, January). *How service learning affects students*. Los Angeles, CA: University of California–Los Angeles, Higher Education Research Institute.

Baca, K. (2002). *Basic writing and service-learning*. Retrieved October 6, 2006, from: www.mhhe.com/socscience/english/tbw/pt/Baca/writing/finalmodule.htm

Bartholomae, D. (1997). Inventing the university. In V. Villanueva, Jr. (Ed.), *Cross-talk in comp theory: A reader.* (pp. 589–619). Urbana, IL: National Council of Teachers of English.

Collins, T. (2002). *Curriculum development and course design.* Retrieved October 6, 2006, from: http://auth.mhhe.com/socscience/english/tbw/ct/collins.htm

Deans, T. (2000). *Writing partnerships: Service learning in composition.* Urbana, IL: National Council of Teachers of English.

Deans, T., & Bacon, N. (2002). Writing as students, writing as citizens: Service-learning in first-year composition courses. In E. Zlotkowski (Ed.), *Service-learning and the first-year experience: Preparing students for personal success and civic responsibility* (pp. 125–137). Columbia, SC: National Resource Center for The First-Year Experience and Students in Transition.

Deans, T., & Meyers-Goncalves, Z. (1998). Service-learning projects in composition and beyond. *College Teaching, 46,* 12–15.

DeGenaro, W., & White, E. (2002). *Assessment and the basic writer.* Retrieved October 6, 2006, from: www.mhhe.com/socscience/english/tbw/ct/degenaro.html

Eyler, J., & Giles, D. E., Jr. (1999). *Where's the learning in service-learning?* San Francisco, CA: Jossey-Bass.

Gates, S. W. (2001). *Increasing basic writers' thinking about and understanding of literacy through literacy-based service-learning.* (Doctoral Dissertation, University of California, Los Angeles, 2001) (University Microfilms No. 3024078)

Heilker, P. (1997). Rhetoric made real: Civic discourse and writing beyond the curriculum. In L. Adler-Kassner, R. Crooks, & A. Watters (Eds.), *Writing the community: Concepts and models for service-learning in composition* (pp. 71–77). Washington, DC: American Association for Higher Education/National Council of Teachers of English.

Herzberg, B. (1997). Community service and critical teaching. In L. Adler-Kassner, R. Crooks, & A. Watters (Eds.), *Writing the community: Concepts and models for service-learning in composition* (pp. 57–69). Washington, DC: American Association for Higher Education/National Council of Teachers of English.

Lu, M., & Horner, B. (2000). Expectations, interpretations, and contributions of basic writing. *Journal of Basic Writing, 19,* 43–52.

McNenny, G. (2002). *Active learning and authentic rhetorical situations in assignment design.* Retrieved October 6, 2006, from: www.mhhe.com/socscience/english/tbw/pt/mcnenny.htm

Sax, L. J., & Astin, A.W. (1997). The benefits of service: Evidence from undergraduates. *The Educational Record, 78*(3), 25–33.

Shaughnessy, M. P. (1997). Diving in: An introduction to basic writing. In V. Villanueva, Jr. (Ed.), *Cross-talk in comp theory: A reader* (pp. 289–295). Urbana, IL: National Council of Teachers of English.

Wurr, A. J. (2002). Service-learning and student writing: An investigation of effects. In S. H. Billig & A. Furco (Eds.), *Service-learning through a multidisciplinary lens* (pp. 103–121). Greenwich, CT: Information Age Publishing, Inc.

14

Meeting the Needs of Those Involved: A University-Based Community ESL Program

Fu-An Lin

In the field of TESOL (Teaching English to Speakers of Other Languages), there is a general acceptance of the need for teachers to be prepared professionally—a consensus exemplified in today's job announcements. As English acquires the status of a lingua franca, professionally prepared teachers are increasingly in demand both inside and outside the United States (Bolitho, 1988; Díaz-Rico, 2000; TESOL, Inc., 2002), and chances to receive favorable job offers have been linked with competitive qualifications. Knowledge of a language alone does not qualify one to teach the language (Braine, 1999; Díaz-Rico, 2000; Phillipson, 1992; Thomas, 1999); an understanding of teaching methodologies, linguistics, and language acquisition commonly forms parts of TESOL professional preparation. While idiosyncrasies exist in the way different programs prepare future teachers, the value of teaching experience in helping a teacher trainee (TT) move towards effectiveness has been much emphasized (e.g., Holten & Brinton, 1995; TESOL, Inc., 2002; Whitaker, 1975).

The need for TESOL professional preparation has been rather adequately addressed by the growing number of programs that lead to a degree, certificate, or other credentials (e.g., see Chris-

348

topher, 2005, for TESOL programs in North America). Teachers have been training in English-speaking and non-English-speaking countries, or even on the Internet (e.g., Nunan, 2002). In contrast, research on TESOL teacher education has not been undertaken at a comparable pace (Freeman, 1996; Johnson, 1996). For example, TESOL teacher preparation and development was still included as one research priority in the beginning of the new millennium (Tucker et al., 2001). Within the context of the value of practical experience and scarcity of empirical focus on teacher development, the current study was undertaken to investigate professional growth that TESOL TTs experienced as they engaged in a service-learning project in a university-based community ESL program. In addition to the focus on teacher trainees, attention is also given to how service-learning could benefit, more than superficially, the community (in this case, ESL students) and university professors.

▪ TESOL Teaching Practicum and Service-Learning

With the rising number of non-English speakers in the United States, local communities where TESOL teacher education programs are located can be promising venues for meeting the emphasis on practical experience in TESOL. A variety of approaches to TESOL teaching practicum have been practiced. TTs could be placed in a school with a mentor teacher (Holten & Brinton, 1995; Johnson, 1996; Kamhi-Stein, 2000). Local English programs offered another possibility (Díaz-Rico, 2000; Kamhi-Stein, 1999; Lopes-Murphy & Martin, 2002), and home tutoring was yet another (Rymes, 2002). Some teacher educators used team work instead of individual placement (Rymes, 2002). Whatever the approach, teacher educators act as supervisors to the TTs, and some have documented what contributed to teacher growth in their work with TTs.

For instance, hands-on experience in practicum has been described to stimulate the TTs' awareness of the gulf between their own and their students' familiarity with instructional materials (Holten & Brinton, 1995; Rymes, 2002; Wilberschied, Bauer, & Gardes, 2003). Through the actual teaching experience, TTs were said to move beyond a student identity and acquire a teacher persona (Holten & Brinton, 1995; Rymes, 2002). TTs' reflection on teaching was also found to be of vital importance (Dong, 2000; Holten & Brinton, 1995; Whitaker, 1975).

Generally defined in the literature as "action and reflection integrated with academic curriculum to enhance student learning and to meet community needs" (Rosenberger, 2000, p. 24), the concept of service-learning has been described as a potentially effective and efficient way for teacher preparation (Root, 1997; Wilberschied et al., 2003). In TESOL, or more specifically in the teaching of ESL, where the recipients of instruction are in great need of the knowledge of the English language, service-learning could readily be the perfect match for TTs' practical experience. Nonetheless, not only are there few instances of such a combination, most TESOL service-learning projects either have had superficial benefits for the community (e.g., Rymes, 2002) or started out with TTs as the sole beneficiaries. With nearly no mention of the community's perspective, Wilberschied et al.'s (2003) five-week summer practicum focused completely on the impacts on those involved as "service" providers in service-learning (see also Lopes-Murphy & Martin, 2002).

In the remainder of this article, a qualitative case study is presented that explored how a community ESL program in central Texas benefited the participants in the program, in terms of the development of TTs as effective ESL instructors, of ESL students as confident language users, and of teacher educators as successful mentors and coordinators. The article will conclude with implications for service-learning in TESOL teacher education.

■ The Community, University, and ESL Program

One crucial aspect of case studies is delimiting case boundary (Merriam, 1998, 2001; Stake, 2005), which for the current study was the community ESL program. Before a description of the program, this section will proceed with a quick sketch of the university and the community for the purpose of contextualization.

The study took place in the Department of Modern Languages in a religious university. Established in the late 19th century, the university was the only higher education institution in a fast-growing central Texas city of 20,000 residents, with Hispanics representing the major minority group. The university had a student enrollment of around 1,500 and conferred a variety of undergraduate degrees. TESOL was offered by the Department of Modern Languages, the core courses being Introduction to Linguistics, Applied Linguistics, and Methods of Teaching. Student teaching was also required in TESOL.[1] Since its establishment in 1997, the TESOL program has enrolled about 40 students, with 15 or so TESOL majors; the rest have worked toward a certificate, an endorsement, or a minor.

The department also directed an academic ESL program that had served approximately 150 international students. At the time of the study, the program was put on hold for university-level administrative reasons. With resources such as the computer lab unused in spring 2002 three individuals who embraced the university's mission to reach out and serve the community—two professors in the department, Dr. Fulton and Dr. Rivera, along with a TESOL TT[2]—initiated the effort to establish a community ESL program for English learners in the city and neighboring towns.

The TESOL TTs' involvement in the ESL program, according to Dr. Fulton, happened by serendipity. Dr. Rivera, a pastor of a Spanish-speaking church, wanted to offer ESL to immigrants because of the importance of English in career advancement. Before long Dr. Fulton, the department chair with extensive ESL experience, was involved. The TESOL TT assisting in establishing the program, who was also taking the Methods class with Dr. Fulton, suggested the possibility of TTs in the class acting as instructors. The TTs' participation in the program was thus accepted as an alternative to the student teaching requirement.

The ESL program met twice a week, from 6 to 7:30, after which was a short Bible study conducted by Dr. Rivera.[3] The program was originally set up after the academic ESL program, i.e., in addition to instruction, students would work on computer exercises and with conversation partners. But the computer and conversation partner components faded out later.[4] During the first semester, spring 2002, when the TESOL Methods class was offered and met two days concurrently with the ESL program, the TTs were told they only had to participate in the ESL program for 30 minutes until 6:30, when the Methods class normally ended, after they had spent one hour in the class (5:00–6:00, including 30 minutes of ESL lesson preparation).

The TTs were in charge of teaching the beginning and high beginning classes.[5] Cooperative teaching was a built-in design, and two or more TTs generally taught one class together. A few TTs who had already taken the Methods class would join Dr. Fulton's class for lesson preparation before teaching the ESL classes. In the second semester, fall 2002, two non-TESOL-trained volunteers participated in the program and taught with the TTs. Dr. Fulton, as the TTs' supervisor, would move between the two classes where practice teaching was ongoing. Occasionally he assisted the TTs by modeling an explanation to the ESL students.

The community ESL program based in the university was a service-learning experience, because it stressed the important aspects in the definition of service-learning. Through their participation in the program as part of their education, the TTs enhanced their professional development and accumulated practical experience. Their involvement in the program was crucial in meeting the needs of the community as "service" and "learning" were given balanced stress in the program, with each strengthening the other (Eyler & Giles, 1999). Reflection—integral to service-learning (Rosenberger, 2000) and symbolized by the hyphen in the term *service-learning* (Eyler & Giles, 1999)— was, as will be discussed later, an implicit but ever-present aspect of the TTs' experience.

■ The Participants

Three groups participated in the current study: the program coordinators, the TESOL TTs, and the ESL students from the community. Non-TESOL-trained volunteers were also included in the study because of their interaction with the other participants. Pseudonyms are used only for the coordinators[6] and the TTs to prevent confusion due to the large number of participants. The following are brief descriptive accounts of the participants.

The Program Coordinators

Dr. Fulton and Dr. Rivera both had extensive experience teaching Spanish. Dr. Fulton also taught TESOL courses; he was responsible for the academic side of the community program, including supervising the TTs. Dr. Rivera took care of the social side of the program such as recruiting students and planning social events. He also conducted the short Bible study after class.

The TESOL Teacher Trainees

Including Laura, the TESOL student who had helped set up the ESL program, seven undergraduate TTs participated in the study. All but one were international students who had completed the academic ESL program before taking college classes. At the time of participation, the international TTs' English proficiency ranged from approximately intermediate high to advanced high according to the American Council on the Teaching of Foreign Languages (ACTFL) proficiency guidelines (Breiner-Sanders, Lowe,

Table 14.1. Backgrounds of Teacher Trainees

	Nationality & 1st Language	Other[1] Languages	Relevant Experience Before Participation	Academic Majors	Initial Participation[2]	No. of TESOL Courses[3]	Teaching During Data Collection (Fall 2002)	Semesters of Participation (up until 2003)	Levels Taught[4] Spring 2002	Levels Taught Fall 2002
Abbie	Taiwan, Chinese	English	None	Music (TESOL cert. completed in fall)	Feb. 2002	3/3	No (graduated)	1 (spring 2002)	B, HB	
Haley	Taiwan, Chinese	English, Spanish	None	TESOL	Apr. 2002	0/2	Yes	2.5 (½ spring[5] & fall 2002, spring 2003)	B, HB	B (with non-TESOL volunteers)
Heather	USA, English	Spanish, Latin, Greek	None	TESOL	Feb. 2002	3/4	No (schedule conflict)	2 (spring 2002, spring 2003)	B (mostly)	
Jessie	Taiwan, Chinese	English	None	TESOL	Feb. 2002 (Methods)	3/4	Yes (graduated fall 2002)	2 (spring 2002, spring 2003)	B, HB	HB
Kazuko	Japan, Japanese	English	Tutoring in Japan	Communication (TESOL cert.)	Feb. 2002 (Methods)	1/2	Yes (withdrew halfway)	2.5 (spring & ½ fall 2002, spring 2003)	B	B (with non-TESOL volunteers)
Kimmy	Taiwan, Chinese	English	None	TESOL (was music)	Feb. 2002 (Methods)	3/4	No (graduated)	1 (spring 2002)	B, HB	
Laura	Mexico, Spanish	English	TA, conversation partner	TESOL	Feb. 2002 (Methods)	3/4	Yes	3 (spring & fall 2002, spring 2003)	B, HB	HB

1) **Other Languages** do not indicate proficiency; 2) **Initial Participation** also indicates if a TT was taking the Methods class with Dr. Fulton; 3) The first number in **No. of TESOL Courses** is for courses taken by spring 2002, and the second by spring 2003; 4) For **Levels Taught**, B stands for beginning and HB for high beginning; 5) Haley, the least experienced TT, first observed from the sidelines while the others taught. Halfway through spring 2002, she began helping the students and took her first TESOL class in summer 2002.

Miles, & Swender, 1999). None of the TTs had taught before participating in the service-learning program. For the TTs who began teaching in spring 2002, they mostly worked in different levels in a rotational manner. In fall 2002, the TTs stayed at the same level throughout. Table 14.1 gives more details of the participating TTs' backgrounds.

Most of the TTs who did not graduate from the university after the first semester of teaching continued teaching in fall 2002, the semester of data collection when no TESOL courses were offered. The TTs who were not teaching were also recruited to participate in the study. By fall 2003, all TT participants in the study had graduated except for Haley and Laura, who continued to teach.

The ESL Students from the Community

Twenty-one students participated in the study: 13 who were attending and eight who had stopped attending the ESL program at the time of data collection. All students had interacted with the TTs extensively, and their proficiency levels were at about Novice Mid to Novice Low on the ACTFL guidelines (Breiner-Sanders et al., 1999). The students, eight males and 13 females, were all immigrants from Mexico.

Non-TESOL-Trained Volunteers

Two non-TESOL-trained volunteers taught with the TTs. One was a native English speaker learning Spanish. The other was an international student from Japan who, after completing academic ESL courses, had also learned to speak Spanish fluently by taking courses and socializing with Spanish speakers. Both had tutoring experience and had an academic interest other than TESOL. They volunteered to teach in the semester of data collection because of their interests in helping people and learning Spanish. They taught the beginning class with Kazuko (before she withdrew) and Haley, and both participated in the program for only one semester.

■ Data Collection and Analysis

Data were collected via observation, interviewing, and document collection. Formal data collection began in September 2002, during the second semester of the community ESL program. Before September, I made several exploratory visits to the program, the classes the TTs were teaching, and Dr. Fulton's Methods class.

The focus of the weekly site visits and participant observation[7] was the beginning and high beginning classes, where the TTs were teaching and Dr. Fulton was supervising. The observations were not quantified, but were recorded in the form of contextualized field notes and later expanded into narratives. Interviewing began in late September with the students who had left the program. With the students who were attending the classes, interviewing did not start until they had had at least 14 classes, or seven weeks of instruction. Interviews with the TTs and non-TESOL volunteer teachers were interspersed among those with the students. The last interviews conducted were with the two coordinators. Informal conversations served as follow-ups for observations and interviews and were added to the field notes and narratives. With the consent of the participants, data were also collected from student attendance records and test results, teacher-made handouts, and email exchanges between participants and me. Other data were gathered from the university's catalogue, U.S. Census Bureau information about the city, and the teaching materials.

Data analysis began with the reading of a small set of interview transcripts. Themes and "connective threads" for participants' experiences were identified (Seidman, 1998, p. 110). Credibility and trustworthiness of the current study were enhanced via triangulation during data analysis by using multiple sources of data to increase the congruency between the findings and reality; the semester-long observation, the initial immersion at the site, and continuous communication with the participants to increase the validity of the findings; and member checks and peer debriefing on the interpretations of data gathered.

■ Benefits of the Community ESL Program

Focusing not only on what TTs took away from the service-learning experience but also on how the community ESL program benefited other participants who played supporting roles in the TTs' professional development, this section is organized by the impacts the service-learning program had on different groups of participants.

For the TESOL Teacher Trainees

> I really felt proud teaching the classes, and besides you built up your confidence in the process. You lay the foundation for how to be a teacher when you really get to practice it. (Kimmy)

Kimmy's pride came from her feeling that she had applied what she learned in practice, had passed on information, and had seen that the students had learned. The foundation Kimmy referred to was the result of a process of growth that originated from the interaction among the participants and among the different features of the program.

The community ESL program began as a semi-volunteer opportunity for the TTs. The TTs participated for the full hour and a half until the ESL classes ended at 7:30, while they only had to stay for 30 minutes. The following semesters were completely voluntary, and many TTs who had not graduated continued to teach. The persistence of those who continued and the fond reminiscence of those who only briefly participated can be attributed to the rewards the TTs felt they had received.

Connecting theory and practice. Like Kimmy, the other TTs appreciated the opportunity to put "theory" that they had learned into practice. Table 14.1 shows that most TTs had had TESOL courses before teaching, and they drew on lectures, textbooks, and discussions in their TESOL classes. Nevertheless, like many new teachers, the TTs weighed their practical experience more than their training (e.g., Johnson, 1996). Heather commented, "I don't think sitting in a classroom reading a book really teaches you how to teach. I think it's good to learn the principles and then to be able to practice them." However, the TTs did recognize the importance of training. The relation between "theory" and "practice" was best expressed by Kimmy: "Use [the theory] for your reference, follow it, and perhaps practice it after modifications."

The opportunity to teach and connect "theory" and "practice" was especially appreciated by international TTs, who were not required to complete TESOL student teaching that was arranged through the College of Education and the local school district.[8] This exemption reflects a complication in placement for international students—a fact seldom mentioned in the literature that centers mostly on American TTs (Liu, 1999). Parish (1976) and Rymes (2002) are two of the rare cases where international TTs' presence in the teaching practicum was addressed, but neither of them was about student placement in the public school system. While socio-cultural factors related to common perceptions of non-nativeness may have contributed to the placement difficulty for international TTs in general, Parish in 1976 described that international TTs he worked with did not feel comfortable teaching but preferred to observe their native speaking peers. In the current study, actual placement of international TTs in an ESL classroom proved to be tremendously helpful. As Jessie put it, "If there were not this pro-gram, like in the past, I wouldn't have any experience and I would just go [into my job] and teach. But now, I have this experience." For international and American TTs alike, the service-learning experi-ence in the community ESL program had served as a catalyst for their development in ESL instruction and for the emergence of characteristics crucial for teachers.

Teacher enthusiasm. One teacher characteristic is enthusiasm. While Heather and Laura had expressed excitement in benefiting the community through their participation, the majority of TTs seemed to have started with a motivation to accumulate experi-ence for their personal advancement. However, every TT soon developed a zeal for student learning. One theme running through the ESL students' accounts dealt with the enthusiasm and patience they observed in the TTs. "Everyone tried hard to help us" summed up the students' opinion.

Regardless of the differences in the TTs' command of English, Dr. Fulton, the supervisor, pointed out what in his opinion outweighed language proficiency:

> enthusiasm, wanting the students to learn . . . you get a thrill because you can see that you have an impact on someone, you're making improvement, and you really get involved in the students' learning . . . so the lack of absolute proficiency at the two basic levels would probably not be a big deal.

He gave an example of how Kimmy's linguistic limitation was almost irrelevant because the students responded to her completely and positively as a result of her engagement in their learning. Also, the TTs regarded Spanish as valuable for the students' learning, and a couple had considered learning Spanish in order to teach more effectively. For example, Kazuko asked her mother to send her Spanish textbooks from Japan, and Haley started taking Spanish in fall 2002. The TTs reported frustration when they did not help the students and a "thrill" when they did.

Like many community ESL programs, student attendance tends to drop as the semester progresses. When asked about how student dropout rates impacted their teaching, some TTs expressed discouragement and disappointment because, like Heather said, "the students were making progress, and they stopped coming. I started to wonder if they were going to learn anymore." Kimmy attempted to find out from Laura and Dr. Fulton the reasons for student dropout: "Because they didn't have time, they couldn't allocate their time. And besides, we had a long [spring] break and people became lazy." Whether they knew why the students stopped or not, the TTs' enthusiasm for teaching was not completely diminished. As Jessie put it, "as long as there are people who are willing to listen to me, I will teach."

One important factor that had sustained the TTs' enthusiasm and fostered their professional development was the students' positive attitudes. *Respectful, polite, appreciative, friendly, expressive, motivated, cooperative,* and *participatory* were the words the TTs used to describe the students. Dr. Fulton, through his supervision and observation, commented, "the ESL students know that [their teachers] are beginners, they understand that and it doesn't seem to bother them as far as I can tell. They accepted that and supported that."

The students did realize that the TTs were practicing. Nevertheless, they enjoyed the instruction and appreciated the TTs' efforts because the TTs knew more English as well as how to teach. One student, who was a school principal in Mexico, remembered, "in the very beginning, I was thinking how are we going to learn? These are not even teachers. But after a while, they put so much effort into helping us learn that they're actually doing a good job teaching." The students' positive attitudes were beneficial. For example, Abbie and Heather perceived a connection between the students' friendliness and their own ability to teach without feeling nervous. The friendliness also ameliorated international TTs' anxiety in using their second language to teach. The atmosphere in the entire service-learning program was positive. There was laughter constantly in the classes. Dr. Fulton suggested that "the whole environment is very relaxed, which is a good environment for learning, especially for the TTs to learn how to teach."

Acquiring teacher identity. Since the beginning of the service-learning program, the TTs had enjoyed great freedom and were allowed to make many teaching-related decisions. "I didn't have to do things 'by order.' I was not told how I was to proceed . . . I could transfer what I had learned in class to my knowledge base and decide how to teach the students," commented Kimmy. The TTs enjoyed being in charge of what they did in class, and the autonomy granted to them had certainly fostered their growth and acquisition of a teacher persona. However, the TTs perceived a teacher identity differently, and most had a rather conservative definition.

Abbie considered herself a helper, not so much a teacher in essence. Haley and Kazuko considered themselves as teachers only when they were teaching. Heather, Kimmy, and Laura thought of themselves as "teachers." When comparing her role now to when she was taking ESL classes, Laura mentioned having to worry about her English more as a teacher. For Kimmy, autonomy was especially important, which was missing when she taught in Taiwan. As a result, she lost her sense of teacher identity because "they mandated the things you teach, the way to teach them ... I felt like I was only there to maintain the classroom order."

While the autonomy to be in charge had helped the TTs acquire a teacher persona to different degrees, they had also taken a learner stance and viewed themselves as apprentices. Jessie thought "I am a teacher and also a student. When I am teaching, I am also learning." Through the service-learning experience, the TTs refined both their teaching skills and their knowledge of the subject matter. Furthermore, the willingness to learn and to improve on the part of the TTs was manifested in their attitudes toward Dr. Fulton's supervision. When Dr. Fulton helped by giving explanations, the TTs recognized the opportunity to sharpen their own teaching by observing a more experienced teacher.[9]

In addition to learning from their supervisor, the TTs learned from their coteachers and students. Haley's words illustrated the value of peers clearly. "When I first began teaching, I didn't know a lot. At first I would stand aside watching. . . . When I encountered problems, I would ask Abbie or Heather because they had been teaching for a while." The presence of students contributed to familiarizing the TTs to classroom reality. Kimmy said, "I think I have learned a lot. When you teach, you would pay attention to how the students are feeling, how they respond to you ... I was sensitizing myself to student reaction." Some TTs also let their students know that they were learning themselves. Laura told the students, "We are all here to learn. I let them know I don't know everything; it's OK to ask questions. I am learning to teach better, to be a better teacher."

Most of the TTs felt the students looked at them not only as teachers but as friends. Haley was the only one who was uncertain in this aspect. "I don't know . . . I think maybe yes . . . I don't know how to describe it." An absolute majority of the students did consider the TTs "real" teachers from whom they had learned much, while also recognizing the TTs' good intentions and enthusiasm. The only exceptions were two students who were teachers themselves in Mexico. However, they also acknowledged the TTs' efforts and respected them.

Experiencing professional collegiality. Teacher development is more than becoming an autonomous professional. Collegiality and autonomy both have a place in teacher development (Bullough et al., 2003). Since the beginning of the community ESL program, the TTs had been teaching with their colleagues. They took turns instructing the class and giving the students individualized attention. So in addition to a teacher persona, the TTs were developing as professionals. Cooperative teaching, in the TTs' own words, was a valuable experience because they supported each other, prepared for their teaching better, and as a result, class time was used more efficiently.

Cooperative teaching also gave the TTs an opportunity to observe and reflect. Jessie thought, "When you teach, you don't know what you have done, but when I watch others, I know [what works and what doesn't]." This is similar to what Roth (2002) views as the occasion where teachers could carry out "reflection in action" (Schön, 1987) right in the middle of teaching, which is otherwise impossible when a teacher teaches alone.

Even with the benefits, there was a negative aspect to cooperative teaching. Abbie, a TT who was drawn to the ESL program because of its practical value, felt the weak transition and coordination among TTs teaching together could be an obstacle for student learning. "Everyone teaches differently. Although what we taught was suppose to connect to each other, it's harder for the students to see the connection." The ESL students perceived coteaching in a more positive way than negative. Different teachers who taught differently could make the class more interesting, and a few students claimed to learn more through the exposure to different teachers. However two students suggested they got confused sometimes; for example, when one teacher was better than the others. Another one thought "it should be just one teacher . . . because you could get used to that person and ask more questions."

Cooperative teaching was also problematic for some TTs. Before Kazuko withdrew, she was not teaching much, which was also Dr. Fulton's observation. Her feelings of isolation in working with the two non-TESOL-trained volunteers and Haley prompted her decision to discontinue. She talked about not knowing what to teach, and when she asked for information, "they don't tell me . . . I don't know why." She often felt that she did not know what to do after a string of Spanish explanations were given by the Spanish-speaking volunteer. She expressed the hope that there would be more students and classes. But Kazuko did return to teach the following semester. According to Dr. Fulton, Kazuko performed best when she was "her own boss."

Jessie, coteaching with Laura in the second semester, remembered feeling bored when Laura used Spanish to teach. "I don't know how to help [the students]. I can't explain it to them; I don't know what their problems are." Luckily, Jessie did not feel isolated, since her relation with Laura was more harmonious. Haley's coteaching experience was also dampened by language-related issues. After Kazuko's withdrawal, Haley taught with the two non-TESOL-trained volunteers and felt strongly her inadequacy as a teacher to this group of beginning students that she and her co-teachers had been teaching. While one volunteer used his

Spanish to relate to the students and the other acted as a model for native pronunciation, Haley sensed her unneeded presence when teaching with them. Unlike Kazuko, Haley did persist in her desire to be trained professionally.

Dan Lortie's (1975, 2002) extensive studies of school-teachers showed that teachers are often isolated from one another, and collegiality is desirable but at the same time hard to develop. The coteaching arrangement in the service-learning program had given the TTs first-hand experiences with collegiality—both pleasant and unpleasant. Better coordination and intervention on the part of teacher educators will be important in their work with TTs in order for cooperation to be present in cooperative teaching.

Fostering reflectivity. Reflective teaching has become the "banner slogan" in TESOL teacher education (Johnson, 2000) and is believed to result in continuous teacher development (Freeman, 1990; Richards, 1998). Carrying out research projects (Hones, 2000; Lopes-Murphy & Martin, 2002), using journals (Jarvis, 1992; Lo, 1996; Lopes-Murphy & Martin, 2002; Moon, 1994), and conducting observations (Day, 1990; Richards, 1998) are among various approaches to facilitating reflection in TTs.

The TTs in this study were not explicitly required to reflect on their teaching. But reflectivity was genuinely a spontaneous part of the TTs' service-learning experience, which generally happened afterward as "reflection on action" (versus "reflection in action;" Schön, 1987). Jessie was the only one reporting instances of "reflection in action:" "Sometimes I will stop a little and think if there are any better ways to teach." For most TTs, "reflection in action," as mentioned, was made possible through the arrangement of cooperative teaching.

The TTs' reflection seemed to be below the surface of consciousness and was retrieved via discussion. The existence of reflectivity in the TTs was ascertained by the fact that when asked to talk about their teaching experience, the TTs promptly articulated reflective accounts to reconstruct the reality and share their insights. For example, Jessie constantly spoke of the "thoughts" she had been considering about the students' level, teaching topics, and materials. The TTs' reflectivity was ubiquitous throughout the interviews. Reflection, integrated with action as in a well-designed service-learning project, was considered by the TTs to have fostered their development because it had made their practice more effective.

Moving toward and beyond effectiveness.

> I was pleased that the majority of the teachers were confident, showed aptitude, were friendly, and, to me, had the right attitude to work with the students. They liked the students and they wanted the students to do well. The majority, when they were teaching particular concepts, seemed to be able to do that, they knew what they were doing, especially the ones in the methodology class [in the first semester]. (Dr. Fulton, personal communication, December 10, 2002)

In their self-evaluation of effectiveness, the TTs' opinions varied. Most of the TTs considered their teaching effective overall. Examples of ineffectiveness can be seen in Abbie's case, when the students did not react to her explanation or when she did not know how to explain. Laura remembered the students attributing their progress to the fact they had a great teacher, although she commented, "I don't know if they know that they have a good teacher or not." Kimmy's self-evaluation was, "[Based on] what I taught in the States, I think I could say very confidently that I was a very good teacher. But in Taiwan, I think I am very frustrated."

Haley was the most uncertain about her teaching, again because of her experience in the second semester. She referred to her inability to relate her teaching to the students, which the Spanish-speaking volunteer was able to achieve. Insecurity about her pronunciation also drove her to the conclusion that "the most important thing is to better my pronunciation." In fact, not only Haley, but all the TTs were able to pinpoint areas they needed to work on through their contact with students.

The TTs' perceptions of their teaching and development seemed to indicate that some had advanced to the phase of "mature" concerns that center on student gain and self-evaluation (Fuller, 1969). Clearly, others might still be lingering at survival-teaching-level concerns: personal gain and evaluation by others (Fuller, 1969). Among the TTs in this study, Kimmy and Laura seemed to have developed philosophies underling their teaching behavior that were derived from their learning and teaching experience. While both intended to lead their students into fuller participation in English by first building up their confidence, they had different philosophies. Kimmy attempted to achieve the goal with a more communicative stance. Her intention was to show her students that they could use the language without worrying about accuracy. Her frustration in Taiwan could perhaps be attributed to the discrepancy between her philosophy and the teaching situation: Her teaching was mandated and her students did not perceive the need to communicate in English. Laura, however, moved toward her goal with a more traditional posture. She began by imparting linguistic knowledge as a way to build confidence in students and chose instructional content that reflected her philosophy.

The other TTs appeared to have a more generic objective in their teaching: to make the students understand. It is possible that they had developed an underlying philosophy that had not been revealed during interviews or observations. But through the service-learning experience, the TTs did gain "a clearer sense of where they are headed professionally, and [began] to formulate their own perspectives on their future career" (Kaufman, 2000, p. 65). For the TESOL majors, the opportunity to teach had helped them confirm their vocational orientation. Haley's many "I don't know, maybe . . . " answers acutely revealed her self-doubt. However, she stood firm on her goal to become an English teacher and felt "maybe because this was the first time I taught, I didn't know what to say [to explain], but the more I come, the more I teach, the more confidence I will have." For Abbie and Kazuko, who took TESOL for certification, they found out they "could actually be a teacher," even though they were not certain that TESOL would be their future career.

For the Students From the Community

The students from the community attended the ESL program because they wanted to advance their linguistic abilities. They felt they were taught by people who were nice, kind, patient, helpful, professional, and knowledgeable and believed they had received effective instruction from effective teachers. Examples they gave for how the instruction they received had helped them included increased security and frequency in using English, enhanced job performance, ability to help with children's schoolwork, independence, and accuracy. A relatively objective measure to evaluate teaching effectiveness was through the students' test results. The students took a test Dr. Fulton constructed at the beginning and again at the end. However, the results of only three students who took the test twice were located: 32% to 78%, 52% to 82%, and 56% to 68%.

All students expressed enjoyment of the immense amount of time and attention the TTs gave them in the classroom. Several mentioned how the presence of more than one teacher facilitated their learning. A majority complained about insufficient time to learn because the classes met only twice a week, but they were all satisfied with how the limited time was spent in the classrooms. The students also felt that their teachers were sensitive to the affective aspect of learning a language, and a few noted how the international TTs were more patient and understood better their efforts.

The students also benefited by the fact that their comments modified the program. Dr. Rivera commented that "since the atmosphere is very relaxed and informal, we have received quite a bit of feedback from the community that we took into consideration as we prepared for the second semester." For instance, Dr. Rivera remembered the frustration most students had with computer exercises.

> [The students] didn't spend that much time in the lab this semester because last semester was so incredibly frustrating to many, especially the older ones. And that's what they kept saying. So Dr. Fulton wisely paid attention to that, and then since they enjoyed being in the classroom so much, that's why there was more classroom time this semester than last semester.

For the Teacher Educators

Unlike the other participants in the ESL program, the two teacher educators who coordinated the program were faced with many obstacles. However, as Dr. Rivera said, "you work with what you have" in keeping the program going. And like the others, the professors had also benefited via their involvement in the program. Starting the program with an altruistic motivation, the professors, especially Dr. Fulton, were gaining more experience in supporting TTs via mentoring. "I was very pleased with the combination of the Methods class and the opportunity for practice teaching. I thought it was tremendous, outstanding. I've never had anything like that when I was learning. It would've helped me a lot." Through his supervision of the TTs, Dr. Fulton continued to encounter situations where individualized support was needed. He realized, "When [Haley] was on her own, she did develop and she did do well. And I tried to set up things [that way]." Kazuko was also provided support once Dr. Fulton recognized the importance for her to be her own boss.

Realizing how the TTs' training assisted their teaching and how a common schedule and location helped with communication and coordination, he planned to structure TESOL courses to coincide with the community program "so that we can use that sequence to help the students to become better teachers." Following Dr. Fulton's model, in the third semester of the ESL program Dr. Rivera was in charge of a Spanish program for the community that involved students who were learning Spanish as instructors.

Implications for Service-Learning in TESOL Teacher Education

> This is the only program in town that really has all the potential to be successful in the long run, because . . . you are doing this in a college and you are bringing professional teachers and you have the resources; this is the program that is bound to be the only one successful in this town.

This quote is Dr. Rivera's paraphrase of the feedback from an advanced-level student whose wife attended the high beginning class. What is significant is the perception that, like many well developed service-learning projects, the community ESL program had the potential to last beyond one semester as part of a course.

The service-learning experience in the current study was significant in yet another way: It was institutionalized. Compared to the common practice of sending students out into the community (Boyle-Baise, 2002), it was based in a university where resources were more readily available. As a result, the project did not end when the university class ended and had a deeper impact on the community than short-lived ones. Although the project began with a religious intent, the scholarship of engagement that has evolved from what Ernest Boyer proposed as the scholarship of application (Rice, 2002; Ward, 2003) is what is needed to sustain a service-learning project, since coordinating a project demands time, attention, and commitment on the part of educators. In addition, a strong professional knowledge base and a commitment to teacher trainees' professional preparation on the part of teacher educators are, as in the case of this study, essential ingredients for a well-developed service-learning program.

Feeling rewarded is another important factor. In this study the service-learning experience benefited its different participants based on what they were concerned about most, and everyone was learning and giving service at the same time. The ESL students became more confident and effective users of the language they needed to master while providing the TTs a friendly learning environment. Perhaps the reason why conversation partners from the community discontinued lies in the lack of a mutually beneficial relation, that is, "learning" was missing from service-learning in their case.

Advocates of community-based service-learning programs may argue that a setting drastically different from the university has the potential to foster reflection in students (e.g., Boyle-Baise, 2002). The current study has shown that reflection could be nurtured even in a familiar environment where the contact with the community takes place and where, as in the current study, the community plays a role in directing the service-learning program.

The current study is noteworthy for another reason: the enthusiastic engagement of international TTs. Placement of international TTs in practicum is often not addressed in the TESOL teacher education literature, and the institutionalized service-learning project reported here was a highly effective approach to enhancing professional preparation for TTs, including international ones. However, with international TTs it is vital for teacher educators to sensitize themselves as well as the TTs to the social and cultural contexts where the TTs will find themselves at the end of their training (Roberts, 1998; Liu, 1999).

As the current study has shown, having TTs who are undergoing training teach a free ESL program in the community creates a win-win situation. In the city where the study was conducted, there have been a couple of other free ESL programs; though both had admirable goals, neither was very successful because good intentions were not enough without the capacity to help as well (e.g., Judd, 2000; Schlusberg & Mueller, 1995; see also Illich, 1968). As was evident in the current study, the ESL students from the community learned from teachers who were more professionally capable as well as more adequately guided by experienced teacher educators than many undertrained ESL volunteers. In addition, a free program that benefits students also facilitates a positive student-teacher relation, and thus a less nerve-racking environment for the TTs. As the demand for qualified and experienced English teachers becomes higher, there is an immense opportunity in the combination of service-learning and teaching practicum.

▪ Endnotes

1) The student teaching requirement was waived for international students due to placement difficulties. Student teaching placement for international TESOL TTs will be discussed later in the chapter.

2) The two professors' names are pseudonyms, as are the names used for the other participants in the study. All the participants in the study had been informed of the protection of confidentiality and had given their consent for the researcher to refer to them with pseudonyms. The use of the title "Dr." for the two professors corresponds to how they were addressed by the other participants in the study.

3) Dr. Rivera considered the Bible study to be separated from other components of the program, which were all academic.

4) Although some ESL students enjoyed the novelty of computers, the majority voted for time spent in the classroom as their favorite. Volunteers from a local church served as conversation partners for the students. However, weak coordination and time commitment had caused many to stop participating. In fall 2002, a few continued coming, but soon the conversation partner segment was abandoned because of the lack of volunteers.

5) There was an intermediate/advanced class in the second semester, which was taught by Dr. Fulton and Dr. Rivera.

6) Although there were three founders of the community ESL program, the coordinators in this study refer to the two professors, Dr. Fulton and Dr. Rivera. The other founder, the TESOL student, is included as a teacher trainee.

7) My role as an observer was never covert although my stance shifted from a more observer-oriented one to one of a participant observer, as the TTs would discuss teaching-related issues with me both in and outside of the classroom, and I began helping the students with their in-class exercise activities.

8) With Dr. Fulton's help, Heather and another international TESOL TT were placed in a local elementary classroom to practice-teach for one semester (Dr. Fulton, personal communication, November 2004).

9) Some TTs and students sometimes felt interrupted by Dr. Fulton's modeling. Overall, the TTs perceived more benefits than harm in his supervision, and the students liked the fact that he was doing "quality control" and making sure they learned.

■ References

Bolitho, R. (1988). Teaching, teacher training and applied linguistics. *Teacher Trainer, 2,* 4–7.

Boyle-Baise, M. (2002). *Multicultural service learning: Educating teachers in diverse communities.* New York, NY: Teachers College Press.

Braine, G. (Ed.) (1999). *Non-native educators in English language teaching.* Mahwah, NJ: Erlbaum Associates.

Breiner-Sanders, K., Lowe, P., Miles, J., & Swender, E. (1999). ACTFL proficiency guidelines—Speaking, revised 1999. *Foreign Language Annals, 33,* 13–18.

Bullough, R., Young, J., Birrell, J., Clark, D., Egan, M., Erickson, L., Frankovich, M., Brunetti, J., & Welling, M. (2003). Teaching with a peer: A comparison of two models of student teaching. *Teaching and Teacher Education, 19,* 57–73.

Christopher, V. (Ed.) (2005). *Directory of teacher education programs in TESOL in the United States and Canada* (13th ed.). Alexandria, VA: TESOL, Inc.

Day, R. (1990). Teacher observation in second language teacher education. In J. Richards & D. Nunan (Eds.), *Second language teacher education* (pp. 43–61). Cambridge, U.K.: Cambridge University Press.

Díaz-Rico, L. (2000). TESOL education in the context of diversity. In K. Johnson (Ed.), *Teacher education* (pp. 71–84). Alexandria, VA: TESOL, Inc.

Dong, Y. R. (2000). Learning to see diverse students through reflective teaching portfolios. In K. Johnson (Ed.), *Teacher education* (pp. 137–153). Alexandria, VA: TESOL, Inc.

Eyler, J., & Giles, D. E., Jr. (1999). *Where's the learning in service-learning?* San Francisco, CA: Jossey-Bass.

Freeman, D. (1990). Intervening in practice teaching. In J. Richards & D. Nunan (Eds.), *Second language teacher education* (pp. 103–117). Cambridge, U.K.: Cambridge University Press.

Freeman, D. (1996). The "unstudied problem": Research on teacher education. In D. Freeman & J. Richards (Eds.), *Teacher learning in language teaching* (pp. 351–378). Cambridge, U.K.: Cambridge University Press.

Fuller, F. (1969). Concerns of teachers: A developmental conceptualization. *American Educational Research Journal, 6,* 207–226.

Holten, C., & Brinton, D. (1995). "You shoulda been there": Charting novice teacher growth using dialogue journals. *TESOL Journal, 4,* 23–26.

Hones, D. (2000). Building bridges among university, school, and community. In K. Johnson (Ed.), *Teacher education* (pp. 11–27). Alexandria, VA: TESOL, Inc.

Illich, I. (1968). *To hell with good intentions.* Retrieved October 22, 2005, from: www.bicyclingfish.com/illich.htm

Jarvis, J. (1992). Using diaries for teacher reflection on in-service courses. *ELT Journal, 46,* 133–143.

Johnson, K. (1996). The vision versus the reality: The tension of the TESOL practicum. In D. Freeman & J. Richards (Eds.), *Teacher learning in language teaching* (pp. 30–49). Cambridge, U.K.: Cambridge University Press.

Johnson, K. (Ed.) (2000). *Teacher education.* Alexandria, VA: TESOL, Inc.

Judd, E. (2000). English Only and ESL instruction: Will it make a difference? In R. Gonzales & I. Melis (Eds.), *Language ideologies: Vol. 1. Critical perspectives on the official English movement* (pp. 163–176). Mahwah, NJ: Lawrence Erlbaum Associates.

Kamhi-Stein, L. (1999). Preparing non-native professionals in TESOL. In G. Braine (Ed.), *Non-native educators in English language teaching* (pp. 145–158). Mahwah, NJ: Lawrence Erlbaum Associates.

Kamhi-Stein, L. (2000). Integrating computer-mediated communication tools into the practicum. In K. Johnson (Ed.), *Teacher education* (pp. 119–135). Alexandria, VA: TESOL, Inc.

Kaufman, D. (2000). Developing professionals: Interwoven visions and partnerships. In K. Johnson (Ed.), *Teacher education* (pp. 51–69). Alexandria, VA: TESOL, Inc.

Liu, D. (1999). Training non-native TESOL students: Challenges for TESOL teacher education in the West. In G. Braine (Ed.),

Non-native educators in English language teaching (pp. 197–210). Mahwah, NJ: Erlbaum.

Lo, R. (1996). The place of internship in ESL teacher education in Hong Kong. *Prospect, 11,* 37–49.

Lopes-Murphy, S., & Martin, D. (2002). Community service learning: Making the match between preservice teachers and ESL students. In E. Auerbach (Ed.), *Community partnerships* (pp. 41–54). Alexandria, VA: TESOL, Inc.

Lortie, D. (1975, 2002). *Schoolteacher: A sociological study.* Chicago, IL: University of Chicago Press.

Merriam, S. (1998, 2001). *Qualitative research and case study applications in education.* San Francisco, CA: Jossey-Bass.

Moon, J. (1994). Teachers as mentors: A route to in-service development. *ELT Journal, 48,* 347–355.

Nunan, D. (2002). Teaching MA-TESOL courses online: Challenges and rewards. *TESOL Quarterly, 36,* 617–621.

Parish, C. (1976). A basic format for ESL practice-teaching utilizing video tape. *TESOL Quarterly, 10,* 327–339.

Phillipson, R. (1992). ELT: The native speaker's burden? *ESL Journal, 46,* 12–18.

Rice, R. E. (2002). Beyond scholarship reconsidered: Toward an enlarged vision of the scholarly work of faculty member. *New Directions for Teaching and Learning, 90,* 7–17.

Richards, J. (1998). *Beyond training: Perspectives on language teacher education.* Cambridge, U.K.: Cambridge University Press.

Roberts, J. (1998). *Language teacher education.* London, U.K.: Arnold.

Root, S. (1997). School based service in teacher education. In J. Erickson & J. B. Anderson (Eds.), *Learning with the community: Concepts and models for service-learning in teacher education* (pp. 42–72). Washington, DC: American Association for Higher Education.

Rosenberger, C. (2000). Beyond empathy: Developing critical conscious-ness through service learning. In C. O'Grady (Ed.), *Integrating service learning and multicultural education in colleges and universities* (pp. 23–43). Mahwah, NJ: Lawrence Erlbaum Associates.

Roth, M. (2002). *Being and becoming in the classroom.* Westport, CT: Ablex.

Rymes, B. (2002). Language in development in the United States: Super-vising adult ESOL preservice teachers in an immigrant community. *TESOL Quarterly, 36,* 431–452.

Schön, D. (1987). *Education the reflective practitioner.* San Francisco, CA: Jossey-Bass.

Schlusberg, P., & Mueller, T. (1995). English as a second language in volunteer-based programs. *ERIC Digest.* Washington, DC: National Clearinghouse for ESL Literacy Education. (ED385172)

Seidman, I. (1998). *Interviewing as qualitative research: A guide for research-ers in education and the social sciences* (2nd ed.). New York, NY: Teach-ers College Press.

Stake, R. (2005). Qualitative case studies. In N. K. Denzin & Y. S. Lincoln (Eds.), *The Sage handbook of qualitative research* (3rd ed., pp. 443–466). Thousand Oaks, CA: Sage.

TESOL, Inc. (2002). *Career Counsel 2002–2003: Practical information to help you start, continue, and enhance your career in TESOL.* Alexandria, VA: TESOL, Inc.

Thomas, J. (1999). Voices from the periphery: Non-native teachers and issues of credibility. In G. Braine (Ed.), *Non-native educators in English language teaching* (pp. 5–12). Mahwah, NJ: Lawrence Erlbaum Asso-ciates.

Tucker, R., Lightbown, P., Snow, C., Christian, D., de Bot, K., Lynch, B., Nunan, D., Duff, P., Freeman, D., & Bailey, K. (2001). Identifying research priorities: Themes and directions for the TESOL interna-tional research foundation. *TESOL Quarterly, 35,* 595–616.

Ward, K. (2003). Faculty service roles and the scholarship of engagement. *ERIC Digest*. Washington, DC: ERIC Clearinghouse on Higher Education. (ERIC Doc. No. ED480469)

Whitaker, S. (1975). Simulation and stimulation. *ELT Journal, 30,* 1–6.

Wilberschied, L., Bauer, L., & Gardes, C. (2003). Emergency room mode: A service-learning case. *Academic Exchange Quarterly, 7,* 97–105.

15

Confidence to Contribute: Service-Learning in ESL

Erin Whittig, Aileen Hale

A recent opportunity to create and teach a new course, an English as a second language-designated section of first-year composition, compelled me to seek out and consider new pedagogical approaches. In "Community-Service Pedagogy," Julier (2001) describes her own similar situation and finds the possibilities of service-learning pedagogy "immediately compelling":

> I began to see how in teaching my course...I might engage students in first-hand experiences with local agencies and organizations that dealt directly with the issues about which we would be reading, writing, and researching. I intuitively sensed that such first-hand experience would at best subvert and at the very least complicate the often-pat constructions and commonplaces upon which so many first-year college students relied as they composed writing for the academy. (p. 132)

As an instructor, I also immediately anticipated the many ways my English as a second language (ESL) students might benefit from such first-hand experience. In my previous experience teaching ESL, I had practiced methods for teaching conversation and spoken grammar, but not composition. I had noticed that experiential learning always yielded better lessons, ones that the students themselves said were most helpful. Why role-play a shopping experience when my students could simply walk across the street and go shopping? I found that students were less enthusiastic about listen-and-repeat exercises, and more engaged when lesson topics directly related to their personal interests and experiences. If the goal was for students to communicate naturally and comfortably both verbally and in writing, then why not involve them in "real-world," relevant, and natural communication situations? Thus arose the integration of service-learning into my ESL composition course (ESL-101).

■ The Course

Since this was the first time Boise State University (BSU) had offered an ESL-only section of 101, I had to consider how the course might differ from the writing courses already offered to ESL students. A series of three writing courses (which I term the "ESL progression") is geared toward preparing ESL students for the writing they will encounter in first-year composition, and the students I would be teaching in ESL-101 had either passed most of these classes or taken a placement exam. With the creation and implementation of ESL-101, I was faced with the task of distinguishing it from the ESL progression. The integration of service-learning certainly separated my course from the other ESL writing courses.

I also believed that a "real" tangible service experience would at best clarify the more abstract concepts of the course curriculum, and at least diminish the anxiety of deciding *what* to write. I suspected that all students shared these issues and would benefit from the pedagogy. Rationalizing service-learning in composition, Heilker (1997) addresses the importance of a "real" experience for students of writing. He writes that students "desperately need *real* rhetorical situations, real audiences and purposes to work with" in order to revise their notion that "writing has nothing to do with 'the real world'" (p. 71). Although Heilker (1997) is not specifically addressing ESL writers, his suggestion easily applies to them; perhaps it is even more applicable to them. Consider Leki's (1992) observation that, for the ESL writer, "the reader is a real stranger, someone from another culture" (p. 4). An effort to make the unfamiliar reader—and the unfamiliar context—more familiar seemed a necessary function of an ESL writing course. I anticipated that service-learning in ESL-101 could enable such a function.

■ Research Questions

The range of students' reactions to service-learning over the semester led me to wonder, "What's going on here?" Peter thinks "service-learning sucks," and then goes on for an hour and a half to explain the problems and needs of Fort Boise Mid-High School, where he served more than the required 15 hours over the semester. Keiko wonders whether the course has been "academic enough" and thinks service-learning "belongs in sociology." Reyhaneh, my youngest student, says, "It's more real," and attempts to help the others in the class when they seem frustrated with their service experiences.

Herrington and Curtis (2000) stress a researcher/participant relationship which I strive for in this study: "We do not claim to speak *for* [the participants], but we do aim to speak *with* them" (p. 45). I want to articulate with my students how service-learning has affected them as ESL students and writers, and how that knowledge then influenced my practice. I developed broad research questions in order to leave room for significant outcomes to emerge:

- What are the affective outcomes for students when service-learning pedagogy is integrated into a first-year ESL composition course?
- How can we as educators use our findings to improve our practice and the context in which our practice occurs?

Methodology: Ethnographic Case Study

I chose to employ ethnographic data-gathering techniques, which "demand attention to human subjectivity" (Bishop, 1999), because my research was driven by students' experiences. Interviews, observations, and student texts are central to this study because I wanted to collaborate with my students to create "a more workable practice" (Root, 2003, p. 177).

Bishop implies that ethnography as a composition research methodology is less a stable category and more a continuum, on which several methodologies may fall. The researcher "decides what degree of affiliation" (p. 41) she has with ethnographic techniques. Bishop (1999) cites Lucy Calkins' taxonomy of case studies to illustrate just a few of the ways we may negotiate ethnography:

> In descriptive case studies, subjects are asked to solve a carefully designed problem or to do a preselected task. . . . In ethnographically oriented case studies, researchers become participant-observers in a natural setting, spending at least a semester . . . as live-in observers. . . . In teaching case studies, the practitioner-researchers usually begin with tentative theories that inform their practices, and they observe the results of those practices. (p. 41)

Within this contextual ethnographic framework, I identify my own study as a *teaching case study* in which I employ ethnographic research and writing techniques to describe what happened to the students in my ESL-101 class. One of the reasons I chose to represent my findings in case study form was that case study, with its ethnographic orientation, provided an effective way for me to deeply explore the experiences of students in my class.

In order to foreground student voices in service-learning and ESL research, I've emphasized students' writing and interview comments in each case study. As I began reviewing ESL and service-learning literature, I noticed a dearth of research on service-learning in an ESL context, as well as little focus on student voice, experience, and perspective. In foregrounding the students' texts and interview responses in the case studies, I hope to address Leki's (2001) claim that:

> many of these studies talked about the students but never gave evidence that the researchers spent any time talking to the students, never asked them one on one what all this (whatever feature of L2 writing was under study) meant to them. (p. 18).

Leki grants that these conversations must have taken place in some studies, but "they did not end up in the public record in any detail" (p. 18). Fox's (1994) *Listening to the World* reminds me that the field is not completely devoid of student voices, and case studies are gaining recognition (Belcher, 1997; Harklau, 1999; Silva, Reichelt, Chikuma, Duval-Couetil, Mo, Vélez-Rendón, & Wood, 2003).

In the field of service-learning, Goodburn (2003) argues for the inclusion of more student voices in Deans's (2000) *Writing Partnerships*. Goodburn claims these voices would lend credence to some of Deans's assertions about student attitudes and performance (p. 121). Goodburn cautions that "composition teachers looking for ideas to incorporate into their own courses might be disappointed by the lack of student examples" (p. 121). In agreement with Goodburn, any assertion I make about a student's attitude naturally becomes more convincing when the reader is exposed to the original source: the student herself.

The students. When I first designed the course, I imagined that the students, because they were non-native speakers of English, would have certain needs in common. Based on this assumption of commonality, I suspected service-learning could be effective in the course. I never thought that I might discover just the opposite.

Leki (1992) points out that ESL students "differ so much that it is not an exaggeration to say that sometimes the only similarity they share is that they are not native speakers of English" (p. 39):

> ESL students are graduate students and undergraduates; forty-five years old and eighteen years old; highly educated doctors, lawyers, teachers in their home countries and naïve, inexperienced teenagers; newly arrived immigrants, graduates of U.S. high schools; poor writers in English but good writers in their L1, poor writers in their L1, or illiterate in their L1; those hoping to remain in the United States, those eager to get back home; those extremely critical of life in the United States or U.S. foreign policy and those wholly in support of anything the United States does. (p. 39)

Tin and Noriko are no exception. Noriko is an accomplished academic; she has likely read and written extensively in her first language, Japanese. She is, by marriage, a United States citizen, continuing her research at an English-speaking university. Tin is a Burmese refugee; he learned English on his own, knowing he would need it to resettle in Boise; he's a confident and determined writer; he's a United States citizen, but plans to return to the area near his home country sometime in the future.

▪ Case Study #1: Noriko

> When did I start to fear writing? . . . My memories about reading and writing trace back to my childhood. Before I started junior high school I often went to the small library in my hometown . . . the books filled me with dreams. . . . My memories of the time I spent in the library can be equated to a nap in the flower garden under the

> peaceful sky. . . . It is a safe house, where is no judgment,
> but are only my own sense of value.

Early in the semester, I found out that Noriko had her Ph.D. in bio-chemistry and worked as a researcher for our university. I antici-pated that her writing would be stiff, formal, and dry, devoid of any deeply personal revelations or explorations, revealing my precon-ceived notions about scientific writing. Instead, her homework and first essay explored her fear of writing with honesty and shameless vulnerability. I was excited by the possibility that service-learning might help Noriko overcome some of her fears. However, this was Noriko's first college course in the U.S., and as Noriko said in our first interview, the unorthodox pedagogy was not what she had expected. Although she had written some short papers in English for her dissertation, Noriko admitted, "I still don't have confidence about grammar . . . so I take this class, but it's not what I want to do." Like other older students in the class, Noriko had expected the class to focus on more technical aspects of writing.

In assessing the effects of service-learning, I examined all of Noriko's writing from the class. It is necessary to encounter Nor-iko's early-semester expectations, assumptions, and beliefs as these influenced her responses to service-learning pedagogy. Over the semester, I sensed that Noriko was divided between an expecta-tion to learn "skills" and her deeper, conflicting desire to recall the "safe house" where she felt confident and secure in her own evalu-ation of herself and her abilities. The case study revealed that Nor-iko's service-learning experiences affected both.

Fear of an Unknown Pedagogy

As a pedagogy that is grounded in students' prior experiences and knowledge, for Noriko, service-learning seemed terrain without explicit rules. In fact, Noriko's friend in the class, Keiko, implied as much when she expressed reservations about service-learning. Keiko described herself as a student who liked to know what she was expected to learn before she learned it, and with service-learning it is imperative that the students first have the experience and then later examine what has been learned. This unpredictability unnerved her. Noriko expressed a similar skepticism in our first interview.

Noriko's first homework assignment reveals reasons why she may have felt this skepticism. Before writing, she read the first chapter of Deans's (2003) *Writing and Community Action,* which claims that "one common view [of] learning to write means learning a set of rules—rules for grammar, rules for structure, rules for research . . . once *you* know the rules, the thinking goes, you can write effectively" (p. 1).

Noriko's response reflects a similar notion of writing, but she also seems to be aware that Deans's definition is too simple.

> I know that it is difficult to explain the language rule. I thought that we get knowledge of language by experience and memorization, so we often cannot explain language logically. This is why I do not like to study language. If [advice] includes the rule of writing with examples, it should be the best for me. I can apply the rule to another situation. I can memorize the rule of language by the experience from example.

Noriko's belief that "we get knowledge of language by experience *and* memorization" contrasts to her emphasis on rules. She's aware that not everything in language learning is logical or follows simple rules, and yet she also desires the rules and wants them to be simple, memorizeable, and applicable to other situations. In another early homework assignment, she adds a postscript to me: "For solving my writing problem, could you tell me what textbook for English grammar is good?" Her message indicates a belief, at this point in the semester, that grammar is her "writing problem," and the problem has a "textbook" solution. Noriko's "study strategy" in Japanese junior high "was based on memorization of theory and answers," which she admits, "did not work for writing."

Fear of Others' Evaluations

Noriko also claimed to fear writing and others' responses to her writing. In a response to two assigned readings, Noriko immediately mentions the authors' mutual "fear to write about themselves" and she concludes that "they were afraid of what other people thought about them." Thus, Noriko introduced her similar fear: "In Japanese culture everyone wants to be identical. No one wants to stand out in the crowd. . . . People start caring about what other people do and what other people think about them."

Noriko concludes that writing the personal essay may be a way to alleviate a fear of others' judgments or evaluations of her. She identifies her early education as the point when this fear began to develop:

> I always fancied that someone looked at me behind the wall to evaluate me. Authority which was teacher at junior high school, had absolute power, and we could not disobey it, because we needed to good recommendation to get in university. We tried to be better than others by getting good scores which means to have no mistake . . . So I feel fear when I start writing . . . because I am afraid of what others will think, and that I am wrong.

Later, Noriko reveals that she not only fears others' evaluations, but depends on them to give her confidence:

> After graduate school, I have always been afraid of something which is invisible. I changed jobs a couple of times, moved to America, and got married, but I still did not have any confidence in my future. After writing this essay, I realized that . . . all my education made me lose confi-

dence in myself. I have had confidence only from others admiration in my life.

Noriko also cites others' judgments as catalysts for her lack of confidence. She longs for her "safe house" where there "is no judgment" and only Noriko knows her value. She welcomes the "opportunity for self-evaluation" with the personal essay, perhaps because she recognizes this as a way to weaken her dependence on others for confidence.

Fear of Uselessness

Noriko concludes her personal essay: "I know writing and research are not to find 'right' answer, but are to leave what I do, what I think, and what I find for the next generation." Noriko's desire to be useful and contribute something to society, however, was often disrupted by her low confidence, especially in her English ability. She regularly attended Toastmasters', a speech club, because her work often required her to present in public. Noriko wrote about the club because she thought it may be "good for ESL students" to read about it.

> To write about the Toastmasters club is good for ESL students who are struggling to improve their English communication. On the other hand, I hesitated to write about the Toastmasters club because I do not speak English well, even though I went to Toastmasters club. Who would believe the benefit?

Noriko admits that her English speaking skills caused her to question the authority with which she could write about Toastmasters, but goes ahead anyway. She was unhappy with her first draft because she felt it had "no message to reader." Noriko's main concern was affecting the reader, not producing a flawless draft. In the introduction of the essay, Noriko addresses a similar point:

"Although public speaking is very stressful, if you can move [the audience's] heart, you must feel accomplished and happy." But in order to have that effect, Noriko writes, "I need to improve my English and overcome my fear of speaking in public." Again, Noriko sees her English ability as an obstacle to her ability to contribute.

Service-Learning: From Fear to Confidence

> Before I went to [Fort Boise Mid-High School] I thought that I was useless or cannot contribute to regular American community ... because I cannot speak English very well. When I showed the student how to play guitar, I felt very happy that I could help someone else. I was excited and my heart was heated. I realized that I cannot speak English very well, but I can still help someone else.

Noriko's first service-learning journal entry shows her revising her notion that she is "useless" because she "cannot speak English very well," and that revision is prompted by the positive service-learning experience. This attitude revision could also have implications for her writing, where she may begin believing that she can produce useful, effective writing without achieving native-like proficiency. One commonly held assumption in first-year writing is that "a student's attitude about herself as a learner will influence her learning." Pajares and Johnson (1994) assert that "what people do is often better predicted by their beliefs about their capabilities than by measures of what they are actually capable of accomplishing" (p. 313).

Pajares and Johnson stress the "development of . . . students' self-efficacy" (p. 327) and when it comes to ESL students, educators must pay special attention to students' "beliefs about their capabilities." Leki (1992) suggests that L2 (second language) acquisition "can take place in a setting which seeks to minimize fear, nervousness, and self-consciousness" (p. 17), perhaps aiding the development of "self-efficacy." Indeed, Noriko's first service-learning experience enabled that development and helped "minimize" some of her fear.

Noriko's increased confidence was apparent during one group reflection session. A man in the class who was also volunteering at Fort Boise had a negative impression of the students there and voiced several generalizations about them based on a few he had tutored. After he had spoken uninterrupted for more than five minutes, Noriko stopped him. This was the first time she had spoken extensively in the class. "I have very different impression," she began, and then related her own experiences and suggested that he was perhaps underestimating the kids, to their detriment. She clearly felt sympathy for the students, and was concerned that his characterizations would be taken as truth by the rest of the class. Noriko was beginning to gain a sense of authority over her service-learning experiences—"demonstrating authority over subject matter" is also one objective in our first-year composition courses. Noriko felt compelled to defend the Fort Boise students, and to convince her classmates of another viewpoint. In comparing her actions in this situation to her attitude toward the community essay, there is a definite change in Noriko's belief in her ability to persuade her audience: "I hesitated to write about the Toastmasters club because I do not speak English well, even though I went to Toastmasters club. Who would believe the benefit?"

Service-Learning: Actualization of Confidence

In her evaluation of the final assignment, Noriko describes how her team worked together to decide on their project:

> We thought that a brochure introducing Fort Boise Mid-High School and service-learning was a good idea. It allowed us to improve our writing skills and contribute to helping students who need more supports. Personally, to make a brochure that will recruiting volunteers is a good

project to show my appreciation to the teachers and students who gave me a good time.

Noriko was absent during early stages of the project, so team members emailed and asked for her suggestions. Noriko wrote in her evaluation:

> I usually hesitate to give my opinion when I have been absent from a meeting, and I am afraid that I do not understand what went on at the meeting I missed. I realized that to give an opinion was most important, and to have contribution from others members.

Noriko realized that, in order to produce a successful document, she had to overcome this fear of speaking up and contributing, even when she wasn't absolutely sure about her opinion.

The two teams who were working on projects for Fort Boise experienced frustration during initial planning. One class period, I remember running back and forth between the two Fort Boise teams, answering questions about the project. Finally, Noriko took over for me. She recognized that she was in a better position to help the others than I was. Her service experience had, in effect, made her the expert, and she recognized that she was equipped to handle the other team's problems.

If she had more time, she "would like to have party or projects to interact with [Fort Boise] students." Noriko said, "In America, there is a lot of opportunity to go volunteer, and it's easy to go . . . to communicate with native speaker." Clearly, Noriko longed to speak more with the students. Her evaluation implies something more: "As we are international students, I wanted to have international projects, such as origami craft projects which we make a thousand cranes to send to Hiroshima for peace, international music party, and panel discussion about international subjects." Noriko wants to push service-learning's reciprocal potential, to share her time and her culture, while practicing her English and expanding her knowledge of American education.

Service-Learning: Passionate Learning

The experience at Fort Boise allowed Noriko to rethink her own abilities and assumptions about the students there, with whom she sympathizes:

> So the students at Fort Boise Mid-High School lost their confidence in their ability like me. They need more attention and support from others. They need your help to give their passion back in their future life!

These last lines of her last essay are as much about Noriko's struggle with recovering her confidence as they are about encouraging the reader to help the Fort Boise kids recover theirs. By identifying with them, Noriko implies, "I need help, too. I need support from others to get my confidence back." Her Toastmasters essay suggested as much. But the difference between that essay and this one is that here, Noriko is not getting her confidence from the Fort Boise students' admiration or evaluations of her. Instead, she gets it from recognizing and actualizing her ability to give them the same kind of support that she needs. I am not suggesting that one semester eradicated Noriko's confidence issues, but she did gain a new perspective on her role in "American life" and her ability to contribute something to that life.

> When I think about this English class, I reminded why I took [it] and what I expected to learn from [it]. Ever since coming to America 3 years ago I have felt uncomfortable and stressed, because I could not communicate with Americans like a native English speaker . . . I did not have confidence in American life. I thought the reason was that I could not speak or write what I wanted to say in English.

After this class, I realized that this was a mistake. I met a lot of ESL students who are in the same situation that I am. I saw how much passion [they] have in their life, and how hard they try to learn how to fit into the American community. I also deal with students from Fort Boise Mid-High School . . . who have been kicked out of regular school. Unlike the ESL students, the students at Fort Boise lack passion for school and learning. We can overcome everything through our passion, even language barriers.

Noriko identifies "passion" as an impetus for learning and comes to a conclusion about how people learn and how we make learning successful. She recognizes what some ESL experts suggest about learning English—that motivation is perhaps the single most important factor determining a language learner's success (Leki, 1992)—and comes to the conclusion that this, and not a deficiency of hers, is what will determine her "confidence in American life."

Elwell (2001) reports similar results among her ESL students who participated in a service-learning project in conjunction with their regular reading class: "Students began to see themselves as valuable, contributing members of a society who, even as mere students with less than fluent English skills, could make tangible, much-needed contributions to society" (p. 60). In a similar project, Heuser (1999) claims that "service gave students a purpose and role for interacting in the community as more than observers. As a result, they gained confidence in themselves and their abilities, which was fundamental to their development of higher communication skills" (p. 67). For Noriko to have such an experience in English potentially changes her relationship to the language—to successfully communicate with or contribute to an English-speaking community increases her connection to that community, perhaps fostering more opportunities for natural language use.

■ Case Study #2: Tin

> As a result of my belief in social justice, and intolerance in
> unfairness, I enthusiastically recruited people and actively
> participated in the demonstrations for democracy against
> the Burmese government on the streets in my home town
> in Burma. The military took over power followed by
> abusing, interrogating, killing, torturing, and prosecuting
> people. And those who participated in democracy move-
> ments were handed with heavy jail terms without trials
> nationwide.

Tin himself was imprisoned when he was 18 years old. He fled for
Thailand after his release six years later and began the long process
of applying for refugee status in the United States. Steve Rainey,
the director of the English Learning Center (ELC), who helped
Tin's resettlement, remembers Tin's arrival.

> When he first got here, he was much more reserved. . . . He
> was the only Burmese when he arrived here, there was
> no other, anyone else to help his resettlement. Of course,
> they're grateful and happy to be in a place that's safe, but
> with almost any refugee, there's just an overwhelming
> feeling of being lost.

Almost five years had elapsed between Tin's arrival in the U.S.
and the first day of our first class together. Tin had become less
"lost" during that time; he had a full-time job at Micron, he had a
car and an apartment, he'd taken GED tests to get a U.S. diploma,
and he had already taken two ESL writing courses. When he
enrolled in ESL-101, he had also just applied for his U.S. citizenship
and was preparing for the test, which he took in the spring while
he was enrolled in my English 102 course. On March 17, 2005,
Tin Shwe passed the citizenship test and became "Tim Strick-
lin," an official citizen of the United States. Tin's progress through

ESL-101 and English 102 is punctuated by the transformation—refugee to citizen—that was made official in March.

Tin's experiences as a refugee influenced how he responded to ESL-101 and English 102. Both semesters, he chose to serve at the very same agency that had resettled him when he first arrived as a refugee in Boise in 1999. That choice immediately put him in a position of greater authority as a writer, since he had insider knowledge of the agency and the experiences of the clients; but it also complicated his status as a refugee and a service-learning participant. Through various aspects of his service at the ELC, Tin had the opportunity to negotiate the multiple positions with which he identified.

Service-Learning: Negotiating Service

Tin's initial service-learning experiences at the ELC consist of Tin negotiating his new position—no longer relying on the Center, but instead, offering them his assistance. In his journal, he recalls how, on the first day at the Center, he observed students breaking one of the Center's rules, and he said nothing. But he soon overcomes his hesitancy and displays more assertiveness in his new role, asking students if he can help them and openly offering his assistance.

At this time, Tin was working on an essay about World Relief, an organization that had helped him resettle. He negotiates a similar role shift in the essay, where he is now an outsider looking in. He uses his new perspective to reevaluate World Relief's programs:

> I had no idea how this class was useful and handy to deal with real job at the time I was a student in that class. I thought it was easy and I knew it already. I felt bored in the class . . . but [the] class really helped me get a job at Micron where I have been working for nearly five years.

This outsider perspective gave Tin the opportunity to assess where he has been, how far he has come, and the factors that have influenced his progress. This could be incredibly persuasive to a particular audience. Indeed, Tin employs it in a later essay discussing how refugees can benefit from learning English, and his status as one-who's-been-there is very convincing.

While the ELC offers Tin this opportunity for reflection, Steve Rainey suggested that the current refugees may also be affected by Tin's presence:

> I think one of the really exciting things about using students who came as refugees [in service-learning placements] is that . . . one of the effects of trauma is that it creates a "foreshortened future," a kind of inability to see—not necessarily to make goals—but to see how you can possibly get to them. So having students come back that have been here, who are now working successfully, supporting themselves successfully, attending university, and being able to give back, having that time and it's a choice of theirs, I think is really, really valuable.

Steve suggests that by simply being there, Tin is serving a purpose at the ELC. This view of service is what Deans (2003) might call "charity" and mainly consists of "delivering a direct service to individuals" (p. 257), such as assisting refugees with computers. Tin's service-learning writing assignment also falls under this definition.

Service-Learning: Negotiating Purpose

For the service-learning writing assignment, we decided that student teams should schedule meetings with their agency contact to assess the agency's needs:

> At that time I talked to Steve and Steve told me, "What you want to do?" and I tell him, "Something useful to you, how you need?" I told him other people doing brochure or advertisement and he told me I can do that but I said, "No! What you guys really need? What your immediate need?"

The most important part of this project, for Tin, was to do something really useful for the ELC. That kind of motivation is significant, perhaps especially for ESL students, as Knutson (2003) observes that increased motivation can lead students to "work harder and spend more out-of-class time on [a] project and speaking in English" (p. 59). In Tin's case, he was motivated to become the group leader. He was frequently in contact with Steve, acting as a proxy for the ELC and his team. His teammates were both Bosnian, so this meant that all of their exchanges also occurred in English.

When Steve explained to Tin that the center was running dangerously low on diapers (they provide day care for refugee children), Tin agreed to help with a diaper drive.

> We came up with a few ideas such as put a short advertisement in the local newspaper, ask to talk to department store managers and present an official letter from the Center. Our backup plan was to send out e-mail messages to the managers. Adhnan and I would go to the stores with the letter and Muhidin would write e-mails and send to the managers.

Although the team's main objective was not to produce a final document, Tin fulfilled other requirements for this project: that students get to know their agencies' needs, create relationships within them, and learn to work collaboratively. Tin also displays some discursive awareness in his assessment of the project and in deciding the best way to tackle the diaper drive. But his main purpose, as he said, was to provide something that the ELC genuinely needed.

Beyond ESL-101: Negotiating Audience

Reflecting on ESL-101, Tin mentions how "stubborn" and closed-minded he had been in his first peer review session. He explained that he revised his position afterward:

> My attitude changed ... and I want to know what other
> people think, and how they view my writing. I just want
> to listen ... because, with writing, your idea is true by you,
> but if you want to be connecting with other people, you
> have to listen to what they have to say.

After completing ESL-101, Tin enrolled in my English 102 course,
which also employed service-learning. He chose to continue working with the ELC, where he became more involved with the clients.
The attitude change Tin mentions—"I want to know what other
people think"—indicated an increased awareness of his audience
and their needs, and in 102 led him to purposefully interview multiple refugees for both major class assignments, and to shift his idea
of service away from charity and toward advocacy.

In the second assignment for 102, I asked students to reflect on
the people represented by our different agencies, the issues faced
by those people, and the possible solutions for how their agencies
could address the issues. The essay culminated in oral presentations. We invited agency contacts to the class and students worked
together in teams to present research findings that, we hoped,
would mutually benefit the agency.

> I notice every time I went to the Center, I see new students
> coming out of English classes. Steve told me that most refu-
> gees are working and do not have time to come to class; even
> though, they want to continue improving their language
> skills. Steve attentively told me it will be enormously helpful
> for those working refugees if the Center delivers an Eng-
> lish class near where the majority of refugees reside. Steve
> told me that we would need to do some research to find
> out where most refugees reside, what time is convenient for
> them and how many of them will show up to class. Based
> on a research result, we can write a proposal to get funding
> from the government or other organizations.

Tin's expertise on the center increased, through close observation and involvement. His relationship with Steve became more like colleagues than the previous semester. Tin's project leans more toward Deans's (2003) notion of "social change," which Deans writes is "sometimes called advocacy" and addresses "root or structural causes of social injustice" (p. 257) While Tin's project was not directly addressing the injustices that cause people to become refugees, he was addressing an issue that has wider social implications. Providing more convenient English instruction for refugees could open up employment and educational opportunities they might not otherwise have considered.

In the essay, he uses personal experience to illustrate how important it is for refugees to learn English, and then goes on to briefly describe the situation at the ELC, and finally concludes with interview results from seven Burmese refugees. The result is Tin's most rhetorically complex and sophisticated piece yet. He combines a number of strategies to produce a document that he ultimately hopes will help the Center apply for grant money.

Beyond ESL-101: Negotiating His Role

I really want to see the center will be granted necessary funding to teach English to those unfortunate people near where they live at their [convenient] time. I also learn how I can be helpful for people who are in need and decided that whenever I have time I will put my effort to help the dream of wonderful people who want to help others and those poor and disadvantaged people get better lives.

Tin's position in the concluding lines of his second essay is complex—he is both refugee and ELC advocate, able to sympathize with the interviewees, but also to align himself with the Center and their mission. He can "be helpful" to the refugees and to the Center. Aligning himself as both insider and outsider places Tin in a unique position—one that is, for this essay, very persuasive, for he can speak from both places with authority. As a refugee, he understands the importance of convenient access to English instruction; as a volunteer for the Center, he recognizes the lack of funds and the problems the ELC faces in trying to implement new programs.

Tin's unique position allows him to recognize his potential beyond the English Learning Center, as evidenced by a comment he made during our second interview. Discussing his long-term goals, Tin said recently he'd been thinking about going back to the Thai-Burma border to teach English to children in refugee camps. Tin took advantage of his service-learning to push beyond being an example to the refugees, using the experience and the assignments to develop his potential to offer something substantive to the Center and its clients. He clearly still identifies himself as a refugee, but, as Steve reminded me, there are varying degrees of refugee status, and Tin's biggest change, he said, was "going from total reliance on everyone else to being an independent person." Through service-learning, Tin negotiated his role as a citizen and a refugee and found a balance between the two that became powerful and purposefully met a community need.

■ Conclusions

Affective Outcomes

Through the integrated service-learning ESL-101 course, both Tin and Noriko not only achieved certain first-year writing objectives, but also demonstrated personal changes necessary to cultivate their more "academic" achievements. Katznelson, Perpignan, and Rubin (2001) categorize personal development as one affective outcome that students often report experiencing in first-year composition classes. They suggest that instructors might attempt to "facilitate the conditions for developing such learning" (p. 157), and learn more about the benefits of these developments in our students. As a pedagogy that is adaptable to individual students' needs and abilities, service-learning certainly "facilitate[d] the conditions" for Noriko and Tin each to develop in their own ways.

Noriko became aware of and eventually overcame fears of writing and speaking in English. In her first service-learning experience, she discovered that she could help someone despite her perceived weak English abilities, and she revised her notion that her English proficiency alone determines her success and ability to contribute something to society. At the end of the semester, Noriko writes, "We can overcome everything through our passion, even language barriers," and adds that, through service-learning, "I received ideas on how to develop myself through volunteer work."

Marton (1989) writes that "regarding oneself as a more capable person implies a fundamental change from seeing oneself as an object of what is happening . . . to seeing oneself as an agent of what is happening" (as cited in Katznelson et al., 2001, p. 293). This "fundamental change" is evident in Noriko's comments—she asserts that a learner's attitude is a key determinant of the learner's success, and becomes an agent of her own learning.

Tin underwent a similar change; however, rather than overcoming a fear of writing or speaking, Tin appeared to regard himself as "capable" from the first day of ESL-101. However, shifting his service purpose from charity to advocacy demonstrates an increase in Tin's awareness of his ability to effect change. His continued service at the ELC and his plans to teach English in the Thai-Burma border refugee camps indicate Tin's recognition of himself "as an agent of what is happening."

Understanding and Improving Our Practice

In a reflective essay for 102, Tin gives advice to future students for making their service-learning experience more successful: "I suggest you work for communities you live in and you will find yourself happy." Both Tin and Noriko chose freely where they wanted to serve, and each of them developed (or already had) a personal identification or connection with the people they were serving.

It seems important that the agencies should hold some personal relevance for the students—whether students identify themselves as members of the group the agency serves, like Tin, or have had similar experiences as the agency's clients, like Noriko.

As instructors, we can help cultivate this personal connection by asking students early on to reflect on their own backgrounds and beliefs in relation to their service. How are they similar to and different from those of the people they are serving? What do they already know about the groups represented by their agencies? What do they want to know? Asking these kinds of questions early in the semester helps students make the personal connection between the course curriculum and the service experience. Kennedy-Isern (2004) suggests that "it is vital that students take ownership of their service, reflection, and post-service products," as this ownership leads them to take pride in their academic and service work. Tin and Noriko both completed projects that genuinely helped their agencies, each having cultivated a loyalty to the clients and staff members. Furthermore, the service enabled significant growth in their writing and speaking skills.

Reflecting on our own practice in light of this study, we are compelled to consider the notion of an ESL-only writing course. Although BSU students have the option to determine whether or not they enroll in the ESL-101 designated course, offering a special section based on their being "non-native speakers of English" may lead instructors to overlook the unique experiences and skills students bring to our classrooms, as Tin and Noriko certainly did bring. The separation also sends the message to ESL students that their grammatical English proficiency alone determines the effectiveness of their writing skills and abilities, and they may begin to believe it. Zamel (1998) might label this a "deficit model of language and learning," and postulates that working under this assumption also has the potential to turn ESL and writing courses into "gatekeepers" for our institutions (p. 193).

In contrast, Noriko and other students said the ESL-101 class was "more comfortable" because "we have the same experience." Comfort in the classroom is especially significant for ESL students (Krashen, 1982), and factors such as "fear, nervousness, and self-consciousness" (Leki, 1992, p. 17) greatly impact students' learning. If ESL students feel more comfortable with others who, as Noriko says, "also have trouble with English," then it cannot be entirely detrimental to reserve classes for them, creating comfortable environments, and likely increasing their chances of success (Braine, 1996).

Integrating service-learning into ESL-only courses may help educators maintain a safe classroom environment, and still recognize that our students bring widely differing backgrounds, skills, and expectations to our classes. Both Tin and Noriko demonstrated that they were able to achieve certain first-year composition objectives (increased confidence, and heightened awareness of purpose and audience), even though each came with different skills and attitudes. Service-learning was an effective pedagogy for both Tin and Noriko because it was adaptable to their individual needs and goals. Having the freedom to choose the agency where they served is important, as it sends an immediate message to students that they will have some control over their learning in the course. Choice also communicates the instructor's confidence in the students' variety of skills, backgrounds, and previous knowledge. Additionally, encouraging students' belief in their abilities to make a difference beyond the classroom, especially for ESL students, is critical to building the self-confidence necessary for long-term academic success.

References

Belcher, D. (1997). An argument for nonadversarial argumentation: On the relevance of the feminist critique of academic discourse to L2 writing pedagogy. *Journal of Second Language Writing, 6,* 1–21.

Bishop, W. (1999). *Ethnographic writing research: Writing it down, writing it up, and reading it.* Portsmouth, NH: Boynton/Cook.

Braine, G. (1996). ESL students in first-year writing courses: ESL vs. mainstream classes. *Journal of Second Language Writing, 5,* 91–107.

Deans, T. (2000). *Writing partnerships: Service-learning in composition.* Urbana, IL: National Council of Teachers of English.

Deans, T. (2003). *Writing and community action: A service-learning rhetoric with readings.* New York, NY: Longman.

Elwell, M. D. (2001). The efficacy of service-learning for community college ESL students. *Community College Review, 28*(4), 47–62.

Fox, H. (1994). *Listening to the world: Cultural issues in academic writing.* Urbana, IL: National Council of Teachers of English.

Goodburn, A. (2003). The value and role of community-writing practices. *Pedagogy: Critical Approaches to Teaching Literature, Language, Composition and Culture, 3,* 15–23.

Harklau, L. (1999). Representing culture in the ESL writing classroom. In E. Hinkel (Ed.), *Culture in language teaching and learning* (pp. 109–130). New York, NY: Cambridge University Press.

Heilker, P. (1997). Rhetoric made real. In L. Adler-Kassner, R. Crooks, & A. Watters (Eds.), *Writing the community: Concepts and models for service-learning in composition* (pp. 71–77). Urbana, IL: National Council of Teachers of English.

Herrington, A., & Curtis, M. (2000). *Persons in process: Four stories of writing and personal development in college.* Urbana, IL: National Council of Teachers of English.

Heuser, L. (1999). Service-learning as a pedagogy to promote the content, cross-cultural, and language-learning of ESL students. *TESL Canada Journal, 17,* 54–71.

Julier, L. (2001). Community service pedagogy. In G. Tate, A. Rupiper, & K. Schick (Eds.), *A guide to composition pedagogies* (pp. 132–145). Oxford, U.K.: Oxford University Press.

Katznelson, H., Perpignan, H., & Rubin, B. (2001). What develops *along with* the development of second language writing? Exploring the "by-products." *Journal of Second Language Writing, 10,* 141–159.

Kennedy-Isern, K. (2004). Making writing relevant. *Language Magazine, 4,* 20–22.

Knutson, S. (2003). Experiential learning in second-language classrooms. *TESL Canada Journal, 20,* 52–64.

Krashen, S. (1982). *Principles and practice in second language acquisition.* New York, NY: Pergamon.

Leki, I. (1992). *Understanding ESL writers: A guide for teachers.* Portsmouth, NH: Boynton/Cook.

Leki, I. (2001). Hearing voices: L2 students' experiences in L2 writing courses. In P. K. Matsuda & T. Silva (Eds.), *On second language writing* (pp. 17–28). Mahwah, NJ: Lawrence Erlbaum Associates.

Pajares, F., & Johnson, M. (1994). Confidence and competence in writing: The role of self-efficacy, outcome expectancy, and apprehension. *Research in the Teaching of English, 28*(3), 313–331.

Root, S. (2003). Teacher research in service-learning. In S. H. Billig & A. S. Waterman (Eds.), *Studying service-learning: Innovations in education research methodology* (pp. 173–185). Mahwah, NJ: Lawrence Erlbaum Associates.

Silva, T., Reichelt, M., Chikuma, Y., Duval-Couetil, N., Mo, R. J., Vélez-Rendón, G., & Wood, S. (2003). Second language up close and personal: some success stories. In B. Kroll (Ed.), *Exploring the dynamics of second language writing* (pp. 93–114). New York, NY: Cambridge University Press.

Zamel, V. (1998). Questioning academic discourse. In V. Zamel & R. Spack (Eds.), *Negotiating academic literacies* (pp. 187–197). Mahwah, NJ: Lawrence Erlbaum Associates.

16

Learning How to Knock:
Cross-Cultural Service-Learning
With Older Students

Robin Glenn Walker

> When we walk our way and encounter a man who comes
> toward us, walking his way, we know our way only and
> not his; for his comes to life for us only in the encounter.
> (Buber, 1923/1970, p. 124)

I have always wondered about literacy in my family, especially that of my older relatives. Coming from a large, extended, rural, Southern, Catholic family that lived about an hour from the area where I grew up, I had many occasions to experience a little of the communal, agricultural society that my grandmother knew as her culture. Many of my relatives made a study of work. In rural North Carolina, work meant all the labor involved with farming.

Coming from this background, the word "smart" meant that one was an extremely hard worker and also skillful in interpreting the world around her. My grandmother exhibits both definitions of smart; she is as hardworking as they come and extremely knowledgeable about her world. Literacy, or being taken with books and the written word, is something that just never interested my grandmother, she stopped attending school at 12. My grandmother is a reader, but can read only through great pains with her weak eyes and thick glasses. She sounds words out and reads each line aloud slowly. She has her children and grandchildren write out her checks and read any contract she signs.

When I was younger, I never noticed our differences regarding words. She was a social magnet in the community, managed all her affairs as a fifty-something widow, and even passed the driver's test, a major literacy test in American society. When I was older and had discovered how important words were to me, I began asking my grandmother if she wanted me to teach her how to improve her reading fluency. She was not interested, and for a very long time I could not understand why. Older people have such a strong sense of themselves through the accumulation of experience that they can, at this stage in their lives, define the parameters of identity through actions that fit their conceptions of themselves. As a successful member of her community, my grandmother rejected an activity (reading) that would not have any tangible benefits in her world.

Based on my grandmother's experience of goal-seeking outside of literacy, I wanted to incorporate life goals in a service-learning project with older immigrant learners. I wanted to help the students in the learning process by connecting one of their goals (learning English) with their new world. I felt that this would connect the English class to the circumstances of their daily lives, just as my grandmother developed her skills of socialization to be successful in her daily life. However, I wondered how the older students would adjust to the TESOL classroom culture and curriculum because of the necessity of teaching conversational English in its American cultural context.

What marks of their culture would appear on their learning as refugees from the former Soviet Republic and Vietnam? How would becoming a teacher to older immigrants differ from my past experience as a tutor to younger immigrants? How would I communicate my respect for their traditions while teaching them the local culture embedded in conversational English? An important goal for service-learning was to see if I could teach English idioms and serve as a cultural mediator in a collaborative learning environment to a culturally diverse group while also respecting their identities and goals as older learners. I planned to assess learners through classroom interaction with the subject matter and interviews in the extended refugee community.

■ Whose Knowledge in the Classroom?

Older immigrant learners have unique and often contradictory relationships to assimilation in the TESOL classroom in that they recognize through education and experience that language learning requires some sacrifice of their earlier identity. Because of persecution in their home countries, refugee learners have hard-won and overlapping ethnic, personal, and social identities. Additionally, because they have experienced being centered in their ethnicities while being persecuted for the same designations, they desire to hang on to aspects of their identities deeply rooted in their home cultures.

I set out to see if the experience of learning casual English and English idioms could be made to fit the goals of my students while allowing them to keep and maintain their unique identities. I also wanted to see how they would teach me what their goals were, just as my grandmother did earlier. TESOL teachers to refugee populations negotiate between the institutional necessity to have their students achieve the expected level of English for citizenship and the desire to have their students find and meet a personal goal. The problem lies in finding out what the goals of the students are. In the case of my grandmother, I was mature enough only later in life to discern what her goals in life were and to realize that my goals for her did not match her own.

There are several challenges in teaching older adults because they have such a strong sense of self, and this is especially important to consider when teaching older immigrants and refugees. Older people in society function as the holders of traditions. A good part of their deep knowledge about their own society comes from having gained increasing levels of experience in their cultures, creating a well-developed knowledge of the self. As older people in their own cultures, they are repositories of experiential knowledge. This status is challenged when refugees come to host countries. Suddenly everything seems different, and their identity can seem to be in danger. They feel pressed to assimilate to the new environment. Even the TESOL classroom can seem to be a challenge to their ways of knowing. Unlike in the youth-oriented culture of the United States, many immigrants come from cultures where great status is accorded to older people. The experiential knowledge of older adults is losing great social status in the United States, in favor of specialized professional and advanced degrees, especially in the business sector.

As classrooms in the United States continue to swell with non-traditional learners, it is important to have a means of assessing the goals of nontraditional students through intergenerational exchange. Nontraditional learners can have widely divergent goals in pursuing an education, from instrumental goals (e.g., finding employment) to personal goals to connect with learning as a means of self-improvement. Because goals can vary so widely, qualitative assessment can be a valuable tool in a classroom of nontraditional, refugee students. I decided to conduct an ethnographic study using qualitative assessment as a methodology because I felt it was the best way to incorporate classroom observation, interviews in the local language community, and intergenerational dialogue into my study.

▪ Home in the Host Country

Greensboro is a medium-sized metropolitan area located in central North Carolina. It has been known as a center of industrial activity, mainly in the area of textile production. Recently, Greensboro has been a federal resettlement area for recognized political refugees.

Because of changing political landscapes worldwide, "Since 1975, the U.S. has resettled 2.4 million refugees, with nearly 77% being either Indochinese or citizens of the former Soviet Union—the two groups in whom the U.S. has had particularly strong humanitarian and foreign policy interests during the past three decades" (Office of Refugee Resettlement, 2002).

Vietnamese and Montagnard Refugees

One of the main groups seeking asylum here are the Montagnards from Vietnam. The Montagnard community is well established in North Carolina: "North Carolina is the largest resettlement site [for Montagnards] in the Western hemisphere" (Banks, 2002, p. 6). They differ from other Vietnamese people ethnically and are Christians, making them a minority in Vietnam. Montagnards are a group of tribal people from the central highlands of Vietnam and are considered indigenous people in Vietnam. They were converted to Christianity from animism due to the settlement of missionaries starting in 1928 (Smith, 1993). According to Reverend Y Hin Nie, a religious leader in the local Montagnard community, they are victims of oppression in their home country because of their religion, political beliefs, and ethnicity; many have crossed the border to live in Cambodian refugee camps or as a last resort have fled to the deep jungle to live.

There are some strong similarities between the situations of the Montagnards and the Vietnamese refugees, although they are different ethnic groups. Because of the United States' interest in its wartime allies, "the U.S. faced the challenge of resettling hundreds of thousands of Indochinese using an ad hoc Indochinese Refugee Task Force, and temporary funding" (Office of Refugee Resettlement, 2002). Many Indochinese fought on the South Vietnamese side against the North, as the Montagnards did, and are considered political refugees by the United States. According to Father Thanh, a Vietnamese-American priest, the Vietnamese Christians feel that they lack the freedom to practice their religion in their home countries. Both groups are considered traitors by the official government. Reverend Y Hin Nie explained the situation of enemies of the government in Vietnam:

> If you stay in the village you will be killed or sent to prison. I don't want to go to prison because I am Christian or worked with the old regime. They accused everyone of working with the CIA.

Older Russian Refugees

The group of Russian refugees in Greensboro is not as well established as the Vietnamese and Montagnard communities. The refugees from the former Soviet Union in the Greensboro area are Jewish. They fled their home countries due to ethnic persecution. The cultural upheavals in the former Soviet Union have left Jews and some other ethnic groups (e.g., Ukrainian Tartars) vulnerable to ethnic hatred. During my interview with Lana Gradenko, she noted that there was a recent case of the hate-based murder of a Jewish father and his daughter while they were leaving a skating rink in the central Asian country, Tajikistan.

Unlike some other refugee groups that are made up of younger people, such as the Sudanese, "Soviet immigrants had the highest percentage of elderly among immigrant populations, about 17% at their time of arrival in the USA" (Persidsky & Kelly, 1992, p. 419). Their acculturation experience is complicated by the fact that they are also adapting to a strongly youth-oriented culture in the United States. Interestingly, "in the European part of the Soviet Union the elderly (aged 60 or over) represent 16–17% of the general population in their regions of origin" (Bezrukov, 1990, as cited in Persidsky & Kelly, 1992, p. 419), and, once here, they find it is difficult even for older Americans to make their place in American society.

Background of the English Conversation Course for Refugees

The classroom where the students from Russia and Vietnam attend English conversation classes is located in the Senior Resources of Guilford County Building in the downtown Greensboro area near a recently renovated bus station. The English conversation class is designed to address both instrumental and social uses of English, as well as to give the students some cultural background about the host country. There is an open-door policy, since attending this class is not a requirement for retaining their refugee status. It is held in the same building as their citizenship class. This class is essentially supplemental to the citizenship classes that refugees take for the citizenship exam that they must pass within seven years of arrival in the United States. It is a 15-week course held for an hour on Thursday afternoons each week.

The mission statement of Senior Resources of Guilford County is "Senior Resources of Guilford County is committed to providing a continuum of quality services and enriching opportunities which support the independent living of older adults in Guilford County." There is a sign on the wall of the waiting area that informs readers about Older Workers' Week. In addition, there is a very official-looking black marquee, similar to the ones that hotels use to advertise events in their conference centers, listing the days that cake decorating classes, piano lessons, movie days, and guest speakers will be available.

Attending almost every class are two older women, June and Linda. June is African American and is a native of North Carolina, and Linda is Caucasian and a native of North Carolina as well. They enjoy speaking with the older foreigners and hope to make them feel more comfortable in their host country by attending and participating in the conversation classes. One wears a small, religious pin each day, and they both stress that they want to be good neighbors to the newcomers.

The older students and older community participants make up the majority of the class. The two moderators of the English conversation club are young women. I am the more inexperienced of the moderators. Ashley has been teaching the class longer and is very experienced in teaching classes of TESOL learners. We both have been very active in teaching ESL (I tutor immigrants and Ashley teaches classes at Glenwood library in TESOL) for some years and both of us have an interest in aiding immigrants in establishing a place in their new country. Ashley was training me to take over the class because she was spread thin with her many responsibilities.

■ Theoretical Tango

Being a teacher-researcher poses some challenges to the nature of ethnography. While objectivity is desired, it is not entirely possible in practice. Teachers can get so involved in their own role as teachers that it is likely that their personal identity as a teacher quickly becomes the only lens through which they view differences. This is especially true for beginning teachers. Because I was conducting a qualitative study with my own observations about my students, I was continually scrutinizing each observed detail of my teaching interactions with a great deal of self-criticism. It is natural that both teacher and student will bring their personal insecurities regarding language and the teaching process to the exchange, but it is equally important that ethnography shows the blind spots (communications impasses) of the researcher. I delved into my blind spots through a combination of theoretical and community research, using the other members of the Russian, Montagnard, and Vietnamese groups as cultural insiders.

"Goin' Through the Big 'D' And I Don't Mean Dallas"[1]

In "Literacy, Discourse, and Linguistics: Introduction *and* What Is Literacy?," James Paul Gee (2001) argues that it is not mere language that communicates the beliefs and wishes of a speaker but a whole arrangement of language, gestures, clothing, personal associations, cultural beliefs, time, and place that communicates a message. He makes a distinction between Discourse (with a capital *D*) and discourse (with a lower case *d*). Gee writes:

> At any given moment we are using language we must say or write the right thing in the right way while playing the right social role and (appearing) to hold the right values, beliefs, and attitudes. Thus, what is important is not language, and surely not grammar, but *saying (writing)-doing-being-valuing-believing combinations*. These combinations I call "Discourses," with a capital "D" ("discourse" with a little "d," to me, means connected stretches of language that make sense, so "discourse" is part of "Discourse"). Discourses are ways of being in the world; they are forms of life which integrate words, acts, values, beliefs, attitudes, and social identities as well as gestures, glances, body positions, and clothes. (p. 526)

In short, it is the area peripheral to language that actually communicates to others the speaker's message.

Refugee students are asked to negotiate the daily language world of small talk and instrumental literacy, as well as the institutional forms of literacy used by the INS, the Department of State, and the Office of Refugee Resettlement while inhabiting a way of being that may clash with their long-held beliefs about who they are. Gee (2001) calls this a Discourse identity kit: "A Discourse is a sort of 'identity kit' which comes complete with the appropriate costume and instructions on how to act, talk, and often write, so as to take on a particular role that others will recognize" (p. 526). Thus, I must look like, dress like, speak like, and eat like an academic researcher, and my students must dress like, question like, act like, and live like immigrant students.

Gee pinpoints the Discourses possible within individual languages as potential places of contention within an individual's identity as a part of a distinct group. This is even more problematic for older refugees, considering that one must take on, as an identity, the ways of being that characterize the Discourse, crossing linguistic barriers as well as discourse barriers. The taking on of a Discourse also challenges the older adult's desire for independence. They have to depend on a cultural interlocutor or initiator, usually a younger member of their own ethnic group. There are degrees of identity investment in each individual rooted in the Discourses in which they functioned for long periods of time, and older refugees have invested the most in their identities over time. They are separated from their host countries linguistically and often socially by living in communities with other members of their language community, making mastery of both a new language and various discrete Discourses very difficult.

The dissonance between who they are and the Discourse community they are expected to join is profoundly alienating. It can be so alienating to some immigrants that they take extreme measures to obscure the previous identity. There are countless stories of first-generation immigrants who give up using their mother tongue, teach their children English only, and even change their ethnic-sounding surnames. This extreme model of assimilation is fairly widespread in the United States.

However, extreme assimilation clashes with cherished American beliefs about social, economic, and personal mobility. "Americans tend to focus on the individual, and thus often miss the fact that the individual is simply the meeting point of many, sometimes conflicting discourses that are socially and historically defined" (Gee, 2001, p. 539). If one must inhabit a position so seamlessly to communicate a message, can one keep a strong identity? Mobility is the main issue here, and it is not possible to be mobile in any of the above forms without acquiring a Discourse (institutional usually) to give the speaker/actor an entrée.

My Place in the English as a Second Language (TESOL) Discipline

I find that teaching yields an exhilarating combination of self-reflection on home culture, an intimate window on the cultures of others, and a strong basis for the development of friendship. Almost all my students and former students are my friends. However, I had never once considered how different teaching a class of students, especially older students, might be from teaching students approximately my age individually. Because my earlier tutoring experience was so personalized, maintaining a degree of respectful distance for the older immigrants was not something that I had consciously considered. My previous experience with older people had consisted of casually interacting with family members and visiting older people in rest homes.

I gradually gave much thought to my presence as being a part of an institutional structure. I think that I viewed the first classes with the older immigrants as very personal interactions without necessarily seeing myself in the personal web of social support networks within the world of refugees seeking citizenship. This is a mistake that many beginning TESOL and other teachers make when entering the classroom. Given these beliefs about personal interaction and teaching, and my newness to the practice of ethnography, my lack of attention to the institutional structure that I was a part of was very understandable but naive.

Cultural Beliefs About Good Teachers

The cultural mythology that surrounds teaching is an important element to consider in any ethnography that takes literacy on as a subject. The American cultural beliefs about good teaching tie into key beliefs about social and class mobility. The cultural beliefs we have in America about good teachers center around those teachers who single-handedly defeat or challenge institutional forces that have dehumanized and cheated their students. In the popular 1988 film *Stand and Deliver*, Jaime A. Escalante, a high school calculus teacher, takes a group of low-performing, low-income students from East Los Angeles and trains them to pass the difficult Advanced Placement calculus exam (Menéndez & Musca, 1988). This film also shows the cultural belief that a good American teacher cares for his or her students on a very personal level, as shown by the lengthy after-school tutoring sessions that Escalante created for his students. The ideal of American teaching closely resembles the tutor/student relationship, highly geared to individual students. The most revered quality in American teachers is to treat all students as individuals. A hierarchal relationship between a student and teacher is not the norm in the United States; a student expects a more informal and politely casual relationship with the teacher.

I expected my students to engage the class and solicit comments and questions during class presentations, even though I didn't know how these learning activities would have been done in their homelands. I discovered at some point in the interaction that I knew little about the backgrounds of my students, even though we frequently discussed cultural and artistic characteristics of their homelands through informal presentations. I felt uncomfortable asking about the circumstances of their migrations, feeling that it was rude to ask directly. This hesitation spilled over into a lack of inquiry, on my part, about their economic and social backgrounds.

In the book *Fieldworking*, Elizabeth Chiseri-Strater and Bonnie Stone-Susten (1997) observe that ethnography sometimes works by serendipitous discovery and the fieldworker must be open enough to recognize the gap between what was assumed through culture and bias and the information presenting itself:

> For example, you may dismiss the middle-aged woman who sits in your political science class and reminds you of your mother. But when you are assigned to a study group with her, you discover that as an army nurse who has trav-

eled all over the world, she knows more about international politics than anyone else in the group. (p. 216)

It is important to find a way to ask students about literacy in a way that is direct enough for understanding, yet not so direct as to seem invasive. This is a difficult balance, but I found that communicating outside of class yielded many unexpected bits of knowledge through conversation.

Because of the beliefs I had had about the poverty occasioned by the Vietnam War and of the images of Montagnard "mountain people" I had seen on television, I had assumed that the Vietnamese and Montagnard students had had little experience with written language in their home countries. I knew that there were gaps in my knowledge; I did not know the level of education of the Vietnamese and Montagnard students and was sensitive to the fact that many Montagnards and Vietnamese elders might not have had much formal education. Ashley, the other teacher in the classroom, once told me that Lamai, a very sociable and sweet Vietnamese woman, had told her one day, "I was smart when I was young, now I feel so stupid."

Literacy is a deeply personal issue and one's feeling about literacy can affect self-perception in parts of life not directly connected to reading and writing. It affects an individual's perception of his or her own efficacy, as I have shown in Lamai's perception of her own skills. In analyzing literacy in this context, the story of a person's literacy is a personal story of the kind told to a friend. So, it is actually the context of an encounter that tells the story.

In my interview with my priest, Father Thahn, he had said that literacy figures during the French colonial period in Vietnam were low; there was less than 10% literacy in the population. This seems a rather challenging statistic; however, I found out later through Duc Le, a Vietnamese community leader, that Lamai had graduated from high school, the other Vietnamese student had finished high school, and the Montagnard had been a local official in the

French administration. Another student was ethnically Chinese with a similarly high level of education. My assumptions about the backgrounds of the Vietnamese and Montagnard students were completely incorrect.

Indirect and Direct Communication in the Classroom

In ethnography, assumptions about value orientation between the researcher and the participants may differ. This especially affects how one communicates values and expectations cross-culturally. In contrast to other cultural groups, Americans are known for directness. In fact, this is the paradigm that American businesses espouse and require of employees. Looking clients and superiors in the eye and directly stating a grievance or wish is expected in American business culture, and it extends to the general American culture as well. Children are socialized in American schools to look the teacher in the eye when being reprimanded and to tell the teacher when they do not understand the lesson.

Thus, from the time they are young, Americans are expected to value direct communication. For cultures that value indirect communication, a directly expressed want seems to violate the tenets of politeness and group cohesion. Generally, cultures that value direct communication value individualism, and cultures that value indirect communication value collectivism. Triandis, Brislin, and Hui's (1991) discussion explains value orientations:

> Found in most northern and western regions of Europe and in North America, individualism can be summarized as individuals putting their goals ahead of the goals of any group of people with which they may be associated. Individualists are idiocentric in that they pay more attention to their own needs and values than they do to those of a larger group. Collectivism, on the other hand, can be characterized as individual people holding their goals as sec-

ondary to those of a group of people to which they belong. Such people are allocentric in that they use group needs and values as the primary reference point for action. Collectivism can be found in Asia, South America, and the Pacific. (as cited in Ady, 1998, p. 112)

This discussion of intercultural negotiation explains the value orientation of both cultural types. For instance, in America it is considered a character compliment to call someone a "go-getter" or "self-starter." In other cultures, pushing individual wants and needs forward can be threatening to the identity of the group. Thus a difference in communication styles can cause conflict in a TESOL classroom.

I found many of my own cultural values to figure strongly in my teaching style, such as humor in the classroom (friendly joking); expectations of close, individualized relationships between the teacher and students (quick friendships); and a tendency towards games and less stringently academic methods of teaching a subject (games, skits, and performances). With individual and small group tutoring, I had used the same teaching style and strategies. However, I had never had responsibility for such a large group. (The largest group I had tutored up to that point had been three TESOL students.) From my cultural background and my tutoring experience, I felt that my informal, joking style would be popular in a class with adult students.

Conflict in the Classroom

I noticed around the middle of March that there seemed to be tension in the classroom when I was teaching. There did not seem to be much of a problem when Ashley was the instructor. I would plan activities that I hoped would create an atmosphere for lively dialogue; however, many times the students would see the activities as confusing or not relevant to the subject of English.

> The high drop-out rate of older refugees enrolled in many traditional adult education classes attests to the fact that older adults are not willing to tolerate what to them is boring or irrelevant content, or lessons that stress the learning of grammar rules out of context. (Grognet, 1997–1998, p. 3)

I had difficulty showing how some of my planned activities, though informal, were methods that could be used to build skills in English. I turned to differences in humor to try to start a conversation about cultural differences in everyday life.

I had devised a lesson to present the subject matter through a practical exercise highlighting differences in humor in America as compared to humor in their home countries. When I presented one of my ideas for classroom discussion that I had thought over for several weeks, knock-knock jokes, one of the more talkative and assertive students said, "We cannot understand your jokes. Jokes cannot translate into other languages. Our jokes are different." I felt very nervous at that point because my activity had seemed so incomprehensible to the students and I had sensed the relief that the students had felt when Ashley arrived, rushing from another class she was teaching.

I tried very tentatively to explain my praxis to the Russian students. I asked if they had any jokes in their home countries that children enjoyed that played with the sounds of words. I said that in America knock-knock jokes allowed children to play with the way that words are written, the way that they are supposed to be pronounced, and the way that they are actually pronounced in daily conversation, showing ideal and real ideas of language pronunciation. I hoped to engage the students in a fun activity that would allow them to make mistakes and learn from them in a non-threatening context because they were simply joking and shouldn't feel pressure to be serious.

The Vietnamese and the Montagnard students were receptive, but I could not catch the attention of the Russian students. They began to chat in Russian and would not separate into groups for the activity. I felt my confidence sink. Ashley took over and began writing anagrams on the board to keep with the spirit of my assignment, word play. They were receptive to this activity and I gradually started to add anagrams to Ashley's anagrams as we worked together. She wrote on the erase board, and I sat with one of the former teachers in the class from Azerbaijan.

The class ended with a presentation on music. They really enjoyed recounting the different kinds of music from their homelands, from light opera to popular dance music from the 1950s to classical music. I noticed that they explained carefully that some music was popular music and some music was valued as art, illustrating to me the distinction between music that was simply to entertain teenagers and music that was designated as culturally important and not written purely for entertainment.[2]

I noticed this hierarchal thinking and thought of how I had been trying to present conversational English to the students in such a typically American, informal way. I now noticed such a strong division between what the Russians saw as high culture and low culture, but I did not see this distinction working among the Vietnamese and Montagnard students. Ashley emphatically agreed that she saw these beliefs about culture operating in the classroom. The Russians liked to talk about politics, composers, music, and higher education, but when they were given a more informal assignment they tended to be less involved. Sometimes, they would even reject the activity outright as a group, saying that it was impossible for them to grasp. The students began to indirectly reject me as an authoritative teacher as well by not showing up for class as a group several weeks in succession (classes were cancelled for all students if there were not enough to fill the bus). This nonverbal rejection made me consider how I was using and presenting my praxis. I was not communicating well interculturally.

This made me also wonder about my Vietnamese and Montagnard students. I wondered if they considered my activities useful. My priest, Father Thanh, explained to me in an interview the ideas of education in Vietnam. He explained that Vietnam was colonized by China for one thousand years and Vietnamese people subsequently absorbed many tenets of Confucianism. Confucianism stressed a respect for authority and civil figures in society, such as teachers, policemen, and others who serve the community. There is an understanding of roles. He told me, "the teacher and the students have a filial relationship, with the students seeing the teacher as a source of knowledge and as a mentor." I was afraid that the Montagnard and Vietnamese students were not getting anything valuable out of my activities, but were not letting me know out of respect for me as their teacher.

I was having a difficult time adjusting to my new role as teacher. As a new teacher, I was very unsure of myself. I had announced to the class at the beginning that I was a new teacher and would be learning from my students about my field. I learned from Lana, an employee at the senior center, in an interview that students in Russia were used to a very hierarchal structure in the classroom, with the teacher as a strong authority figure who would not have expressed her insecurity and inexperience.

Collaborative classrooms, such as the one I shared with Ashley, would have been very rare in the Soviet educational system due to ideas about hierarchal organization in the classroom. I had been creating a classroom without strict hierarchies, an act that would call my teaching abilities into question for my Russian students. In the article, "Educational Revolution on the Volga River," Perkins and Stickney (2004) give an account of trying to get a class of Russian professionals to use classroom dialogue as a way to learn in a week-long conference designed to get different sectors of society to come together and form solutions to the problem of pollution in the Volga river. Heavily influenced by Paulo Freire's idea of education being a liberating force in the daily lives of students, the consulting group attempts what they term "dialogue education." They write:

> Some participants expressed concern that a less formal method of teaching, which included so much dialogue, might appear unprofessional. . . . The course became an exciting departure from the traditional Russian educational practice of disseminating information. (Perkins & Stickney, 2004, p. 272)[3]

This model, common in American education, did not fit my students' expectations about teaching.

The Russian students would tell the intercultural advisor, Lana, that they did not like my class but would not tell me what they perceived as the problem. Ultimately, they were rejecting what they saw as an unprofessional classroom. I found that my learners used indirect communication strategies to communicate their expectations and goals when they started to miss classes. To try to understand the problem in the classroom, I began to interview members of the community that worked at Senior Resources who had already experienced the immigration process and had the eyes of two cultures.

Communication problems can sometimes be handled by bringing in other community members as co-ethnographers. During my interview with Reverend Y Hin Nie, as I looked with foreign eyes on his culture, he was analyzing his own culture through the lens of my questions about literacy. He became a bicultural advisor to me. In the case of the Russian students, a bicultural point of view turned out to be necessary to turn the stilted communication in the classroom into open communication and dialogue. Lana, the coordinator for the Russians, served as a much-needed mediator. She explained that older Russians generally relied on group consensus to determine if something is valuable. If one student in the group rejects the class, the others will not attend class.

Lana was able to get the students to respond directly to the aspects of the class that they disliked. (The Asian students were absent that day.) After the uncomfortable experience with knock-knock jokes, the students gave me suggestions about how they wanted to learn English in the classroom. I made columns on the board labeled "likes" and "dislikes." The main dislike that students agreed on was jokes, the most informal element in the class. They felt that the activities associated with jokes did not belong in the classroom. The use of jokes was insulting to their identities as accomplished professionals. This touched on an important idea about identity for me and illustrated how identities can be strongly tied to professions.

My students held strongly to their professional identities. They listed giving presentations on their home countries as a "like" in the likes and dislikes column. A large part of giving these presentations was to talk about their occupations in their countries of birth. Because so many of the Russian students had terminal degrees, they were very upfront about their educational backgrounds in class. Most had been scientists or engineers. Professional identities are extremely important to immigrants from the former Soviet Union.

Living in the former Soviet Union, a scientist or engineer occupied one of the most valued positions in society. I was very intrigued on several occasions when one of my students pulled out pictures of a tunnel that he had engineered through the steep cliff of a mountain, just as an American might show pictures of his or her family. (He had pictures of his son, who was also an engineer, in one photo). Professionalism was such a part of Soviet culture that it was expected in every discipline.

My students indirectly told me what they valued, having a professional identity, by explaining the difference between high culture and low culture in the field of music. Popular music was a simply a diversion while classical and opera music was the hallmark of a professional composer. The speech and values of my students' professional identities can be understood through Gee's

(2001) Discourse theory. This theory of Discourse includes indirect communication through values and beliefs. Their preferences in the class showed the professional aspect of their identities.

There were lessons that were unusually popular. The class really enjoyed proverbs and loved to tease meaning out of something that bridged a gap between academic, textual knowledge and the cultural, everyday knowledge of idioms. I used proverbs dealing with being open to experience and learning from your experiences in life as a compromise to meet the academic orientation of my Russian students and my desire that all of my students develop cultural literacy in Americanisms through language. The unraveling of meaning was a challenge. Not surprisingly, two of the proverbs had alternate connotations of the word "knock." I used "Don't knock it 'til you've tried it," and "I come from the school of hard knocks."

The students puzzled over the proverbs in groups. Evstafy and his wife got the very hard one, "the school of hard knocks," and Evstafy knocked on the table and said, "I don't understand school of hard knocks." He had halfway decided that it meant corporal punishment in school. The other groups figured out what "don't knock it 'til you've tried it" meant when I asked them if they could really know about an experience that they had never tried.

When we again assembled into groups, I pantomimed for Evstafy and Natalia the feeling of a really tough lesson in life; it feels like a hard knock! The group of two men explained their interpretation of the proverb. When I wrote on the board all the different uses of the word "knock" that they had seen in the class, smiles broke out. As Leon was leaving he tried to show me a Russian proverb: "To live is not crossing a field." We worked on bridging the meaning of this idiomatic expression in English, playing with the differences in English and Russian syntax. I had some idea that the proverb meant that life is not straightforward. When I added the word "just" as a restrictive element, I immediately understood the meaning, "Living is not *just* crossing a field!"

◼ Discussion

Inexperience Is the Best Teacher

My title for this chapter, "Learning How to Knock," reflects the experience of a classroom with multiple perspectives. I really had to consider what it must be like to be an older immigrant, used to the respect that age and lifetime employment confers on older people in their countries. I had to understand that their desire for structure in the classroom was implicitly a desire for deference to their wealth of experiential knowledge. Conversely, the students had to learn to be more direct with me as a teacher and to see that open communication was a sign of respect in my eyes as an American teacher.

Knocking took on significance to me in the classroom. *Knock* was used several different ways throughout the class. It was used to describe a type of pre-scripted joke, dealing with language play and unique to the English language. Knock-knock jokes are a cultural phenomenon, but also serve the same purpose as an idiomatic expression, a set expression or event that is marked not by a strictly routine use of language.

I see "knocking" as a metaphor for the practice of respecting each individual's integrity. To knock implies that the other person has the ability to respond to a request from another person who is respecting their personal space and choice in the matter. Without understanding the subtext of indirect communication, it is easy to mistake intentions. For instance, the students were not directly telling me that something was wrong, but used their collective absences as a form of communication.

My intention was to have a class with open communication and real discussion about difference; however, my reading of the situation, or metacommunication, was culturally bound. I was unable to confront the issue without the mediating role of Lana, who worked to tease out the difficulties the students had with my teaching style, and Y Hin Nie's, Father Thanh's, and Duc Le's information about Vietnamese and Montagnard beliefs about teachers and students. Lana, Y Hin Nie, Duc Le, and Father Thanh served as a doorway into the set of beliefs and expectations at work in the class. Using people as resources from respective communities can help a TESOL teacher see her and her students' assumptions about language more clearly. Bicultural advisors are invaluable to TESOL teachers.

In addition to exploring communication practices, idioms also expressed the multiple layers of meaning in an encounter that I wanted my class to consider. In her seminal work *Ways with Words,* Shirley Brice Heath (1983) writes about the process that an infant used to differentiate between the denotations and connotations of words in her analysis of "Tracktown," a small, African-American community in the Piedmont area of North Carolina. Lem, a Tracktown child, had to learn the shades of meaning in the word *keep* by reading the behavior and actions of Tracktown's mayor, depending on the mayor's intonation and behavior:

> He had also to learn the literal and conveyed meanings of *keep.* The mayor played on the double meaning of the word—retain indefinitely, and protect. As Lem got older, the mayor would try to reopen his old game with Lem, saying, "Come on, I keep it for you." Lem would retort: "You ain't *keep* nut'n, you eat it." (Heath, 1983, p. 85)

Contextually, words like *knock* became idioms that my students mastered through context as well.

The multiplicity of words (something I am sure they understand in their native languages, but can easily be forgotten as they deal with their frustration with their daily use of the English language) was a daunting, though exhilarating, subject to teach. I felt that this was valuable to them in their daily lives in the community as well as in their dealings with the INS and other refugee agencies. Analyzing how language is used in their new communities can give refugees a sense of being insiders, increasing their sense of independence in a new country. The students become "bicultural" learners and observers through their understanding of idioms. It is important to stress that creating bicultural perspectives necessarily advocates an accommodationist perspective to immigration. Students choose what will be incorporated into their identity from the new culture. The respectful TESOL teacher and established members of their communities, as cultural initiators, can help them to understand the perspectives of the new culture while respecting the degree of closeness they want to maintain with it.

That is the essence of teaching idioms and idiomatic expressions. Students respond to the proverbs, because they reflect the knowledge of the insiders, the Americans, who recognize the word associations easily as American cultural expressions.[4] It allows the student a sense of mobility as well as giving them an insider's view of language through discovery, like when Evstafy discovered that "the school of hard knocks" was actually a metaphorical, rather than a literal and physical description of challenging life experiences. It can become a student-centered goal-fulfillment exercise.

Using idioms in a class of well-educated and highly intelligent older students can be liberating in that it addresses the instrumental and daily usage of language as well as more advanced applications of cultural wisdom imparted through language. Older learners "are more able to make higher order association and generalizations, and can integrate new language imputs into already substantial learning and experiences" (Grognet, 1997–1998, p. 1). It is hard not to impinge upon their identities because of what we have to teach them. It is necessary to incorporate familiar elements with the new knowledge into the classroom environment in order to open the value orientation in the class to include the values of the older learners and help them to understand the values of their new country through the eyes of the old country.

■ Endnotes

1) Rogers and Wright (1994).
2) Russian scientists are remarkably well rounded and knowledgeable about the fine arts as well as their own fields of study.
3) The Perkins and Stickney article seems to present a slightly oversimplified account of the resolution of cultural differences in the classroom. While the article makes some very important points about the benefits of dialogue education, the actual practice tends to be more complicated.
4) To give an example of idioms and instrumental language from a third culture, a Spanish-speaking friend of mine said that the Spanish word for bureaucracy, burocracia, changes in pronunciation to burrocracia, with the emphasis on the stubborn mule, burro, only when the speaker is embroiled in a bureaucratic impasse.

■ References

Ady, J. C. (1998). Negotiating across cultural boundaries: Implications of individualism-collectivism and cases for application. In T. M. Singelis (Ed.), *Teaching about culture, ethnicity, and diversity: Exercises and planned activities* (pp. 111–120). Thousand Oaks, CA: Sage.

Banks, M. M. (2002, July 7). Montagnards finish journey to Triad. *Greensboro News and Record,* p. A1.

Buber, M. (1970). *I and thou* (W. Kaufmann, Trans.). New York, NY: Charles Scribner's Sons. (Original work published in German in 1923)

Chiseri-Strater, E., & Stone-Susten, B. (1997). Researching people: The collaborative listener. In E. Chiseri-Strater & B. Stone-Susten, *Fieldworking: Reading and writing research* (pp. 215–234). Boston, MA: Bedford Books of St. Martin's.

Gee, J. P. (2001). Literacy, discourse, and linguistics: Introduction and what is literacy? In E. Cushman, E. R. Kintgen, B. Kroll, & M. Rose (Eds.), *Literacy: A critical sourcebook* (pp. 525–544). Boston, MA: Bedford Books of St. Martin's.

Grognet, A. G. (1997–1998). Elderly refugees and language learning. In A. Keltner, *ELT: Technical Assistance for English Language Training Projects*, (pp. 1–5). Washington, DC: Office of Refugee Resettlement.

Heath, S. B. (1983). *Ways with words: Language, life, and work in communities and classrooms*. Cambridge, U.K.: Cambridge University Press.

Menéndez, R. (Director/Co-writer), & Musca, T. (Co-writer). (1988). *Stand and deliver* [Motion picture]. United States: Warner Brothers.

Office of Refugee Resettlement. (2002). *U.S. Resettlement Program—An Overview*. Retrieved October 9, 2006, from the U.S. Department of Health and Human Services web site: www.acf.hhs.gov/programs/orr/programs/overviewrp.htm

Perkins, P., & Stickney, M. B. (2004). Educational revolution on the Volga River. In J. Vella & Associates (Eds.), *Learning as a personal victory in the new Russia* (pp. 269–280). San Francisco, CA: Jossey-Bass.

Persidsky, I. V., & Kelly, J. J. (1992). Educational perspectives for elderly migrants: A case of Soviet refugees. *International Review of Education, 38*, 417–425.

Rogers, R., & Wright, J. (1994) Goin' through the big D [Recorded by Mark Chesnutt]. On *What a Way to Live* [CD]. Nashville, TN: Decca.

Smith, D. W. (Director/Producer). (1993). *Vietnam mission: Fifty years among the Montagnards* [Motion picture]. United States: Filmmakers Library.

Triandis, H., Brislin, R., & Hui, C. (1991). Cross-cultural training across the individualism-collectivism divide. In L. Samovar & R. Porter (Eds.), *Intercultural communication: A reader* (pp. 370–382). Belmont, CA: Wadsworth.

Name Index

Subject Index